Quantitative Trading & Money Management

A Guide To Risk Analysis and Trading Survival

Fred Gehm

REVISED EDITION

IRWIN
Professional Publishing®

Chicago • Bogotá • Boston • Buenos Aires • Caracas
London • Madrid • Mexico City • Sydney • Toronto

ISBN 1-55738-585-8

Printed in the United States of America

BS

1 2 3 4 5 6 7 8 9 0

JB

For Celia and Alex.
with love.

The race is not to the swift, nor the battle to the strong, nor bread to the wise, nor riches to the intelligent, nor favor to the men of skill; but time and chance happen to them all.

Ecclesiastes 9:11

The race is not always to the swift, nor the battle to the strong—but that's the way to bet.

Damon Runyon

Table of Contents

Foreword

This book is most important for those who have the least interest in opening the cover. If you have gotten to this point, you will find great rewards in going farther. *Money Management* is filled with common sense about the most critical topic in finance, *risk*. For most traders, risk is an unpleasant subject. It is as unpalatable as the child's bad-tasting medicine. It lacks the glamour of big profits, but it is absolutely essential for anyone interested in financial longevity. Money management is about risk and, with increasing price volatility and constant reminders of mismanagement in even the largest institutions, risk reduction is much more important to us now than it has ever been.

One of the ironies of money management is that, as the world markets open and become more liquid, there is less diversification. Along with globalization has come interdependence. You can, of course, find some risk reduction in the daily fluctuations of your portfolio when you select a sample of Japanese, U.S., and European shares or financial markets. But during a crisis, such as the 1987 stock market plunge, Gorbachev's abduction, or Iraq's attack on Kuwait, everything moves together. There is no diversification just when you need it the most. Combine that with the added problem that most of the markets able to accept large pools of funds are all financial and therefore interrelated, risk reduction should be a very real concern.

If I were to choose the most important section in this book, it would be "Catastrophic Risk," because it is the least forgiving. It is tempting to ignore events that occur infrequently. There is not enough attention given to catastrophic risk. It seems difficult to invest the effort in a situation that may only occur once in five years. But those five years will come, and at some point all your skill and planning will be tested.

Competition for better short-term returns force traders and managers to take chances that will not survive the large, correlated price shocks that are inevitable. Investment reality does not often live up to expectations. When you see performance as returns and risk, it is the risk portion that is most often miscalculated. This book helps you to understand what to expect. It gives you a critical piece to solve the investment puzzle.

We now have very powerful tools for developing investment strategies. In many cases, these computerized programs are difficult to control. They allow mass testing of large data sets, and can apply countless rules to identify supposedly significant relationships of cause and effect. But common sense says that it doesn't work that way. You must control these tools. First, you observe a market action and determine its cause. You then consider whether this situation repeats itself, and under what conditions. The tools, or computer program, are now used to validate your idea by applying your rules to the data. You control the process, rather than the process controlling you. It is the same with money management. If you cannot clearly state the risk expectations, you will always be on the defensive; you will always be underleveraged, or worse, overleveraged.

Gehm discusses the virtues of accepting proof of error. To recognize that we have been operating incorrectly, or drawing the wrong conclusions, is a normal part of learning. It is an interesting trait that we tend to question losses much more than profits. When a strategy is back-tested, we pay particular attention when the results are disappointingly bad, or a single event causes a large loss. We learn why in order to correct the problem. When results are surprisingly good we are not as inclined to question them. They are viewed as the reward justifying the effort. Yet, errors can cause profits as well as losses.

A large part of money management is accounting for change. Past performance is not likely to be the same as current results. Volatility fluctuations, variations in noise, new participants, new tools, and even fundamentals that drive the markets all orchestrate changing patterns. This means that your expectations should be adjusted to market conditions, and you need expectations to control risk and measure performance. It will tell you whether your investment approach is better than a passive portfolio, or worse than doing nothing. Fred Gehm gives you insight into recognizing change and adapting to it, but most important, understanding the need to evaluate risk.

You won't need to be adept at math to use this book. Although the mathematics is there to support the author's statements, the concepts are fully illustrated by extensive commonsense examples. Fred Gehm's writing is full of simple truths. It is not necessary to be precise about probabilities—a rational guess is a good start. Often, any risk management is an improvement over doing nothing. As Gehm says, "the reality is that the best answer is still an approximation." It is clear that understanding the ideas is more important than solving the formulas. I found that simply recognizing that "Aha! It's a formula," did not detract from any of the sections in this book. As Gehm himself says, "A statistical technique, like a car or a computer, will work whether or not its user understands why."

This book has been revised and brought up to date with more familiar examples. It was strange that, when I read about the risk in the Mexican peso devaluation, that I could not tell whether it was 1976 or 1995. Change is often a subtle concept. I hope you find this as easy to read as I have. It is filled with valuable information and stays focused on its purpose, risk management. Even the chapter on "Nuts and Bolts of Building a Trading Method" will bring a refreshing change from other discussions of moving averages. It looks at ways to arrive at new ideas and valid methods.

If you already have a familiarity with risk management, beginning at the end might make sense. Chapter 12 is a practical discussion of diminishing returns and marginal cost, which is typical of the author's practical approach. Gehm is very realistic about his solutions, not suggesting that you put in more effort than the expected reward.

You must come away from this book with a greater and healthier respect for risk. As Gehm states, "we need to worry," because it provides the motivation to reduce risk. We need to plan, because there is no other way to objectively assess results to distinguish a sensible trade from a careless one. Most of all, you will understand that "part of the risk a trader must accept is not knowing the full extent of the risk."

Perry Kaufman

Preface

I wrote this book to help traders make better, more professional, more profitable trading decisions. This is a "how to" book.

This is not an introductory textbook. I have assumed that the reader has some familiarity with trading, that he or she is willing to dedicate time and money to trading, and that he or she is seriously interested in winning. The amount of money the reader is willing to dedicate to trading is not overly important; the amount of time and energy is.

In this book, I have presented the money-management approach to trading. As the words are usually used, "money management" has little real meaning. Although many traders claim to practice money management, not all of them do. At least, many who claim to use money-management techniques do not use the best investment technology available, and many use no technology at all. This is unfortunate. Over the past 30 years or so, traders, economists, statisticians, mathematicians, and financial theorists have created many useful and practical techniques for managing trading funds. Unfortunately, much of this material is buried in technical journals that few, if any, traders will ever read. My intention is to present traders with the most practical and useful of this material, including techniques such as statistics, probability theory, marginal analysis, and portfolio theory.

These techniques can improve a trader's performance. A detailed written trading plan, for example, can reduce a trader's uncertainty. If the trader can forecast the market with some accuracy, diversification can increase a trader's return, reduce his or her risk, or both.

This is not a matter of opinion: Money-management techniques are more than common sense; they are tools and techniques that allow the trader to solve difficult and important problems in valid but sometimes unobvious ways.

There is no magic involved. Few traders use all of the available information, and fewer still use the available information correctly. Many trading decisions are therefore *necessarily* bad. In all cases, the trader who uses the techniques in this book will make decisions that are at least as profitable as those who do not. In most cases, the trader will make much better decisions. The rewards are real and obtainable.

The rewards are not easily obtained, however. The money-management approach is a business approach, and that means work. The money-management approach is also a technical approach, that is, it involves the use of highly sophisticated and technical tools. It is as difficult to trade profitably without using these tools as it is to pour steel successfully without using metallurgy.

Some of the tools are conceptual; some are mathematical. The conceptual tools are the most difficult and important. Conceptual tools involve thinking about the market in new and different ways and asking new questions. Asking new questions is no assurance that the right questions will be asked, but there is no other place to start. Moreover, asking the right question is no assurance of getting the right answer, but then there is no "right" answer to a wrong question.

I believe that the reader will find that an understanding of the concepts in this book is critical; the mathematics, on the other hand, is merely useful. In this book I have stressed the quantitative approach to money management. Most of the time, quantitative means numeric. Profit and loss are numbers. The relationships between profits and losses are not always obvious. Sometimes we can clarify the relations mathematically. When we can, the cost of not doing so is often great.

It is possible to overstress mathematics, of course. Mathematics is a tool, and not always the most useful one. Thus, the book is about *numeric* trading and money management only to the extent that using numbers produces results, that using numbers makes money management more professional. Not all quantitative techniques are numeric; when numbers fail to give value, I will use something else.

Most of the mathematics in this book makes use of techniques that produce the best or nearly the best possible solution for a given problem, such as determining the proportion of trading capital that should be committed to the market at any given time. It is possible to guess, of course. But when a mathematical solution is available, guessing is invariably costly.

Fortunately, although the mathematics is sometimes tedious, it is not difficult. A little high school algebra is needed, and not much of that.

Unfortunately, even the use of managerial techniques such as marginal analysis and portfolio theory cannot guarantee market success. Nothing can. The most these techniques can do is increase a trader's probability of success or increase the trader's average return. But these are advantages of no small importance.

Can money-management techniques really be of use?

As gambling theorist Richard Epstein would say, "You can bet on it."

Fred Gehm
Abu Dhabi, UAE

Acknowledgments

A writer must credit those who influence him. But I will not relegate to text or footnote those who have helped me most; I would like to thank them here.

I would like to thank my wife Celia, who typed and critiqued many versions of this book. Without Celia's help and support, this book would never have been written.

Thanks are also due to my mother, who not only did a great deal of the typing but who made my life easier while I wrote.

Thanks go to Obaid Al-Nasseri and Hussain Al-Sayegh for putting up with me, among other things.

The theoretical and practical difficulties that statistics present are considerable, and I would like to thank Dr. David Mirza, Dr. Jerry Funk, Dr. Norman Johnson, Ted Clay, Subramanian, and Lingeswaran for helping me with the problems involved.

Frank Pusateri, Jim Marzano, and Keith Day all checked the book for technical and historical errors, which says something for their tolerance for pain. Thanks guys.

I would like to thank the late great Jim Alphier—the market's greatest mind. Had I not met Jim early in my career, this book might never have been written.

Finally, I would like to thank Paul Pekin, who taught me how to write.

1

Introduction: What Is Money Management?

If the articles and advertisements in the trade press are any indication, "money management" is currently a popular approach to trading. Among the claims made for money management is that it can guarantee, or almost guarantee, trading success. Are such claims valid?

To some extent, money management is merely the attitude that trading should be taken seriously, that is, professionally. Risks, for example, should only be taken when the potential reward justifies them. Trading, in other words, is a business venture, and the trader is a business manager or an entrepreneur.

Clearly, money management is essential to successful trading. But just as clearly, money management will *not* guarantee success. Both business managers and entrepreneurs fail on occasion.

The reason money management cannot guarantee success is that the approach is managerial rather than entrepreneurial. Money management focuses on those tasks where proper management will produce certain or nearly certain benefits. Unfortunately, entrepreneurial tasks cannot really be managed. They can only be accepted and acted upon. They demand not so much analysis as creativity; they demand not so much tools and techniques as ideas and action. Managerial tasks are important, but not critical. Entrepreneurial tasks are critical.

The trader's only necessary entrepreneurial task is to produce trading ideas, that is, forecasts. Without forecasts, trading profits are impossible.

Indeed, without entrepreneurship, profits are impossible.[1] Entrepreneurship, and therefore profits, depends both upon the imperfections of the market and upon innovation, that is, ideas. If innovation were impossible and competition were perfect, there would be no profits at all. There would be no profits because no rational individual would loan to, sell to, or work for another if he or she could earn more without doing so. Competition would therefore quickly drive prices down to costs, including, of course, the costs of the owner's own money, goods, and work.

"Profits" would still be reported, of course. But the reported "profits" would not contain a single cent of real profit; rather, the reported profits would just equal the implicit interests, rents, and wages.

The fact that competition is imperfect does not mean profits are guaranteed, only that they are possible. Profits are made by innovation, that is, by ideas. But innovation is pointless if profits are impossible.

The fact that competition is imperfect ensures that profits will not be immediately competed away; that is, that profits will last some period of time. Nevertheless, profits are remarkably ephemeral. Profits are only possible as long as the ideas they are based on are uncommon. For that reason, profits dissipate as the ideas they are based on disperse (see Figure 1–1).

The available evidence suggests that the investment markets are remarkably efficient in disseminating information. In other words, profits are competed away remarkably quickly. For that reason, if a trader knows a way of beating the market, he or she would be well advised to keep it to him- or herself.[2]

In another sense, money management is a group of tools and techniques for managing the rewards and costs of trading. These techniques allow the trader to make decisions at least as

Figure 1–1

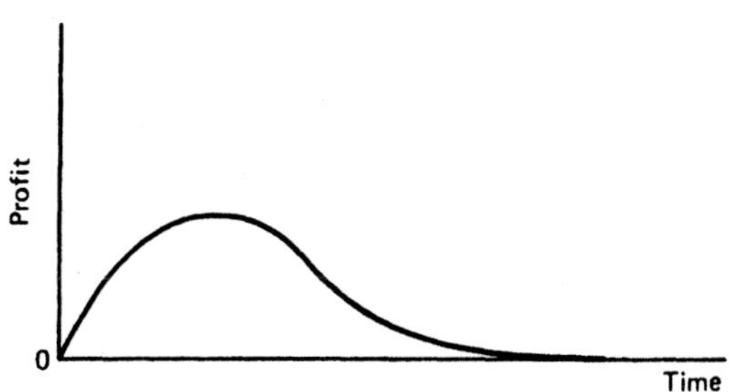

All profits are based on uncommon ideas. As time passes, the ideas disperse, competition increases, and profits diminish.

good, and in many cases much better, than he or she could do otherwise. Ten years ago, these tools were hardly used, even among those who advocated the money management approach. The tools were not used because they were inaccessible; they required a level of sophistication few traders had.

Today, many money management tools are easily accessible. And those that are not probably will be soon. For example, anyone willing to buy a computer and software can now do quadratic programming, a hideously complicated technique. In this sense, the situation has improved remarkably in the last ten years.

In another sense, the situation has gotten worse. There are more posers now than there used to be. Ten years ago, if someone said they were doing quadratic programming, they almost certainly were. Now, it's harder to tell. If someone purchases the right hardware and software, they can do something that they can call quadratic programming. But whether or not they are actually doing quadratic programming, and whether they are doing any good, is another matter.

Money management is not a matter of doing something; it is a matter of doing the right things. A manager has to understand the techniques he or she is using. Which brings us to this book.

This book was written for speculators. It is my intention to provide traders with practical tools, tools that can improve their trading performance. Admittedly, some of the tools provided are difficult to use, but then some of the problems facing the trader are difficult to solve. Worse, almost any error the trader makes will be costly.

In many cases, there are more sophisticated techniques available than those I have presented here. In all cases, however, these more sophisticated techniques are more difficult to use, in most cases *much* more difficult to use. Academicians often stress the theoretical elegance and power of their techniques. Elegance is not important in the "real world"; on the other hand, power, which, roughly, is the effectiveness or the usefulness of a technique, is. However, I believe that practical power is an even more important concept. Practical power is the theoretical power of a technique times the probability of its being used.

Naturally, I selected techniques I felt relatively certain speculators could benefit from. It is for this reason that there are no discussions of individual forecasting techniques in this book. Whereas I can guarantee that a trader who follows a trading plan will be at least as well off as one who does not, I cannot guarantee that any trading methods will ever be profitable. Tomorrow is forever unknown.

This book presupposes that the reader has or can develop forecasting ability. For some readers, this will be a reasonable assumption, for others not. However, the assumptions need not remain assumptions. The discussion in Chapter 6 and the techniques in Chapters 7 and 8 can help the reader decide which group he or she is in. Chapter 6 discusses the efficient market hypothesis. If this hypothesis is true, as is believed by many academic economists, the market is unbeatable and trading is pointless. Chapter 7 discusses building a trading method. Chapter 8 discusses statistical techniques. These techniques allow the trader to judge how likely it is that he or she can really beat the market.

If the reader decides to abandon trading after reading these chapters, his or her money will have been well spent.

However, Chapters 6, 7, and 8 may be difficult to understand if the trader has not read the preceding chapters. Chapter 2 discusses the inevitability of risk. Chapter 3 discusses techniques for discovering the nature of risks that the trader must manage, and techniques for managing in extremely uncertain situations. If the trader can forecast the market, however, the forecasts must be turned into trades. Chapter 4 discusses the trade-offs and choices the trader must make in order to do so. The actual process of transforming a forecast into a trade is discussed in Chapter 5. With the exception of the last chapter, which should be read last, the rest of the book can be read in almost any order.

Chapter 9 discusses how to minimize a particular type of risk, the risk of very large losses. Chapter 10 discusses diversification, a risk reduction technique. Chapter 11 discusses portfolio commitment strategies, which are techniques for diversifying over time. Finally, Chapter 12 discusses managing the work of managing risk, or how to put the rest of this book to work.

This book presupposes that the reader is familiar with the market. Ideally, the reader should have traded for a year or more. Failing that, the reader should put this book down and read an introductory book or two on trading.

This book cannot be read like a novel. (Only novels can be.) If this book is to be of any use to you, the reader, you must understand the techniques and adapt them to your own use. Clearly, the experienced trader has an advantage here that the inexperienced trader can only overcome by thinking long and hard about the problems involved.

On the other hand, the inexperienced trader may have an advantage over the experienced trader. If my experiences are typical, many experienced traders are not open to new ideas.[3] Such traders are likely to reject this book as being too theoretical, too academic, and too mathematical.

Although I have tried to minimize the amount of mathematics in this book, I simply cannot eliminate it. Profit is a numbers game, and there is no way to avoid mathematics.

On the other hand, many business people find academic work irrelevant. Academicians often seem unaware of what is happening in the real world. For example, many academicians do not seem to realize that *every* business decision must be cost-justified. Needless to say, I do not think these criticisms can be applied fairly to my book.

Many business people have the attitude that "no one ever made a dime from theory." To the extent that a theory is wrong or unapplied, this attitude is clearly correct. But nothing is as practical or as profitable as good theory.

Consider, as an example, Thales of Miletus (460?–546 B.C.). Thales was one of the first philosophers and, apparently, out of touch with the real world on occasion. For example, one night while he was gazing at the stars, he fell or walked into a pit. But at other times, he was very much in touch with the real world. According to Aristotle (*Politics* 1259a): "He was reproached for his poverty, which was supposed to show that philosophy is of no use. According to the story, he knew by his skill in the stars while it was yet winter that there would be a great harvest of olives in the coming year; so, having a little money, he gave deposits for the use of all the olive presses in Chios and Miletus, which he hired at a low price because no one bid against him. When the harvest time came, and many were wanted all at once and of a sudden, he let them at any rate which he pleased, and made a quantity of money. Thus he showed the world that philosophers can easily be rich if they like . . ."

What was then philosophy would now be a great many things, including, no doubt, business administration. In a certain sense, philosophy is nothing more than thinking as hard as you can about something. Although I do not believe any amount of thinking can guarantee that a trader will make money, I do believe that those who trade without thinking are certain or almost certain to lose.

What follows is some of the best thinking of which I am capable. I hope it makes you money.

Unfortunately, I cannot assure you that it will. The techniques I have presented will ensure that good decisions, even in some cases the best possible decisions, are made with the information and resources available. Unfortunately, the techniques presented here cannot ensure profitable trading. Nothing can. The best possible decision may be not to trade.

Endnotes

1. This is simply a restatement of the work of Joseph A. Schumpeter, *The Theory of Economic Development* (New York: Oxford University Press, 1961). For an opposing view see, Michael E. Porter, *Competitive Strategy, Techniques for Analyzing Industries and Competitors* (New York: Free Press, 1980). Porter sees profitability as a function of five competitive forces that a business may manage to some extent. Porter's arguments are persuasive, but I can see no trading implications that Schumpeter and the efficient market hypothesis, which is discussed in Chapter 6, do not also imply.
2. Chapter 7 contains a further discussion of this issue.
3. A recent and fascinating study of institutional investors documents the extent to which economic rationales are excuses for behaving one way or another. William M. O'Barr, and John M. Conley, *Fortune and Folly: The Wealth and Power of Institutional Investing,* (Homewood, IL: Business One Irwin, 1992). There is no reason to believe that other investment professionals or other investors are different. You and I are on that list. I worry about that a *lot*. On the positive side, rationality is not a set of beliefs. It is a skill like playing the piano. It is a skill that anyone can acquire, but no one acquires without work.

2

Risk-Free Trading Is Risky Stuff

On a regular basis, investment advisors of various types sell or rent "conservative" and even "risk-free" trading methods or advice. Are such things possible?

Risk-free trading is a very quick road to bankruptcy and suicide. It is not difficult to see why. If there were really no possibility of losing on a given trade, the proper procedure would be to borrow as much money as possible and invest it all in the next such trade. Only a half dozen trades should be sufficient for you to retire if you pyramid your winnings. But assume the odds of success are really a mere 0.9, where one indicates winning is certain and zero that it is impossible. Then the chance of not losing at least one trade in six (and only one losing trade is necessary to send you to bankruptcy court rather than Bermuda) is $0.9^6 = 0.53$. And if the odds of success are 0.6 on a given trade, the odds of a six-trade profitable run are $0.6^6 = 0.05$.

So long as the future cannot be known with complete certainty, there can be no such thing as risk-free trading. What is marketed as risk-free trading is simply trading with the risk understated or ignored. For example, one publicly offered trading method recently advertised allegedly will enable you "to trade on the commodity market without fear of loss of your working capital. . . ." In fact, it will do no such thing. What the author is selling is the same three-zone system that Pugh sold four decades ago. With this system, you identify three zones on the basis of the past several years' price action, and buy when the price is in the lowest of the three zones. The author assumes the price cannot go lower than the lowest zone, which is nonsense unless the lowest limit is zero. The first bear market will wipe out anyone using this method. Worse, the price doesn't even have to drop below the bottom of the lowest zone for you to lose; all that is necessary is that the price drop below your purchase point and stay there.

A better example is that of the Mexican peso fiasco. Buying distant peso contracts and "riding them in" was the short and riskless path to wealth. One adviser even put his clients' short-term funds into peso contracts. But there is no such thing as a free lunch. The risk-free profits were in fact insurance premiums that in many sad cases were insufficient to cover the losses when the Mexican government devalued the peso.

The situation is not much better among allegedly sophisticated institutional investors. No brokerage company or investment management firm would suggest that their approach is riskless, except off the record, and then only if they thought they were talking to a real dummy. But such professionals will stress how conservative their approach is, and they will minimize or ignore real risks. For example, David J. Askin's Granite Fund, a $600 million pool of exotic mortgage securities, recently lost all of its net worth. Askin's fund was sold to institutional investors as a low-risk, "market neutral" fund, designed to produce high, steady returns in bull and bear markets. In fact, Askin's fund was an accident waiting to happen.

Askin's fund was a highly leveraged portfolio of various illiquid mortgage-backed securities. Roughly speaking, mortgage rates follow other interest rates, and mortgage prices follow the prices of other bonds. When they do not, it is because mortgages can be prepaid. Now, brokerage companies have broken mortgages into interest-only investments and principal-only investments, and the price of one often goes in the opposite direction of the other. Askin tried to delicately balance the instruments that went up against the instruments that went down so as to earn high returns wherever the market went. As long as the interest-rate movements remain small, and the markets remain liquid, this can be made to work. But when interest rates jumped radically, the markets went illiquid, and Askin could not make the changes necessary to keep his portfolio balanced. Askin missed a margin call, and brokerage companies seized his investments and sold them at huge losses.[1]

But while risk-free trading is not possible, conservative trading is not only possible, in one sense it is necessary. In *Playboy's Investment Guide* (the best introductory book on investing and speculating I know of), Michael Laurence writes, "Too often we tend to think that millionaires are conservative because they are rich, without considering the equally plausible converse: that they are rich because they are conservative."[2]

"Conservative" here has no political connotation. It refers solely to risk management. Inadequate or nonexistent risk management is probably the reason that most traders lose their trading capital. It is necessary that most traders lose, of course, but it is not necessary for a trader to lose if he or she can forecast the market with some accuracy.

The primary tool of risk management is diversification over time and over investments. Consider an investment that has a 0.50 probability of gaining 0.50 in value and a 0.50 probability of losing the same over a year. Over a period of years, you would expect to lose about 0.13 a year on this investment. But if you diversified by buying a portfolio of two such investments that never moved up or down together, you would raise your return to zero. It is for this reason that a *properly* diversified portfolio is both more profitable and less risky than trading a single investment at a time.

Obviously, diversification depends on investments moving independently of each other. In *this* sense trading can be much more conservative than buying and holding blue chip stocks. Corn and copper, say, are much more likely to move independently than, for example, Chrysler and Kodak. In addition, as there is little dependency between stock or bond price movements and trading profits, the effect on an investment portfolio of trading would be to reduce the total risk.[3] If trading can be done profitably, all portfolios, especially the most conservative ones, might be profitably supplemented this way.

Diversification must be over income sources rather than just investments.[4, 5] For most individuals, there is little relationship between business or salary income and trading profits, so trading can reduce income fluctuations. But some individuals should not speculate. They are, oddly enough, just those individuals who are most inclined to: trading advisers, fund managers, brokers, and hedgers. No doubt, this is one reason for the huge turnover of advisers, managers, and brokers. Even the best advisers or managers can expect to have losing periods, and if their own portfolios are eroding at the same time their incentive fees or subscriptions are drying up, they can be financially ruined. Of course, they could have their own speculative portfolio traded by someone with a completely different approach than their own, but it would be safer to invest in stocks or real estate or, better yet, bonds. For brokers, the situation is similar to the extent that their clients do not make their own decisions. Again, for similar reasons, hedgers should not speculate and hedge in the same or related derivatives. However, there is no reason that a banker, for example, cannot hedge interest rates and speculate in corn and copper.

There is a profound difference between investing and trading. The investor need not forecast. An investor can pick stocks and bonds at random and expect to make money on average. A trader who buys and sells at random will eventually lose. It is in this essential context that there can be no conservative trading. It does not matter that you think your chance of success is considerably better—so do the others.

Profitable trading depends on building and validating a forecasting system. That's a *lot* harder than most traders seem to realize. Almost no traders show an understanding of the formidable statistical (and in some cases accounting) barriers to validation. This is not to say that trading cannot be profitable. It can be gloriously profitable. But these profits, if any, are not so much a return on the investment of money as a return on the investment of brains, self-discipline, and work. The trader is not an investor. The trader is a speculator and business person. The successful ones know it.

Endnotes

1. For details, see "The Market's Revenge," *Business Week* (April 18, 1994): 24–29.
2. Michael Laurence, *Playboy's Investment Guide* (Chicago: Playboy Press, 1971).
3. Katherine Dusak, "Futures Trading & Investor Returns: An Investigation of Commodity Market Risk Premiums," *Journal of Political Economy* (November/December 1973): 1387–1406.
4. Edward M. Miller, "Portfolio Selection in a Fluctuating Economy," *Financial Analysts Journal* (May/June 1978): 77–83.
5. Terry Coxon, "How Borrowing Can *Reduce* Your Risk," *Inflation Survival Letter* (November 30, 1977).

3

The Nature of Risk

Given that investments are risky, how do we manage risk? There are plenty of things a trader can do, of course. Naturally, not all of them work. Consider portfolio insurance, as an example. In its 1987 year-end review, *The Wall Street Journal* noted,

> It was a tough year for "portfolio insurance," a stock-market hedging strategy designed in part to sidestep bear markets. The Oct. 19 market crash came so suddenly that many portfolio insurers couldn't erect hedges quickly enough. Explains Hayne Leland, one of the pioneers in portfolio insurance: Market conditions were so disruptive that most hedging models simply couldn't work well. "One doesn't deal a lot with a 1929 scenario in trying to make decisions."
>
> Trouble is, 18 months earlier, Mr. Leland's firm of Leland O'Brien Rubinstein Associates Inc. said it had all the bases covered. In a marketing display entitled: "What LOR's Sophistication Means," the firm listed the following benefit: "Assurance that all the implications and expectations of the selected strategy are known in advance. No unhappy surprises."[1]

What went wrong? Why didn't Leland O'Brien Rubinstein Associates Inc. deal with the 1929 scenario? In Leland and Rubinstein's famous *Financial Analysts Journal* article on portfolio insurance, the article that created the portfolio insurance industry, footnote 15 says, "Remember that the analogy to insurance breaks down under a sudden catastrophic loss that does not leave sufficient time to adjust the replicating portfolio."[2] In other words, portfolio insurance is useless exactly when you want it the most.

This may seem like a fatal flaw, but it is not. Insurance policies do not protect against everything. For example, if you are a typical homeowner with a typical insurance policy, and your home is destroyed by a typical earthquake or war, you lose. No doubt it is possible to get coverage for earthquake or war, but the cost goes up. Few homeowners think such coverage is worth the money. Similarly, if catastrophic price changes are rare enough, there is no flaw in portfolio insurance, in which case the losses were just bad luck, like getting hit by a meteorite. This is Leland and Rubinstein's argument.[3] But are they correct? More important, did they check?

Leland and Rubinstein claim that they did check and provide some evidence that they did. But many other portfolio insurance professionals certainly did not. At least, in contrast to Leland and Rubinstein, many of the portfolio insurance professionals that I have talked to do not understand the technical problems. There is a moderate-sized literature devoted to the shapes of price distributions. As we will see in Chapter 9, this is where the answer to this question lies, if the answer can be found in the investment or economic or business literatures. And if the answer doesn't lie in this literature, this is certainly the place to start looking. But there are few, if any, references to price distribution literature in the portfolio-insurance literature. For example, *Portfolio Insurance: A Guide to Dynamic Hedging* contains no article or even references to this literature.[4] The portfolio-insurance literature does mention discontinuous prices and jump prices, but there is no way to know how often prices jump or become discontinuous without knowing how prices are distributed.

My point is not that Leland, Rubinstein, portfolio insurance, or any combination thereof is wrong. I think highly of portfolio insurance. And I think highly of Leland and Rubinstein. They are clever and creative people. My point is that, as a group, investment-industry professionals think they know much more about risk than they do. This kind of mistake is absolutely typical of investment-industry behavior. I see several examples of it a month.

Which brings us back to our original question, How do we manage risk? We need to do at least three things. We need to worry, we need to look systematically at what we are doing and try to figure out how it might go wrong, and we need to use investment models that accurately portray the knowledge a trader has and doesn't have. We will discuss each of these in turn.

1. Most important, we *worry*. I saw a cartoon a few years ago where a risk-management firm's client says, "Be careful? The best advice you can give me is 'Be careful?'" The client was not impressed, but he was actually getting excellent advice. If he worries, if he is careful, he has a chance of identifying those risks he is not yet managing. He can then find out what to do and act appropriately. If he is complacent, regardless of how good his risk management technique is, he has no chance at all.

Investment professionals hardly ever worry enough. Over the years, I have seen many professionally managed speculative portfolios blow up. In many cases, the managers claimed the risks were managed in a sophisticated and professional manner. In a sense, many of these claims—perhaps all—were correct. But the manager did not manage all of the risks, and one of the risks he or she did not manage blew the portfolio apart.

Part of the problem is that almost all investment jobs involve selling, and effective selling demands enthusiasm and confidence.[5] An enthusiastic and confident risk manager is not likely to worry enough. Logically, there is no reason a manager cannot appear enthusiastic and confident in public and worry in private, which is what investors pay them to do. But for psychological reasons, this seems difficult or impossible for many.

The other part of the problem is that each of us has a psychological map of the real world. All of our maps differ, each corresponding to the real world in some ways but not in others. Whenever our maps differ from the real world, but we act as if they did not, we get into trouble. An old mathematical joke may make this clearer:

Teacher: "Let *X* equal the number of sheep in this problem. . . ."
Student: "But, sir, what if *X* is not equal to the number of sheep in the problem?"

What if, indeed! Of course, one can tell how many sheep there are by looking at them, by *really* looking at them. But this is much harder than it seems; we tend to see our maps of the world rather than the world itself (see Figures 3–1, 3–2, 3–3, and 3–4).

Ironically, the less seriously a trader takes this problem, the more serious the problem is for him. Conversely, the more fully the trader understands the problem, the less risk of this type he will have to accept. In other words, to the extent that the trader's thinking is influenced by evidence rather than ideology, he will have to accept less of this type of risk.

Figure 3–1

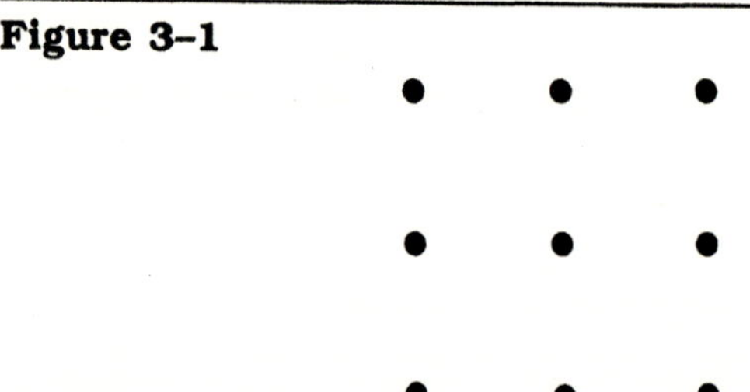

It is quite easy to connect the nine dots above with five continuous straight lines. Nine dots can also be connected with *four* continuous straight lines, but only by those who see the world as it is. The solution is displayed in Figure 3–2.

2. We must look systematically at what we are doing or are going to do, and try to figure out how it might go wrong. There is a technology for doing this. It is called probabilistic risk assessment and was developed by engineers to figure out how likely it was that something would go wrong and what could be done to prevent, or at least minimize that danger.[6] The original work was done by aircraft engineers who apparently had some interest in preventing planes from falling from the sky.

The first step is to figure out what the hazard is. In the technical jargon of probabilistic risk assessment, this is the event you are trying to avoid, such as getting fired or having the planes you build fall out of the sky or, quite possibly, both. As probabilistic risk assessments are expensive, and every hazard requires its own, deciding what the hazard actually is, is of some importance.

A well-defined hazard is clear, intractable, and serious. By clear, I mean that it should be obvious when the hazard has happened, at least after the fact. By intractable, I mean that it should not be possible to manage the hazard directly. If it is possible to manage the hazard directly, you need a hammer, or a blowtorch, or a memo pad, not a probabilistic risk assessment. By serious, I mean that the problem is big. Underperforming the market this month is not a hazard. Losing an account is.

Indeed, I submit that the hazard of interest, for the investor and the trader, is the loss of the account because of underperformance. Losing an account, by itself, is not a hazard. It is no reflection on a trader if an investor closes an account because, say, the client wanted to buy another business. Conversely, it reflects positively on a trader if she closes an account because she does not think she can do a good job. Such an account is often opened later, when the trader thinks she has the problem under control, with considerable investor goodwill.

By itself, underperformance is not a hazard. Indeed, sooner or later, probably sooner, the trader will underperform. Trying to prevent this is likely to prevent performance. It is only when significant underperformance drives the investor to close the account that a hazard takes place.

Notice that focusing on the loss of the account because of underperformance forces the trader to focus on the investor's desires, fears, and constraints. It is the investor's money and he or she deserves to be listened to.

The second step in a probabilistic risk assessment is to figure out what causes the hazard. When probabilistic risk assessment is applied to investment problems, and this can be said dogmatically, this is where the user will make his most important mistakes. Investment professionals tend to depend heavily on their own experience. To a lesser degree, they depend on their education and on the experiences of those they know and trust. Typically, they do not believe that the failures of others, espe-

Figure 3–2

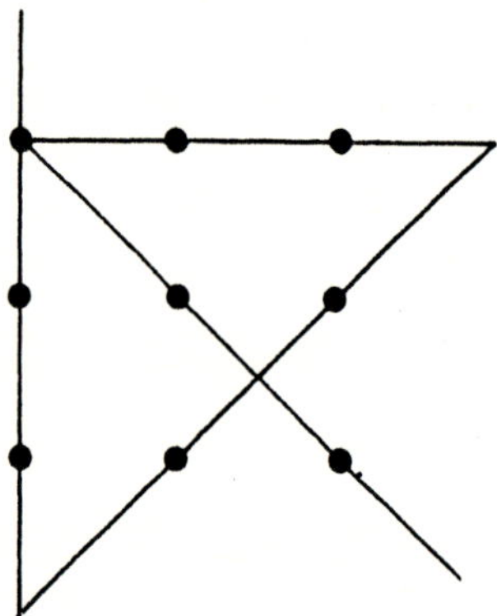

The nine dots above can be connected by four continuous straight lines only by extending several of the lines outside the area bounded by the dots. Most people fail to solve this problem because they assume the lines cannot go beyond this area. This prohibition is not given in the problem itself, however. Solving problems demands seeing the problem itself, not an image or map of the problem. Understand? Then connect the dots above with *three* continuous straight lines. The solution is displayed in Figure 3–3.

cially others they have never met, have anything in common with them. They would never make *their* mistakes. But the sad fact is that we are all condemned to be human, that we all have far more in common than we care to admit.

Put another way, the academic and professional literatures are rich with stories of failure and success. The trader who is more interested in succeeding than feeling successful will read this literature and try to figure out which types of failures his method is prey to. Generally speaking, the answer is most of them. Plus ways that have not happened yet. More specifically, methods that depend on the same economic tools, techniques, and principles will fail in the same ways. Methods that differ will fail in different ways. In order to apply this technique, therefore, the investor needs a deep understanding of his trading method and of the methods described in the literature.

The third step in a probabilistic risk assessment is to organize or group the causes of failure. There are a dozen or so major ways of organizing this information of which, for our purposes, the fault tree is probably the most useful.[7] At the top of the fault tree is the hazard the trader is trying to prevent. Under that hazard are listed all the failures that could lead to it. Under those failures are subfailures that could lead to the failures. And so on. Fault trees are sometimes drawn on their side, which increases or decreases their metaphorical value, depending on your artistic inclinations.

The fourth step in a probabilistic risk assessment is to estimate the probability of each failure or subfailure. Notice that this puts a lower limit on the amount of detail necessary for the analysis. Theoretically, the analysis should continue until the analyst knows how likely each particular failure is. For example, a nuclear power plant is made of, among other things, wires and pipes. The probability of a particular type of wire or pipe failing over a specified period, when used in a certain way, can be estimated with some reliability, in which case the engineer has sufficient detail.

A well-constructed fault tree must include human errors, such as a technician throwing the wrong switch or a clerk giving a buy order when a sell order was needed. Fortunately, it is possible to estimate the types and frequency of simple human error. Unfortunately, this is not the only problem the trader faces. The trader must also estimate how often certain complex judgments made under stress will be wrong. Worse yet, in many cases the trader must estimate how often his or her judgments will be wrong. Most people find it difficult to be objective here. Possibly, because it is impossible.

Thus, it is not at all clear how long the analysis should go on, or how much detail is needed. I am informed that a fault tree for a nuclear power plant can take 20 worker-years. For most traders, this level of detail is probably excessive. Still, a good working rule is to continue working until the project has stopped generating insights, until the trader has lost interest, and then to work awhile longer.

The fifth step in a probabilistic risk assessment is to calculate the total system risk. This is a simple matter of addition and multiplication. When two or more subfailures can each independently lead to the same failure, the probabilities are added. When all of a series of subfailures must take place before a failure

Figure 3–3

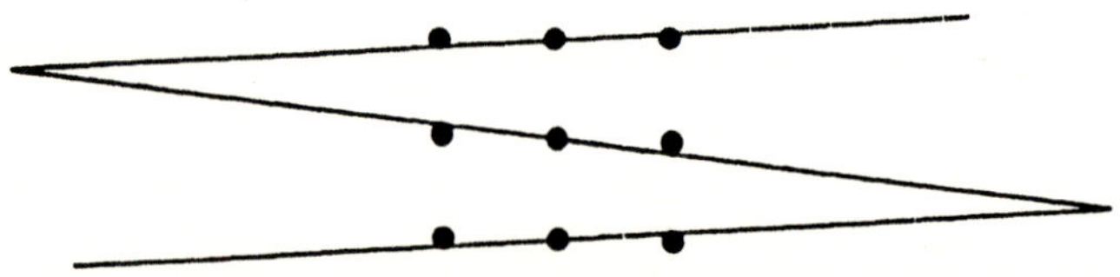

The nine dots above are not really dots at all; that is, they are not mathematical points, but have height and width, thus allowing three straight, continuous, intersecting lines to be drawn through them. Solving the problem demands realizing that our map of the world is not the world itself. Understand? Then connect the nine dots above with *one* continuous straight line. The solution is displayed in Figure 3–4.

takes place, the probabilities are multiplied together (see Chapter 4). Notice that the probabilities do not add to one. Presumedly, the system works some of the time.

Because of the approximations and estimates involved, total system risk is always a guess. Thus, a probability of the hazard taking place of 9.7832 percent over the next 60 months might really mean a probability of say, 5 to 20 percent. Considering that traders, being human, typically overestimate the amount of skill they really have, the higher estimate is probably more accurate. Still, if the analysis is done honestly, it will give the trader some feel for whether he or she wants to use a particular trading method. It is probably better if investors never see a probabilistic risk analysis. It is hard enough being honest in private.

The sixth and final step in a probabilistic risk assessment is to figure out what techniques are available to solve the identified problems. See Figure 3–5. Notice that an analysis of the branches of the fault tree will indicate where the greatest risks are. In many cases, perhaps in all cases, these risks can be lowered and the total risk recalculated.

In many cases, the necessary techniques can be found somewhere in the investment literature. Failing that, they may be buried in some other professional or academic literature. In my experience, none of the problems that traders face are unique. To the contrary, powerful insights and techniques can be found in other disciplines. To find them, the trader must decide who faces similar problems and then find out what they do about them. Failing that, the trader must invent her or his own solutions or accept the risk.

Figure 3–5 is a fault tree for a hedge fund using a systematic technical approach to selecting overvalued and undervalued equities. It was developed by the firm's president, who is also the developer of the trading method. The hazard here is that the client might close the account for poor performance within the next five years. The tree first acknowledges that the account could be closed because the method did not work or despite the method's working. If the method did not work, it would be because the trading method was tested on too small a sample or because the sample was biased. The logic for the other major branch of the fault tree was similarly worked out.

Based on his estimates of individual faults, the president of the firm estimated that the probability of the hazard taking place was 9 percent, which was too high, in his opinion. In an effort to sharpen the numbers, he hired a statistician who added several branches to the tree and reestimated the numbers. The statistician noted that if an improper statistical technique was used, it was because the wrong statistical technique was used or because of unrealistic data assumptions. The statistician also noted that the sample size was too small to make a meaningful decision. The statistician checked the program code and found two major errors. These were corrected, data was bought, the proper statistical technique was used, and the numbers were recalculated. Analysis of various subsets of the data showed no bias. Comparisons of the data against a broader universe showed no biases. A similar analysis, using other consultants, was done on the other section. The results of this analysis is in Exhibit 3–6. The new

Figure 3–4

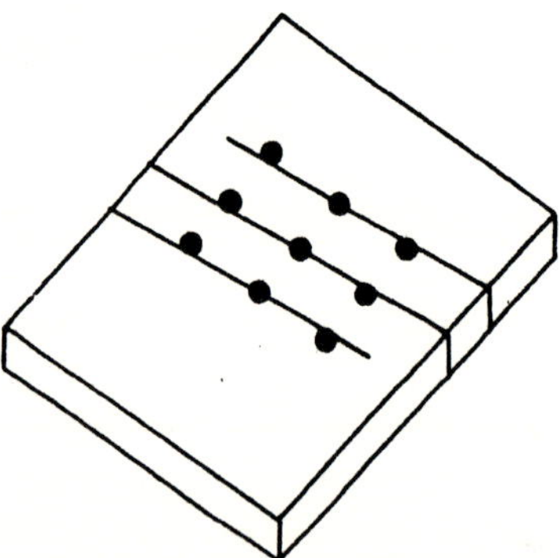

Nine dots can be connected with one straight line either by wrapping the line around the page the dots are drawn on or by drawing a very thick line. Understand? Then . . .

Figure 3–5 Fault Tree A

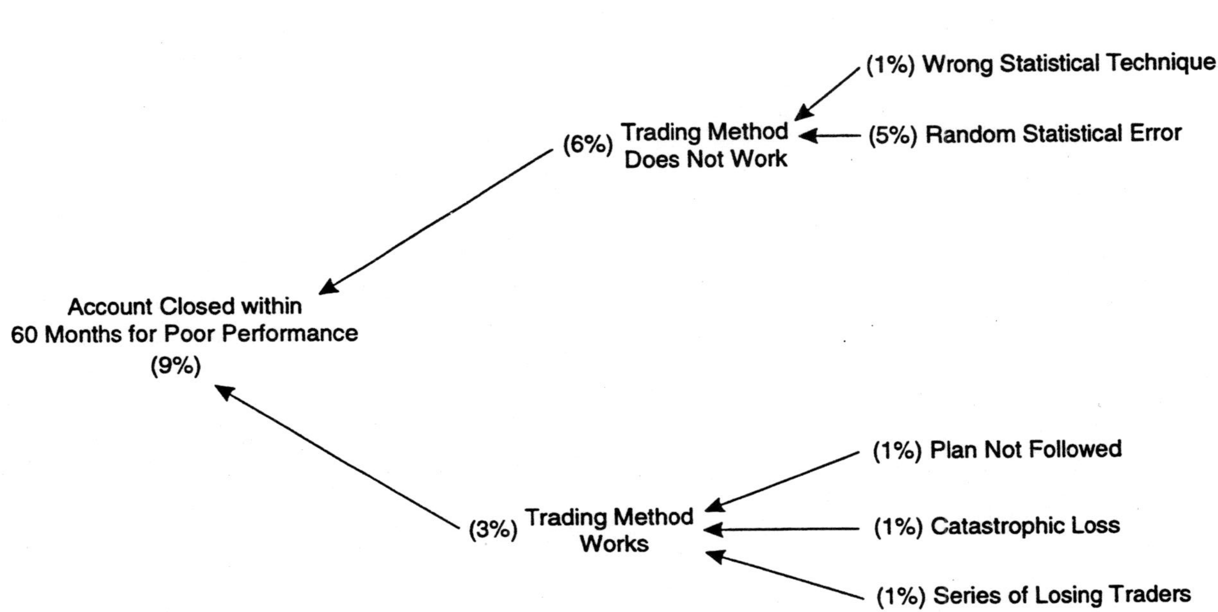

Figure 3–6 Fault Tree B

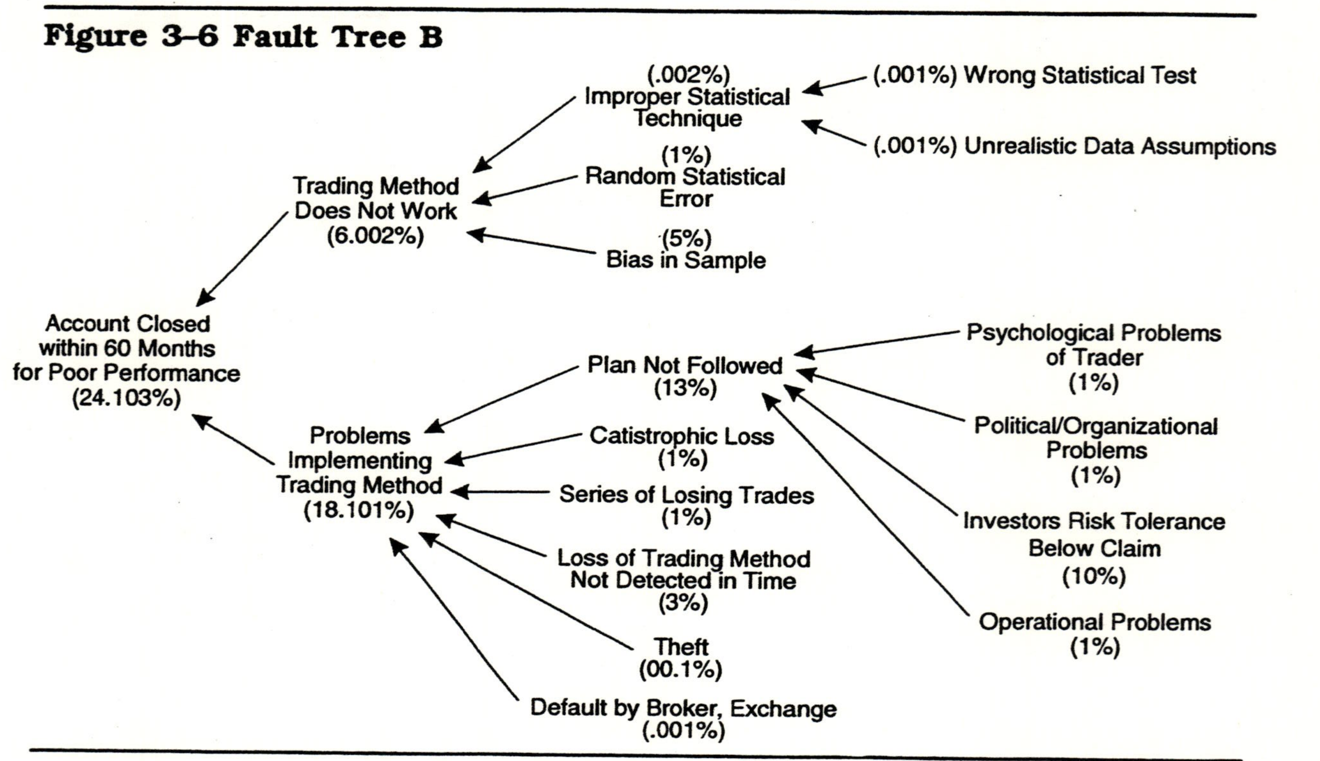

estimate of the probability of the hazard taking place was 24.103 percent. The president decided he had a lot of work to do.

3. The trader can use investment models that accurately portray the knowledge he or she has—and doesn't have. Trading decisions, like all decisions, must be made under one of three broad conditions: certainty, risk, and uncertainty. When a decision is made under *certainty*, the results of all possible actions are known in advance. When a decision is made under *risk*, the results are not known in advance. However, the possible results of any given action are known, and the relevant probabilities are known or can be estimated. When a decision is made under *uncertainty*, the possible results may not be known or may be known incompletely. When the possible results are known, the probabilities are not.

Traders obviously need many types of decision-making techniques. Less obviously, all of the most important investment decisions must be made under uncertainty.[8,9] Unfortunately, almost all decision-making technology is designed for decision making under risk or certainty. This is not because investment scholars are ignorant or biased. Techniques for making decisions under risk are based on statistics and probability theory, which are *very* powerful theories. Techniques for making decisions under uncertainty are based on fuzzy set theory, interval mathematics, or ad-hoc rules. The ad-hoc rules are, in some ways, the most interesting, as they make the weakest possible assumptions. Unfortunately, they do the least work. Fuzzy set theory is more powerful than the ad-hoc techniques, but it is nowhere near as powerful as probability theory. Fuzzy techniques can be more trouble to use than they are worth, so these techniques are relegated to an appendix. Interval mathematics is between the two in ease of use and power. We will discuss the ad-hoc techniques first and then a technique based on interval mathematics.

All of the published ad-hoc techniques implicitly assume that the uncertainty in the decision is inherent; that is, the uncertainty cannot be reduced to risk or certainty.[10] Fortunately, this is not always the case. However, the relevant information cannot always be purchased or cannot be purchased at a reasonable price, and techniques for making decisions under uncertainty are needed.

The published techniques assume further that, given a set of investments, all of the states of nature that might affect those investments and all of the possible results are known with certainty. This is rarely the case, of course.

The investments selected are known with certainty, of course. Theoretically, all of the investments that might be considered should be considered. At least, the more investments considered, the more likely it is that the investment selected will be a good one. On the other hand, since considering investments is costly, the number considered must be kept manageable. Investments might be chosen for consideration on the basis of the states of nature to be considered, on the basis of the trader's forecasting and trading style, or on other bases.

A state of nature is any event or combination of events beyond the control of the trader that affects the results obtained. Theoretically, the states of nature should be mutually exclusive and exhaustive. Unfortunately, the obvious states of nature are almost never mutually exclusive. Worse, the number of possible states of nature is almost always infinite. Simplifying assumptions must therefore be made.[11] If the assumptions made are reasonable, the results will be reasonable. If not, not.

The necessary information must be presented in the form of a payoff matrix. A payoff matrix is a table that shows the results or payoffs if an individual selects one of several investments and then one of several mutually exclusive and exhaustive states of nature occurs.

Payoffs are rarely known with certainty. In most cases, they must be estimated or assumed. The methods to be described do not assume a particular method of deriving possible results (e.g., average returns, consensus of analysis, econometric forecasts, etc.), they only assume that the results have been derived. Analysis based on doubtful data will, of course, produce doubtful results.

Once the payoff matrix has been constructed, it must be examined for dominance and the dominated investments removed. One investment dominates a second if and only if the first will produce a payoff larger than or equal to the second for every possible state of nature and a payoff larger than the second for at least one state of nature. A dominated investment is clearly an inferior investment and need not be considered further. In Table 3–1 investment *D* dominates investment *E* and the latter can be ignored.

A decision rule must fit its users' values and beliefs. The *Maximax* rule is useful if the trader is optimistic or if he believes that nature will conspire with him to produce the results most to his liking. The rule is:

$$\text{Max}_i \, [\, \text{Max}_j \, \theta_{ij} \,]$$

where θ_{ij} is the payoff for the *i*th investment and the *j*th state of nature. Max indicates that the largest value must be located. The procedure is to first locate the most favorable payoff for each investment and then to locate the investment whose most favorable payoff is most favorable. In the case of the example, this would be Investment *B*.

Table 3–1

	State J	State K	State L	State M
Investment A	***50.00***	60.00	140.00	2,200.00
Investment B	200.00	***0.00***	170.00	2,210.00
Investment C	210.00	30.00	***10.00***	2,200.00
Investment D	150.00	***40.00***	130.00	2,190.00
Investment E	150.00	0.00	40.00	2,190.00

Investment E can be ignored as it is dominated by Investment D. The least favorable payoff has been printed in ***bold italic*** for Investments A–D above. The Maximin rule suggests the investment with the largest minimum payoff, Investment A.

The *Maximin* rule is useful if the trader is pessimistic or if he believes that nature will conspire against him to produce the results most to his displeasure. The rule is:

$$\text{Max}_i \; [\; \text{Min}_j \; \theta_{ij} \;]$$

where Min indicates that the smallest value must be located. The procedure is to first locate the least favorable payoff for each investment and then to locate the investment whose least favorable payoff is most favorable, which in the case of the example is Investment A (see Table 3–1).

The *Hurwicz* (1951) rule can be used regardless of whether the trader is optimistic or pessimistic and regardless of the trader's psychology of nature.[12] In fact, the Hurwicz rule contains the Maximax and Maximin rules as special cases. The rule is:

$$\text{Max}_i \; (\phi \; [\text{Max}_j \; \theta_{ij} \;] + [\; 1 - \phi \;] \; [\text{Min}_j \; \theta_{ij} \;])$$

ϕ represents the trader's optimism or pessimism by a number from zero to one inclusive, where zero indicates complete pessimism and one indicates complete optimism. When ϕ equals zero or one, the rule reduces to the Maximin or Maximax rules, respectively.

The procedure, once the trader has quantified his or her feelings by selecting a value for ϕ, is to locate both the most favorable and the least favorable payoff for each investment. Each most favorable payoff must be multiplied by ϕ; each least favorable must be multiplied by $1 - \phi$, and for each investment the results must be added together. The investment with the largest resulting sum is the most desirable. In the case of the example, if, say, ø equals 0.4, the most desirable investment is *A*.

The *Minimax Regret* rule is a radical departure from the rules above.[13] The rule attempts to minimize the cost or regret arising from picking the wrong investment. The rule is:

$$\text{Min}_i \; [\; \text{Max}_j \; \theta_{ij} \;]$$

where θ_{ij} represents the trader's regret that he or she selected the *i*th investment when the *j*th state of nature occurred. The procedure is to first transform the payoff matrix into a regret matrix. This is done by subtracting each payoff from the maximum payoff for its state of nature and tabling the results. Next the maximum regret for each investment is located. The investment with the smallest maximum regret is the most desirable, which in the case of the example is Investment *B* or *D* (see Table 3–2).

In many, perhaps most, real-world situations, the most reasonable procedure would seem to be to select the investment that could be expected to be most profitable on average. One obvious alternative, which oddly does not seem to be mentioned in the literature, is the *MaxMedian* rule.

$$\text{Max}_i\ [\ \text{Med}_j\ \theta_{ij}\ ]$$

Table 3–2

	State J	State K	State L	State M
Investment A	50.00	***60.00*** [a]	140.00	2,200.00
Investment B	200.00	0.00	***170.00*** [a]	***2,210.00*** [a]
Investment C	***210.00*** [a]	30.00	10.00	2,200.00
Investment D	150.00	40.00	130.00	2,190.00
Investment A	***160.00*** [b]	0.00	30.00	10.00
Investment B	10.00	***60.00*** [b]	0.00	0.00
Investment C	0.00	30.00	***160.00*** [b]	10.00
Investment D	***60.00*** [b]	20.00	40.00	20.00

[a]The maximum payoff for each state of nature has been printed in ***bold italic*** above. Each value is subtracted from the maximum payoff for its state of nature and the results tabled below.

[b]The maximum regret for each investment has been printed in ***bold italic*** above. The Minimax Regret rule suggests acquiring the investment with the smallest maximum regret, Investments *B* or *D*.

where Med indicates that the median value must be located. The procedure is to locate the median payoff for each investment and then locate the maximum median payoff. In the case of the example, this is Investment *B*.

MaxAverage rules are similar in concept to the MaxMedian rule. The general form of a MaxAverage rule is:

$$\mathrm{Max}_i \frac{\sum_{j=1}^{N} W_j \cdot \theta_{ij}}{\sum_{j=1}^{N} W_j}$$

where W_j is the weight for the *j*th state of nature, and N is the number of states of nature. The procedure is to multiply each payoff for each investment by a weighting factor constant for that state of nature, to sum the weighted values for each investment, to divide the results by the sum of the weighting factors, and finally to choose the investment with the largest result on average.

The problem is, of course, in choosing a weighting function. One solution that is frequently mentioned in the literature is to weight the payoffs according to the probability of occurrence of the relevant state of nature (i.e., $W_j = P_j$). In some cases, reasonable assumptions can be made, and this can be done. For example, the principle of insufficient reason, also known as the Laplace rule, can sometimes be appealed to. The basic idea here is that unless there is an obvious reason to weight the states of nature unequally, they should be equally weighted. Unfortunately, this assumption seems to be only rarely useful. In most cases, an unequal weighting seems called for, but what unequal weighting to use seems less than obvious.

A second solution is to weight the payoffs according to the importance of the various states of nature to the investments being considered. Clearly, a state of nature with a relatively narrow range of payoffs is relatively unimportant. If that state of nature occurs, it will have mattered little which investment the trader chose. Contrariwise, a state of nature with a relatively wide range of alternative payoffs is highly important.

A *MaxAverage Importance* rule scales the weighting factors to reflect the relative range of payoffs. The formula is:

$$W_j = R_j / Z$$

where:

$$Z = \sum_{j=1}^{N} R_j$$

and:

R_j = the range of payoffs for state of nature j

The range is only one of an infinite number of measures of dispersion, and conceivably another measure might be more appropriate, at least under certain circumstances, although it is difficult to say what those circumstances would be. Still, the choice of the range is not completely arbitrary. The range is the only measure of dispersion that depends solely on the most extreme values. It seems clear that the importance of a state of nature depends entirely or at least primarily on the most extreme values. Also, the range is easy to use.

The procedure is, first, to calculate the weighting factors for the states of nature by dividing the range of the payoffs for each state of nature by the sum of the ranges. Second, each payoff, in turn, must be multiplied by the appropriate weighting factor; that is, the weighting factor for its state of nature. Third, the results must be summed for each investment, and the investment with the largest sum chosen, which in the case of the example is Investment B (see Table 3–3).

Several of the techniques described above are useful when nature, or the people on the other side of the trade, have an interest in the investor's actions. For example, the Maximax rule

Table 3-3

	State J	State K	State L	State M
Investment A	50.00	60.00	140.00	2,200.00
Investment B	200.00	0.00	170.00	2,210.00
Investment C	210.00	30.00	10.00	2,200.00
Investment D	150.00	40.00	130.00	2,190.00
Range[a]	160.00	60.00	160.00	20.00
Sum	400.00	400.00	400.00	400.00
Weight	0.40	0.15	0.40	0.05

	State J	State K	State L	State M	Average[b]
Investment A	20.00	9.00	56.00	110.00	195.00
Investment B	80.00	0.00	68.00	110.50	258.50
Investment C	84.00	4.50	4.00	110.00	202.50
Investment D	60.00	6.00	52.00	109.50	227.50

[a]The first line under the payoff matrix is the range of payoffs for each state of nature. The range divided by sum of the ranges is the weighting factor. Each of the payoffs has been multipled by the relevant weight and the results tabled below.

[b]Summing across the line produces the "average" payoff for each investment, that is, the range-weighted average payoff. The MaxAverage/Importance rule suggests acquiring the investment with the largest average payoff, Investment B.

is reasonable if nature is benevolent. Given the investment markets' reputation for compassion, this is a surprisingly popular rule. Alternatively, the theory of contrary opinion holds that the market acts so as to surprise the greatest number of people.[14] This theory may not be true, but it is reasonable. If true, the theory implies that most traders would be wise to use the Maximin rule.

The other rules are harder to justify. When only two investments are available or when nature is interested in your choice, it makes sense to select investments on the basis of extreme values. But this is not much help. Any trader who must choose between two investments does not get out enough. When nature is not interested, and most theories of the market do not presume this, making decisions on the basis of extreme values makes little sense. One exception is the Minimax Regret rule, which may be of value to the professional trader. Investment professionals are often criticized when their performance is not the best possible for the state of nature that occurs. This technique can help them cope with that unfair situation, at least to some extent.

When nature is not interested, some kind of average makes sense. When the states of nature are equally likely to occur, that is, when Laplace's rule makes sense, a simple arithmetic mean should be used. When Laplace's rule is not acceptable, and no doubt this is most of the time, the MaxAverage Importance technique is the best of the available techniques.

An example may make the virtues and vices of the various techniques clearer. More important, it may clarify how a trader can use these techniques. Consider a trader who developed four different bond arbitrage systems. While the trader has designed these systems to be market neutral, his own research indicates that they are not as neutral as he would like. Method A performs well in high interest-rate, high-volatility markets. Method B performs well in low interest-rate, high-volatility markets. Method C performs well in high interest-rate, low-volatility markets. Method D performs well in low interest-rate, low-volatility markets. Each of the methods performs badly in some combination of interest rates and volatility.[15] Characterizing interest-rate markets as high or low interest-rate and high or low volatility is artificial and arbitrary, but it is a common industry practice. Be that as it may, which trading method, if any, should the manager use?

Clearly, the manager might make or buy a forecast of interest-rate levels and volatility and decide on that basis. But the success of this approach depends on the manager's ability to forecast the market, which is exactly what the manager wanted to avoid when he tried to develop a market-neutral method. Alternatively, the manager can use one of the ad-hoc techniques described above.

The first step in this type of analysis is to construct a payoff matrix. The investments are the four noted earlier plus the option of doing nothing. There are four states of nature, each of which is a combination of interest rate and volatility. The most obvious payoff value is the total trading profit. But the manager wants high risk-adjusted returns. After considering several measures, he decided on Sharpe's Ratio, which is a measure of return adjusted by a measure of risk.[16] The manager reviews the historical studies for the various methods and estimates each method's Sharpe's Ratio for each market type. These estimates are placed in the appropriate matrix cells.

The second step is to examine the matrix for dominance. Unfortunately, none of the trading methods dominates all of the others. Far more often than not, this is the case.

The third step in this analysis is a review of the available decision-making techniques in terms of the economics of the situation and the manager's goals and feelings. Upon consideration, the manager decides that there is no reason to be particularly optimistic or pessimistic about the methods. Nor is there any reason to believe that nature, or other traders, will conspire with or against him. This eliminates the Minimax, the Maximin, and Hurwicz rules.

The manager also decides that he wants a trading method whose risk-adjusted return is as large as possible on average. This means he must use the MaxMedian, MaxAverage Importance, equally weighted, or a probability weighted average. The manager rejects the MaxMedian on the basis that it uses little of the available information. He rejects the equally weighted average because he does not believe the probabilities are equal.

The manager notes that he could use the historic frequency of the various market types as the basis of a probability-weighted average. But he has no reason to expect the probabilities will remain stable. In fact, he uses ad-hoc uncertainty techniques because he wants to avoid that assumption. He therefore decides to use the MaxAverage Importance rule.

The ad-hoc techniques just described permit or allow no probabilities, where probabilities are really needed. By way of contrast, Table 3–4 shows how the decision would be made if we were certain of our estimates of payoffs and probabilities. The expected value for each investment is calculated by multiplying the payoffs for each state of nature by the probability that that state of nature will take place. The values are then summed for each investment. The investment with the highest sum is presumedly the best.

Table 3–4

	State J	State K	State L	Average
Probability	.70	.20	.10	
Investment A	–5,000,000	–10,000,000	7,000,000	–4,800,000
Investment B	–5,000,000	0	0	–3,500,000
Investment C	0	7,000,000	2,000,000	1,600,000
	–3,500,000	–2,000,000	700,000	–4,800,000
	–3,500,000	0	0	–3,500,000
	0	1,400,000	200,000	1,600,000

In the top of the table each return is multiplied by the probability for that state of nature. The result is shown in the bottom of the table. The average return for an investment is the sum across the row..

The technique just described is a standard probability-weighted decision analysis. But what if we do not know the exact probabilities or the payoffs? If we know how high or low the probabilities or the payoff might be, we can replace the standard analysis with an analysis based on interval mathematics.[17] In the standard analysis, we might say that the probability of a certain state of nature taking place is 20 percent, when we mean that the probability is exactly 20 percent. In the interval mathematics variant, we might say that the probability of a certain state of nature taking place is between 15 and 30 percent, inclusive. In other words, the probability of interest is the 15–30 percent interval. Similarly, exact estimates of the various payoffs are replaced with intervals.

When we know the exact probabilities or payoffs, we use the same number on both sides of the interval. Thus, a certain state of nature might be expected to occur 15–15 percent of the time. In the unlikely event we know all of the probabilities and payoffs exactly and still want to use interval mathematics, we can do that, too.

In the current technical jargon, the intervals described above are called intervals of confidence, as opposed to confidence intervals, which is a statistical concept described in Chapter 8. Notice that in interval mathematics, we replace a demand for an exact probability or payoff with a demand for an exact interval. Two exact estimates are needed where one was needed before. This might not seem like much progress, but it is a lot easier to say what something might be than to say what it is.

Presumedly, the more confidence an investor has to have in his or her estimate, the *wider* the intervals will be.[18] Thus, an analyst or trader needs some kind of intuitive definition of confidence, although exactly how confident a trader is, is not important, as long as he or she is consistent. Mathematically, there are no constraints on payoffs. The profits or losses do not even have to be finite, although infinite profits and losses are relatively rare. However, probabilities are constrained. No probability can be below zero, or above one, and the sum must always be one. A relatively easy way to estimate consistent upper and lower probabilities is to do it indirectly. Make two different consistent estimates of the probabilities for the various states of nature. Now, rearrange the probabilities so that one set of numbers contains all the high numbers, while the other set contains all the low numbers. Use this later set for the analysis (see Table 3-5).

Each payoff interval can now be multiplied by the appropriate probability intervals. A payoff interval is repressed as $[a_1, a_2]$, where $a_2 \geq a_1$. A probability interval is repressed as $[P_1, P_2]$,

Table 3–5

	State J	State K	State L
	70%– 50%	20%– 40%	10%– 10%
Investment A	0– –5,000,000	3,000,000– –10,000,000	7,000,000– –5,000,000
Investment B	–5,000,000– –5,000,000	0– 0	3,000,000– –5,000,000
Investment C	3,000,000– 0	7,000,000– 0	7,000,000– –10,000,000

where $P_2 \geq P_1$. Interval multiplication is a bit complicated. There are three multiplication formulas. The results of the multiplication are $[x_1, x_2]$, where $x_2 \geq x_1$. The formulas are:

$$\text{If } a_1 \geq 0 \text{ and } a_2 \geq 0 \quad \text{then } [x_1, x_2] = [a_1 \cdot P_1, a_2 \cdot P_2]$$
$$\text{If } a_1 \leq 0 \text{ and } a_2 \geq 0 \quad \text{then } [x_1, x_2] = [a_1, \cdot P_2, a_2 \cdot P_1]$$
$$\text{If } a_1 \text{ and } a_2 \leq 0 \quad \text{then } [x_1, x_2] = [a_1 \cdot P_2, a_2 \cdot P_1]$$

The resulting intervals for each investment are now added. Fortunately, this is somewhat easier. If $[x_1, x_2]$ is the sum of $[a_1, a_2]$ and $[b_1, b_2]$, then the formula is:

$$[x_1, x_2] = [a_1 + b_1, a_2 + b_2]$$

Table 3–6 is an example.

If the investor were doing a standard probability-weighted decision analysis his, or her work would now be done. In this kind of analysis, the investment with the highest sum is presumedly the best. Sometimes this is the case in an interval analysis. All too often, however, the intervals overlap. Fortunately, the Hurwicz rule, explained earlier in this chapter, is well suited for this type of situation.

Table 3–6

	State J	State K	State L	Average
	70%–	20%–	10%–	
	50%	40%	10%	
Investment A	0–	3,000,000	7,000,000–	1,900,000–
	–5,000,000	–10,000,000	–5,000,000	–8,000,000
Investment B	–5,000,000–	0	3,000,000–	2,200,000–
	–5,000,000	0	–5,000,000	–3,000,000
Investment C	3,000,000–	7,000,000–	7,000,000–	5,600,000
	0	0	–10,000,000	–1,000,000
	0–	1,200,000–	700,000–	1,900,000–
	–3,500,000	4,000,000	–500,000	–8,000,000
	–2,500,000–	0–	300,000–	–2,200,000–
	–3,500,000	0	–500,000	–3,000,000
	2,100,000–	2,800,000	700,000	5,600,000–
	0	0	–1,000,000	–1,000,000

Endnotes

1. Kevin B. Salwen, *The Wall Street Journal* (January 4, 1988): 4B.
2. Hayne E. Leland and Mark Rubinstein, "Replicating Options with Positions in Stocks and Cash," *The Financial Analysts Journal* (July–August 1981): This is the article that started the portfolio insurance industry. It is included in the Luskin book, cited later.
3. I do not believe I am misrepresenting Leland and Rubinstein's view, but that is possible. For an unbiased view see Mark Rubinstein. "Portfolio Insurance and the Market Crash," *Financial Analysts Journal* (January–February 1988): 38–47.
4. Donald L. Luskin, Editor, *Portfolio Insurance: A Guide to Dynamic Hedging* (New York: John Wiley & Sons, 1988). My knowledge of the portfolio insurance literature is not exhaustive, but I know of no mention of the price distribution literature in the portfolio insurance literature. My criticisms here are not anachronistic. Leland and Rubinstein's article was published in 1981. The first edition of this book, which had a review of the price distribution problem, was published in 1983. This material can be found in Chapter 9. The S&P 500 crashed in 1987. In a letter to me, Leland claimed he had considered the issue and he provided some substantiating evidence.
5. Successful salespeople have consistently and enthusiastically told me this. Most of them seemed confident they were right. They may not be, but they sold me.
6. For a review of the available technology see, E. J. Henley and H. Kumamoto, *Probabilistic Risk Assessment* (New York: IEEE Press, 1992).
7. Other alternatives include failure modes and effects analysis, criticality analysis, event-tree analysis, hazards and operability studies, cause-consequence analysis, and whatever risk engineers have come up with since I last reviewed the litera-

ture. Incidentally, none of this has anything to do with so-called "financial engineering." Some of what financial engineers do is reasonable, but the title gives the impression that we know more about what we are doing than we actually do.

8. There is a large amount of literature that *claims* to be concerned with decision making under uncertainty, but even the most casual perusal reveals that the techniques are really valid under conditions of risk, or worse, certainty. Schlaifer's *Analysis of Decisions Under Uncertainty* (New York: McGraw-Hill, 1969) is typical. As far as I can tell, not one of the book's 700-plus pages deals with decision making under uncertainty.
9. The Bayesians are one of the more popular schools of statistics. Bayesians argue that probability theory is the *only* available tool. I'm a frequentist, myself, and I strongly disagree. Nevertheless, they may be right.
10. The material that follows is taken from Fred Gehm, "Techniques for Making Decisions Under Uncertainty," *Journal of Futures Markets* (Spring 1984): 65–73. The original article contains material on other techniques and material on evaluating the techniques.
11. Edesess and G. Hambrecht, "Scenario Forecasting: Necessity, Not Choice." *Journal of Portfolio Management* (1980): 10–15.
12. L. Hurwicz, "Optimal Criteria for Decision Making Under Ignorance," Cowles Commission Discussion Paper. *Statistics* (1951): 370.
13. L. J. Savage, "The Theory of Statistical Decision," *Journal of American Statistical Association* 46 (1951): 55–67.
14. Humphrey B. Neil, *The Art of Contrary Thinking* (Caldwell, Idaho: Caxton Printers, 1954)
15. For a discussion of this issue, see Chris P. Dialynas, "The Active Decisions in the Selection of Passive Management and Performances Bogeys," *The Handbook of Fixed Income Securities* (Homewood, IL: Business One, Irwin, 1991), 882–897.
16. Sharpe's Ratio is explained in Chapter 10.

17. Interval mathematics was designed to manage rounding and truncation errors, as they propagated through calculations. It is a predecessor to fuzzy arithmetic and is now a subset of it. As a subset of fuzzy arithmetic, it is potentially much less powerful. However, given the current state of the art, I believe the analysts will find it more useful. See R. Moore, *Interval Analysis* (Englewood Cliffs, New Jersey: Prentice-Hall, 1966).
18. The logic here is the same as for the confidence interval. See Chapter 8.

4

Trading and Trade-Offs

Many traders fail to plan not because they do not know the virtues of planning, but because they are not sure what a good trade would look like. There is some market folklore on this topic (e.g., don't take a trade unless the potential profit is three times the potential loss), but most of it is either irrelevant or worse, wrong.

Which trades are worth accepting is suggested by probability theory and interest-rate theory. Interest is the time value of money. Simple interest can be calculated as follows:

$$V(t) = V(0)[(1 + i)^t]$$

where

$V(t)$ = the value at the end of t periods
$V(0)$ = the value at time 0
i = the interest rate
t = the number of periods

The order in which the calculations are performed will generally affect the outcome. Calculations within parentheses are performed before calculations outside them. Furthermore, multiplication takes place before division, both take place before exponentiation, and all of these take place before addition or subtraction. Exponentiation is indicated by a superscript such as the *Y* in the expression X^Y. The *Y* indicates that the *X* is to be multiplied by itself Y times; for example, $5^4 = 5 \cdot 5 \cdot 5 \cdot 5 = 625$. Therefore, if $V(0) = 10$, $i = 0.08$, and $t = 15$, then:

$$\begin{aligned} V(t) &= 10[(1+0.08)^{15}] \\ &= 10[(1.08)^{15}] \\ &= 10(3.172169114) \\ &= 31.72169114 \end{aligned}$$

When interest is compounded, the proper formula is:

$$V(t) = V(0)\left[\left(1+\frac{i}{q}\right)^{qt}\right]$$

where

q = the number of times interest is compounded per time period

Therefore, if $q = 4$ and the other numbers are as they were above, then:

$$V(t) = 10\left[\left(1+\frac{0.08}{4}\right)^{(4 \cdot 15)}\right]$$

$$\begin{aligned} &= 10\,[(1+0.02)^{60}] \\ &= 10\,[(1.02)^{60}] \\ &= 10(3.281030739) \\ &= 32.81030739 \end{aligned}$$

When compounding is continuous, q becomes infinite and the formula becomes:

$$V(t) = V(0)[e^{(i\,t)}]$$

where:

e = 2.71828

For example, if $V(0) = 10$, $i = 0.08$, and $t = 15$ as above, then:

$$V(t) = 10[\,2.71828^{(0.08 \cdot 15)}\,]$$

$$= 10[\ 2.71828^{(1.2)}\ ]$$

$$= 10(3.320114243)$$
$$= 33.20114243$$

The interest-rate formula can be used to examine the trade-off between trading profitability and trading frequency. Traders are generally cautioned not to overtrade, but if the trader can trade profitably, frequent trading would seem to be a virtue because it allows the trader to increase return on capital. Indeed, as the trader can compound profits, it would seem that trading frequency is more important than profitability. Experienced traders generally consul against overtrading. Is this just a case of the old fogies (such as myself) being unnaturally conservative?

Actually, the old fogies are right. Or so says this one. Using i as a measure of profitability and q as a measure of frequency, Figure 4–1 illustrates the effect of increasing the frequency of trading.[1]

Notice that while compounding increases the return, the marginal increase—that is, the amount the return is raised by

Figure 4–1

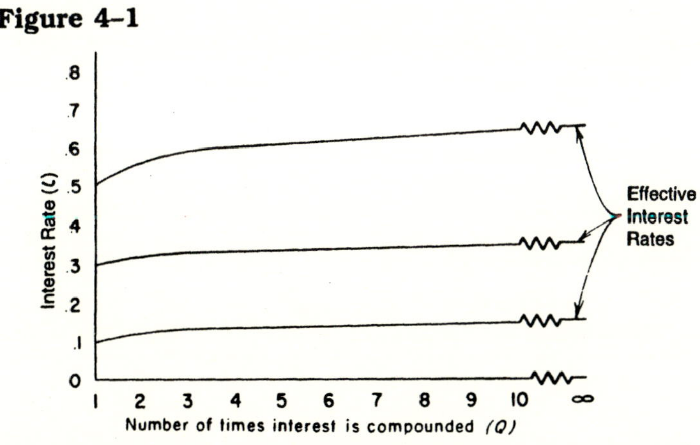

Compounding earnings by frequent trading becomes progressively less important as the rate of compounding increases.

compounding just one more time—continually decreases until it reaches the limit when compounding is continuous. Clearly, it is simply not that important to trade frequently.

On the other hand, Figure 4–2 shows that the marginal return from increasing the interest rate increases without limit. Notice, for example, that the difference between the compound returns for $i = 1$ and $i = 0.99$ in the eleventh year is larger than the compound returns for $i = 0.5$. Oddly enough, as Figure 4–3 shows, even the importance of compounding is a function of profitability. Clearly, most traders would be better off trying to find very profitable trades than trying to trade often.

Figure 4–2

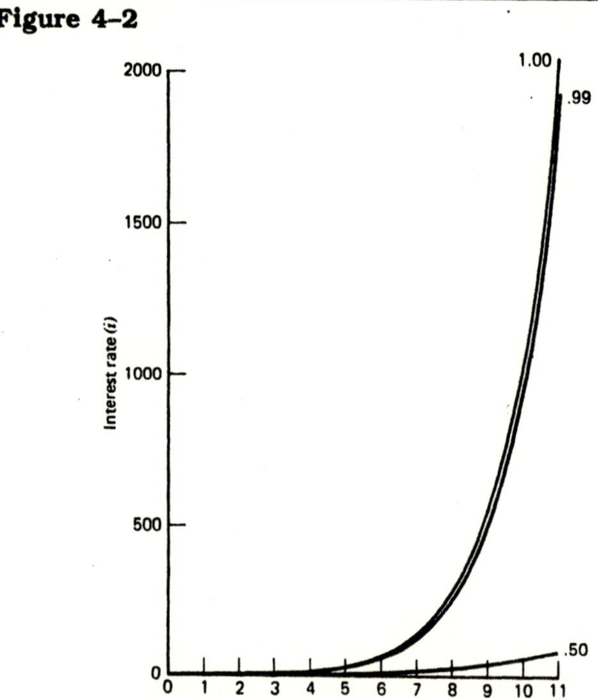

The marginal returns from increasing the interest rate increase without limit.

Figure 4–3

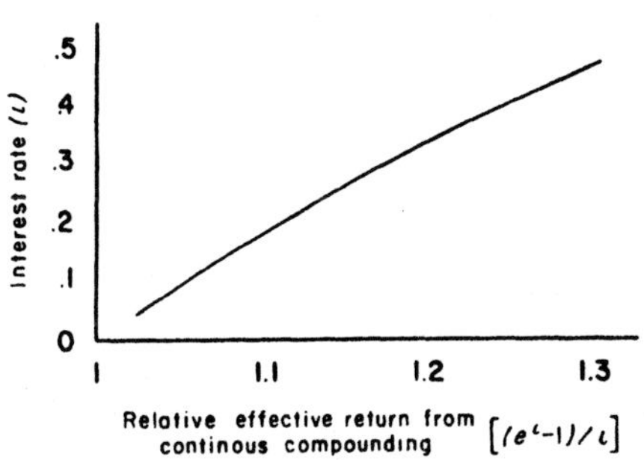

The importance of compounding is a function of profitability.

There is no reason to assume that a very profitable trade need have a large potential gain. Indeed, potential loss is probably more important because it becomes increasingly more difficult to break even, much less profit, with larger and larger losses. In fact, the gain necessary to break even (E) is:

$$E = 1/(1 - \Lambda)$$

where Λ = the proportion of capital lost

If a trader loses 0.2 of trading capital, he or she must then make $E = 1/(1 - 0.2) = 1.25$ on the remaining capital to break even. Figure 4–4 charts this relationship. As the reader will observe, large losses will almost certainly doom a trader.

Nevertheless, it may still be reasonable to risk a large proportion of the available funds if the probability of loss is small enough. The value of a trade, after all, is a probability-weighted average of the trader's potential risks and rewards.

Therefore, unless the trader understands some probability theory, at least intuitively, he or she can't really evaluate a trade. Richard A. Epstein, for example, has cataloged some of the most common and most dangerous financial fallacies—listed below—and, not surprisingly, many of them are misunderstandings of

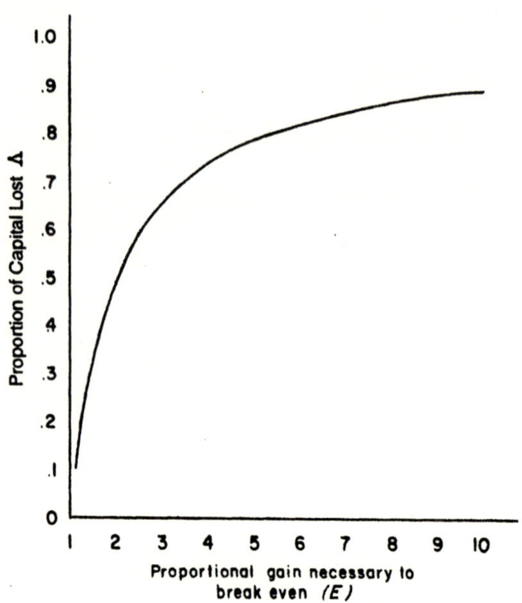

Large losses will almost certainly doom a trader.

probability.[2] The fallacies he presents are "gambling" fallacies, but that is cold comfort indeed; trading is also a gamble.

1. A tendency to overvalue wagers involving a low probability of a high gain and undervalue wagers involving a relatively high probability of low gain. This tendency accounts for some of the "long-shot" betting at race tracks.

2. A tendency to interpret the probability of successive independent events as additive rather than multiplicative. Thus the chance of throwing a given number on a die is considered twice as large with two throws of the die as it is with a single throw. [For example, the

odds of throwing a six twice in succession with a fair die is $(1/6 \cdot 1/6) = 1/36$, not $1/12$.]

3. After a run of successes a failure is inevitable, and vice versa [The Monte Carlo fallacy].

4. The psychological probability of the occurrence of an event exceeds the mathematical probability if the event is favorable and conversely. For example, the probability of success of drawing the winning ticket in a lottery and the probability of being killed during the next year in an automobile accident may both be one chance in 10,000; yet the former is considered much more probable from a personal viewpoint.

5. The prediction of an event cannot be detached from the outcomes of similar events in the past, despite mathematical independence. [For example, the odds of throwing a head with a fair coin is the same both before and after a run of ten heads.]

6. When a choice is offered between a single large chance and several small chances whose sum is equal to the single chance, the single large chance is preferred when the multiple chances consist of repeated attempts to obtain the winning selection from the same source (with replacement); however, when there is a different source for each of the multiple chances, they are preferred. [For example, the odds that a head will appear on one toss with a fair coin and that at least six heads will appear when eleven fair coins are each tossed once is exactly the same. But many people will prefer the latter bet to the former.]

7. The value of the probability of a multiple additive choice tends to be underestimated and the value of a multiplicative probability tends to be overestimated. [For example, the odds of throwing a one or a two or a

three with one throw of a fair die is $(1/6 + 1/6 + 1/6) = 3/6$; whereas, the odds of throwing a one three times in a row is $(1/6 \cdot 1/6 \cdot 1/6) = 1/216$. However, most people underestimate the odds of the first bet and overestimate the odds of the second bet.]

8. When a person observes a series of randomly generated events of different kinds with an interest in the frequency with which each kind of event occurs, he tends to overestimate the frequency of occurrence of infrequent events and to underestimate that of comparatively frequent ones. Thus one remembers the "streaks" in a long series of wins and losses and tends to minimize the number of short-term runs.

9. A tendency to overestimate the degree of skill involved in a gambling situation involving both skill and chance

10. A strong tendency to overvalue the significance of a limited sample selected from a relatively large population.

11. The concept of "luck" is conceived as a quantity stored in a warehouse to be conserved or depleted. A law of conservation of "luck" is implied, and often "systems" are devised to distribute the available "luck" in a fortuitous manner. Objectively, "luck" is merely an illusion of the mind.

12. The sample space of "unusual" events is confused with that of low-probability events. For one example, the remarkable feature of a bridge hand of 13 spades is its apparent regularity, not its rarity (all hands are equally probable). For another, if one holds a number close to the winning number in a lottery, one tends to feel that a terribly bad stroke of misfortune has caused one *just* to miss the prize. Bertrand Russell's remark

> that we encounter a miracle every time we read the license number of a passing automobile is encompassed by this fallacy. The probability of an "unusual" occurrence should be equated to the ratio of the number of unusual (by virtue of symmetry or other aesthetic criteria) events to the total number of events.

Clearly, the trader or gambler who can avoid the fallacies above has a considerable advantage over those who cannot. Statistics and probability theory can be of use here. Statistics will be discussed in Chapter 8. Probability theory will now be discussed.

A probability is a number between zero and one, inclusive, where zero indicates that a given event has no possibility of occurring, and one indicates that the event is certain to occur. Although probabilities can rarely be determined, they can be estimated in several ways:

1. **Judgment.** The simplest and most obvious way of estimating a probability is to guess. Clearly, the usefulness of a guess will depend on the experience and reasoning ability of the guesser. This may not be a particularly rigorous approach, but it's better than nothing, and sometimes it's the only approach possible.

2. **Theory.** In some cases, probabilities can be determined mathematically. For example, if the probability of throwing a head with a fair coin is 0.5, the probability of throwing three heads in a row is 0.125. With this approach, the trader must know the assumptions underlying the theory and must determine or estimate how closely they match the real world. If the assumptions do not match the real world, the theory is irrelevant. In other words, if the probability of throwing a head on a given throw is not 0.5, the probability of throwing three heads in a row is not 0.125.

3. **History.** In many cases, the probability of something happening in the future can be assumed to be the same as or reasonably close to its past relative frequency. For example, if a trading

method was profitable on half of its trades to date, most traders would be willing to assume it will continue to be profitable half of the time.

Several definitions must be learned before the mathematics of probability can be discussed. A *simple* probability is the probability of a given event occurring. It is written $P(\ )$. This is read "the probability of." Events are represented by arbitrary letters; for example, throwing a head with a given coin could be represented by $\ddot{H}$, in which case the probability of throwing a head would be written $P(\ddot{H})$. (The double dots above some symbols are umlauts. Umlauts indicate arbitrary symbols—symbols that are *not* constant from example to example.) A *joint* probability is the probability of two events, say $\ddot{H} + \ddot{T}$, both occurring. If the probability of throwing a tail with the same coin is $P(\ddot{T})$, then the probability of throwing a head and a tail is written $P(\ddot{H}, \ddot{T})$. This probability is zero, of course. A *conditional* probability is the probability that one event will occur, given that another event has occurred; for example, if the probability of throwing a head on the first toss of a fair coin is $P(J)$, and the probability of throwing a head on the second toss is $P(\ddot{K})$, the probability of throwing a head when a head has just been thrown would be written $R(\ddot{K} \mid \ddot{J})$.

Statistical *independence* exists for two events, say $\ddot{K} + \ddot{J}$, if the probability of $\ddot{K}$ occurring does not depend on whether $\ddot{J}$ has occurred. Another way of putting it is that the probability of event $\ddot{K}$ occurring equals the conditional probability of event $\ddot{K}$ occurring, given that event $\ddot{J}$ has occurred. This can be written $P(\ddot{K}) = P(\ddot{K} \mid \ddot{J})$. For example, with a fair coin the probability of throwing a head will not depend on the previous throw; that is, it is independent of the previous throw. Consider, as an example of statistical *dependence*, the probability of selecting at random a coin dated 1980 from six coins, three dated 1980 and three dated 1978. The probability of success on the first selection is 0.5. But note that if the coin is not replaced, the probability of success on the second selection depends on whether the first coin selected was dated 1980. If the first coin selected was dated 1980, the probability that the second one selected will be dated 1980 is 0.4; otherwise the probability is 0.6.

Statistical dependence is important in calculating *joint* probabilities. If two events are statistically independent, their joint probability—that is, the probability that both of them will occur—is the product of their individual probabilities. This can be written as:

$$P(\ddot{K}, \ddot{J}) = P(\ddot{K}) \cdot P(\ddot{J})$$

For example, if the probability of tossing heads with one bent coin is $P(\ddot{U}) = 0.4$, and the probability of tossing heads with another bent coin is $P(\ddot{V}) = 0.1$, the probability of tossing heads with both is:

$$P(\ddot{U}, \ddot{V}) = P(0.4) \cdot P(0.1) = 0.04$$

If two events are statistically dependent, the probability of both events occurring is the simple probability of one of the events occurring (it does not matter which one) times its conditional probability. This can be written as:

$$P(\ddot{Y}, \ddot{Z}) = P(\ddot{Y}) \cdot P(\ddot{Y} \mid \ddot{Z})$$

where $\ddot{Y}$ and $\ddot{Z}$ are arbitrary events.

For example, the probability of selecting a coin dated 1980 from three dated 1980 and three dated 1978 is $P(\ddot{Y}) = 0.5$. The probability of selecting a second coin at random dated 1980 is $P(\ddot{Z}) = 0.4$, where $P(\ddot{Z}) = P(\ddot{W} \mid \ddot{Y})$; that is, where $\ddot{W}$ represents the second coin dated 1980. In other words, $P(\ddot{Z})$ is shorthand for $P(\ddot{W} \mid \ddot{Y})$, the probability that a second coin dated 1980 will be selected at random, given that the first coin selected was dated 1980. Therefore, the probability of selecting two coins in a row dated 1980 is:

$$P(\ddot{Z} \mid \ddot{Y}) = P(0.5) \cdot P(0.4) = 0.2$$

The probability of either of two events occurring is equal to the sum of their simple probabilities minus their joint probabilities. This can be written as:

$$P(\ddot{Z} \text{ or } \ddot{Y}) = P(Z) + P(\ddot{Y}) - P(\ddot{Z}, \ddot{Y})$$

For example, the probability of tossing at least one head with two bent coins when the probability of tossing a head with one is 0.7 and the probability of tossing a head with the other is 0.4 is:

$$\begin{aligned} P(\ddot{Z} \text{ or } \ddot{Y}) &= P(0.7) + P(0.4) - P(0.28) \\ &= P(0.82) \end{aligned}$$

Note that because the coin tosses are independent:

$$\begin{aligned} P(\ddot{Z}, \ddot{Y}) &= P(0.7) \cdot P(0.4) \\ &= 0.28 \end{aligned}$$

If the two events are mutually exclusive, that is, if both cannot occur, then the formula above simplifies to:

$$P(\ddot{W} \text{ or } \ddot{V}) = P(\ddot{W}) + P(\ddot{V})$$

For example, with a fair coin the probability of throwing a tail is 0.5; therefore, the probability of throwing either a head or a tail is:

$$\begin{aligned} P(\ddot{H} \text{ or } \ddot{T}) &= P(0.5) + P(0.5) \\ &= 1.0 \end{aligned}$$

The probability, of course, is not always equal to 1.0.

The virtue of probability theory is that it allows the trader to compare investments and speculations without losing sight of their relative risks. Consider, for example, two bets. The first bet is at odds of 2 to 1 on one flip of a fair coin. The second bet is at odds of 8 to 1 on one flip of a bent coin. The trader, after examining the coin, believes that the probability of it landing in his or her favor is 0.2. Before going further, the trader might consider whether he or she would accept one of the bets and if so, which one and why.

One measure of the potential profitability of a bet is its expected value (EX). This value is calculated by multiplying each potential profit or loss by the probability that the profit or loss will in fact take place.

When the profits or losses can take only two values, the expected value is particularly easy to calculate. The expected value (EX) is:

$$EX = PW - (1 - P)\,L$$

where

W = the potential winnings
L = the potential losses
P = the proportion of winning trades

Therefore, for the first bet:

$$EX = 0.5 \cdot 2 - 0.5 \cdot 1 = 0.5$$

and for the second bet:

$$EX = 0.2 \cdot 8 - 0.8 \cdot 1 = 0.8$$

The fact that the second bet has a higher expected value means that its probability-weighted *average* return is higher. Expected value is a measure of risky returns, but it is *not* a risk-adjusted measure of return; that is, it does not measure how risky the return is.

Consider for example, the following two trading methods:

Method I	**Method II**
$W = 2$	$W = 101$
$L = 1$	$L = 100$
$P = 0.5$	$P = 0.5$
$EX = (2 \cdot 0.5) - (1 \cdot 0.5) = 0.5$	$EX = (101 \cdot 0.5) - (100 \cdot 0.5) = 0.5$

Although both trading methods have the same expected value, the second method is clearly riskier. It is riskier because its profits and losses are more widely dispersed (see Figure 4–5).

Logically, risk is merely a cost of trading. If the cost is excessive, the trader will be ruined. However, even if the cost is modest, the account will *never* grow as quickly as the arithmetic average would indicate. This is called "variance slippage." Variance is the square of the standard deviation, which in turn is a measure of the width or dispersion of a distribution. If the distribution of interest is of profits and losses, variance can be used as a measure of risk. Variance slippage means that as long as there is any risk or variance, the account will never grow as quickly as the arithmetic average of the trading profits would indicate. Moreover, the larger the variance, the more the arithmetic average will overestimate the real growth (see Figure 4–6).

The rate at which the account can really be expected to grow is a useful measure of risk and reward. If E.O. Thorp's strategy for minimizing risk and maximizing the (*e* log) growth of capital is followed, the growth rate can easily be calculated or,

Figure 4–5

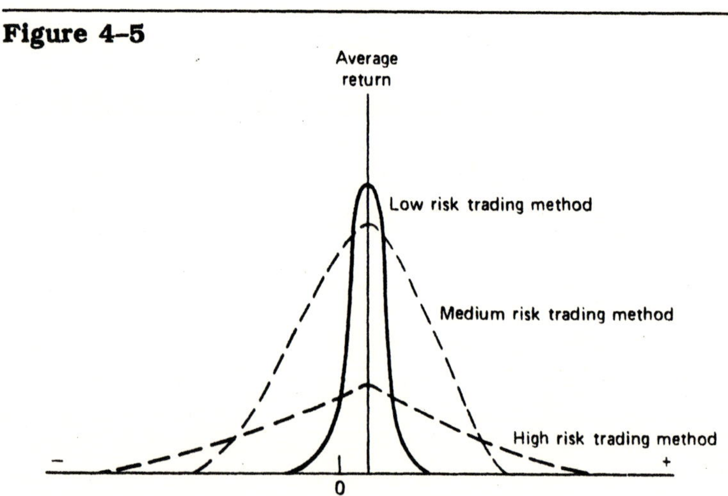

The wider the distribution of returns, the larger the risk.

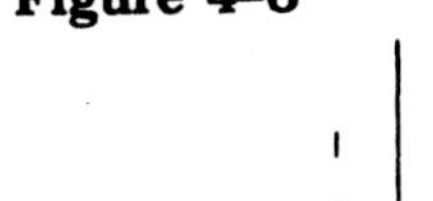

Figure 4–6

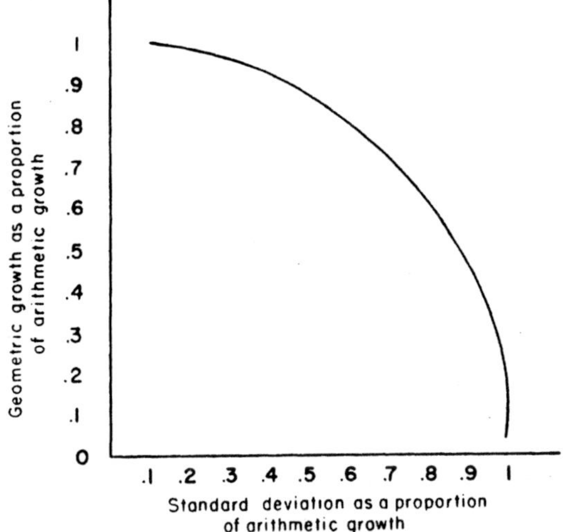

A portfolio's long-term compound growth rate declines as its risk, measured by the standard deviation of returns, increases.

at least, estimated.[3] Actually, Thorp's formula only calculates capital growth correctly when *P*, *W*, and *L* completely describe the distribution of potential profits and losses. Since this is not the case, Thorp's formula will also overestimate account growth, although by a lesser amount. Unfortunately, at the current state of the art, there is no alternative except to use complicated and expensive Monte Carlo techniques. Considering that we are trying to find rules of thumb, Thorp's formula is probably sufficient. Thorp's strategy is to bet a fixed fraction (*f*) of the capital where:

$$f = \varepsilon / B$$
$$\varepsilon = (B + 1)P - 1$$

where

$B = W/L$

and where

W = the potential winnings

L = the potential losings
P = the proportions of winning trades

For example, if $W = 3$, $L = 1$ and $P = 0.6$ then $B = 3$ and $\varepsilon = 1.4$, in which case $f = 0.47$ and Thorp's strategy would be to bet 0.47 of the trading capital.

How quickly capital will grow is a function of B and P. According to Thorp, the growth function (g) is:

$$g = P[\log(1 + Bf)] + (1 - P)[\log(1 - f)]$$

"Log" here refers to the natural logarithm. This function can be found on several pocket calculators. It has also been extensively tabled (see Table 13 in Appendix 2).

$$g = 0.6\{\log[1 + (3 \cdot 0.47)]\} + \{(1 - 0.6)[\log(1 - 0.47)]\}$$
$$g = 0.6(\log 2.41) + 0.4(\log 0.53)$$
$$g = 0.6(0.8796) + 0.4(-0.6349)$$
$$g = (0.52776) + (-0.25396)$$
$$g = 0.2738$$

Clearly, the larger g is, the more quickly capital can be expected to grow. Because these formulas are objective, it is possible to derive some generalizations about what constitutes a reasonable risk or potentially profitable trade.

First, popular rules of thumb such as "don't accept a trade unless the potential profit is at least three times the potential loss" clearly are of no use whatsoever because they do not incorporate the probabilities of winning and losing.

Second, if the expected gross profit (GP) is:

$$\text{GP} = PW - (1 - P)\,L$$

and the expected gross ratio (GR) is:

$$\text{GR} = PW/(1 - P)\,L$$

then the expected gross ratio of profit to loss is of considerably more importance than the expected gross profit. This can be deduced from the fact that the difference between winning and losing is not a part of the formula for *f*, whereas their ratio is. An example may make this clearer. Consider two trading methods with the following properties:

Method I	**Method II**
$W = \$4$	$W = \$3$
$L = \$2$	$L = \$1$
$P = 0.5$	$P = 0.5$

Plugging these numbers into the formulas for GP and GR we obtain:

$$\text{GP} = 4(0.5) - 2(1 - 0.5) = 1 \qquad GP = 3(0.5) - 1(1 - 0.5) = 1$$

$$\text{GR} = 4(0.5)/2(1 - 0.5) = 2 \qquad \text{GR} = 3(0.5)/1(1 - 0.5) = 3$$

Notice that although gross profit for both methods is the same, the gross ratio of profit to loss is higher for Method II. Plugging the appropriate numbers into the formulas for *B*, ε, *f*, and *g*, we obtain:

Method I	**Method II**
$B = 4/2 = 2$	$B = 3/1$
$\varepsilon = [(2 + 1)\,0.5] - 1 = 0.5$	$\varepsilon = [(3 + 1)\,0.5] - 1 = 1$
$f = 0.5/2 = 0.25$	$f = 1/3 = 0.3333...$
$g = 0.058891517$	$g = 0.143841035$

Note that *g* is higher for Method II than it is for Method I. Clearly, Method II is superior.

The analysis above does not consider commission and execution costs, which is a matter of some small importance. It is, of course, the ratio of expected profits to losses after costs that is important, rather than the difference after costs. Nothing unexpected happens when these costs are factored in.

The above analysis implies that prudent trading is a waiting game. The trader must carefully watch and forecast the market but only trade when the potential loss (L) is less than his or her account balance, when the expected loss (i.e., $L(1 - P)$) is a small proportion of his or her account balance, when the expected net ratio of profit to loss is large, and when the commission and execution costs are only a small proportion of the expected gross profit.[4]

Naturally, this approach will not guarantee success. Christopher Culp and Merton Miller argue that Metallgesellschaft, a German commodities conglomerate, lost $1.4 billion using a basically sound oil-derivatives trading strategy. The loss was caused by the panic of bankers and top management.[5] Clearly, there is no such thing as a trade that is too carefully planned.

Endnotes

1. The alert reader will notice that the above analysis does not consider taxes. I have thus implicitly assumed that trading is either tax exempt or that it is the trader's primary source of income, in which case, trading profits are taxed as ordinary income. When this is not the case, which is more often than not, the trader must consider whether trading is worth the effort. It takes considerable skill to make active trading worthwhile. Unfortunately, even the form taxes take is unstable, and it is therefore difficult to give advice on this matter. An article on this subject that may still be relevant by the time you read this is: Robert Jeffrey and Robert Arnott, "Is Your Alpha Big Enough to Cover Its Taxes?" *The Journal of Portfolio Management* (Spring 1993).

2. R. A. Epstein, *The Theory of Gambling and Statistical Logic* (New York: Academic Press, 1977), 393–394. The examples in brackets in numbers 2, 5, 6, and 7 are my own.
3. E.O. Thorp, "The Kelly Money Management System," *Gambling Times* (December 1979): 91, 92.
4. I assume here that the trader is not willing to lose his or her entire trading portfolio. This is generally, but not always, true. I discuss this further in Chapter 9.
5. Merton Miller won a Nobel prize for economics and apparently knows something about finance. See Christopher Culp and Merton Miller, "Hedging a Flow of Commodity Deliveries with Futures; Lesson from Metallgesellschaft," *Derivatives Quarterly*, Volume 1, Number 1 (Fall 1994). See also Christopher L. Culp and Merton H. Miller, "Metallgesellschaft and the Economics of Synthetic Storage" *Journal of Applied Corporate Finance* Volume 7, Number 4 (Winter 1995). Culp and Miller cite other possible explanations.

5

Trading Plans

Introduction

In many ways, trading is a loser's game.[1] The winning trader, like the winner in tennis or war, is the one who makes the least mistakes. Not all mistakes are fatal, of course, but one mistake that will almost certainly doom a trader is to trade without a plan.

Any trading plan will be superior to no trading plan because every plan will consider strategy and tactics in more detail than the trader would otherwise. A trading plan, for example, will never allow a trader to take a position for no reason at all, and then wait to get lucky. Yet, sadly, many traders will do just that.

An unwritten plan is better than no plan at all, and a written plan is better than an unwritten one. This is because a written plan will be more carefully thought out, more detailed, and more conscientiously followed than an unwritten plan.

A written plan will also allow the trader to audit his or her own performance. Periodic audits are critical; a trader who does not perform them will continue to make the same mistakes. However, without a written trading plan, audits are impossible. When important sums of money are involved, it is difficult not to lie to oneself. Worse, the trader who does lie will rarely be able to admit it later unless confronted with evidence, such as a written trading plan.

A written trading plan is a set of documents, forms, and work sheets. A reasonably complete set might include a strategic plan, a tactical plan, a watch sheet, a log book, a work sheet, and an operating statement.

Naturally, a given trader need not use all of the tools described. Nor is there any reason he or she cannot invent others. Clearly, the tools used should depend on the trader's philosophy, psychology, forecasting skills, and capital. The reader should, therefore, feel free to modify the tools presented to fit his or her own style of trading.

Strategic Plans

The strategic trading plan deals with the broadest and most general problems of trading: How much money will I dedicate to trading? How much time? How will I forecast the market? How will I convert these forecasts into trades? How will I allocate money to trades?

A good strategic trading plan should be consistent, viable, authoritative, and enforceable. A consistent plan is simply one with no self-contradictions. For example, it may be reasonable to trade on the basis of fundamentals, to trade a number of investments with different fundamentals, or to spend little time trading, but it is scarcely reasonable to expect to do all three.

A viable trading plan is one that is consistent with the "real world," that is, the trader should really have the skills and resources that the trading plan demands. Any self-delusion here—and many more traders delude themselves than not—will ensure defeat.

An authoritative plan allows the trader to make judgments about tactical plans. A good tactical plan is consistent with the strategic plan; a bad one is not. For example, if for strategic reasons a trader decided to trade only long-term, fundamentally based trends, even to consider technical input would violate the strategic plan.

An enforceable plan is a plan that must be followed. For an individual trader, this means that the trader must have the psychological skills, the tolerances for pain and boredom, that the plan demands. For an organization, this means that someone, probably internal audit, must enforce the plan. A plan that is not enforced is not a plan. At best, it is a symbol of good intentions. More commonly, it is a piece of paper used to distract internal audit for a year or so.

There is nothing sacred about a strategic plan, and if a better one can be constructed, it certainly should be. Nevertheless, the plan should be changed only after a great deal of thought and never to avoid missing a trade.

The reason is essentially mathematical. All trading involves a risk of ruin, a risk that the trader will lose his or her trading capital. This risk can be expressed as a number from zero to one, inclusive, where zero indicates no risk of ruin, and one indicates certain ruin. When wins and losses are equal, the risk of ruin (R) can be calculated from the formula

$$R = \left(\frac{1-A}{1+A}\right)^{\delta}$$

where $A = P - (1 - P)$
P = the proportion of winning trades
δ = the units of trading capital

For example, if the trader wins or loses $5,000,000 each time he trades, and if he wins 0.6 of the time and if, after dedicating the necessary funds, if any, to margin, he starts with $50,000,000, then $\delta = 10$, $P = 0.6$, $A = 0.2$, and $R = 0.02$.

Now assume the same trader finds that a net loss of one unit of capital bothers him so much that he quits trading. In effect, then, this trader had one unit of capital, not 10. The risk of ruin under these conditions is 0.67. Clearly, this trader would have been better off not trading at all.

Changes in the trading plan can decrease the risk of ruin, of course, but changes that are not considered carefully and at leisure almost always do just the opposite.

Tactical Plans

The form of the tactical trading plan should depend on the strategic plan. Some strategic plans need virtually no tactical planning. For example, many trend-following techniques require little more than an order log. Fundamentalists, on the other hand, may need extensive tactical plans.

A tactical plan can be constructed freehand, but the use of forms insures that the trader will consider certain factors each time he trades. Which factors should be considered is a strategic, not a tactical, decision. Figure 5–1 is a fairly general and extensive tactical form. It should work well with exchange-traded investments, especially stocks, options, and futures. It does not provide the details needed for debt instruments, although that information could easily be added. It might work well or poorly with over-the-counter derivatives, depending on the contracts. Since there is no logical limit to what such contracts can include, it's hard to draw up an inclusive example. At least, it's hard to draw an example of finite length. Naturally, the trader should feel free to modify the form to fit his own style and strategy.

The reasons for most of the data in sections A and B should be fairly obvious. The trade number and opening date allow the trade to be located and reviewed later. The closing date ensures that a trade is not forgotten or misplaced.

Section B allows net long and short positions, spreads, options, and multiasset investments to be recorded. A multiasset investment is a forecast that is implemented by trading a number of investments. Spreads and various hedged investments are examples. When a number of investments or trades are all based on the same forecast, they should be managed together.

Figure 5–1 Tactical Trading Form

A. Date opened ___/___/___ Trade No. _____
Date closed ___/___/___

B.

	Long	Short	Long	Short
Investment				
Month (if applicable)				
Number of Units				
Units				
Delta				

C.

	Long	Short	Long	Short
Maximum risk acceptable				
Stop-loss risk				
Probable skid				
Commission				
Net risk per unit				
Number of units				
Total net risk				
Margin per unit				
Marginal worst case skid				
Gross risk per unit				
Number of units				
Total gross risk				

D. All investment exchange traded?

___ Yes.

___ No. Default risk:

Trade implications:

Figure 5–1 Tactical Trading Form (continued)

E. Bullish factors:

Bearish Factors:

Conclusion:

F. Bullish catastrophic risk:

Bearish catastrophic risk:

Conclusion:

G. Entry plan:
Entry log:

Entry No.	Log No.	Date	Order	Fill
1.				
2.				
3.				

H. Exit plan:
Landmarks:
Perils:
Exit log:

Exit No.	Log No.	Date	Order	Fill
1.				
2.				
3.				

I. Trade narrative:
Profit __________ Loss __________
Evaluation:

If a long or a short position is taken, the investments, contract months (if applicable), number of units, and unit (contracts, shares, bonds, etc.) should be listed under the appropriate headings. If a multiasset investment of some kind is taken (the form allows complexes with up to four investments), each investment must be listed under long or short, with the appropriate month, units, and, if the investment is an option, the current delta, listed below.[2] The months and units, not to mention the number of units, are not always obvious, so completing this section might be delayed until sections C through F are completed.

In section C, the number of units traded is calculated. The number of units traded is partly a strategic and partly a tactical problem. Part of the strategic plan should be a money-management system, which should allocate a maximum amount of risk acceptable for each trade. Tactical analysis should then suggest how much risk should be accepted per unit.

The acceptable risk per unit may be larger or smaller than the amount of risk acceptable for that trade. If it is larger, of course, the trade cannot be accepted. If it is equal or smaller, the maximum risk acceptable is divided by the risk acceptable per unit. The result, with any remainder dropped, is the number of units to trade.

The risk a trader must manage at any given time must be calculated on both a gross and a net basis. Most of the time, money must be allocated on the basis of net risk. The gross risk is needed for the operating statement, described later in the chapter. The net acceptable risk is the stop-loss risk, the commission, and the average probable slippage. The gross acceptable risk is the stop-loss risk, the commission, the worst case probable slippage, and the margin needed to trade the contract.

The stop-loss risk is the difference between the entrance price and the stop loss, if any. Stop-loss location is a major trading decision and is worth a considerable amount of thought. Although a stop loss is a money-management tool, its location should somehow be a function of the price forecast. Clearly, a price movement opposite the one forecasted is prima facie evidence that the forecast is wrong. If the trader can decide at what point the evidence is strong enough to abandon the trade, he has his stop-loss point and his stop-loss risk.

Slippage is the difference between the price at which an order is entered and the price at which the order is filled. For example, typically if a trader decides to buy at the opening, she will likely get the price at the top of the opening range. If she sells, she will likely get the price at the bottom. How much slippage a trader will incur will depend on the order used, the size of the order, the investment, and the volatility of the market at the time of the order.

Less obviously, the estimate used can be the average probable slippage or the worst-case probable slippage. For example, in S&P 500 futures, the average slippage on one futures contract is currently about $75.00. A worst-case estimate might be tens of thousands of dollars per contract. When risk is measured on a gross basis, the worst-case estimate is used. When risk is measured on a net basis, the average is used.

The net acceptable risk is the stop-loss risk, the commission, and the probable skid. In contrast, the gross acceptable risk is the stop-loss risk, the commission, the worst-case skid, and the margin. These values must be estimated for each investment traded and then summed. Net risks are adjusted for the correlations and deltas involved. Gross risks are not. Depending on what the operating statement says, the number of contracts taken is decided on the basis of either the gross or net risk.

In section D, the default risk is recorded or at least noted. If the trader limits him- or herself to exchange-traded futures and options, there is almost no default risk. With over-the-counter derivatives, the default risk is considerably larger and much more difficult to evaluate. If the trader's credit exposure is material, he or she should prepare a credit-risk analysis on a regular basis. (Credit analysis will be discussed later in this chapter.) This information should be used as input to the tactical plan. Theoretically, a default might happen at any time, which means the trading implications are minimal. But assuming the trade contributes to your counterparty's default, the default is likely to happen at the worst possible time, that is, when your trade is most profitable. This clearly affects the reward estimates. A narrative summary of the credit risk and its effect on the reward and risk estimates should appear in this section.

Section E is the most important part of the trading plan. All rational trading is based on an explicit or implicit forecast. When the trade and the forecast are not identical, the forecast must somehow be transformed into a trade. Clearly, the more explicit the forecast, the easier this will be to do.

Less obviously, perhaps, unless the trade and forecast are identical, which is not always the case, the trader will lose money on some trades that he should have made money on, and vice versa. Assuming the trader is skillful, that he really can forecast the market successfully on average, he will lose more than he gains. This means that the trader must forecast first and then create a trade that matches the forecast as closely as possible.

For example, assume a trader believes the Nikkei is overpriced, given the current world economy, but that a political change in Europe would be extremely favorable to Japanese business, and thus to the Nikkei. Further, assume that the trader believes this change will happen in the next three months or not at all. Finally, assume all options on the Nikkei are fairly priced given the current world economy, in which case, the trader would want to buy a three-month or longer call option on the Nikkei. This would give him the right to buy a fixed amount of stock at a fixed price for a fixed period. The trader would not want to buy the stock itself. The trader would not want to buy a lookback option that gave him the right to buy a fixed amount of stock at its lowest price for a fixed period. Nor would he want to buy an Asian option that gave him the right to buy a fixed amount of stock at its average price over a fixed period. The stock and the lookback and Asian options have their uses, but they do not look like the trader's forecast.

The format presented requires the trader to evaluate the bullish and bearish factors in narrative form. Forcing oneself to evaluate the arguments against a desired trade can have a sobering effect. Another approach that some traders may prefer is a check-list format, requiring the trader to evaluate certain indicators or data each time a trade is contemplated. Which data and indicators are evaluated is a strategic question, of course.

The conclusion should be the direction and distance the price is likely to move, the investments that should be traded, and the location of the stops. In addition, the data necessary to structure the portfolio, such as the probability of the trade being profitable, must be estimated.

In section F, the economic arguments for extremely large or catastrophic price changes are examined. Depending on the trade, extremely large bull and bear moves might be possible or one type only or perhaps, neither. The probability of an extremely large move will almost certainly be small. But if the probability of a move of the wrong sort is not extremely small, the trader may have to forego the trade. Catastrophic losses and price changes are examined in Chapter 9.

Once sections A–F are completed, the trader can initiate the trade. This cannot be done without giving orders, and the trader will find it virtually impossible to consider too carefully the orders he might give and the conditions under which he might give them. Naturally, not all brokers or exchanges will accept all types of orders.

Section G consists of an entry plan and entry log. An entry plan is simply a narrative analyzing the orders to be given and conditions under which they will be used. Because it is sometimes necessary to initiate several orders before obtaining a fill, a moderately long entry-log is provided. A more detailed description of the trading orders can be provided in an order log, which is discussed later. The reader should note that the entry log and the order log should be cross-referenced.

If a position is accepted, it must eventually be exited. This will happen for one of five reasons, and the exit plan in part G must provide for all of them.

1. **The Trade Shows a Loss.** At some point, at least, when money is leveraged, a loss will become larger than the trader can afford, and the trade will have to be abandoned. This loss can be planned or unplanned. A planned loss is better than an unplanned loss because no reasonable plan will allow a significant portion of the capital to erode. Yet unplanned losses often do just that.

If the risk on an individual trade is limited, and the trader can afford to write off the entire investment, he or she does not need a stop. This may well be a sensible action. But such risks should not be taken without thought. A stop loss ensures that the loss will be planned. Although stop losses are critical, they are not the only means of exiting a losing trade. Conceivably, the reader may have an indicator or method of analysis that will indicate that the forecast is no longer to be trusted. If so, the exit plan for losing trades may read, "Exit when indicator $\ddot{X}$ gives a signal or when a stop loss at price $\ddot{Y}$ is touched, whichever comes first."

2. **The Trade Is Profitable.** Ideally, both a risk level and a profit objective should be determined before the trade is begun. Unfortunately, for some trading methods there is no reasonable way to set objectives. An alternative might be an indicator or method of analysis that signals when profits should be taken.

Again, having more than one method of exiting a trade has its advantages. A reasonable plan might read, "Exit when the price reaches $\ddot{Y}$ or indicator $\ddot{X}$ gives a signal or when a stop loss at price $\ddot{Z}$ is touched, whichever comes first."

3. **Nothing Happens.** Occasionally, the price will float between the stop loss and the profit objective without touching either. In some cases, this will indicate that the analysis was wrong and the trade should be closed. In other cases where the forecast indicates only the direction of the trend and not its extent or timing, theoretically it would not be valid to close out the trade without an exit signal.

Many investments have limited lives, and every trade using them must be closed eventually. If manipulating stops and profit objectives is not a viable way of closing the trade, an arbitrary date must be picked and the trade closed on that date. Money may be moved to a similar investment on that date, if that is the plan. Choosing the closing date when the trade is initiated has the advantage that the trader will not be affected by price movements irrelevant to his or her analysis.

4. A Better Trade Becomes Available. Prudent money-management allows only a certain proportion of the funds available to be committed to the market at any one time. If more good trades become available than can be supported, theoretically the trader should upgrade his portfolio, closing his worst open trades and accepting the best new ones. If the trader does not have the discipline to do this—if, for example, he keeps his worst trades while accepting others—his chances of success are almost nonexistent.

On the other hand, upgrading is difficult and expensive, and the benefits need not exceed the costs. If the marginal costs—that is, the commission and execution costs—exceed the marginal profits, the portfolio should not be upgraded.

Some traders should not upgrade even if this is not the case. Upgrading demands that the trader realistically evaluate trades in progress. Unfortunately, when hard cash is on the line, objectivity can be difficult or impossible for many traders. A good trading plan must consider a trader's psychology as well as his or her finances.

5. The Situation Changes. Every trade is based on an explicit or implicit forecast. Clearly, if the forecast is no longer reasonable, the trade should be closed, whether it is profitable or not.

It is critical that every conceivable reason the trade might be abandoned is considered in the trading plan. Not to do so ensures that the estimates needed for money management will be wrong. It also ensures that decisions on whether to close a trade will sometimes have to be made while the trade is still open; for many traders, perhaps even most, this ensures that the decision will be made irrationally.

A trade may no longer be reasonable because of foreseeable or unforeseeable events. A foreseeable event might be a government crop report that differs from the expected. An example of an unforeseeable event cannot be given, of course. If an example could be given, it would be foreseeable. Still, it's safe to say that many traders might not even consider the possible effects of a radical change in government policy on a potential trade. For those traders, if a radical change in government policy took place, it would be unforeseen.

How the trader should handle the unexpected is partly a strategic and partly a tactical problem. The trader has only two choices. He can act on what limited information he has at the time, or he can ignore the situation. If the trader decides to act, he must act quickly or not at all. To do this rationally demands ice water for nerves and an encyclopedic knowledge of market fundamentals.

For most traders, a more reasonable approach is to ignore the situation. If the trader has a stop in place, and if a catastrophic price change does not take place, she cannot be hurt too badly. Although the trader might lose money that she would not have lost if she had acted quickly, over the long run she will lose less. If a trader cannot make decisions rationally, she must give up trading or she must find a way to trade rationally without making those decisions.

Another alternative is to make decisions only within limits set before the trade begins; the sections "Landmarks" and "Perils" prescribe these limits. Landmarks are events indicating that the trade is going according to plan; perils indicate that it is not. The distinction is somewhat arbitrary. For example, a government crop report might be both a landmark and a peril. Still, the distinction is useful enough to be worth keeping in mind.

Somehow the exit plan must be executed. This cannot be done without giving orders; a log is provided for recording them.

Section H provides for a review of the completed trade. The profit or loss must be recorded, the actions taken summarized, and the trading plans and trade reviewed. Separating the trade narrative and the evaluation should be useful. The actions taken will never change, but the evaluations will, as the trader grows.

Watch Sheet

One drawback of tactical plans is that the market changes as plans are developed. By the time a perfect plan could be constructed, if one could be constructed at all, the opportunity would probably have disappeared.

One solution to this problem is to scale down the tactical plan to reach some kind of compromise between urgency and completeness. Another solution is the watch sheet.

The watch sheet is simply a dated listing or summary of whatever news, announcements, data, information, analysis, or gossip the trader thinks might help to forecast the market. Along with the trader's own ideas, analyses, and forecasts, the original unsummarized data can be clipped and kept in an appended file.

Which data should be recorded, how long the data should be kept, what form the data should be kept in, and how the data should be used, all depends on the trader's strategic plan. There is no reason that the trader must record every piece of data, just as there is no reason that the trader must always be able to forecast the market. The trader must merely be right, on average, when he or she does forecast the market.

Currently, a popular approach is to scan incoming data for information that can be put into particular places in a tactical plan. Data that do not fit into the available pigeon holes are ignored. In many ways, this approach is particularly well suited to large organizations using quantitative, fundamentally based strategies.

A second approach is to watch the data until a clear bullish or bearish pattern emerges and then create a tactical plan to exploit the data. A third approach would be to watch the market until it makes a mistake and then trade against it. In this case, it is not enough that the trader disagree with the market's price; the trader must also understand why the market prices as it does and disagree with its analysis. The trader then develops a tactical plan to exploit the market's mistake.

In any case, the watch sheet will allow the trader to develop the tactical plan in far more detail and far more rapidly than without it.

Order Log

A trading order converts a plan into a trade. Regardless of how well wrought a plan is, if the order is ill-conceived or carelessly given, the trade is almost certainly doomed.

Because the order and limits given can change a trade's reward/risk ratio, sometimes drastically, it is nearly impossible to consider too carefully which orders to give. (See Figures 5–2 and 5–3).

Some strategic plans allow the trader few or no alternatives. Such plans may give the trader no choice of orders and even no choice of tactics. In such cases, there may be no reason to have a tactical plan, and the simplest of order logs will suffice.

Exchange propaganda to the contrary, traders do not buy and sell physical and financial assets. It just looks that way. Traders buy and sell information, knowledge, insights, and perhaps wisdom. At one extreme, traders act because they have information they believe other traders lack. Such traders must act quickly, before the information they possess becomes generally known. For example, in 1982 Salomon Brothers purchased $400 million worth of bond futures 90 minutes before their influential economist Henry Kaufman publicly changed his outlook on interest rates.[3] At the other extreme, traders act on the basis of value. Such traders do not have to act quickly, but they must act at the right price. For example, a comparative analysis of dis-

Figure 5–2

Where various trading orders may be placed in relation to current trading price. Adapted from J. R. Maxwell. *Commodity Futures Trading Orders.* Port Angeles, WA: Speer Books, 1974, 22.

tressed securities might indicate that a particular firm's debt should be bought at any price under 30 cents on the dollar.

In a way, information, knowledge, insight, and wisdom are all information; they differ only in their permanence. If the information ages quickly, the order must be executed quickly, which is costly. If the information does not age quickly, less-costly techniques can be used. The selection of market and order is the analysis of this trade-off.[4]

In other cases, there will be no reason to keep an order log. The trading plan must contain entry and exit logs; the trade could hardly be analyzed without them. If only one or two investments are traded at a time, the trader hardly needs both a tactical plan and an order log.

Figure 5–3 Usable Order and Limit Combinations

Type of Order	Relation to the Market		Class of Order		Usable Limitations		
	Above	*Below*	*Day*	*Open*	*Price*	*Life*	*Time*
Market			X		X		X
Market-if-touched	S	B	X	X	X	X	X
Fixed-price	S	B	X	X	X	X	X
Stop	B	S	X	X	X	X	X
B = Buy, S = Sell, X = Use is permitted.							

Useful Combinations

Above the Market	*Below the Market*
Buy stop	Sell stop
Sell MIT	Sell stop
Buy stop	Sell MIT
Buy stop	Fixed-price buy
Fixed-price sell	Sell stop

MOC Combinations

Market-if-touched, fixed-price, and stop orders may be placed with the "or market on close" stipulation.

From J.R. Maxwell. *Commodity Futures Trading Orders.* Port Angeles, WA: Speer Books, 1974, 54.

However, many traders, especially active traders, will benefit from using both. Having a separate order log allows the trader more control. For example, it allows him or her to analyze the performance of the brokerage firm executing the orders apart from the performance of the trades.

An order log may be arbitrarily complex. How complex it should be depends on the number of alternatives the trader wishes to consider every time he or she trades.

For many traders, all or part of a log like the one in Figure 5–4 should suffice. An all-inclusive example is not possible; the number of markets and investments and constraints is simply too large. Fortunately, the principles are universal. The order number allows the order log to be cross-referenced with the tactical plan. The date column should contain the date, and the time the order is given to the broker. This information can be useful if there is a problem with the fill. The trade number and the entry/exit number allow the tactical plan to be cross-referenced with the order log. If the trade requires more than one attempt for entry or exit, which is often the case, these data can be important.

The order column should list the investment, the contract month, if applicable, the number of contracts or shares, the type of order, and whether the order is a buy or sell. If the investment is traded on more than one exchange or market, this should be listed in the next column.

Any limits on the order should be indicated in the next column. Limits can be useful in shifting the reward/risk ratio. The use of a special column ensures that the trader will at least consider limiting his order before he places it.

The fill column should indicate if an order is canceled. If the order is filled, the column should indicate the date of the fill, the time, and the price at which the order was filled. These data can be useful in evaluating the cost of placing various types of orders, your skill at placing them, or your broker's efficiency in having them executed. Unfortunately, if the data indicate a problem, it's not always easy to tell where the problem lies.

In the market-conditions column, the trader describes the market around the time the order was filled. A sell stop in a bear market should get a bad fill. An MIT order to buy should not. Alternatively, the trader may wish to append a chart of that day's price action. Well-financed traders may wish to append detailed price logs.

Trading orders must not only be carefully considered, they must be carefully given. Any error here will destroy the trading plan. However, properly used, the order log will ensure that the

Figure 5–4 Order Log

Order No.	Date	Trade No.	Order	Exchange	Limits	Fill	Market	Conditions

Adapted from J. R. Maxwell. *Commodity Futures Trading Orders*. Port Angeles, WA: Speer Books, 1974, 2.

orders a trader gives his broker are the orders he intends to give. If the order is not sent electronically, then the trader should write the order in the log and then *read* the order to his broker. The broker should then record the order and repeat it, and the trader should confirm it. The word *not* should not be used.

Work Sheet

Money is a trader's largest and most important tangible asset. Money can take several forms, such as equity, margin, or net trading power. If funds are not in the right form at the right time, interest will be lost or trades foregone or abandoned. As funds can generally be changed into different forms only at a price, the trader would be well advised to watch his or her funds carefully.

It is simply impossible to manipulate something meaningfully unless you know what you are manipulating. Many traders, and not just small traders, control their funds on the basis of a monthly account statement from their brokerage firm and an occasional question to their account executive. This information is neither detailed enough nor frequent enough for meaningful control. If trading decisions are made daily, funds must be managed daily or even on a moment-to-moment basis. Software is now available for managing multiple accounts at multiple brokerage firms in real time. This may seem to make the paragraphs below irrelevant. Unfortunately, they are not. It is not necessary that you do the accounting, as long as it gets done. But it is necessary that you understand it.

An operating statement and a work sheet should be prepared daily, at least. Because information from the work sheet is needed to complete the operating statement, the work sheet must be completed first.

A work sheet may be part of a tactical plan. Figure 5–1 includes part of a work sheet. When a work sheet is not part of the tactical plan, it consists of a number of short, identical, numbered forms. How many of these will have to be filled in on any given day will depend on how many trades are open after the close, or whenever the sheets are filled in. If no positions are open, no forms are filled in. In which case, the work can be done in no time at all. (See Figure 5–5.)

The number at the top of each segment ensures that the segments are completed in the proper sequence. This number and the date ensure that the previous day's data are not included in the current analysis.

Listing the investments and position ensures that the sign and values for the calculations that follow are correct. The current open profit or loss is the latest price or, at least, the previous day's closing price minus the entry price, times the dollar value of a unit change, if the trade was long. The dollar value will depend upon the number of units traded and the units. No surprises here. If the trader was short, the sign of the results must be changed. If spreads were traded, price differentials rather than prices must be recorded. The mechanics, however, are the same.

Subtracting the stop-loss point from the last close gives the open risk; whether the trader is long or short, the open risk is always positive. Notice that the security is marked to market daily. The accounting system should always reflect the current market value of the securities. If it is not possible to mark the security to market, possibly because there is no market for the security, the trader must estimate the price him- or herself.[5]

If the trader is not using a stop loss, his or her losses are potentially unlimited. For budgeting purposes, the trader must select some arbitrary amount as his or her open risk. Prudence demands a *large* arbitrary amount.

Operating Statement

Much of the data necessary to calculate an operating statement may be part of a trader's tactical plan. In this case, the accounting system should generate an operating statement automatically. Failing that, the trader should complete an operating statement

Figure 5–5 Daily Work Sheet

Date:	*No.:*
Units:	*Position:*
Last close	$ ________
minus entry price	________
Difference (correct for sign)	$
times dollar value unit change	________
Open profit or loss	$
Last close	$ ________
minus stop loss	$
Difference (ignore sign)	$ ________
times dollar value unit change	________
Open risk	$ ________

The double line is an accounting convention that indicates that the numbers below the line are not related to the numbers above. Consider a trader whose 74th trade was short one contract of December wheat on the Chicago Board of Trade. The value of each one-cent change for one contract is $50.00. Assume that the trader had sold the wheat at $5.12, put in a stop at $5.20, and that the contract last closed at $5.14. The form is completed as follows:

Date: October 22, 1982	*No.:* 74
Number contracts held: 1	*Commodity position:* Dec. wheat
Last close	$ 5.14
minus entry price	$ 5.12
Difference (correct for sign)	–$ 0.02
times dollar value unit change	$ 50.00
Open profit or loss	–$ 100.00
Last close	$ 5.14
minus stop loss	$ 5.20
Difference (ignore sign)	$ 0.06
times dollar value unit change	$ 50.00
Open risk	$ 300.00

each day he has a position open after the close. The object of the calculations is the trader's net trading power, or his ability to accept new trades.

Before a new position is accepted, the trader must calculate how much net power, or capital net of all commitments, the trade will demand. If this demand exceeds the trader's net power, the trade cannot be accepted. As Teweles, Harlow, and Stone note:[6]

> Failure to consider net power can force a trader to choose among three choices, none of which are good:
>
> 1. depositing more money than he wishes to utilize for trading
> 2. reducing or eliminating an open position too soon, or
> 3. changing stops which were set logically
>
> Such an approach makes an already difficult game almost impossible to win.

Many professional investment funds, perhaps most, do not calculate net power. Net power calculations are based on gross risk figures; while professional investment risk-management is generally done, if it is done at all, on net risk. When used to allocate money among investments, net risk is almost always superior. Gross risk uses worst-case slippage estimates, as opposed to probable slippage estimates. And then it adds margin, if margin is demanded, as if it were a measure of risk. But worst-case slippage estimates are almost always overly pessimistic. And margin is not at risk. If a trader is well financed, margin, if it is demanded, does not affect trading. Prudent money-management demands that a certain proportion of the trading capital be kept from the market at all times. If these funds are large enough, they can be used for margin, and margin need not affect the number of units traded.

Gross risk calculations are clearly irrelevant if a fund is well financed. Since most investment funds are well financed, at least, in the opinion of those running them, net power is irrelevant. Except, there is no way of knowing whether a fund is well financed without calculating net power. At least, it is remarkable how often seemingly well-financed funds turn out to be underfunded. Typically, this comes to light when the fund cannot make its margin call. Apparently, this was the case with the $600 million Granite Fund (see Chapter 2).

Fortunately, net power is easy to calculate. We will do so now (see Figure 5–6). The available trading capital are the funds dedicated to trading, and accessible in time to meet margin calls. Interest earned, commissions committed, profitable and unprofitable trades, and additions and withdrawals of capital all affect the available trading capital. If for any reason the trader cannot get at the funds in time to make margin calls, he must reduce the trading capital by that amount. For example, the German Bankhaus Herstatt failed in the middle of a business day because too much of its cash was in the wrong time zone. Conversely, the trading capital must be increased for secure credit lines. The result, of course, is the account balance.

If the trader did not have any open trades, the account balance and the gross trading power would be equal. When there are open trades, the account balance must be decreased by the margin needed to sustain those trades and increased or decreased, respectively, by the open profits or losses. Margin levels, unfortunately, are not constant, and if the trader believes they might be raised, he or she should increase his or her allowance for margin.

The gross trading-profit minus the commissions, the open dollar-risk, and the execution costs gives the net trading-profit. The open dollar-risk has already been calculated, and commissions are easily available. The execution costs of a trade are the slippages between the trading order and its execution. If the trade is still pending, execution costs on both the open and close must be estimated; otherwise, only the close need be. Execution costs, of course, depend on the liquidity of the market. Market liquidity can change rapidly, and it can be expensive to underestimate the net power. Thus, it is better to overestimate execution costs than underestimate them.

Exhibit 5–6 Operating Statement

Available trading capital	$
minus inaccessible funds	________
Account balance	$
minus margin	
plus open profits	
minus open losses	________
Gross trading power	$
minus open $ risk	
minus commission	
minus execution costs	________
Net trading power	$ ________

Consider as an example a trader who has $11,043.00 committed to trading of which $3,000.00 is in a certificate of deposit. Assume that the trader had three open positions, the wheat trade discussed in Figure 5–4, a corn trade and, an oat trade. The margin for these trades is, let's say, $750.00, $600.00, and $400.00, respectively, and the margin total is $1,750.00. The wheat trade has an open loss of -$100.00. The corn and oat trades have open profits of $12.00 and $233.00. The open risk for the contracts is $300.00, $200.00, $350.00, respectively, for a total of $850.00. The commissions are $50.00 apiece for a total of $150.00. The execution costs are estimated as $50.00, $64.00, and $40.00, respectively, for a total of $155.00. The form is completed as follows:

Available trading capital	$ 11,043.00
minus money market reserve	3,000.00
Account balance	$ 8,043.00
minus margin	1,750.00
plus open profits	223.00
minus open losses	100.00
Gross trading power	$ 6,416.00
minus open $ risk	850.00
commission	150.00
execution costs	155.00
Net trading power	$ 5,261.00

A trader's gross trading-power is the amount of money the trader might use to open new positions or even withdraw from the account—if he or she is certain of never losing a trade. If the trader believes he or she might occasionally lose a trade, he or she should use net power instead.

Credit Analysis

Traders face default risk from the exchanges, from brokers and dealers, and from the investments themselves. Defaults rarely happen. But when there is a default, the costs are huge. Worse, traders are not compensated for taking credit risk, the way they are in the bond market, say.[7] Prudence thus demands that the trader monitor credit risk on a regular basis and set limits on the money he will risk with any given exchange, broker, dealer, or investment. He must then enforce those limits.

How often a trader should review his credit risk depends on how much money he has at risk and what other actions he takes to defend himself. Credit reviews are costly. For all but the largest traders, monthly or even quarterly analysis should be sufficient. Depending on the results of the analysis, small traders must decide whether to accept or reject a particular exchange, broker, or market. Large and moderate traders may alter their diversification strategy somewhat, change their cash-management strategy, or perhaps seek legal solutions.

There is almost no risk of an exchange default. The exchanges stand as seller to each buyer and buyer to each seller, and the exchanges are very well financed. Defaults have taken place, of course, and will certainly take place in the future, whenever the exchanges think it is in the best interests of some of their members to allow them. The exchanges cannot afford to let this happen more than once a decade, or so, but it does happen.

On the other hand, unless the trader is extremely well financed, it is unlikely that she can do a better job of assessing the risk than her brokerage company. Generally speaking, brokerage companies do not give credit information on the exchanges, other than forwarding public information to their customers. Although brokerage companies might make exceptions for large and demanding customers, it is not in their best interest to cast doubts on any market a trader might want to use. Brokerage companies do provide such information indirectly, in the form of commissions they charge and margins they demand. In extreme situations, they may even prevent a trader from using a particular exchange.[8]

The risk of a brokerage house default is considerably larger, but as long as the exchange is culpable, and the exchange does not default, you will get your money back. Eventually. Unfortunately, whether or not the exchange is culpable depends on how exchange officials read certain legal documents. A trader or investor who disagrees with the exchanges interpretation can sue. A typical example, to the extent there is a typical example, is that of the Comex and Volume Investors. Volume Investors was a brokerage firm with a seat on the Comex. Several of Volume Investors' customers had sold naked options and could not make their margin call. Because of this, Volume Investors could not make its margin calls. The Comex had a choice of (1) liquidating all of Volume Investors' accounts, almost all of which were held by innocent third parties, and using the money to make the margin calls, or (2) transferring all properly margined accounts to other brokerage firms and charging the other clearing members of the Comex for the margin money. Comex chose the first alternative.[9] Eventually, under threat of a lawsuit, and because they really are a bunch of really swell guys, Comex did refund the money to the innocent third parties.

At best, default is an inconvenience and the trader should avoid it when possible. If the brokerage firm is publicly owned, it must produce balance sheets and income statements on a regular basis. These can be analyzed using traditional credit-analysis techniques.[10] In the case of the larger brokerage firms, the trader does not even have to analyze the statements him- or herself. Many brokerage firms produce research reports on their competition.

If the brokerage house is not publicly owned, it probably does not publish its balance sheets and income statements. If the house does business in the United States, it must file financial statements with the CFTC and SEC, which are accessible with a freedom of information act inquiry. If the brokerage house is not publicly owned and does not do business in the United States, it probably does not publish its financial statements. In this case, the trader must depend on innuendo, rumor, and reputation. In the opinion of most reputable observers of the industry, these are not reliable sources. Better to go elsewhere.

With over-the-counter derivatives, the default risk is larger still, and much more difficult to evaluate. Triple-A credit ratings give remarkably little succor. Currently, derivatives do not appear on the balance sheet. Moreover, the leverage and the lack of a cash commitment means that a dealer can quickly do immense damage. Proctor and Gamble lost $102 million on *one* interest-rate swap.[11] No doubt, given the leverage dealers enjoy, a determined dealer can find ways of losing much much more.

The default risk from individual investments varies widely. Individual stocks and bonds have individual default risks, of course. Nothing new here. But strictly speaking, derivatives do not. An exchange-based futures or options cannot default without the exchange defaulting. Similarly, an over-the-counter derivative cannot default without the dealer defaulting.

Roughly speaking, there are two types of over-the-counter derivative default risk. The first is the risk of a default today. This is the cost of reestablishing the position today, including whatever payments would be received or disbursed today. Measuring this cost, summing across investments and reporting, is relatively easy. Better yet, in all or almost all cases, this risk is a small fraction of the face value of the trade.[12]

The other type of default risk is the cost of replacing the trade at some unspecified time in the future. In most cases, the maximum cost is not at the start or end of the trade, but sometime in the middle (see Figure 5–7). There is no easy, low-cost way to figure out what the cost is likely to be ahead of time. In

Figure 5–7 Swap Replacement Costs

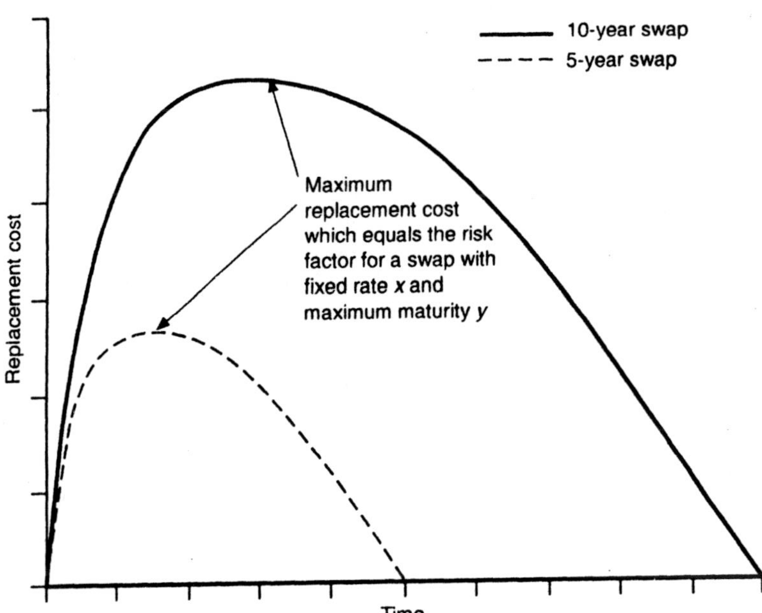

Source: Reprinted from Erik Banks. *Complex Derivatives*. Chicago: Probus, 1994, 211.

fact, there is no hard, high-cost way to get a good answer. The best available technology involves horribly complex Monte Carlo simulations, loaded with assumptions that are difficult or impossible to check.[13]

If default risk with a particular counterparty is excessive, there are only three obvious remedies, the trader can reduce the cash at risk, diversify over counterparties, and seek legal remedies. We will discuss each of these actions in turn.

Small traders can reduce the cash at risk only by reducing the size of the account. For small traders, other solutions are simply too expensive. Moderate and large traders can sweep the account of excess cash on a regular basis, say, daily or weekly. Any money in the account over what is necessary for margin can be wired somewhere safe. Or placed under a mattress.

In addition, the trader can diversify over exchanges, brokers and dealers, and investments. Given that the trader does this anyway, as a way to minimize market risk, or as part of his or her search for opportunity, the cost may be nothing or almost nothing. On the other hand, if the trader is not already doing this, the cost might be quite high.

Credit risk is supposed to be firm specific, which would be lovely, if it were true. In this case, a trader could diversify until his or her risk was nothing, or almost nothing. Unfortunately, in addition to various firm-specific causes, of which meaningful examples cannot be given because they are firm specific, credit risk is a function of various large-scale economic trends and events. This is why all assets of a particular class sometimes deteriorate simultaneously. This happened to California municipal bonds, for example, when the state economy deteriorated.[14]

Conceivably, all brokers and dealers, or all of the brokers and dealers that you use, could default simultaneously. This almost happened in September 1970, a time of high profits and full employment, when broker Hayden Stone almost destroyed the United States brokerage industry.The United States brokerage industry was saved by Jack Golsen of Oklahoma City who agreed to a deal he *knew* was not in his best interests. The next person or institution that holds the fate of Wall Street in its hands might not be so civic minded.[15] Clearly, money swept from an account should not be kept at another broker or dealer.

Legal actions are probably only cost-effective with over-the-counter derivatives. The trader should use one master agreement for all over-the-counter derivative transactions with a given dealer. Moreover, the master agreement should state that, regardless of who defaults, all cash flows will be netted. This means that you may have to pay money to the gentlemen and ladies, if that is the correct descriptive phrase, who defaulted. This is not fair. Worse, it rewards people for defaulting, which is not prudent behavior. But the alternative to netting is considerable legal risk.[16]

All trades should be collateralized or, at least, margined.[17] In the current technical jargon, a trade is collateralized when you and your dealer place liquid securities, equal to the face value of the derivative, in escrow accounts that you can access in the case of the other's default. Margin is usually a small fraction of the value of a contract. Generally speaking, it is only large enough to ensure compliance with the contract. If margin is reasonable, it will ensure compliance under normal circumstances. It will not protect a trader against a catastrophic price change.

Until recently, margin was set by exchange officials, who would look at price charts and fundamentals and then specify a dollar amount that they thought would ensure compliance. As exchange officials are in intimate contact with the market, this actually worked fairly well. But with the development of the options market and the increasing complexity of the relationships of investments in many portfolios, even an intimate personal knowledge of the markets was not enough.

In 1988, the Chicago Mercantile Exchange developed SPAN, their risk-based performance bond system.[18] This system is now used by at least 20 other exchanges. SPAN stands for Standard Portfolio Analysis of Risk. The SPAN system is complicated, and individual traders do not make the calculations themselves, they download arrays of values from the exchanges daily and multiply the number of contracts they own of various investments by the proper array values. Quite obviously, something like the SPAN system could be used in the over-the-counter market. If the SPAN system could not be used by others, other exchanges could not use it. On the other hand, the SPAN system is complicated and developing a version for a particular use is probably expensive. An alternative is J. P. Morgan's RiskMetrics® system.[19] If the RiskMetrics® or the SPAN system, or something like it, is not available, the best thing to do is to use some fixed fraction of the collateral values, say 25 percent.

In either case, the security should be marked to market. Any material difference between the value of the securities and the value required for collateral or margin should be corrected. If it is not possible to mark the security to market, margins should be set relatively high.

When a trade is collateralized, the dealer and the securities placed in escrow must both default before the investor is hurt. Unfortunately, this is not as unlikely as it sounds. Beginning in 1978 or 1979, depending on how you read the story, the Hunt brothers tried to corner the silver market. They bought silver bullion and silver futures, pushing the price of silver up as they bought. Unfortunately for Conti & Company and Bache & Company, two of their brokers, they used silver bullion as margin for silver futures. When the price collapsed, the futures and the margin collapsed together, bringing Bache to the edge of ruin and destroying Conti and several other brokerage firms that could not make their margin calls.[20] A trader can avoid a similar fate by making sure the derivative, the dealer, and the collateral or margin have nothing in common. If the trader is buying a heating oil option from a Wall Street firm, then prudent collateral might be, say, Japanese government bonds.

Endnotes

1. Charles D. Ellis, "The Loser's Game" *The Financial Analysts Journal*, Vol. 31, No. 4, July/August 1975, pp. 19–26.
2. The delta of an option is the amount an option changes given a one dollar change in the underlying investment. So, if a call option on IBM has a delta of .6, and the price of IBM goes up a dollar, the price of the call option will go up 60 cents. If an investor has bought a share of IBM and sold a call with a delta of .6 against that share, and if the price of IBM goes up by one dollar, the net effect is that the value of the investment goes up by 40 cents. Delta values necessarily range from zero to one, exclusive. Deltas are not constant.

3. Thomas Petziner, Jr., et al, "Risky Futures," *The Wall Street Journal* (February 16, 1984): 1, 23.
4. Jack L. Treynor was the first to make this point. See Jack L. Treynor, "What Does it Take to Win the Trading Game?" *Financial Analysts Journal* (January–February 1981): 55–60.
5. In this case, the trader should consider whether he or she actually wants to make the trade. If it is not possible to mark the security to market, the chance of fraud is much greater than average.
6. Richard Teweles, et al., "Notes from a Trader," *Commodities* (December 1976): 30.
7. It is not clear that the brokers and dealers are compensated for taking credit risk either.
8. For example, Merrill Lynch destroyed the New Orleans Commodity Exchange when it quadrupled margin requirements overnight and accepted orders from customers on a liquidation only basis. At the time, Merril Lynch had more than 53 percent of the open interest. See "Down, Not Out," *Commodities* (August 1983): 23.
9. C. R. O'Dea, "The Guarantee That Wasn't There," *Intermarket* (July 1985): 38ff.
10. See Sumner N. Levine, *The Financial Analyst's Handbook,* Irwin Professional Publishing, 1988.
11. As a result, Proctor and Gamble replaced its treasurer. Kashima Oil, a Japanese firm, lost $1.5 billion trading foreign exchange derivatives. *The Economist* (May 14, 1944): 21ff.
12. A pilot study by the International Swaps and Derivatives Association, "surveyed 14 leading derivatives dealers at year end 1993 and found the net replacement value of outstanding interest rate and currency swaps was $101.3 billion, or about 1.22 percent of the total $7.6 trillion notional amount. The gross replacement value was $178.4 billion, or 2.15 percent of the notional amount." *Derivatives Week* (June 13, 1994): 2.

13. For more detailed analysis, see Erik Banks, *Complex Derivatives* (Chicago: Probus, 1994).
14. See, for example, Dennis Waltens, "Localities and California Need to Learn a New Dance," *Bond Buyer,* (October 7, 1993): p 44f.
15. The Federal Reserve bailed out Wall Street during the crash of 1987, but it did not have to do this, and it might not do it next time. In 1933, Henry Ford did not respond to the requests of Treasury Secretary Ogden L. Mills and subordinate his demand account at the Union Commerce Bank, which caused the bank's failure and the 1933 panic. Mr. Ford, who was not as civic minded as Mr. Golsen, stated, "If a panic and crash will come from all this, so be it. Let it come." See Charles D. Ellis, *The Second Crash* (New York: Simon and Schuster, 1973).
16. This is the opinion of the Group of Thirty. Considering that the group is dealer dominated, and that dealers face greater credit risk than their clients, this is a remarkably impartial recommendation. Group of Thirty, *Derivatives: Practices and Principles Global Derivatives Study Group* (Washington, D.C. 1993): 16.
17. A third-party guarantee is an alternative. Unfortunately, while dealers may demand guarantees, they do not like to give them. Moreover, there is always the risk of your guarantor defaulting. If you do get a guarantee, do not get one from an organization that uses derivatives.
18. Chicago Mercantile Exchange, *SPAN—A Risk-Based Performance Bond System* (Chicago: 1992).
19. J. P. Morgan, RiskMetrics®—Technical Document (New York: JP Morgan), 1994. Incidentally, Jim Alphier developed a system similar to RiskMetrics® more than 15 years ago. Personal communication (no date).
20. See Stephen Fay, *The Great Silver Bubble* (London: Hodder and Stoughton), 1982.

6

Forecasting Theory: Insight and Irony

Successful trading demands successful forecasting. Forecasting is not always explicit. For example, trend followers do not forecast the extent or timing of price movements. But all trend following methods are based on the implicit assumption that from the time a buy signal is given until the time it stops, prices will rise on average. And prices will go down on average from the time a sell signal is given until the time it stops.

Similarly, someone selling a delta-neutral option spread is implicitly forecasting that price will not go too far up or down. More, he or she is forecasting that volatility will go down. *If the trader cannot successfully forecast the market, on average, all of his or her other trading skills are useless.* Unfortunately, because the future is forever unknown, the trader can *never* be certain that he or she can really forecast the market.

On the other hand, if it seems reasonable or likely that the trader can, on average, forecast the market accurately, trading is still a reasonable business venture. How reasonable or likely it is that the trader can successfully forecast the market is a matter of probabilities and statistics, of course. Although both topics are discussed in this book, the trader should be aware that many individuals who understand these topics best believe that the probability is zero or almost zero that the trader can beat the market.

Many academicians argue, in effect, that no one can make money in the market *precisely* because anyone can make money in the market. An account can be opened for a few thousand dollars. Fortunes can be made on hardly any investment at all.

Precisely because of this, much *is* invested in beating the market. Billions of dollars have been invested in speculative funds and accounts of various kinds. Decades of computer time have been dedicated to price analysis. Tens of thousands of man-hours a year are invested in collecting and analyzing data. More important, some of the finest minds in the world are working full time trying to beat the market. Possibly, the net result of this effort is that all potential profits have been beaten out of the market.

If all potential profit has been beaten out of the market, the market is "efficient." When the market is efficient, the current price will always, or nearly always, be the most reasonable one possible, in terms of all currently available information.

This theory is known as the *efficient market hypothesis*. One particularly well-known form of this theory is the random-walk theory. A market that follows a random walk will be an efficient market, but an efficient market will not necessarily follow a random walk.

"Random" has a special meaning here. It does not mean irrational. Rather, it means that there is no pattern or structure to the data. Consider, for example, the following number series:

6 9 0 1 4 8 4 5 8 3 0 7 6 7 2 5 2 5 6 4
1 1 1 1 1 1 1 1 1 1 1 1 1 1 1 1 1 1 1 1

The first series clearly is random; the second series clearly is not. The first series is random because it does not have a pattern or structure; the second series does. Because the first series lacks any pattern, it can be communicated only by repeating each digit in order. The second series can be communicated the same way, of course, but it can also be communicated as follows: "Construct a number 20 digits long consisting solely of ones."

The sentence above is a simple verbal algorithm. The algorithm, which is an explicit and exhaustive set of instructions, generates the number series; that is, it contains all the information in the original data but in a more economical form.

Randomness and nonrandomness involve the presence and absence of patterns. More explicitly, a number series is random if and only if there is no algorithm to generate the series that can be transmitted more economically than the series itself (see Figure 6–1.)

Figure 6–1

```
1   REM PROGRAM NUMBER 1
2   READ A1
3   PRINT A1
4   GO TO 2
5   DATA 6, 9, 0, 1, 4
6   DATA 8, 4, 5, 8, 3
7   DATA 0, 7, 6, 7, 2
8   DATA 5, 2, 5, 6, 4
9   END

1   REM PROGRAM NUMBER 2
2   FOR N=1 TO 20
3   PRINT "1"
4   NEXT N
5   END
```

Both of the above programs are written in the programming language BASIC. The first program prints out a list of 20 random numbers. The second program prints out the number "1" 20 times. The fact that the second program is shorter and more efficient than the first indicates that the second number series is less random than the first.

If prices follow a random walk, they cannot be dependent upon or correlated with past price changes. Curiously enough, the efficient market hypothesis allows prices to be dependent upon past price behavior as long as such dependence is not of a form that allows trading profits; for example, the efficient market hypothesis would allow the size, but not the sign, of today's price change to be dependent upon yesterday's price change. The random walk theory would allow neither.

A distinction between the random walk theory and the efficient market hypothesis is necessary only if the theory or hypothesis is to be tested. Evidence that will contradict the random walk theory will not necessarily contradict the efficient market hypothesis. Indeed, although there is evidence that the market is not a random walk, there is little evidence that the market is not efficient. Fortunately, in terms of trading implications the theories are almost identical.

The most important trading implications[1] are:

1. **The Value of Price Analysis.** When the market is efficient, prices are appropriate, at least in terms of the available information. When this is the case, there is no profit potential to exploit and, therefore, no value to price analysis.

2. **The Value of Speculation.** On a gross basis, speculative markets are a zero sum game: Every dollar won by one player must be lost by another. Worse, on a net basis, the market is a negative sum game. In other words, not every dollar lost will be won, the difference going to the speculative industry. The industry—that is, the brokerage companies, the money managers, and the trading advisors—are playing a positive sum game. On average, the industry makes money. On average, traders do not.

Trading cannot be a valid business venture for the average trader, but it can be a valid business venture for those who can forecast the market successfully on average. If this cannot be done, trading is clearly valueless.

3. The Value of Large Portfolios. The importance of this concept depends on how large the fixed costs of trading are; that is, how large those costs of trading are that are independent of the size of the trading portfolio. Much of the trading literature assumes that fixed costs are small or nonexistent. But surely this cannot be the case. If the market can be beaten at all, surely it cannot be beaten by obvious and unsophisticated means. Unfortunately, obscure and sophisticated techniques are likely to be expensive. Moreover, their expense is almost certain to be independent of the amount of money traded. For example, an advisory service that charged $1,000 a year could as easily be used to trade one futures contract as a hundred, but the average cost—that is, the cost per contract—will drop as the number of contracts traded rises. If the gross profit per contract is constant, it clearly makes more sense to trade a large portfolio than a small one.

4. The Relative Value of Technical and Fundamental Analysis. If the market is efficient, the current price will be the most reasonable one possible in terms of all currently available information. What trading implications the theory has depends on what information is considered available. Currently, the theory takes three forms: the weak, the semistrong, and the strong.[2]

The weak form of the theory alleges that the present price of an investment reflects all past price, volume, and open interest trends. If this is true, such data cannot be used to forecast the market, and technical analysis is therefore of no use.

The semistrong form of the theory alleges that the current price reflects all publicly known information. If this form of the theory is true, neither technical analysis nor any method of fundamental analysis based on public data, such as news or corporate reports, is of any value.

The strong form of the theory alleges that the price of an investment reflects everything that is knowable about the investment. If this form of the theory is true, even a private survey of supply and demand would not give the trader an edge. If this form of the theory is true, there is no rational reason for trading.

A fourth alternative, of course, is that the current prices may not even reflect past price trends, much less other data. If this is the case, both technical and fundamental analysis could be used to forecast the market.

Given these alternatives, it is clear that whereas both types of analysis may be of value, neither type need be. It is also clear that if technical analysis is of value, fundamental analysis must be also but that the converse is not necessarily true.

The overwhelming academic opinion is that the above theory is almost certainly true in its weak form and true to at least some extent even in its strongest form. The overwhelming opinion of the investment community is that regardless of form, the theory is a piece of trash.

For years, the investment community has heaped scorn on the efficient market hypothesis. This is understandable, because if the theory is true, or almost true, almost all the products and services the community provides are completely without value. Nevertheless, this scorn is misplaced. The theory is perfectly reasonable, though it may not be true.

Over the years, a large number of articles and books have attempted to discredit the efficient market hypothesis. Unfortunately, few of the writers seem to understand the theory. This is, of course, understandable. Few individuals are willing to invest the considerable effort necessary to understand a theory that they believe is wrong. Although this may be good time-management, it is rotten science. A theory must be refuted, if at all, in its own terms. For example, I may believe that numerology is worthless, but I would never commit myself to that in print without attempting to understand numerology in its own terms; that is, in terms numerologists themselves understand and use.

The most common misunderstanding of the efficient market hypothesis is probably the belief or intuition that the market must provide at least some valid trading opportunities if only because it provides so many opportunities to trade. Actually, *none* of the numerous opportunities the market provides need favor the trader.

Consider, by way of analogy, a wager on three fair but bizarrely numbered dice.[3] None of the dice are numbered from one to six; but for each of the dice, the probability of the die landing on any one of its six faces is one in six. You will be allowed to examine the dice and select one. Your opponent will then select one of the two remaining dice. You will both then roll your dice, and the player with the higher number wins.

The wager certainly seems fair. Surely, at worst the dice are equally likely to win, in which case it does not matter which die you choose. At best, one of the dice may be more likely to win than the others, in which case you can surely determine which die is favorable by examining them. Since you select the first die, you should find the bet at least fair and possibly favorable. Right?

Wrong. This analysis assumes that the relationship among the dice is transitive; this is, if the first die beats the second die on average and the second die beats the third die on average, the first die will beat the third die on average. It seems reasonable to assume that the relationship among the dice will be transitive because most betting situations are transitive. If, to give an example from poker, four of a kind beats a full house and a full house beats two pair, then four of a kind beats two pair. Unfortunately, not all bets are transitive.

For example, consider three dice with the following faces:

1, 1, 4, 4, 4, 4
3, 3, 3, 3, 3, 3
2, 2, 2, 2, 6, 6

No matter which die the trader selects, there is another that will beat it on average. On average, the first die will beat the second die, the second die will beat the third die, and the third die will beat the first die.

It is not clear whether the market resembles the above example. What is clear is that the fact that the market provides many trading opportunities does not necessarily imply that any of them are desirable.

A second common misunderstanding of the efficient market hypothesis is the belief that price behavior should be lawful, that unlawful price behavior is somehow unnatural or irrational. In a sense unintended by its advocates, this belief is certainly true. Prices may or may not obey causal laws; that is, they may or may not be forecastable, but they certainly obey the laws of probability.

A third common misunderstanding is the belief that obvious market "trends" are somehow prima facie evidence of market inefficiency. For example, one trader writes, "can anyone deny that the silver move that started late in December, 1973 and ended in March, 1974 showed a well-defined trend? If that was a random walk it was one up the side of a mountain!"[4] (See Figure 6–2.)

But there is nothing whatsoever unnatural or illogical about a random walk over mountainous terrain, however. Indeed, some random walks look exactly like this (see Figure 6–3).

In other words, a trend may be nothing more than a drift. A price series has a drift if, *in retrospect*, the price changes are positive or negative on average. But a drifting series can only be said to have a trend or trends if the drifts could have been successfully forecasted, on average. Silver may have indeed trended from December 1973 to March 1974, but if so, it is far from obvious.

A fourth misunderstanding is the belief that the theory is somehow self-contradictory. Actually, the theory does allow a number of delightful ironies and paradoxes. For example, the theory has the curious property that it can be true only to the extent that it is not believed; that is, to the extent that traders continue to trade. But this does not imply that the theory is false, as some writers believe or wish to believe. A paradox is not a contradiction. The paradox only implies that *if* the efficient market hypothesis is true, traders cannot really understand the nature of the market, at least not to the extent that academic econo-

Figure 6–2

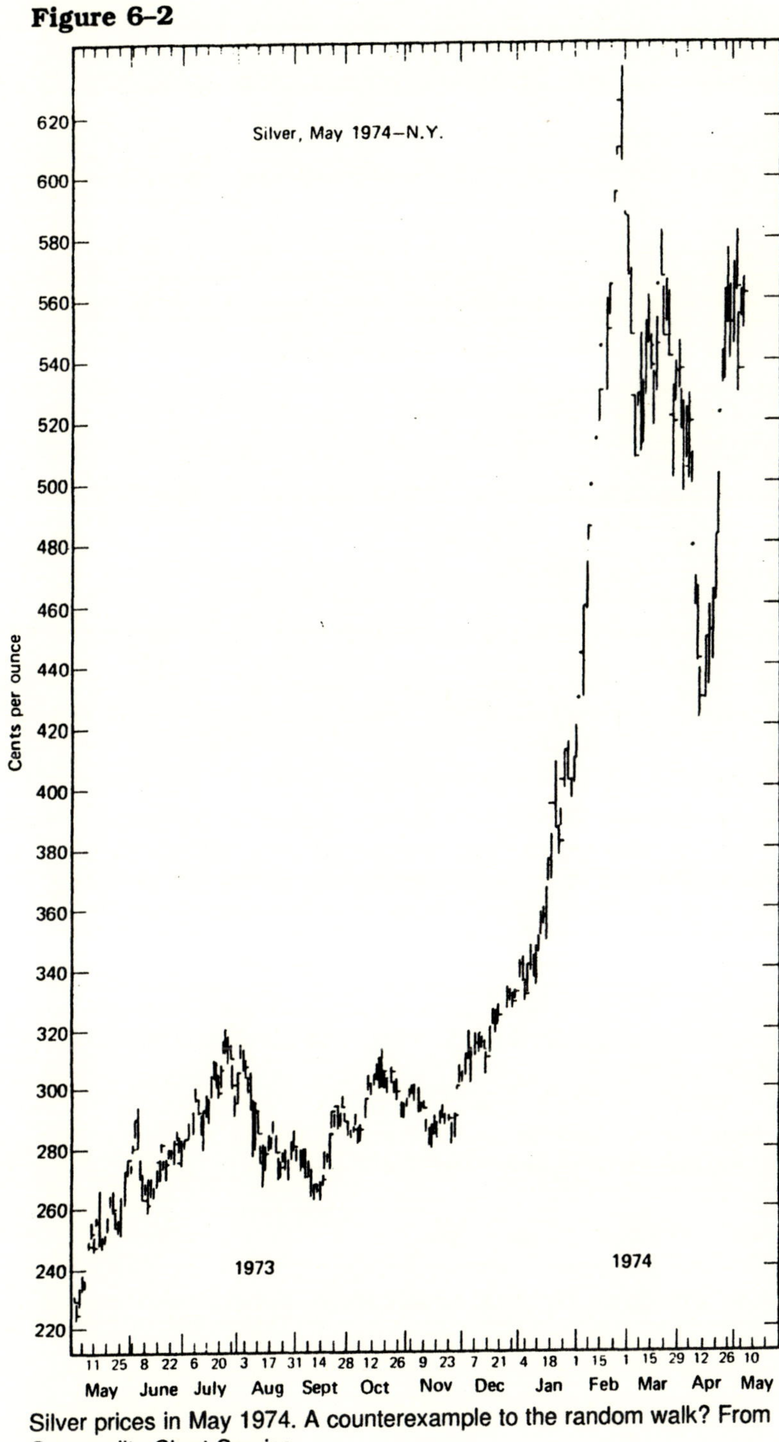

Silver prices in May 1974. A counterexample to the random walk? From Commodity Chart Service.

Figure 6–3

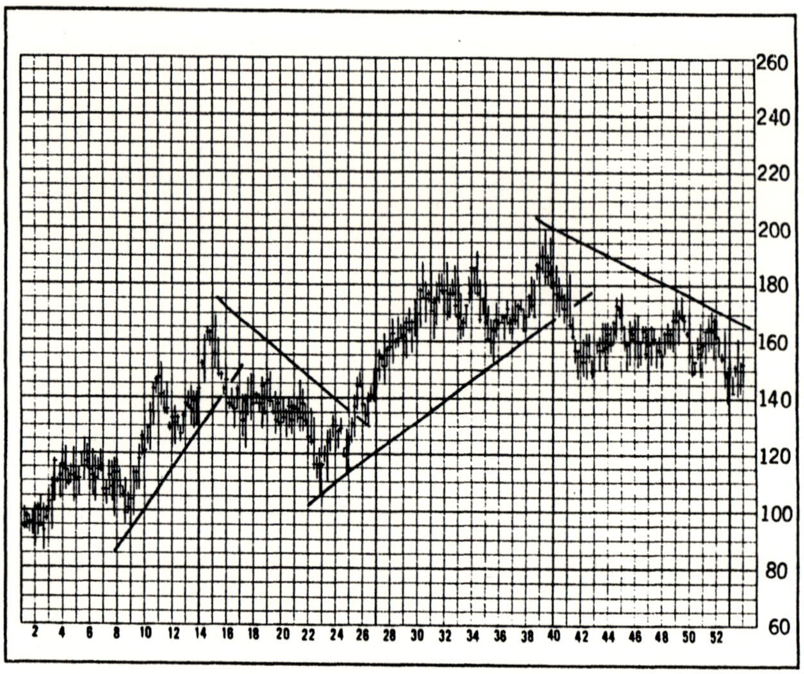

Notice the chart patterns and trend-like behavior, yet the chart was constructed from randomly generated data. From A. Sklarew. *Techniques of a Professional Commodity Chart Analysis.* Commodity Research Bureau Inc., 1980, p. 12.

mists do. No doubt, economists find this flattering, but the theory is not necessarily false for this reason. The theory is quite capable of being true.

A theory that is capable of being true must be accepted or rejected on the basis of how well it describes the real world; that is, on the basis of evidence.[5] For example, to the best of my knowledge, astrology has no internal contradictions, but there is also no evidence that it works.

Oddly enough, traders and academicians produce the same type of evidence: historical studies showing that a given method did or did not work over a given period. Traders have presented so many studies showing so many ways of beating the market that the reader may well wonder why anyone loses. On the other hand, academicians have presented many studies showing that many popular trading methods have not worked after all.

Since the academic literature is considerably more rigorous than the trading literature, it would seem prudent that the trader either get acquainted with the academic literature or give up trading.

Academicians, of course, have *not* proven that the market is random. Moreover, they never will. All they have proven is that certain types of nonrandom price behavior do not appear over certain historical periods. If these periods are representative—that is, if they have been randomly selected—these types of nonrandom price behavior are unlikely to appear in the future. Other types of nonrandom behavior may well appear, however.

The academician is in the same position as an ornithologist who tries to prove that all ducks are black. Clearly, one nonblack duck, say a white or a tan one, would disprove the theory. But although each black duck observed strengthens the theory, no number of black ducks can prove it. Even if the ornithologist examined every living duck, he or she could not prove the theory because it is always possible that ducks had been or might be born some other color than black.

Clearly, if science demanded absolute proof, there would be no science. Scientifically, statistically significant results—that is, results that are reasonably unlikely or improbable—are sufficient. For example, the ornithologist's belief that all or almost all ducks are black would seem justified if each of a thousand randomly selected ducks were found to be black. Similarly, the academician's belief that the market is random would seem justified if each of a large number of randomly selected trading methods were found to be useless.

Over the years, so many forecasting and trading methods have been found useless that many academicians lost interest in the issue. It just wasn't fun any more. But that, of course, does not prove that the market is random. The methods selected for testing have never been selected randomly. They have, of course, been selected in order of their obviousness and testability. It is not reasonable to conclude that the market cannot be beaten when a less obvious or more expensive method might do so.

More recently, a number of academicians have found methods that appear to beat the market. If these methods really beat the market, the efficient market hypothesis is disproved. It only takes one white duck to prove that not all ducks are black.

Unfortunately, it is not completely certain that these methods work. Critics note that any test of the efficient market hypothesis is actually a joint test of the hypothesis and an asset pricing model. In other words, in order to show that market prices are wrong, you need to know what the right price should be, which is what an asset pricing model does. An alleged proof that the market is efficient could be a proof that the asset pricing model is wrong. Thus, other academicians believe that the available evidence indicates not profit opportunities, but errors in the way risk is measured.[6]

The problem is logically unsolvable, but fortunately it is not particularly serious. The academic tests of the efficient market hypothesis and the various asset pricing models are high-quality work. And even if they were not, it is hard to see why someone who believed in market inefficiency could take comfort in that.

Still, in a certain sense the market is almost certainly not random. Surely, at any given moment there are numerous obscure facts that could be exploited profitably. No doubt, methods could be found to eke profits from even the most available and analyzed data. But such methods should not be easy to find. *If the cost of finding a method of beating the market exceeds the potential profit, as it does for many, perhaps most, traders, the market is in effect random.*

The question, therefore, is not whether or not the efficient market hypothesis is true, but to what extent it is true. The evidence in favor of the hypothesis is considerable—but not overwhelming. There is almost certainly some truth to the weakest form of the theory. Certainly, the most obvious and naive forms of technical analysis are barren. On the other hand, it seems unlikely that the theory is true in its strongest form. Surely, at any given moment, there are numerous obscure facts that could be exploited profitably—if only one knew what those facts were.

The extent to which the efficient market hypothesis is true depends upon the logic of the hypothesis and the validity of the assumptions. When the logic is flawless, which in this case is almost certainly true, the truth of the hypothesis depends on the validity of the underlying assumptions. If the assumptions are true, the hypothesis must be true.

The consensus among academicians is that the efficient market hypothesis depends upon five assumptions.[7] These assumptions are sufficient but not necessary; that is, the market must be efficient if these assumptions are true, but the market can be efficient without these assumptions being completely true. On the other hand, if the market is not efficient, one or more of the following assumptions must be false.

1. **Low Transaction Costs.** This means that commissions, execution costs, and taxes must be low enough so potential traders and hedgers are not prevented or inhibited from acting. This seems to be the case. Commissions and execution costs are quite low for most markets. Trading profits are currently taxed at moderate rates, of course, but moderate or even high rates do not seem to excessively inhibit trading, at least if the market's growth in recent years is any indication.

2. **High Liquidity.** This means that individual trades must not excessively affect the market price. For a great many markets, this also seems to be the case. In T-Bonds, for example, the trading volume is high enough that even large buy and sell orders cause little more than ripples.

3. **Effective Information Flow.** This means that news must flow quickly and freely to all real and potential traders and hedgers. This is not quite the case. Generally, news is available at a rela-

tively low cost, but it is not available free. News is available to anyone willing to pay for it, but not all traders are willing.

More important, in many markets there is no "inside information," other than the actions of our own and other governments. For example, in the agricultural futures markets, the most important influence is the U.S. Department of Agriculture, which takes considerable pains to ensure that the information they procure is released simultaneously, after the market's close, to all concerned. Other agencies may not be so scrupulous.

There is no other inside information because there is no inside. Commodities can scarcely be produced or consumed in secret. Individual producers and consumers may act in secret, of course, but there are so many producers and consumers of most commodities that this scarcely matters. Thus, while it is possible for a trader to consistently get market news before others, in fact it rarely appears to happen.

Life is not always so idyllic in the corporate world. Insiders know things outsiders do not. It is illegal for insiders to act on such knowledge, but, alas, the law is not always a barrier.

In any case, traders worried about the efficient market hypothesis can take no comfort here. Anyone possessing inside information will not worry about the efficient market hypothesis. Those of us without such information find the cards stacked against us.

4. Rapid Price Adjustments. This means that the price must change rapidly when new information indicates that a change is appropriate. This seems to be the case.

5. Rational Traders and Hedgers. This means that traders and hedgers must recognize prices that are too high or low in terms of the available information. The assumption here is that all or almost all traders and hedgers will not make the same errors. Clearly, whenever traders and hedgers with the same information disagree, at least some of them must be in error. If all or almost all of them are in error, the assumption is violated.

Without a doubt, this assumption is the most dubious of the lot. Indeed, in the past, traders and investors have been frequently and unanimously wrong; that is, they have frequently and unanimously been stupid and irrational.

Irrationality is the substitution, in whole or in part, of greed or fear for reason. For example, during the 17th century, tulip bulbs became a major focus of the Dutch economy. Tulips were attractive, exotic, and potentially profitable as an export item. They were valuable and had the potential of becoming even more so.

The profit potential was large, but it was not infinite. Yet in many people's minds, the profit potential quickly became infinite, or nearly so. More and more money was paid for tulip bulbs, until fortunes were paid for individual bulbs. In one of many sad cases, a farmer traded all of his worldly goods, including "a farm of 38 acres, cattle and sheep, hundreds of pounds of cheese, lard and butter, all of the furnishings of the farmhouse, and a gold drinking cup . . ." for a single tulip.[8]

Eventually, there was no more money for tulips. The tulip boom crested and shattered, leaving the Dutch economy in ruins. Bulbs that had once sold for fortunes now sold for pennies.

Unfortunately, the Dutch tulip boom was not unique. It was followed by the Mississippi land frauds and the South Seas bubble, which almost bankrupted 18th century France and England, respectively. The South Seas bubble was a stock fraud large enough to retire the English national debt. During the boom, stock was sold in ventures to supply England with sea coal, to rebuild every home in England, to build a perpetual motion machine, and most fascinating of all, to develop "a company for carrying on an undertaking of great advantage, but nobody to know what it is." Apparently, speculators could buy shares at 100 pounds each, each of which would produce an annual return of 100 pounds and each share of which could be purchased with only a 2-pound deposit. Within five hours, the issue was oversubscribed. Naturally, the promoter left England that evening and was never heard of again.

The Mississippi land fraud and the South Seas bubble were followed by the Florida land boom, the 1929 stock market collapse, and scores of other booms and busts (see Figure 6–4). Historically, mass irrationality has been so prevalent that it is sometimes difficult to believe that the market is basically rational. Indeed, irrationality has been so frequent that it is sometimes difficult to believe that the market price is ever appropriate.

The market price during a boom or bust is virtually never appropriate. Indeed, the market price could only be appropriate if the millennium or the apocalypse were approaching.

Sometimes, of course, the millennium or the apocalypse is approaching. For example, holders of Czarist's bonds should have sold when they saw the Russian revolution coming, regardless of price. Come the revolution, the bonds had become worthless or virtually worthless. Only hope or delusion gave the bonds value.

More often, the millennium or the apocalypse does not arrive. Jensen describes the nonarrival like this:

> When the pressure to sell is the greatest, that is when I start shaking my head and state, 'It should hold here.' When I rush to the brokerage office a half hour before opening time to be sure I am there to watch the crash, when I feel my stomach turn and food doesn't appeal to me, when the blood is rushing to my head and my breathing is a little short because I know I must make a decision, possibly to salvage what is left, when my broker's voice is trembling, when the faces in the board room are full of fear, then, I have learned this is not the time to sell. THIS IS THE TIME TO BUY.[9]

It generally becomes clear sooner or later that the millennium or the apocalypse will not arrive during the near future, and prices return to normal. Clearly, anyone with the foresight to buy during a crash or sell during a boom will earn extraordinary returns. But this is not easy to do. It not only demands considerable foresight, it demands courage.

Figure 6–4

The number of objects that have been used for speculation is too large to catalog here. The following list is partial and suggestive:

BRITISH GOVERNMENT DEBT: Amsterdam, 1763.
SELECTED COMPANIES: South Sea Company, Compagnie d'Occident, Sword Blade Bank, Banque Generale, Banque Royale, 1720; British East India Company, 1772; Dutch East India Company, 1772, 1783.
IMPORT COMMODITIES: sugar, coffee, 1799; 1857 in Hamburg; cotton in Britain and France, 1836, 1861; wheat in 1847.
COUNTRY BANKS: England, 1750s, 1793, 1824.
CANALS: 1793, 1820s in Britain; 1823 in France.
EXPORT GOODS: 1810, 1816, 1836 for Britain.
FOREIGN BONDS: 1825 in London; 1888 in Paris; 1924 in New York.
FOREIGN MINES: Latin American in Britain, 1825; German in Britain and France, 1850.
FOREIGN DIRECT INVESTMENT: by U.S. companies, 1960s.
BUILDING SITES: 1825 in France; 1857 in the United States; 1873 in Austria and Germany; 1925 in Florida; 1970s in Florida, Arizona, and New Mexico.
AGRICULTURAL LAND: *biens nationaux* (noble land confiscated during the Revolution in France), speculated in from 1815 to 1830s.
PUBLIC LANDS: United States, 1836, 1857; Argentina, 1888–90
RAILROAD SHARES: 1836, 1847 in Britain; 1847, 1857 in France; 1857, 1873 in the United States.
JOINT-STOCK BANKS: Germany, 1850s and early 1870s.
JOINT-STOCK DISCOUNT HOUSES: Britain in the 1860s.
PRIVATE COMPANIES GOING PUBLIC: 1888 in Britain; 1928 in the United States.
EXISTING AND MERGED COMPANIES: 1920 in Britain; 1928 in the United States; conglomerates in the United States, 1960s.
COPPER: 1888 in France; 1907 in the United States.
FOREIGN EXCHANGE: the mark in 1921–23; the franc in 1924–26; sterling in 1931, 1964, etc.; the dollar in 1973.
GOLD: 1960s, 1970s.
NEW INDUSTRIES: the United States in 1920s, 1960s.
BUILDINGS: hotels, condominiums, office buildings, nursing homes, retirement villages.
COMMODITY FUTURES.
STOCK PUTS AND CALLS (options).

Source: Charles P. Kindleberger. *Manias, Panics and Crashes: A History of Financial Crisis*. New York: Basic Books, 1978, pp. 45–46.

Stupidity is the misunderstanding of market economics. In a sense, stupidity is unavoidable. Understanding is a map, and no map completely describes its territory. Still, some maps are better—that is, more accurate or more useful—than others.

Consider, for example, the slot machine. The slot machine is one of the most popular forms of gambling. In Las Vegas, according to Richard Epstein, "They outnumber all other forms of gambling by more than 10 to 1." This popularity is remarkable, considering the slots are one of Las Vegas's least favorable games. If we disregard the entertainment these machines provide, the slot machine players clearly are acting irrationally.

The slot machine player has only two obvious alternatives: to bet or not to bet. If the player bets, he or she can choose the size of the bet but nothing else. As all bets have the same apparently negative expected value, there seems to be little point in betting. Indeed, it can be proven that there is no betting system or strategy that will allow the trader, on average, to beat the machine.

Yet slot machines have been beaten. They have been beaten because the map or description above was, and perhaps still is, wrong.

All bets on the slot machine are not necessarily equal and negative. The manufacturers, of course, attempt to ensure that this is the case, but they are not necessarily successful. Profits are possible if the machines have:

> mechanical imperfections. One example is the celebrated 'rhythm method.' Discovered in 1949 by an Idaho farmer who had aided a friend in repairing slot machines, this method rested on the fact that certain symbols would reappear after a certain number of seconds if they had previously stopped near the pay line. A player could insert a coin, pull the handle, pause for the correct time interval, and pull the handle a second time. The concomitant payoff was approximately 120 percent of the funds invested. By 1951 the slot machine manufacturers had installed a 'variator,' which caused the symbols to appear at varying intervals, thereby destroying the effectiveness of the 'rhythm method.'[10]

Slot machines have been beaten only by individuals who understand their workings better than their manufacturers. Similarly, the market can be beaten only by those who understand market economics better than average.

Roughly speaking, this can be done in only three ways. Profitable trading must be based on exploiting information that other traders do not possess or on exploiting their irrationality or stupidity.

Unfortunately, theory provides little help in constructing profitable trading systems; that is, there are no other obvious attributes that *every* successful trading system must have, although there are certainly attributes that any given trading system must have. Therefore, if a trading system is to be constructed rationally, the underlying theory must be analyzed in terms of criteria intrinsic to the theory itself. Trading implications must be developed in the same way.

For psychological reasons, this is difficult to do. Many, perhaps most, people tend either to apply one set of criteria to all situations or to apply ad hoc, more or less arbitrary rules to individual situations. Sometimes this is exactly the right thing to do, but sometimes it is not.

Perhaps the distinction between intrinsic and extrinsic criteria can be clarified by the dog-show metaphor. In a dog show, awards are given to the best of each of several breeds, and a second award, the best of show is given to one of those winners. Each breed is judged by different extrinsic criteria. Dachshunds, for example, are judged by the blackness or brownness of their coats and the shortness of their legs. Irish Setters are judged by the redness of their coats and the length of their legs. But the dog awarded the best of show may have black hair or red, long legs or short; it doesn't matter. What does matter is whether the best Dachshund is more like what a Dachshund should be than the best Irish Setter is like what an Irish Setter should be. The best of show is judged by intrinsic criteria.

Trading methods must be analyzed in terms of intrinsic criteria. The goal, of course, is always the same—a valid set of buy and sell signals—but the way the theory is developed and the trading signals derived will necessarily vary from theory to theory. A risk-managed arbitrage method must be analyzed in a different manner than an econometric method, which must be analyzed in a different manner than the Elliott wave method.

Any or all of these techniques may be of value; at least, there is no reason to believe that if the market can be beaten at all, it can be beaten in only one way. If the market can be beaten at all, surely there are numerous valid approaches, numerous valid points of view (see Figure 6–5).

Interestingly enough, an individual who has spent the last 10 years studying the market does not necessarily have an advantage over a beginner, for much of his or her knowledge was rotting as it was acquired. The way wheat is grown and consumed, for example, is hardly the same now as it was a decade ago.

Figure 6–5

Is the figure above a leftward looking bird or a rightward looking rabbit? Actually, both views and perhaps others are equally valid. From N. P. Hanson. *Patterns of Discovery*. London: Cambridge University Press, 1961.

It is not simply that the nature of the game changes over time; rather, the act of playing the game changes its nature. When slot machines are beaten, they will be redesigned and rebuilt. When some traders beat the market, others will anticipate them. Ultimately, the profit will dissipate.

Ultimately, the market cannot be beaten, but money can be taken before the market's nature changes. At least, money can be taken by those who understand market economics best.

Market knowledge is therefore relative. The market is a zero game, a game that can be won only by those with superior knowledge. Market knowledge is therefore a zero sum game. It is for this reason that traders with average or below average knowledge are doomed. In effect, they know nothing or less than nothing about the market.

The average or below average trader is doomed. Yet we may be that trader. Unfortunately, we cannot know.

Consider the slot machine example above. The slot machine is a relatively simple game and yet there are at least three levels of insight or understanding possible, each of which implies its own tactics. On the first or simplest level, the player plays because he or she does not understand that the slot machine offers only bad or unfavorable bets. On the second level, the player refuses to play precisely because he or she does understand that. On the third level, the player plays because he or she understands that if played in a certain way, the machine really does offer good bets.

The third level is the correct level, of course, at least if there are no higher levels. This seems to be the case, but then, individuals on the first two levels also seem to believe they are on the top level. The market allows both insight and irony.

For that reason, ultimately, we cannot know whether the bets the market offers are good ones. Things are not always as they seem. Damon Runyon puts it this way:

> Son, no matter how far you travel or how smart you get, always remember this: Someday, somewhere, a guy is going to come to you and show you a nice brand-new deck of

> cards on which the seal is not yet broken, and this guy is going to offer to bet you that the Jack of Spades will jump out of this deck and squirt cider in your ear. But, son, do not bet this man, for as sure as you do, you are going to get an earful of cider.[11]

In many ways, the market is a confidence game. In most confidence games, the victim plays the game only as long as he believes he understands the game better than the other players do. For example, the victim may be allowed to cheat another player who is, of course, one of the confidence men. Sadly, ironically, justly, the victim is cheated as he attempts to cheat someone else.

The market is not a confidence game because of a conspiracy of hedgers and floor traders and dealers and specialists and so on. The truth is worse: the con is in the nature of the game.

The only rational people to play the market are those who expect to win. Yet the nature of the game demands that some of them lose. A zero-sum game demands losers, and anything that prevents losers from entering the game must necessarily stop the game or turn potential winners into losers. As long as there is a market, there can be no way of knowing who will win and who will lose.

Yet fortunes can be made *precisely because* no one knows and no one ever will know how the market can be beaten. *All profitable trading methods are dependent upon some bias among market participants; this bias both creates profit opportunities and inhibits their discovery.* This is the principle of contrary opinion, a principle necessarily more subtle than most market participants realize. A curious corollary to this principle is that most traders are likely to select just those trading methods least likely to be profitable.[12] Indeed, if you've discovered a strong enough bias among traders, you could publish your discovery in *The Wall Street Journal* and still trade it profitably forever, for it will be disregarded by all, or almost all, other traders.[13]

Endnotes

1. See James H. Loris and Mary Hamilton, *The Stock Market—Theories and Evidence* (Homewood, IL: Richard D. Irwin, 1973).
2. Fama created this nomenclature, *cf.* Eugene F. Fama, "Efficient Capital Markets: A review of Theory and Empirical Work," *Journal of Finance* (May 1970): 387–388. Fama has since suggested another nomenclature that fits the way the market has been studied better, but is not as clear and obvious as his first choice. *Cf.* Eugene F. Fama, "Efficient Capital Markets: II," *Journal of Finance* (December 1991): 1575–1617.
3. Gambling involves the creation of risk; speculation does not. Economically, legally, and morally, speculation and gambling differ. Nevertheless, from the gambler's or speculator's point of view, the economic characteristics are identical. Therefore, because gambling examples are often simpler, they will be used when possible.
4. Don Jones "The Misbehavior of Commodity Prices," *Commodities* (August 1975): 20.
5. Although a review of the evidence would seem appropriate, it would shift the subject from money management to trading methods, and it is emphatically not one of the functions of this book to recommend individual trading methods. Moreover, it seems unnecessary, as 50 to 90 percent of the professional literature concerns trading methods.
6. A typical example is Arbel Avner, "Generic Stocks: An Old Product in a New Package," *The Journal of Portfolio Management* (Summer 1985).
7. See footnote 2 this chapter.
8. M. Shapiro, "Trading in Tulips?" *Barron's* (August 26, 1968): 1.
9. Edward S. Jensen, *Mass Psychology,* quoted in James Dines, *How the Average Investor Can Use Technical Analysis for Stock Profits* (New York: Dines Chart Company, 1972): 83–84.

10. Richard A. Epstein, *The Theory of Gambling and Statistical Logic* (New York: Academic Press, 1977): 118.
11. Damon Runyon, *The Idyll of Miss Sarah Brown*. Incidentally, in many ways the gambling literature, including gambling fiction, is more honest and insightful than the investment literature.
12. This is not completely theory. According to Dennis Dunn of *Dunn & Hargitt* (personal communication, no date), few of the purchasers of their $500 pork belly trading systems were still using the system a year after purchase. Yet according to *Dunn & Hargitt*, the system had been profitable, on average, in the interim. Presumably for different reasons, *Dunn & Hargitt* no longer uses the system itself.
13. Another curious corollary to this theory is that if the theory is true, it should be difficult to believe and therefore difficult to publish. Unsympathetic reviewers should keep this in mind.

7

The Nuts and Bolts of Building a Trading Method

Developing an investment approach or an investment method means (1) generating investment ideas, (2) quantifying these ideas, (3) obtaining relevant data, (4) testing the ideas for validity, (5) optimizing investment methods, (6) protecting the method produced, and (7) abandoning the method when necessary. Each of the steps will be discussed below.

Generating Investment Ideas

Generating ideas is a two-step process.[1] The first step is to gather raw material. The second step is to combine the material in new and unusual ways.

There are at least three ways of generating investment ideas. The easiest way to gather raw material is to steal it, that is, to read the investment literature. Many of the ideas presented in the investment literature are reasonably good; that is, they might reasonably be expected to make money if implemented. This is not to say that they will make money, of course, that is another question.

Unfortunately, the vast majority of the ideas presented are bad; they are unreasonable and unlikely to work. Fortunately, this is not completely relevant. The fact that a given idea does not work as presented may mean nothing more than that the idea's originator could not make it work and published it in order to get something back on his or her time and investment. It does not mean that the idea cannot be reworked into usable form.

A second way to generate investment ideas is to look at investment data. An enormous number of ideas can be generated by those who are willing to do the necessary work. Oddly enough, the necessary work is rarely done. Part of the problem is that we almost always think we know what the data must look like. When this is the case, actually looking at the data is superfluous, of course. But in far more cases than we let ourselves realize, the world does not look or act as we think it must. All or almost all of us are unobservant of even the most common and ordinary experiences. Which dials on your stove turn on which burners, for example? Precisely how is the dashboard on your car arranged? When water empties down a drain, does it flow clockwise or counterclockwise?

Investment data are under no obligation to look the way we think they must look. Investment methods are under no obligation to act the way we think they must act. The fact that it seems reasonable for indicator Ẍ to predict purchase points if it predicts sale points and vice versa does not mean that is what it does. The fact that indicator Ÿ requires three months of data and indicator Z̈ requires two days of data does not mean that indicator Ÿ must be an intermediate-term indicator and indicator Z̈ is a short-term indicator. To the contrary, if these constructions forecast anything at all, indicator Ÿ may well forecast nothing more than the next day or two, while indicator Z̈ provides forecasts of the market over the next few years.

The problem is not simply one of laziness. Looking at the data is not as easy as it sounds. We tend to see what we want to see or what we believe we should see rather than what is really there. For example, read the following sentence *once* and note the number of times the letter *F* appears in it.

Finished files are the result of years of scientific study combined with the experience of many years.

How many times does the letter *F* appear in the sentence above? On one reading, most people will state that it appears only two or three times. The correct answer is six. Most people do not see the *F* in of, for example because it is pronounced V.

There are problems within problems here. The example above still gives the impression that looking at data is easier than it is. The correct number of *F*'s can only be found by looking at each letter in the sentence and counting, but it can be found easily and mechanically. In this situation, at least, it is clear what an *F* is and what a letter is. In many investment situations, it is not clear exactly what one is looking at and what the implications are.

Worse, even when what we are looking at is clear or at least appears to be clear, the implications may not be. Consider, for example, the following puzzle. A man goes on a bear hunt. After making camp, he sets out and goes five miles due south. Seeing no bears, he turns and goes five miles due east. Still finding no bears, he turns again and goes five miles due north. Arriving back at his camp, he sees a bear. What color is the bear?

The puzzle does not seem to contain enough information to tell the color of the bear; yet it does. There is only one place one can go five miles due south then five miles due east and then five miles due north and wind up where one started: the North Pole. Any bear at the North Pole must obviously be white.

Similarly, there is always, or almost always, more information in investment data than there appears to be. Bennett Goodspeed writes:

> A small article that appeared on the second page of *The Wall Street Journal* in October 1979 stated that without warning the Saudis suddenly had changed their shipping requirements on all incoming containerized freight. Conventional containers, which measured forty feet and contained two

> doors, were now required to be scaled back to just twenty feet and had to have four doors. Not only that, but Saudis went from inspecting 20 percent of the incoming containers to 100 percent.
>
> Because the Saudis were taking such dramatic action, they had to be worried about illegal arms shipments, and therefore about the security of their country. One professional investor took this piece of intelligence and mulled it over. He realized that if the Saudis were that concerned they would switch part of their vast wealth into gold.[2]

On the basis of this analysis, the investor bought gold at $372 per ounce and sold it six weeks later at $610 per ounce.

A third and final method for generating ideas should be mentioned. It is always worth considering why an idea that looks like it should work does not or why an idea that looks like it should not work, does. In almost all cases, one finds nothing more than dirt or noise or error. But on occasion one finds gold. In fact, *all* major scientific advances have been made because something that should have happened did not or because something that could not have happened, did. Consider an entirely typical case, the discovery of x-rays. Thomas Kuhn writes:

> The physicist Roentgen interrupted a normal investigation of cathode rays because he had noticed that a barium platinocyanide screen at some distance from his shielded apparatus glowed when the discharge was in process. Further, investigations—they required seven hectic weeks during which Roentgen rarely left the laboratory—indicated that the cause of the glow came in straight lines from the cathode ray tube, that the radiation cast shadows, could not be deflected by a magnet, and much else besides. Before announcing his discovery, Roentgen had convinced himself that his effect was not due to cathode rays but to an agent with at least some similarity to light.[3]

In Roentgen's case, the anomaly was relatively obvious, at least in retrospect. The platinocyanide screen could not be glowing. There was no known physical mechanism that would explain the glow. Yet the screen glowed. In many cases, the anomaly is not even clear in retrospect. For example, Henry Guerlac writes:

> Richards, like other chemists, was puzzled by the fact that the atomic weights, when accurately determined, were not always whole numbers. Thus the most precise methods gave an atomic weight for lead of 207.2. Independently of Soddy, Richards demonstrated that lead derived from uranium-rich ores had an atomic weight of 206, while that from thorium ores had a weight of 208. Thus ordinary lead was seen to be a mixture of these two isotopes, of two kinds of atoms having identical chemical properties but differing slightly in weight.[4]

The anomaly could well have been caused by dirt or noise or error. Richards, however, did not assume that it had been. It is worth noting that in a remarkable number of cases other investigators noticed these phenomena too, but all but one *did* assume, without checking, that the cause was dirt or noise or error. Investment researchers often face the same situation.

The second stage is to masticate the material gathered, to combine and recombine the material in new and unusual ways, to generate new ideas. Judgment must be suspended. Any idea is a good idea as long as it is new. Speculation and fantasy, the far-out and the seemingly irrelevant, all have value here. What if we replaced our computer with an abacus? What if we looked at the relationship between real-estate prices and poetry styles? Is there anything in *Women's Wear Daily* that might help us forecast interest rates?

I suspect that few paragraphs in this book will draw as much disagreement, or inaction, as those on generating ideas. With almost no exceptions, investors, especially investment professionals, believe that investment ideas must be rational and that to get rational ideas you must generate them "rationally." For most investors, generating ideas rationally means grinding the same investment theories over and over again, trying to figure out what to do with them. In effect, it means that few investors really look at market data or think about the market. Rational investment ideas are necessary, of course, but this does not mean that they have to be generated rationally. Any procedure that generates valuable ideas is of obvious value. You do not have to tell anyone that you wave magic wands, or read entrails. In turn, this means that those that do, presupposing that waving magic wands and reading entrails helps generate ideas, will possess a real and important advantage.

Most ideas, especially most fantasy, will be stillborn, but so what? Most ideas are wrong, anyway. Being wrong in a bizarre, unprofessional manner is no worse, and it is certainly more entertaining, than being wrong in a more mundane manner. More correctly, it is no worse financially. There are other costs, however. Far more often than not, advancing unconventional ideas is professional suicide. The cost can be high even for an individual investor. It is simply impossible to generate new and valuable ideas without generating many useless and stupid ideas, too. Innovators generate more bad ideas than anyone else; they just throw the bad ones away.

Unfortunately, it will not always be clear why a particular idea is stupid until someone else explains exactly why. If you chose your friends and coworkers wisely, they will not point and giggle, although this is what many ideas deserve. Still, an unavoidable and unfortunate side effect of generating valuable ideas is that quite often you will look quite foolish.

Anyone who is not willing to look foolish on a fairly regular basis is either not telling anyone their ideas or, much more likely, is not taking enough intellectual risks. Just as it is impossible to get a high return on your investment dollar without taking risks, it is impossible to get a high return on your thinking without taking risks. Yet this is something that few are willing to do. Most investors, including most who are willing to risk their money, including almost all investment professionals, are not willing to risk their ideas or their image.

Quantifying Investment Ideas

Ideally, we would like to know that our investment ideas will work, at least on average, before we implement them. But that is not possible. The best we can do is to test those of our ideas we can test and to use them only if there is strong evidence that they can be expected to work on average.

However, before ideas can be tested, they must be capable of being tested; that is, they must be quantified. Every meaningful investment theory can be quantified; that is, it can be operationally defined and, if the data are available, tested.

Conversely, if a theory cannot be operationally defined and tested, the theory has no meaning. Such a "theory" may have meaning, perhaps, as a sales piece or a piece of market philosophy, but it can have no meaning as market theory. Put another way, if the theory cannot be operationally defined, how can it be used in practice? How will the people who are supposed to follow the theory know what to do?

A theory that cannot be operationally defined cannot be tested. An investment theory that has been operationally defined can be put in a form so unambiguous that a computer or a clerk can use it. According to B. F. Skinner, one of the original advocates of operationalism:

> Operationalism may be defined as the practice of talking about (1) one's observations, (2) the manipulative and calculational procedures involved in making them, (3) the logical and mathematical steps which intervene between earlier and later statements, and (4) nothing else.[5]

Operational definitions are not the only type of definitions. They are not even the most common or useful type. But they are the only type that can produce unequivocal tests.

Obviously, some market theories are easier to test than others. Trend-following theories are easier to test than charting theories. Less obviously, many theories that might seem almost completely metaphysical are, in fact, vulnerable to testing. They just need a little thought and work. For example, at one time, and perhaps still, Elliot Janeway maintained that one and only rule can be trusted to predict stock-market movements:

> The rule, simply stated, holds that when the president and the congress work in harmony together, and when the president proposes and the congress disposes, no negative pressures to which the stock market is subject can keep it down; and that, contrariwise, when a breach develops between the president and congress, when the president moves but doesn't lead, and when the congress advises but doesn't consent, no expansive pressures which conventional analysis identifies as constructive can hold the market up.[6]

Mr. Janeway may or may not be right. As the idea is presented, it is impossible to test. What does it mean to say that the president and congress are working in harmony? Mr. Janeway explains this idea by talking about the president proposing and the congress disposing, but what do these words mean? No doubt, Mr. Janeway knows proposing and disposing when he sees them, but many of the rest of us may not be so perceptive. Surely, all presidents lead in some ways and lag in others. How are such things to be weighted and acted on? Mr. Janeway must explain his explanation. What precisely is it that we must look at and count? What precisely must we do?

This is not to say that the ideas Mr. Janeway presents are meaningless. They are not. As long as an idea or some derivative of it can be tested, an idea is not meaningless. Mr. Janeway's ideas can, indeed, be tested, although not without doing some violence to them. For example, we might ask a number of congressional historians to judge, given the evidence available at the time, on a one-to-ten scale, the extent to which the president and the Congress could have been said to "be working in harmony together" for the months beginning January 1, 1900; February 1, 1900; March 1, 1990; and so on. Alternatively, the degree to which the president and Congress are working in harmony might be approximated by the proportion of bills submitted to the president that are signed by him in a given month or quarter. The relationship between either of these indexes and subsequent stock-market movements might be tested by a number of means, such as regression analysis. If Mr. Janeway's theory has any merit, there must be some relationship between these indexes and subsequent stock-market behavior.

More correctly, such a relationship must exist if the indexes above capture the essence of Mr. Janeway's theory. As noted, the indexes described are somewhat arbitrary. Neither quite does justice to Mr. Janeway's theory. But this is not completely relevant. Rarely, if ever, does a test completely capture the theory it is supposed to capture. For that reason, multiple tests are almost invariably necessary. If multiple tests are necessary, and if each of the tests captures at least one important feature of the theory, and if none of the tests distort the theory in any material manner, then each of the tests must provide some information on the value of the theory. If the tests all show the same answer, even if each test is flawed in its own way, then that is the answer.

Obtaining Relevant Data

The next step is to buy or generate data on which to test the theory. Data can always be bought or generated, of course. Thousands of time series are commercially available. Experiments can be run. Surveys can be taken. Unfortunately, the data available never seem to measure what we want measured as well as we want it measured. There is always dirt and noise and error. No data, at least no significant amount of data, are absolutely clean.

Data quality ranges over many orders of magnitude. The available evidence indicates that the best-known price series are almost always correct, and when they are not, the error is minute, say, a cent or two in the case of wheat prices. On the other hand, estimates of the gross national product should always be expected to be in error, and the error should be expected to be one of tens or hundreds of billions of dollars.

The range of errors is large in proportional terms, also. The errors in many price series can be expected to be a percent or two. On the other hand, many corporate earnings reports have an expected error of 50 percent or so. The fact that a company's annual report states that earnings per share were, say, $2.53 per share means that corporate management has estimated the earnings to be $2.53 per share, based on the available data, and given certain accounting judgments and assumptions it has made. Alternative assumptions and judgments might well produce earnings estimates anywhere from, say, $1.25 to $3.75 per share.

The examples above give an unfortunate impression that the problem is more objective than it is. To a large extent, the size of the errors in a given data series depends on what, exactly, you mean by error. For example, if the fact that the gross domestic product does not measure the underground economy, the household sector, leisure, and many other sectors of the economy is important, then the reported GDP might underestimate the actual GDP by as much as 20 to 40 percent. Worse, the degree to which the reported GDP underestimates the actual GDP is almost certainly constant over neither time nor location. Leisure, for example, appears to be taking up more and more of our time. If this is true, and if there are no important countervailing forces, then the reported GDP is progressively underestimating the actual GDP. On the other hand, if the technicalities mentioned above, and many other technicalities, can be ignored, and if quarter to quarter changes in the GDP are of interest, then the error rate can probably be assumed to be a percent or a fraction of a percent.

How serious an error problem is obviously depends on how the data will be used. Someone trying to forecast changes in the interest rate on commercial paper a year or two ahead need not be bothered by errors of billions of dollars in the GDP. Conversely, many short-term-following systems are based on statistical techniques that can be seriously affected by even minute errors in daily price series.

A knowledge of the extent and type of errors that the data of interest contain can obviously be useful, at least insofar as we are interested in forecasting, say, the price of General Motors, rather than the price of General Motors as it will be recorded in *The Wall Street Journal*. By definition, there are two and only two types of error: systematic and random. Systematic errors involve a bias in the data. In other words, the population that was supposed to be sampled was not. For example, for many investment purposes, information on the distribution of individual or family income would be of interest. Unfortunately, the most obvious source of such data, tax records, is of dubious value. Such records must be biased; at least, they must be biased as long as it is in the best interests of the taxpayer to lie. The IRS does what it can to make sure the records are accurate, of course. But as long as it operates in a hostile environment, what it can do will be strictly limited.

Random errors are errors that are not systematic. For example, when data are being keyed in, the wrong key will be hit a certain portion of the time. An entry of $5.01 might be entered as $5.04 or $5.02. If one type of error is no more likely than another, the errors are random. If the data errors are small and random, they are not important. More precisely, small and random errors can easily be controlled using standard statistical techniques.

The types of systematic errors that data can be expected to contain depend on the types of data, of course. There are far, far too many types of errors to even allude to them all here. Still, most investors are interested in only quantitative time series, and these can contain at least four important types of systematic errors. First, the data source itself can be in error for any of a number of reasons. For example, the data can be outright lies, as income and manager-performance data sometimes are. Alternatively, the idea may be misspecified, as national productivity figures are. Productivity, which means output per worker hour, would be of obvious and considerable interest, if only we knew how to measure it. We can obviously measure the productivity of a steel mill or power plant. But how do we measure the productivity of a bank or a brokerage firm? Considering that three out of four Americans are working in service-related businesses, this is obviously not a minor technical problem.

Second, even if the data source is correct, the data may be recorded or transcribed incorrectly. For example, a computer program may only allow two digits for a price that requires three digits. If the digit on the left is shaved off, a price of 166 becomes a price of 66.

Third, even if the data are, strictly speaking, correct, they may not be complete. Price series are especially susceptible to this problem. Worse, it may be obvious only to relatively sophisticated users that the data are incomplete. For example, complete information on the price per ton for specialty steels must consist not only of the steel's price per ton, but of all the rebates, discounts, and kickbacks available, not to mention the various types of special services the manufacturer may perform. Many price series are not just one number.

Fourth, the data may not have really been available on the date the records state. For example, unfavorable earnings reports are frequently released late. Note also that historical summaries frequently present revised data, without noting that the data have been revised. Revised data are data that have been corrected on the basis of information available after the release of the report. Many macroeconomics forecasts and indexes are revised, sometimes repeatedly, after they are released.

There are two and only two ways of locating data errors. First, the data can be checked against information in the datum or data series itself. No datum is infinitely surprising; it is always more or less expected. There are always qualities that each datum in a series must have, and the data should always be checked against these qualities. For example, most price series are represented by numbers larger than zero.[7] For these series, any datum that is not a number or that is a number less than zero is clearly an error. Relationships within the data should also be checked. For example, on any given day, a stock's high price must be equal to or larger than the stock's low price. When this is not the case, one or both of the prices must be in error. Such relationships can be arbitrarily complex.

There are also qualities that the data need not have, but are likely to have. A value that is not impossible but simply unlikely is usually worth checking. Thus, the larger and smaller values in any series are worth checking. Relationships among the data can also be checked. For example, scatter plots of pairs of data series will often reveal points that seem unusual and are therefore worth checking.

Second, if the observation can still be made, the data can be checked against the original observation. If the observation cannot be made, which is obviously the case with time series data in all but the last observation and sometimes even then, the data must be checked against whatever historical traces they have made. For example, the price that General Motors closed at on July 19, 1985, is no longer observable, and price traces in the New York Stock Exchange records will contain errors themselves, but this is the best we can do. If the errors are independent, observing multiple traces are almost as good as looking at the original data. On the other hand, if the errors are dependent—if, for example, *The Wall Street Journal* simply transcribed the stock-exchange records—observing multiple traces adds no information. In fact, each time the data is copied, another layer of error will be added. To whatever extent possible, therefore, error checking must return to the earliest possible source of the data.

No matter how carefully errors are tracked down and corrected, there will still be errors in the data. The *residual biases* and *error rate* are the biases and the proportion of errors that remain after the data has been corrected. Unless the residual biases and error rate are known, it is dangerous to try to draw conclusions from the data. An estimate of the residual error can be made by sampling the uncorrected data and comparing each datum in the sample to the original observation or at least to the best available traces. Such an estimate should indicate whether the data should be abandoned, cleaned further, or trusted.

One important source of bias information is the correction procedure itself. All correction procedures introduce their own biases into the data. For example, any procedure that checks for price-change outliers—that is, any procedure that checks all large price changes regardless of whether the changes are positive or negative—ensures that small price-changes will be wrong more often than average. This bias may or may not be important. It is not likely to affect most econometric methods, but it is likely to affect many technical systems.

While data can almost always be bought or generated, good data cannot always be, at least not at a reasonable cost. When this is the case, the project must be either dropped or modified. Among the ways a project can be modified is to use surrogate data series: series that are like the series that are really of interest. In one sense, almost every data series is a surrogate for the series that we really want, if only it were available. We might really want, say, a daily survey of small-investor market opinion, but we settle for weekly odd-lot purchases, sales, and short-sales data. In this sense, buying or generating data involves balancing what is desirable, what can be done, against cost. If acceptable surrogate series are cheap enough, a project is cost-effective.

Since a researcher knows little or nothing about what he or she will find until after he or she has found it, benefit/cost analysis is of far less use here than it is elsewhere. Nevertheless, important choices must somehow be made. Indeed, no decision can be better than the data it is based on. Given the cost of failure, therefore, unless there are strong reasons to do otherwise, it would seem prudent to either buy or develop high-quality data or to buy or develop no data at all.

Testing the Idea for Validity

The next step is to test the idea for validity. Investing on the basis of an untested idea makes a mockery of the rest of the investment plan because it assumes that the idea is valid, even though we know that most investment ideas are worthless, that they represent momentary aberrations if they represent anything at all.

In a sense, a test is a way of asking questions. This analogy cannot be taken too far, unfortunately, for final answers are not forthcoming. No matter how much data we collect, there is always the chance that our results are a fluke. Still, if there is strong evidence that a given investment is valid, then investing on the basis of that idea is reasonable (see Chapter 8).

Some answers are easier to find than others. Unfortunately, the answers that are of the least interest are the easiest to find. More precisely, it is much easier to show that a theory is false than to show it is true. This is one of several reasons why there is never a shortage of critics.

For example, it would be of some interest to know whether or not "growth stocks," defined as, say, stocks whose average return on net earnings over the last four years has been at least $\ddot{X}$ percent and whose growth in unit sales volume has been at least $\ddot{Y}$ percent over the same period, provide a larger average total-return than the S&P 500 does. On the one hand, it would be relatively easy to show that growth stocks do not provide superior total-returns by showing that growth-stock returns have been equal to or lower than the S&P 500's total return over some reasonably long and representative period. On the other hand, showing that growth-stock total returns are higher is a much harder problem. Growth-stock returns being higher than the S&P return over some reasonably long and representative period does not prove that the responsibility lies where we think it lies, in stocks with high rates of growth in net earnings and unit sales. It may well be that the stocks we selected for study were only coincidentally profitable. It may well be that it is not sales and net earnings that are important but, say, the capitalization of the stock—that, on average, small-capitalization stocks produce large profits and large-capitalization stocks produce small profits and that, by accident, we included many small-capitalization companies in our study.

The question of what caused or produced the extraordinary profits is only an academic one as long as, and only so long as, the various causes coincide. In the example above, it is academic as long as small-capitalization stocks are growth stocks. But the fact that they coincided during the study is hardly proof that they will coincide from now on. More likely than not, the causes will diverge at some point in the future, probably when the investor has more money riding on his or her system than ever before.

This is not an uncommon problem. The fact is that every possible phenomenon has multiple explanations. If the number of possible explanations is not infinite, it is nearly so. It is not even limited by the imagination of the investigator. It would be possible to prove that growth stocks provide superior returns if and only if we could somehow manage to prove that there are no other possible causes. This would be difficult. Probably because it is impossible.

Still, the problem may seem more difficult than it is. The fact that even the most thoroughly confirmed theory can be wrong applies to all types of research, not just investment research. This problem has not stopped other types of research, such as, say, drug research, from being valuable and profitable. But successful researchers in other areas do at least two things that investment researchers do not.

First, and more important than anything else, successful researchers are honest. The history of science is the history of people admitting errors. For example, Einstein introduced a "cosmological constant," a repulsive force between particles, into his early steady state model of the universe. The cosmological constant kept gravity from collapsing the universe. Later, when it became obvious that the universe was expanding, Einstein abandoned the cosmological constant, calling it, "the chief blunder of my life."[8] Gottlob Frege's life's work was *The Fundamental Laws of Arithmetic*, in which he placed mathematics on the firm, logical foundation of set theory, a more interesting and important task than it may seem. The second volume of Frege's work was at the printer when a letter from logician Bertrand Russell arrived. Russell described the liar paradox, which struck at the heart of set theory. Mr. Frege had only time to insert an appendix in his book. The appendix started, "A scientist can hardly encounter anything more undesirable than to have the foundation collapse just as the work is finished. I was put in this position by a letter from Mr. Bertrand Russell."[9] Perhaps it is my imagination, but I hear tears behind these words. More to the point, I suspect that most investment researchers would not be able to do this; they would manage not to understand the evidence that proves them wrong. In contrast, the stories above are absolutely typical of scientific research.

Scientists are not always honest, of course. They are human. When it is difficult to be honest, they structure their research so that their own personal problems do not affect their research. The research is blinded. For example, in a single-blind drug test, a potentially useful drug will be given to one group of patients, and a placebo, a drug with no known effect, will be given to another group. The patients do not know which group they belong to. The results are then compared. Notice that patient bias no longer counts.

There are other kinds of bias, of course. In a double-blind test, a potentially useful drug is given to one group of patients, and a placebo is given to another group. Neither the patients nor the doctors who give the drugs know which group a given patient belongs to. In a triple-blind test, neither the patients nor the doctors nor the analysts comparing results know who took what drug. The analysts compare the results of drug A and drug B without knowing what the codes mean.

There are obvious investment-research analogues to single, double, and triple-blind tests. Real investment-results can be compared to random results, for example. More important, the analyst can compare results without knowing which results represent real data. Indeed, given a trader's need to get positive research-results, it is dangerous not to do this.

Second, successful researchers attempt to rule out all other "likely" causes and as many "not-so-likely" causes as possible. What constitutes a likely or not-so-likely cause depends on the current state of theory in the field, of course. A theory that is internally consistent, strongly supported by the evidence, and has no serious competitors is assumed true.

The fact that a theory is assumed to be true does not mean it is true, of course. Nor does it mean that the theory cannot be questioned. To assume a theory is true means nothing more than that the theory will be the working basis of all future research and that the burden of proof is on those who wish to challenge the theory.

As long as it is understood that there are no final answers, it does no harm to talk about asking questions of the data. Indeed, this kind of language does much good, as it focuses attention where it belongs: on the analyst's work and responsibility. Answers are not "found," that is, research is not a passive activity. Research is not a question of collecting data and more data and still more data, until slowly or quickly the answer reveals itself. Sometimes the answer is obvious, of course. More often, it is not. An analyst's job, therefore, is to ask questions in such a manner that whatever answers the data possess reveal themselves. This is not an easy task.

Research never involves asking just one question. No one question is right; or if one is, it is never clear what that question is. Far more often than not, the available evidence is ambiguous, that is, if it reveals anything at all. Research, for that reason, is always a process of trial and error, of asking many questions or of asking one question after another until sooner or later, something of importance is revealed.

There seem to be three and only three solutions to this problem. One is to ask only one question. The oldest statistical techniques, such as the T-test, were designed for just this purpose. If, for example, it is important to know whether the average yearly profit from investment method $\ddot{X}$ is larger than zero, this is the kind of method to use. Naturally, few researchers have only one question they want to ask.

A second solution is to ask one question after another and whenever a particular result seems to be of value, test it again on new and different data. An investor interested in developing a trend-following method, for example, might test a number of such methods on the Dow Jones averages. If he or she found a method that seemed to be of particular value, he or she could then test the method on, say, cash silver. If it worked on silver, it might be worth committing real money to. If it did not work on silver the investor could go back to testing methods on the Dow Jones averages until he or she found another method that seemed to be of value. This new method could then be tested on silver.

But even here there is the possibility of fooling oneself. Sooner or later, just by accident, a worthless method will pass both tests. If the second set of data is going to be used more than once, there must be a third set of different data, say the Financial Times Ordinary Shares Index, which is a British stock-market index. There must be one final set of data that will be used only once.

A third solution is to carefully structure the question-asking process so that the very powerful methods of modern statistics can be used. If the researcher is sufficiently skillful, a number of questions can be asked simultaneously. A statistical technique known as the analysis of variance allows a trader to do this. For example, the technique might help a researcher decide whether or not profits from trend-following method $\ddot{X}$ were really greater in some years than others or were really greater in some investments than others.

Monte Carlo techniques can help an investor who is interested in only one investment cope with the fact that one question after another will be asked. Consider the investor who is only interested in the price of gold. Such an individual may well test a number of methods on cash-gold data. If the methods are operationally defined, if the sequence of tests is known, and if the rules by which one moves from one test to another are known exactly, it is possible to decide just how likely it is that the results obtained were obtained by chance.

For almost all investors, the second approach is best. Whatever approach is used, however, it is simply impossible to be too careful or prudent.

Logically, validation would seem to come first and optimization second. At least, finding the best way of doing this or that would not seem to make sense unless you know that what you are doing is of real value. However, this does not mean that an investment method must be tested and then optimized, although this is a possible approach. Unfortunately, all but the simplest and most obvious methods are too complicated for this approach. Unless the method is extremely simple, it is easier to build the method in pieces, with each piece being validated and optimized in turn. But there is danger in a piecemeal approach, of course. It is all to easy too build into a valid method some untested and disastrous feature. It is best, therefore, to end a research project by testing and then optimizing the method as a whole.

Optimizing Investment Methods

To optimize an investment method is to make it the "best" method possible. More precisely, it is to find the "best" parameter values for that method. The word *parameter,* in the sense it is used here, means a variable under the investor's control.[10] For example, many trend-following methods involve the use of one or more moving averages. The length of a moving average is a parameter, a value that the investor chooses.

More precisely, a parameter is a value an investor must choose, although he or she does not have to choose wisely. An investor might choose a particular parameter value at random, or for ease of use, or because he or she believes a certain value is lucky or attractive or has some particular numerological or mystical value. Notice that if an investor does not explicitly choose a parameter value, in effect he or she chooses at random. This is not necessarily a wise thing to do. Roughly speaking, an investment method is optimized by testing a number of alternative parameter values for each parameter and then choosing the best combination of values.

Optimization has received a considerable amount of attention over the years. This attention makes sense; the argument is reasonably sound. If an investment method is of value, then some of the method's parameter values may be better than others, if only marginally. If the differences are nonexistent or marginal, the trader need not worry about finding the best values. Conversely, if the differences are not marginal, the trader had better worry. For example, if some parameter values are profitable while others are not and if the trader cannot determine which parameter values are profitable, then of what conceivable use is the trading method? In effect, the trader is making commitments on the basis of a method that may or may not be profitable on average. This does not seem prudent.

I have met traders who believe that optimization is the *only* thing of value a trader can do. This is nonsense, of course. Validation, not optimization, is critical. A valid but nonoptimal investment method should make money on average. An unvalidated but "fully optimized" investment method will not necessarily make money on average; that is, it will make money for its owner only if he or she has been lucky enough to optimize an investment method that, by chance, really works.

Oddly, while the arguments for optimization are reasonably strong, there is little evidence one way or another. Louis Lukac has done several interesting studies where he compared the results for a particular trading method with random and optimized parameters. Mr. Lukac determined the best parameters for a particular trading method for the past N years, and then compared the results over the next year to the results from a method with randomly chosen parameters. Mr. Lukac found no added value.[11] This seems to imply that, while finding the best parameter values is a pleasant way to spend one's time, especially for someone who knows a great deal about programming and operations research, it is of little practical value. Other studies have shown similar results.

Unfortunately, the situation is not that simple. Robert Pardo, who argues that optimization is one of the most important things a trader can do, sells software that incorporates a test similar to Mr. Lukac's.[12] Presuming that Mr. Pardo has some satisfied customers, the evidence cannot be completely one-sided.

One part of the problem is that such tests are conclusive *only* if the methods tested are valid trading methods. Unfortunately, this is never certain. The other part of the problem is that in many studies at least one of the periods compared is relatively short, say, a year or two. But surely, the relative worth of the various parameter values is determined the same way profits and losses are determined, in which case, over any moderate amount of time the best parameter values are largely determined by chance.

No reasonable person demands that a valid investment method invariably beat the market. Instead, he or she demands that the method beat the market, on average, over some reasonably long period. Similarly, no reasonable person demands that the relative worth of various parameter values stay stable over short periods.

On the other hand, if decades of data are compared, parameter values should be stable. If it really does not matter what parameter values are chosen, the data will show this. If a trader cannot find out which parameter values, if any, are of real value and prove, beyond a reasonable doubt, that such values are stable over some reasonably long period of time, then either the method of investing is wrong, the method of searching for good parameter values is wrong, the method of proving parameter values are stable is wrong or, quite possibly, all three. Such an investor would be well advised to find out which is the case.

Determining whether or not an investment method is valid is dealt with elsewhere in this chapter and in Chapter 8. Proving that parameter values are stable is almost the same as finding them, except that an investor trying to locate parameter values might not consider time, while someone trying to prove values stable must. We will therefore consider these questions together. Selecting parameter values and proving them stable involves at least three problems.

First, which parameter values are best obviously depends on what the word *best* means. Most traders believe the answer is obvious: The best method is the one that produces, say, the largest total-profits over the period of study. Other traders have other answers, of course; but whatever answer is given, it is always given as though it were obvious, as though there were no other serious alternatives. Actually, the only thing obvious about the problem is that all the obvious criteria are either irrelevant or, worse, dead wrong. To the extent that optimization is performed on the basis of such criteria, the results must be irrelevant, or worse. (Criteria are discussed in Chapter 4.)

Second, it is not always clear what the parameters of a particular method are. It may well be clear that a particular method is a moneymaker, without it being clear why the method makes money. This is particularly likely to be true in the early stages of an investigation. An investment method only makes money if it somehow embodies an economic or investment law. A given method may well embody the law poorly, in which case any attempt to optimize the method is an attempt to find the best values for a group of parameters, of which, perhaps, one or two are of real worth.

If some but not all of the parameters of a method are stable, the method probably needs rebuilding. The method may have too few parameters or too many or, quite possibly, both. A method has too few parameters if profits are a function of some economic factor that the method does not consider. Perhaps the method does not work when interest rates are high, in which case adding an appropriate interest-rate filter to the method should stabilize profits. The filter might be something as simple as, Don't trade when interest rates are above $\ddot{X}$ percent.

Alternatively, the method may have too many parameters. The trader may believe that profits are a function of eclipse paths or interest rates, when they are not. A method has too many parameters when a trader adds filters without evidence that the modifications add value or when a trader develops and tests a method that he or she does not really understand. In which case, subtracting a filter, or simplifying a rule or weighting scheme in an appropriate manner should stabilize profits.

Third, somehow the best parameter values must be chosen. If only one criterion, say, the method's ratio of profits to loss, is of interest, then choosing the best parameter values means nothing more than testing many variants of the same method and using the parameter that seems to be the best value, in this case the parameter with the largest total-profits. But assuming some randomness in the data, a very high or very low measure of value does not necessarily indicate the best parameter. Consider Figure 7–1. The hypothetical trader who created that exhibit was

Figure 7–1

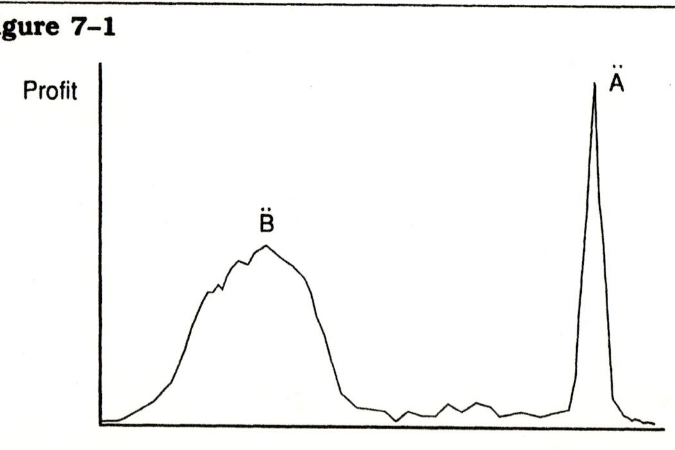

Despite the fact that profits are higher at point Ä, Point B̈ is the safer parameter value.

interested in one parameter and one measure of goodness: total profit. Notice that point *A* has the highest total profit, but it is probably a fluke of some kind. Point *B* is probably not.

If more than one criterion is of interest, the problem is more complex. If no one set of parameter values is clearly better than all others in terms of *all* of the criteria of interest, which is almost always the case, then there is no best set of parameter values. At least, no one set of values is objectively best. For example, if a given method is to be optimized on the basis of its average return and the standard deviation of returns, and one particular set of parameters has both the highest return and the lowest standard deviation, then that set of parameters is best. On the other hand, if no one method has both desirable properties, a selection must be made from those sets of parameters that are most desirable. Decisions can still be made, of course. But the decisions are now subjective.

But the judgments have to be made on the basis of summary statistics, which on the one hand, leave out important details, and on the other, do not summarize enough.[13] Obviously, return and risk should be measured for the various parameters of interest, perhaps over time, and over whatever universe of investments seems relevant. Notice that two dimensions are needed for reward and risk data, assuming only one measure of each is used; one more dimension is needed for time; one more for each of the investment parameters; and one for the various investments, if there are more than one. If the analyst intends to graph the data, this means a graph of five or more dimensions, quite possibly many more. This is within the capability of a well-programmed personal computer. Unfortunately, it is remarkably difficult to find high-quality plotting paper with more than three dimensions.

Given the current state of the art, there are only two obvious approaches. One alternative is to use nonparametric, multivariate analysis of variance techniques.[14] These techniques are exactly as easy to understand and use as they sound.

The other alternative is to use graphic techniques. Although the data may exist in some unimaginable world of five or more dimensions, clever graphing-techniques can give an impression of more than two or three dimensions.[15] Moreover, the problem can be approached in pieces, in which case returns are graphed for two parameters or for one parameter over time and a variety of investments. If all of the graphs show roughly the same results, that is the answer. If the results are not approximately the same, the trader needs to find out why.

If the arguments above are correct, optimization is a useful, if not essential, technique. Nevertheless, optimization is dangerous. First, optimization encourages overly optimistic money-management estimates, and that is extremely dangerous. Optimization may add no value; even if it does add value, it almost certainly adds less value than it seems to. It is possible to estimate how much value is added, but these techniques are extremely complicated.[16]

An easy way to avoid this problem is to assume, for money-management purposes, that no value is added, in which case the trader uses parameter averages as money-management estimates. For example, assume the trader has a one-parameter method, where the best parameter produces profits of (P = .6, W = 4, L = 1), while an average parameter produces profits of (P = .50, W = 1.5, L = 1). Here P = probability of a win, W = the average win, and L = the average loss. A conservative trader would use the buy and sell signals that the first method generates but would use the parameters of the second for money-management purposes.

Second, an overenthusiastic optimizer can turn a valid trading method into a worthless trading method. In fact, it is so easy to do this that some traders deliberately select their parameters at random, a decision that otherwise makes no sense. The danger is that the trader will modify a valid method on the basis of almost no evidence. In many cases, perhaps most cases, the method is repeatedly modified and optimized. Probability being what it is, sooner or later one or more of those modifications will subtract value. Quite possibly, a lot of value. The solution to this problem is to demand significant evidence before modifying a method and to test the new method on new data.

Protecting the Method Produced

Intellectual property laws give investment innovators little or no protection.[17] A legally active investor might, say, prevent a former employee from selling a method that is not really his; but if the method is widely known, the investor can hardly prevent other investors from using it. There is one and only one way to really protect a valuable investment idea and that is to *shut up*.

Unfortunately, it is almost impossible to shut up and make money. Certainly, I haven't been successful at it. For investment professionals, career and business success depends heavily on demonstrating expertise. And this cannot be done without giving out information. For example, portfolio-insurance pioneers Leland and Rubinstein found a great deal of early investor interest in their product, but professional investors were not willing to act. Developing business demanded persistence and education. Eventually, their business grew. Leland and Rubinstein note:

> . . . our willingness to risk explanation of our procedures even to potential competitors, and publication of a pedagogic article in the *Financial Analysts Journal* inevitably took its toll: We had our first competition from two well-established firms. Ironically, neither firm met with much success but inadvertently helped to legitimize the product in the minds of many firms who later became our customers.[18]

Notice that the competition helped their business, although it did not help their clients. Sooner or later, popularity will probably destroy portfolio insurance, if it hasn't done so already. But from a business person's point of view, this does not matter. Compound interest being what it is, a few years of big profits starting right now can be worth more than 20 years of small profits. From a business person's point of view, revealing how portfolio insurance works was the right thing for Leland and Rubinstein to do.

It is worth thinking over what information is worth keeping secret and what information is not. An amazing number of things people try to keep secret are not worth knowing. Even when something is of value, it may not be worth keeping secret. Most investment information can be given away freely, as it does not keep anywhere near as well as fish. In contrast, extremely powerful strategies may not age at all. If the strategy is really powerful it may be almost impossible for someone else to discover it. This would seem to make them candidates for keeping secret. If it's a strategy that someone else will discover eventually, you are probably better off disclosing it.

Abandoning the Method When Necessary

No reasonable person trades without evidence that he or she can beat the market. But evidence is not certainty, and prudence demands that a trader abandon a trading method when evidence accumulates that it has stopped working. But what kind of evidence? And how much? Sooner or later, generally sooner, all trading methods lose money. To abandon a trading method at the first loss, or string of losses, is to all but ensure failure. Unless a trader has remarkable self-restraint, he or she will find it impossible to make reasonable decisions during losing periods. For those without such restraint, including, perhaps, some readers of this book, it is better to decide under what conditions a method should be abandoned before trouble starts. A trading method might have to be abandoned because of any of four reasons, and a trader needs a policy for each.

First, cumulative losses or even a single catastrophic loss might be so large that the investor loses faith in the method and closes the account. An account or fund should have a stop loss for the same reason a trade should have one. All losses are evidence that something is going wrong. Sooner or later, the evidence will be strong enough to justify abandoning the method. Generally speaking, the lack of a stated account stop-loss does not mean there is no account stop-loss. It means that the trader does not know what the account stop-loss is. If an account or fund does not have a stop-loss strategy, it should be because the investor deliberately decided not to have one.

The exact level the stop loss is set at determines the risks the trader can take. Otherwise, it has no importance. Theoretically, if a trader uses proper money-management techniques, he or she should be able to reduce the probability of loss to a comfortable level. Of course, these techniques cannot turn a losing method into a winning method. If the trader insists on using a losing method, all money-management technology can do is prolong the agony.

However, from the trader's point of view, it is critical that once the investor decides on a stop-loss strategy, he or she does not change it. Trading the market is difficult work. If a trader has to alter his or her trading strategy to match the whims of his or her investors, he or she will not beat the market. It does not matter whether the investor and the trader are the same person. If an investor must change a stop-loss strategy, he or she should announce the change way before changing it.

Second, a priori evidence might indicate that the trader should no longer trust a once valuable technique. Occasionally, this evidence is obvious. For example, a trading method might depend on a report that the government no longer publishes. More often, the evidence is not obvious—for example, stock market short-interest figures used to indicate investor psychology. But with the development of the options and futures markets, it is not at all clear that it still does. If a trading method depends on such data, and if the trader is convinced that the economics of the market have changed, he or she should abandon the method.

Third, the method's profit and loss pattern over time may indicate that the method is not under control, that it is not acting the way it should. Whether or not the method is making money does not matter here. For example, if the method is supposed to follow trends, does it buy when the price rises and sell when the price falls. If not, the method is out of control. Conversely, if the method is following a pattern it should not follow, the method is probably out of control. For example, a fundamental approach to buying distressed securities has nothing in common with trend-following. But if such an approach usually buys when distressed-security prices rise and sells whenever such prices fall, it is probably out of control. An out-of-control method is an extraordinary research opportunity and an extraordinary financial risk.

Fourth, the distribution of profits and losses may indicate that the method is not under control. Whether or not the method is making money may not matter. If the distribution of profits and losses is relatively stable over time, the distribution can be plotted at regular intervals (see Figure 7–2). If the shape of the distribution changes, something unexpected is happening; something in the underlying economics is changing. In this case, the trader must act. Unless the trader understands what is happening, and it is in his or her favor, he or she should probably stop trading.

Oddly enough, manufacturers face the same problem, and manufacturing engineers developed statistical quality-control for managing it.[19] Typically, at regular intervals someone will draw a small number of objects from a production run and measure one or more qualities that are important to the customers. He or she will then calculate descriptive statistics, plot the values, and analyze the plots. This generally takes less time to do than to describe.

A trader will want to measure profits and losses and anything that indicates whether or not trading is under control, and possibly several other things, such as slippage. A trading method is under control if it is behaving according to expectations. The only way to know whether the method is behaving according to

Figure 7-2

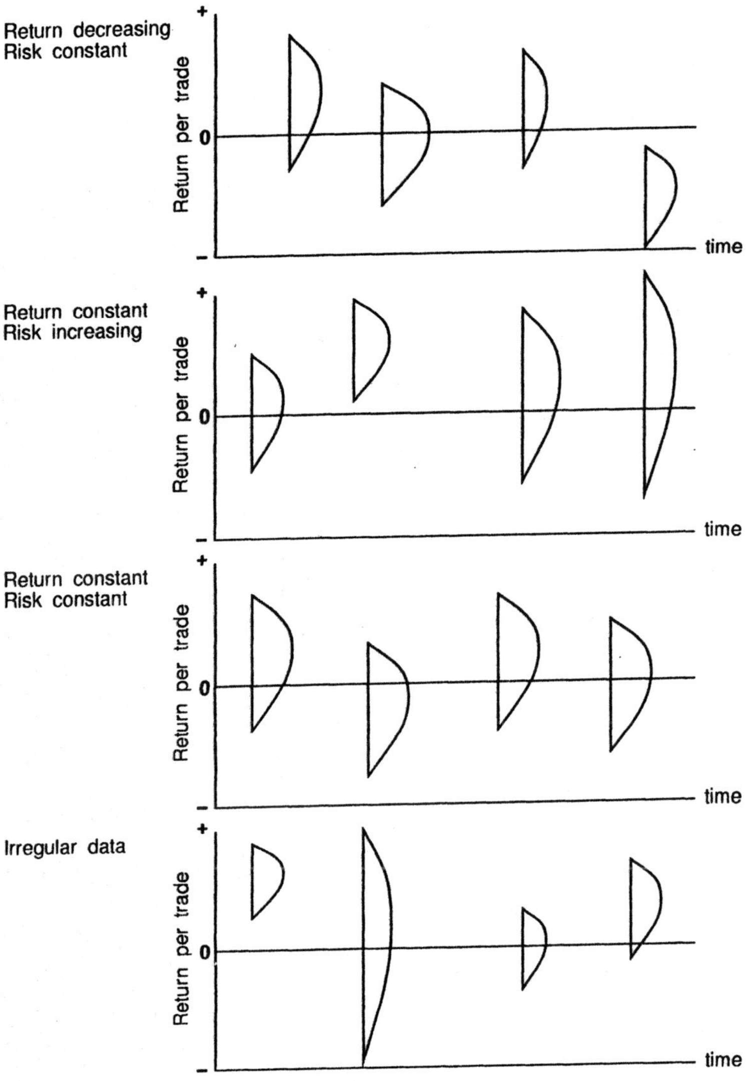

A distribution may change over time.

expectations is to run the simulation real time and compare it to real-world results. Every simulation makes at least one assumption that is impossible to check. The assumption is that the person on the other side of the trade is randomly drawn from the population of other traders. In fact, he is self-selected. He selects himself because he thinks you are stupid. It is of some importance to know whether or not he is right. If he behaves the way the simulation says he should behave then he is stupid and you are not. The profits, losses, and whatever else is measured have to be normalized so that the trader can compare results across time and investments. Profits and losses can be normalized by dividing them by some lagging measure of market risk or volatility.[20]

Figure 7–2 implies that the trader should study the entire distribution of profits and losses or whatever is measured at regular intervals. Unfortunately, reliable statistics for skewness and kurtosis demand large sample sizes. Usable statistics for the location and scale, fortunately, do not. Typically, in manufacturing studies a sample size of four or five is drawn, something or other is measured, the mean and the range of whatever is measured are calculated and plotted and analyzed.

The mean and the range are sensitive to extreme data, more so when the sample is small. Thus, if something unexpected is happening, the manufacturer finds out fast. Of course, manufacturing data are typically much better behaved than investment data are. Thus, the trader may want to use a larger sample-size and more robust statistics, such as the median and the interquartile range. Larger sample-sizes are especially appropriate if the trader trades frequently. This will give slower warnings but fewer false warnings.

Whatever sample size the trader picks, he or she should be constant. The sample should not be, say, four or five trades; it should always be four or always be five or whatever number the trader decides on. This eliminates the need for certain statistical adjustments. And every trade should be part of one sample or another.

The trader must estimate an average value for whatever measure of location is chosen and an upper and lower limit. This should be done before trading starts. The data used to validate the system can be used to estimate these values. The data are then plotted on paper, or some other media, with these scaling (see Figure 7–3). Figure 7–2 shows typical patterns and what they indicate.

Figure 7–3

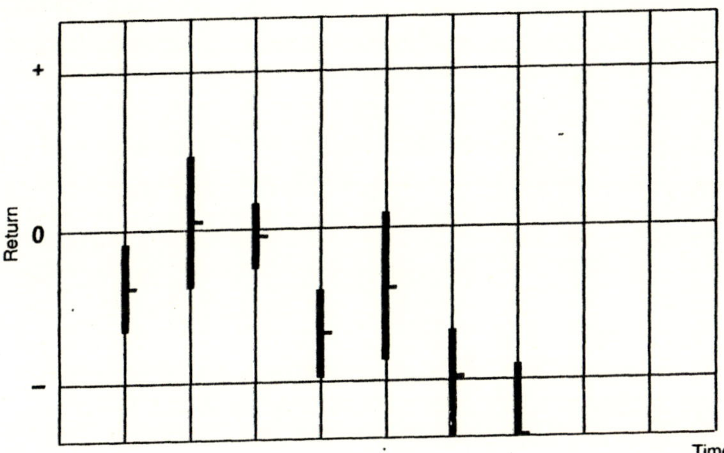

Bars on chart represent mean return and range of returns for last five trades. Upper and lower bands on charts are 95 percent and 5 percent confidence limit.

Endnotes

1. Most writers on creativity have their own way of classifying the process. The most useful books on this topic are not the academic studies, but books that try to unsettle the reader.

See for example, Roger von Oech, *A Whack on the Side of the Head* (New York: Random House, 1983).

2. Bennett W. Goodspeed, *The Tao Jones Averages* (New York: Penguin, 1984), 98–98.
3. Thomas Kuhn, *The Structure of Scientific Revolutions* (Chicago: University of Chicago Press, 1970).
4. Henry E. Guerlac, *Radar in World War II* (American Institute of Physics, 1987).
5. B. F. Skinner, "The Operational Analysis of Psychological Terms" *Psychological Review*, 52 (1945), pp. 270–77. Operationalism is a psychologist's version of logical positivist philosophy. Operationalism and logical positivist philosophy are powerful tools for avoiding nonsense and error. Indeed, it is hard to overstate how powerful these ideas are. Nevertheless, they have limits. One problem with almost all investment management research is that uncertainty is operationally defined, and everything that is not defined is ignored. But if uncertainty is really everything that the investor cannot foresee, then any operational definition of uncertainty must define away much, if not everything, of importance. Not incidentally, notice that defining uncertainty as everything that the investor cannot foresee is a useful, but nonoperational definition.
6. Michael Laurence, *Playboy's Investment Guide* (Chicago: Playboy Press, 1971).
7. Some things are of less than no value, such as a nuclear power plant that needs decommissioning.
8. Martin Gardner, *Gardner's Whys & Wherefores* (Oxford: Oxford University Press, 1989): 170.
9. Martin Gardner, *Order and Surprise* (Oxford: Oxford University Press, 1984): 160. Most observers of science share my opinions. For the opinion of someone who does not, see William J. Broad and Nicolas Wade, "Science's Faulty Fraud Detectors" *Psychology Today* (November 1987): 51–57.

10. This use of the word *parameter* should not be confused with statisticians' use of the word.
11. See for example, Louis P. Lukac, B. Wade Bronsen, Scott H. Irwin, "A Test of Futures Market Disequilibrium Using Twelve Different Technical Trading Systems," *Journal Paper of the Purdue Agricultural Experiment Station* (July 1987) 119–127.
12. Robert Pardo, *Design, Testing and Optimization of Trading Systems* (New York: Wiley, 1992).
13. When the number of data dimensions are small the data can be graphed. When the number of data dimensions are large, the trader must depend on diagnostic statistics to tell him when the summary statistics cannot be trusted. Diagnostic statistics are less trustworthy than graphs.
14. I don't know of any books on nonparametric multivariate analysis of variance, but this is not fatal. Parametric multivariate analysis of variance, which is generally known as analysis of variance, can be turned into nonparametric multivariate analysis of variance by replacing the original data values with rank values. The literature on analysis of variance is huge and the titles unimaginative. See for example, H. Scheffe, *The Analysis of Variance* (New York: Wiley, 1959).
15. There are ways of encoding data so that a flat page shows more than three dimensions, or seems to. See for example, Brian Everitt, *Graphical Techniques for Multivariate Data* (New York: North-Holland, 1978). Curiously enough, most of the most interesting work is done by cartographers. See for example, Mark Monmonier, *Mapping It Out* (Chicago: University of Chicago Press, 1993). However, by far the most remarkable work in this field is by a graphic artist. See Edward R. Tufte, *Envisioning Information* (Cheshire Connecticut: Graphics Press, 1990).
16. One approach is to use James-Stein Estimators. Bradley Efron and Carl Morris, "Stein's Paradox in Statistics," *Scientific American* (May 1977) 119.

17. One of many books on this subject is Ramon D. Foltz and Thomas A. Penn, *Handbook for Protecting Ideas & Inventions* (Cleveland: Penn Institute, Inc., 1994).
18. Luskin, Donald L., Ed., *Portfolio Insurance: A Guide to Dynamic Hedging* (New York: Wiley, 1988): 8.
19. The literature on statistical quality control is large and accessible. One of many excellent books on the subject is Eugene L. Grant and Richard S. Leavenworth, *Statistical Quality Control* (New York: McGraw-Hill, 1988). Thomte and Company was probably the first to use statistical quality control as an investment risk-management technique. Thomte and Company called their techniques, which they did not reveal, *damage control,* but their promotional material sounded a lot like statistical quality control. Thomte and Company is no longer in business.
20. Jim Alphier, personal communication, no date.

8

Statistics and Certainty

Theory

Statistics is a body of methods for making wise decisions in the face of uncertainty.[1] Given this definition, statistics is clearly an important trading tool. After all, there are few areas outside of trading where uncertainty is as prevalent or where wise decisions are as profitable.

A wise decision is one that effectively uses the available data; it will not necessarily be the "correct" decision, that is, the decision that in retrospect would have been best. For example, if you are interested in acquiring money and if you accept 1 to 100 odds on a flip of a fair coin, you have accepted a bad bet and made a bad decision; it will not become a wise decision if, by chance, you win.[2]

Chance is an important concept. Indeed, it is another word for probability, and probability theory is the basis of statistics. A probability is a number between zero and one, inclusive, where zero indicates that a given event has no possibility of occurring and one indicates that the event is certain.

The trader will find that most of the most interesting events *do not* have probabilities of zero or one. On the other hand, in most of the most interesting cases, the trader will have to act *as if* an event had a probability of zero or one. For example, no reasonable individual will trade who does not believe that he or she can forecast the market accurately, on average. Yet that probability will never be one, for no matter how much evidence the trader accumulates, there is *always* the possibility that the results are a fluke. However, if it is unlikely the results are a fluke, that is, if the probability is, say, 0.99999999, the trader may well be willing to act as if the probability were one.

In many cases, the evidence is so extensive that the trader may confidently act as if the probability were one or zero. On the other hand, often the evidence is less persuasive than it seems. For example, Edson Gould's seasonal stock-market price-change data are presented in Figure 8–1. Presumably, he believed the data to be of value or he wouldn't have published them. Unfortunately, he was wrong. A statistical test of the data shows no evidence of seasonal patterns.

Statistical techniques are useful in just those cases where the trader is not willing to depend on his intuition. In other words, statistical techniques are most useful when it is costly to be wrong and when the data are meager or ambiguous or expensive to collect. Under even the most impoverished conditions, statistical techniques will allow the trader to estimate how likely or unlikely an event is, so he can make a decision and take action.

Two of the most important classes of statistical techniques are estimators and tests. An estimator is a rule or strategy that estimates the value of a carefully defined population on the basis of a carefully defined sample. A test is a rule or strategy that accepts or rejects a hypothesis about a carefully defined sample. Consider, for example, the percentage of pricing errors in the trade log of a particular trader. A pricing error is any price in the trade log that differs from the price in some verified source. An estimate of the number of pricing errors for a particular manager's log is 3 percent. A hypothesis is that the percentage of pricing errors is 3 percent. A test of that hypothesis could determine if the number of pricing errors in the trade log is likely to be significantly larger than 3 percent or significantly smaller than 3 percent.

Figure 8–1

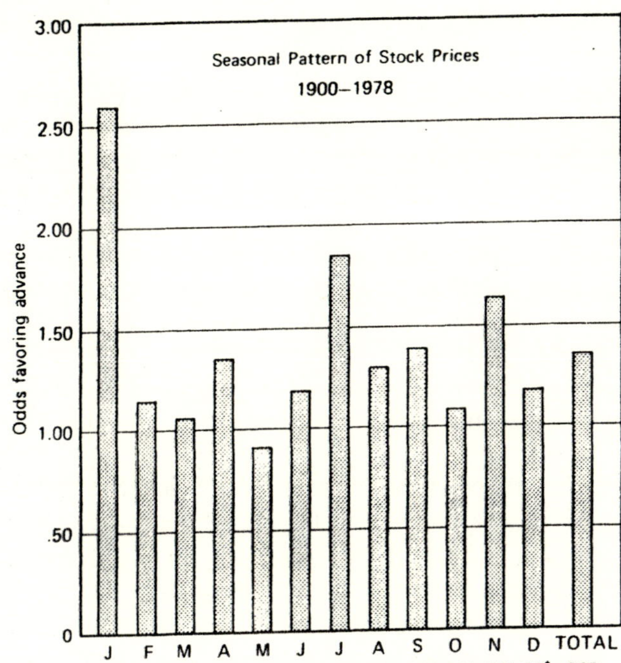

	J	F	M	A	M	J	J	A	S	O	N	D	TOTAL
Total number of months	79	79	79	79	79	79	79	78*	78*	78*	78*	78†	943
Total plus months‡	57	41	40	46	37	43	51	44	45	40	48	42†	534
Total minus months‡	22	38	39	33	42	36	28	34	33	38	30	36†	409
Odds favoring advance (plus months ÷ minus months)	2.59	1.08	1.03	1.39	0.88	1.19	1.82	1.29	1.36	1.05	1.60	1.17	1.31

†Figures as of 1977.

*One fewer month; New York Stock Exchange closed July 31 to December 12, 1914.

‡Plus months are those showing advance from previous month; minus months are those showing decline from previous month.

NOTE: Figures based on monthly mean of Dow Jones Industrial Average.

These data look important, but are not; the results are statistically insignificant. From E. Gould. *Edson Gould's 1979 Forecast.* New York: Anametrics, 1978.

Notice the distinction between sample and population and between statistic and parameter. In the example above, the population is the trader's entire log. The sample is that portion of the log actually tested. The parameter is the number of pricing errors in the entire log. The statistic is the number of pricing errors in that part of the log tested.

Theoretically, it might be possible to test each item in the log. A more reasonable approach is to compare, say, a couple of hundred items to a verified source. The couple of hundred items are the sample. The percentage of errors in the sample is the statistic.

It is clearly unreasonable to expect the statistic and parameter to be identical. However, if the sample is selected correctly, that is, randomly, and if the sample is large enough, the statistic should be reasonably close to the parameter. How close, on average, the statistic will be to the parameter will depend on the sample size, the statistic used, and the population's size and distribution.

A distribution is a description of a variable that relates the probability of the variable, taking a given value, to each value the variable might take. If the variable is discrete, that is, if it can take on only certain specific values, the distribution can be pictured by a histogram. A histogram is a graph of vertical bars where the areas are proportional to the probabilities represented. If the bars are equally wide, the heights alone can be used to represent the probabilities (see Figure 8–2).

If the variable is not discrete, that is, if it is continuous, the distribution can be fairly represented only by a frequency curve. In a sense, a curve is a histogram with an infinite number of infinitely thin bars (see Figure 8–3).

If a variable is continuous, the probability of the variable taking on any given value is zero. For that reason, a frequency curve cannot be used in the same way a histogram can. However, a curve can be used to represent the probability of a variable taking on a *range* of values. For example, a Krugerrand is supposed to contain a troy ounce of gold. But no Krugerrand ever contains *exactly* an ounce of gold. In other words, the probability of a given Krugerrand containing exactly one troy ounce is zero.

Figure 8–2

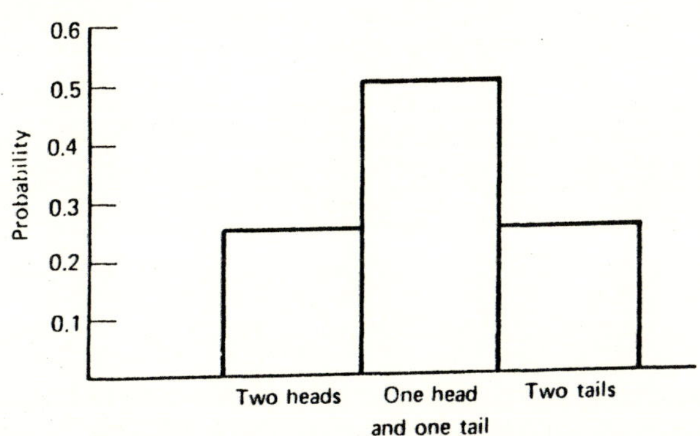

A histogram represents frequencies or probabilities by the area of vertical bars. The probability of two fair coins landing in various ways is represented above.

However, the probability of an unseen coin containing between, say, 1.000 troy ounce and 1.010 troy ounces might be .95.

Histograms are useful, but statistics are even more useful. The two most popular and useful groups of statistics are measures of location and dispersion. The most obvious and popular measure of location is the arithmetic mean. It is calculated by adding up all the sample values and dividing by the sample size.

The most popular measure of the dispersion or width of a distribution is the range. The second most popular measure, and a measure that is technically superior, is the standard deviation. In Figure 8–4, the various curves all have the same mean and area, but they have different widths. The narrower curves have the smaller standard deviations.

In the same way a population has a distribution, a statistic has a distribution. In the same way a population can have a mean and a standard deviation, a statistic can have a mean and a standard deviation, although the standard deviation of a statistic is called a standard error.

Figure 8–3

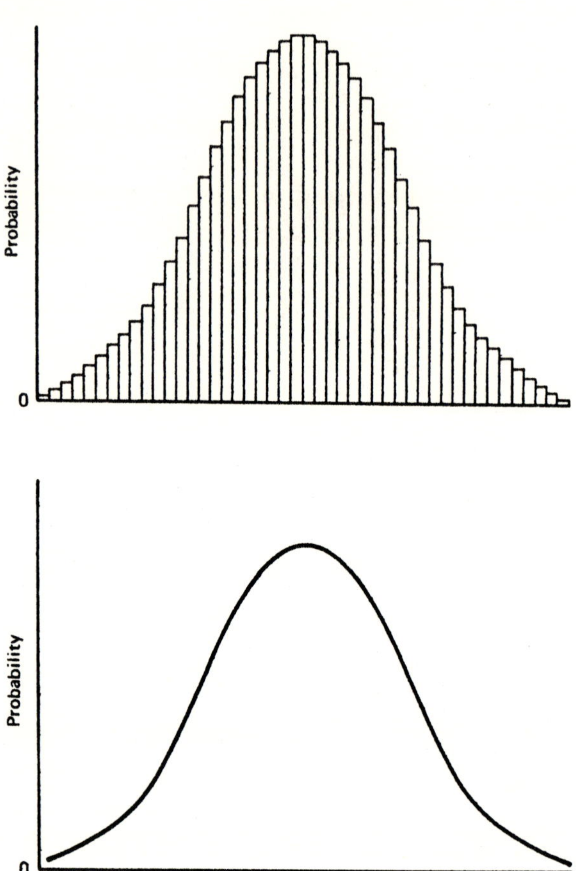

A frequency curve is a histogram with an infinite number of infinitely thin bars.

Any given sample mean may or may not equal the population mean, of course. On average, however, the sample mean will equal the population mean as long as the population has a mean (populations without means and standard deviations are dis-

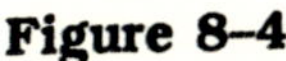

Figure 8–4

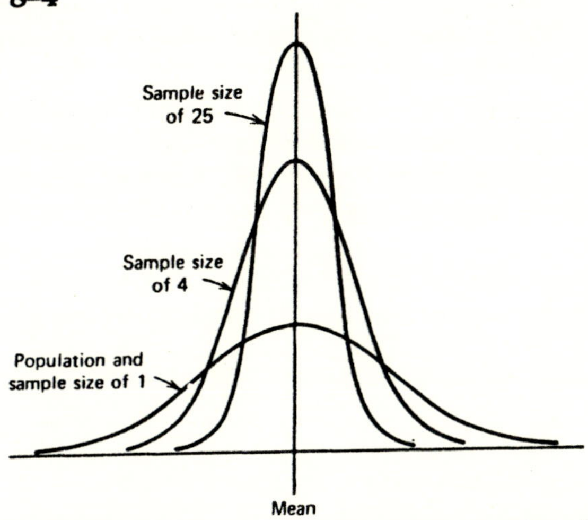

The larger the sample size, the more closely the sampling distribution clusters about the mean.

cussed in Chapter 9), and the sample is randomly selected from the population of interest. However, only when the sample size is one will the standard error of the sample mean equal the standard deviation of the population. Whenever the sample size is larger than one, the standard error will be smaller than the standard deviation. Notice in Figure 8–4 how the distributions of the sample means cluster progressively tighter about the population mean as the sample sizes increase.

It is generally easier to think in terms of confidence intervals, which are multiples or fractions of the standard error, than in terms of the standard error itself.[3] A confidence interval is a range of values within which the parameter has a known probability of appearing. This probability is called the confidence coefficient and it is known because it is chosen. A confidence coefficient can be chosen between zero and one, exclusive, where numbers approaching one indicate virtual certainty, and numbers approaching zero indicate almost no probability. For example, if a confidence coefficient of .5 is chosen, on average only half of the confidence intervals calculated will have the parameter within them (see Figure 8–5).

In a sense, the confidence intervals of a statistic are a measure of how useful the statistic is. If for a given confidence coefficient the confidence limits are relatively narrow, the statistic will be a relatively good estimate of the parameter. On the other hand, if for a given confidence coefficient the confidence limits are relatively wide, the statistic will be a relatively poor estimate.

Tests are another method of measuring the usefulness of a statistic. A test is a procedure for deciding which of two mutually exclusive hypotheses are true. Two hypotheses are mutually exclusive if and only if one of the hypotheses must be true and the other false (e.g., a given trading method is either profitable on average, or it is not).

Figure 8–5

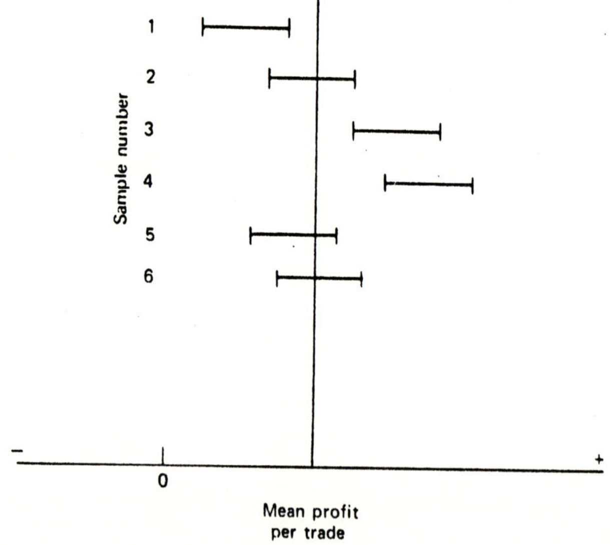

On average, half the 0.50 confidence intervals contain the parameter.

By convention one of the hypotheses, called the null hypothesis, is assumed to be true until it is proven false. A legal analogy may make this clearer. The null hypothesis is put on trial, in a sense, where the trial consists of obtaining a sample and calculating a statistic. The null hypothesis is assumed to be innocent, that is, true, until it is proven guilty, or false.

Guilt need not be proven beyond any possible doubt but only beyond a reasonable doubt. A reasonable doubt is a chosen probability value, a chosen level of significance [i.e., $(1 - \alpha)$] [0.1, 0.05, 0.01 and 0.001 are popular values for $(1 - \alpha)$]. If the probability of obtaining a result at least as extreme as the one obtained is smaller than the level of significance chosen, the null hypothesis should be considered false and the alternative hypothesis true.

Suppose a trader wished to know whether a given coin was fair. If the trader flipped the coin 20 times and heads appeared each time, the answer would be obvious. The answer is obvious because it is easy to see intuitively that when the coin is fair, the probability of obtaining such an extreme answer is very small.

On the other hand, if, say, 15 heads had occurred, the answer would have been less than obvious. It is less than obvious because it is less than obvious how the probabilities involved should be calculated. If the probabilities are represented by a distribution, the problem becomes how to divide the distribution into those probabilities that favor a fair coin and those that do not. In this case, the proper distribution is the binomial distribution. Figure 8–6 shows the probabilities involved. If the probability of throwing 15 heads is considered evidence that the coin is unfair, certainly the probability of throwing 16 heads also should be. It is certainly not reasonable to consider it evidence that the coin is fair. Therefore, the probability of throwing 15 or more heads is the probability that the coin is unfairly weighted to fall heads. If this amount is relatively small, the coin should be considered unfair. Of course, if it is also possible that the coin might be weighted to fall tails, the possibilities of 5 or fewer heads (15 or more tails) must also be considered.

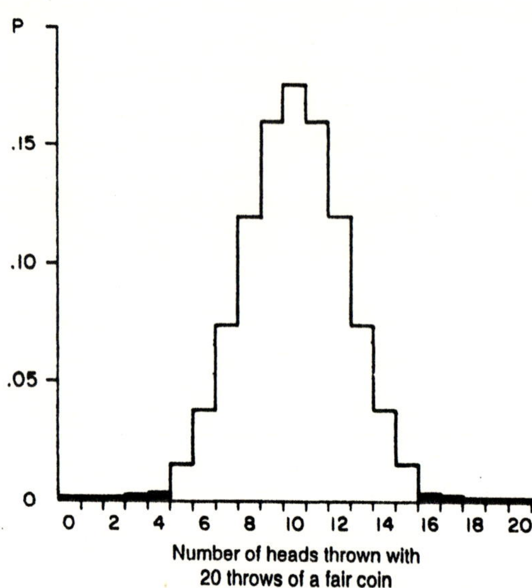

Histogram of probability distribution of 20 throws of a fair coin. Shaded area represents 5 or fewer, or 15 or more heads.

If the null hypothesis is that the coin is fair and the alternative hypothesis is that the coin is not fair, and if the trader accepts a (1-0.99) or 0.01 level of significance, the evidence indicates that the coin is *fair*; that is, as the probability of 15 or more heads or 5 or fewer heads (i.e., 0.042) is larger than the level of significance chosen, the null hypothesis cannot be rejected.

The level of significance chosen and the hypothesis designated as the null hypothesis are questions of value, not questions of logic or fact. The correct decision depends on the economics of the decision that the trader must make. The null hypothesis should be the hypothesis that the trader would find prudent to assume true if there were no evidence. For example, it is clearly prudent for a trader to assume that any given trading method is worthless until proven otherwise. The hypothesis that a given trading method is worthless would be the null hypothesis. The alternative hypothesis would be that the trading method has value. The level of significance desirable depends on the cost of being wrong. More precisely, the higher the cost of acting as if the alternative hypothesis is true when it is not, the higher the level of significance should be. As it is obviously expensive to trade with useless trading methods, relatively high levels of significance seem prudent.

In a sense, tests and confidence intervals are mirror images of each other. Whereas tests provide more information on how certain a result is, confidence intervals provide more information on the results. Whereas the trader will find it useful to know that it is 0.98 certain that the probability of success on a given trade will be larger than 0.5, he or she will, perhaps, find it more useful to know with 0.95 certainty that the probability of success on a given trade will be larger than 0.55. I suspect, therefore, that the trader will find confidence intervals more useful than tests.

How useful tests and confidence intervals will be depends on how large the sample size is, of course.

Clearly, for a given confidence coefficient, the larger the sample is per se and the larger the sample is as a portion of the population, the smaller the confidence limits will be. However, unless the sample is a relatively large portion of the population, say larger than 0.1, the sample size as a portion of the population is considerably less important than the sample's size per se. This is fortunate, because in all of the most interesting cases there is no way of knowing how large the population really is. Indeed, in all interesting cases the population could, theoretically at least, be infinite.

For example, we might be interested in the average price change of the S&P 500 after a certain chart pattern. In this case, the sample would be the price behavior of the S&P 500 for some years past. But clearly, the population we are really interested in encompasses the future of the S&P 500. Who can say how large that will be? In practice, therefore, the trader will find that statistics rarely need be, or can be, adjusted for population size.[4]

Notice how the sample and population differed in the example above. The population of interest consists of the future price behavior of the S&P 500, but the sample consists solely of past price-behavior. By definition, *not a single member of the population of interest can be sampled in a forecasting problem.*

This does not imply that past data are necessarily useless, but rather that they are not necessarily helpful. To extrapolate, it is necessary to assume both that the sample was randomly selected and that the population that was really sampled is essentially the same as the population of interest.

This last assumption is a dangerous one. There are an infinite number of ways the population sampled can differ from the population of interest. For example: (1) future investment markets may not have the same mix of trading and trending markets as in the past, (2) a trading method may depend on information that is not really available when it is needed, (3) a trading method may depend on executions that cannot be obtained.

I do *not* mean to suggest that the last assumption should never be made, but I do believe the trader should think about it long and hard. Moreover, such thinking should be done *before* a research project is begun. Research projects are expensive; unless the project is carefully designed, the expense can easily be wasted.

A popular rule of thumb among researchers is to allocate 20 percent of research funds to planning and analyzing. One planning technique many researchers find particularly useful is to consider how an individual who did not want to believe their conclusions would criticize them. What kind of evidence would convince a rational but unfriendly critic?

However, even if it is reasonable to assume that the population sampled is reasonably similar to the population of interest, it is not reasonable to assume that the population of interest will be like any given sample unless that sample was randomly selected. Partly, this is because a random sample is likely to be a representative sample. More important, however, if the sample is random (but *only* if it is random), the mathematical laws of probability can be applied. These are powerful laws that make it possible to make *objective* generalizations from the sample to the populations. In other words, if the sample is random, reasonable statements can be made about the population. However, if the sample is not random, these statements cannot be made, no matter how large the sample is.

If the efficient market hypothesis is true or approximately true, past data have been randomly distributed. Therefore, a method that works with *unseen* past data should work on the market itself. Unfortunately, even with the best will in the world, it is difficult not to select methods to fit the data or to select data to fit the methods. For that reason, it is generally advisable to replicate successful studies on unseen data. Of course, the best, though most expensive data are the market itself.

Research is expensive. Although research, on average, will produce better decisions, better decisions are not infinitely valuable. The trader, therefore, should give some thought to how much time and money to invest in research.

Clearly, if a sample is randomly selected, the larger the sample size, the more useful the research will be. Indeed, the usefulness of any admissible statistic will increase with the square root of the sample size (see Figure 8–7).

Figure 8–7

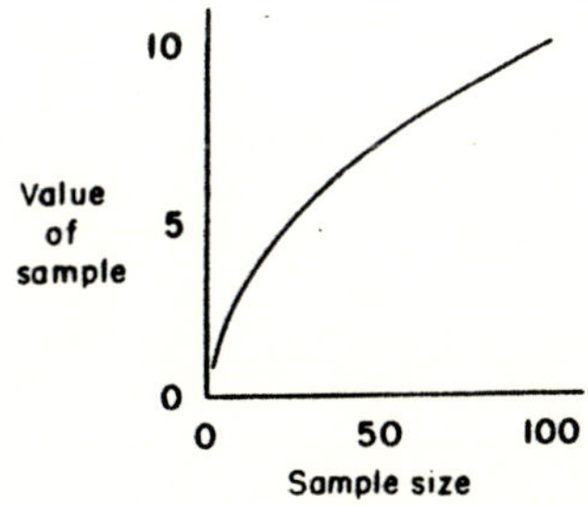

The value of a sample increases with the square root of the sample size.

On the other hand, the cost of taking a sample will almost never increase with the square root of the sample size. Almost invariably, the cost of taking a sample will consist of a fixed cost; that is, a cost that increases directly and linearly with the sample size.

This implies there is an optimal size for any sample. What that will be depends on the cost of being wrong and the costs of taking a sample. If the cost of being wrong is small enough and the costs of taking a sample are high enough, the optimal sample size may be no sample at all (see Figure 8–8).

More often, some sample will be worth taking. However, even when this is the case, not every sample is worth taking. Notice in Figure 8–9 that when the sample is either very small or very large, the total-cost curve is above the sample-information value curve.

The optimal sample-size is the point where the sample-information value curve most exceeds the total-cost curve. This is the point where the marginal reward from gathering a larger sample size just equals the cost of gathering it. For example, the

Figure 8–8

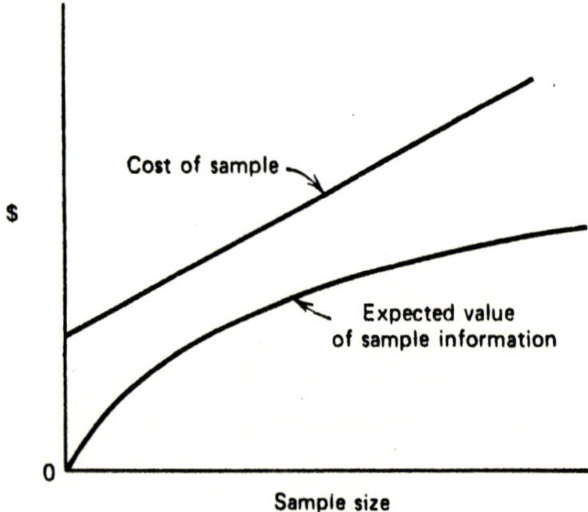

Figure 8–9

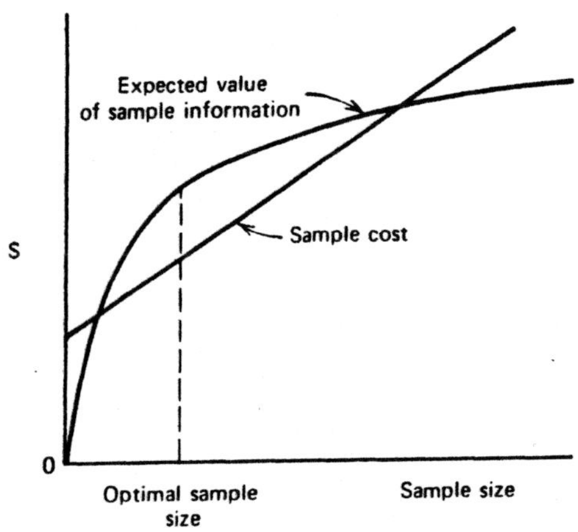

Very small and very large samples are rarely worth taking. Moreover, there is a "right" sample size.

optimal sample-size will be the point where the value to the trader of narrowing the confidence intervals will just equal the cost of increasing the sample size by one.

There are, of course, formulas for calculating the optimal sample-size. Unfortunately, they are difficult to use and make assumptions that may not be true. If the trader puts some care into guessing, he or she probably will be almost as well-off.

Practice

Statistics is an applied science. Still, if the trader has decided to begin his study at this point in the text, he has made a mistake. Statistical techniques work only because they are applications of theory. If the trader does not understand the applicable theories, he will be unable to meaningfully apply the techniques.

On the other hand, what theory statisticians find of most interest is of no practical importance. A statistical technique, like a car or a computer, will work whether or not its user understands why.

The trader should look at a statistical technique as a black box (see Figure 8–10). It is not important that the trader understands what goes on in the box, but it is important that the trader understand what goes into and what comes out of the box.

Figure 8–10

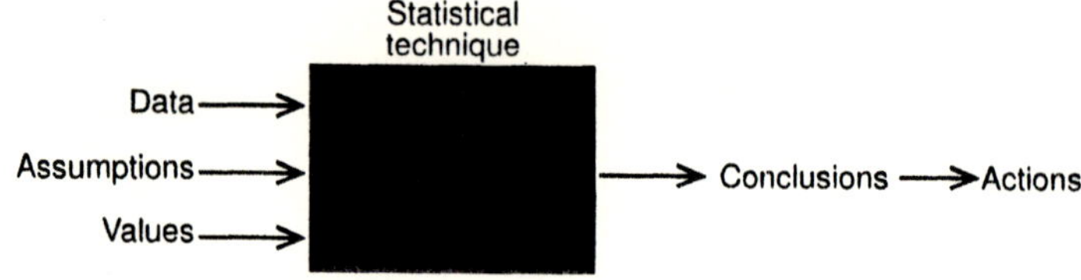

It is important that traders understand the assumptions and values of statistical techniques. It is not important that they understand the theory.

It is necessary that the trader understand how to perform the needed calculations, or use software that will do the calculations for him, but it is not necessary that the trader understand the logic of the calculations. For example, the formula for the Spearman's rank correlation coefficient (r_s), which will be explained later, is:

$$r_s = 1 - \frac{6 \cdot \Sigma di^2}{N^3 - N}$$

The trader must understand how to use this formula but need not understand why, for instance, di^2 is multiplied by 6 and not 7.

Part of the input for each technique is a group of assumptions. If these assumptions are in fact met, the output can be relied upon. Clearly, the trader should carefully consider the assumptions of the available techniques before he uses them.

It is for precisely this reason that alternative methods are presented. If the assumptions of one technique are not appealing, the assumptions of another might be. Of course, if the assumptions behind none of the methods presented are appealing, the trader must seek out more sophisticated and difficult methods, if they exist, or guess.

A great deal of important data are dichotomous. In other words, the data can only take one of two forms: yes or no, in or out, up or down. Even when this is not the case, data can often be reduced to a dichotomous form: a person has blue eyes or he does not, a person is born in England or he is not.

Frequently, it is important to estimate what portion (P) of a given dichotomous population has a certain characteristic. (Note that parameters are printed in boldface while statistics are printed sans serif, that is "T" rather than "T," with the exceptions of "N," "P," and X^2. Note also that with the exceptions of "N" and "R," none of the symbols used in this chapter are used elsewhere.) For example, for money-management purposes, it may be important to estimate what portion of risk-arbitrage trades will be profitable.

There are several ways to estimate **P** if it can be assumed that:

1. Each event can be classified into one of two groups: Y and ~Y.

2. The probability **P** of an event being classified Y remains constant from event to event.

3. The *N* events are independent.

4. The *N* events have been randomly selected.

The most obvious estimator is *P'* (the ' merely indicates that it is the first indicator considered. The " indicates it is the second indicator considered, etc.), where

$$P' = Y/N$$

P' has a number of virtues. The first and most obvious is that it is easy to calculate. Its second is mathematical. It can be shown that the sample statistic is more likely to be P', if in fact the population parameter is **P**, than it is if it is any other value. In other words, if, say, $P' = 0.4$, this is more likely to occur when **P** = 0.4 than it is at any other time.

Unfortunately, when N is small, P' is sometimes clearly unreasonable. For example, if a speculator has made three risk arbitrage trades, but has traded successfully each time, then

$$Y = 3$$

$$N = 3$$

and, given certain assumptions, his probability (P') of profiting on any given trade would seem to be

$$P' = \frac{3}{3}$$

$$= 1.0$$

which is clearly unreasonable.

A more prudent procedure would be to use P' as an estimate of **P** but to construct a confidence interval about P'. Clearly, it is more reasonable to use P' as an estimator of **P** than to use any other estimator. On the other hand, it is clearly unreasonable to expect P' to exactly equal **P**. A confidence interval is a way of showing how reasonable an estimate of **P** the estimate P' really is.

If the sample is relatively large, say larger than 30, confidence limits can be easily calculated. How this is done will be described later. Unfortunately, these techniques are not valid when the sample size is small, in which case Table 1 in Appendix 1 must be used. The small-sample procedure will now be described.

1. Select a confidence coefficient α. If no value is acceptable, use the next largest value.

2. Calculate Z. If only one confidence limit is to be calculated, $Z = \alpha$. If both are calculated, $Z = 1 - ((1 - \alpha)/2)$.

3. Locate the section of the table where N is equal to the sample size.

4. Under column Y locate the row where Y is equal to the number in the sample with the attribute of interest.

5. The lower confidence limit $PL(\alpha)$ is the value where the selected row and column intersect.

6. Under column Y locate the row where Y is equal to $N - Y$.

7. The upper confidence limit $PU(\alpha)$ is one minus the value where the selected row and column intersect.

For example, assume that a trader has traded IBM options twice, but both times successfully. In this case, *P'*, of course, is 1. Assume the trader wishes to locate the 0.9 confidence intervals. Using Table 1 in Appendix 1 and following the procedure above, the confidence levels located are $PU(\alpha) = 1.0000$ and $PL(\alpha) = 0.224$.

Clearly, the most likely value for **P** is 1.0000. Unfortunately, there is a 0.9 probability that **P** is as large as 1.0000 or as small as 0.224. Considering the size of this range, it does not seem reasonable that *P'* is a reliable estimate of **P**.

However, when $N \geq 30$, confidence intervals can easily be calculated. We shall do so now.

1. Decide whether one or both confidence limits are to be calculated.

2. Select a confidence coefficient α.

3. Calculate Z. If only one coefficient limit is to be calculated, Z = α. If two, Z = 1 – [(1 – α)/2].

4. Locate $\tilde{Z}$. $\tilde{Z}$ is the number of standard deviations from the mean that has a probability of Z. These values can be found on Table 2 in Appendix 1.

5. Calculate:

$$Pu(\alpha) = P' + \tilde{Z}\sqrt{\frac{P'(1-P')}{N-1}}$$

$$PL(\alpha) = P' - \tilde{Z}\sqrt{\frac{P'(1-P')}{N-1}}$$

For example, assume that a trader wants to be 0.95 certain of both the upper and lower confidence limits when $P' = 0.6$ and $N = 100$. Therefore:

$$\alpha = 0.95$$

$$Z = 1 - [(1 - 0.95)/2]$$

$$\tilde{Z} = 0.975$$

Using Table 2 in Appendix 1, if Z = 0.975 then $\tilde{Z} = 1.96$

$$PU(0.95) = 0.6 + 1.96\sqrt{\frac{0.6(1-0.6)}{100-1}}$$

$$= 0.6 + 1.96\sqrt{\frac{0.24}{99}}$$

$$= 0.6 + 1.96 \cdot \sqrt{0.0024242424}$$

$$= 0.6 + 1.96 \cdot 0.049236596$$

$$= 0.6 + 0.096503728$$

$$= 0.696503728$$

$$PL(\alpha) = 0.6 - 1.96\sqrt{\frac{0.6\,(1-0.6)}{99}}$$

$$= 0.6 - 0.096503728$$

$$= 0.503496272$$

All of these techniques assume that the events are independent. In many cases this is a reasonable assumption. In many cases, however, it is not.

There are two types of dependency, positive and negative. Positive dependency means that large values are followed, on average, by large values, and small values by small values. Negative dependency means that large values are followed, on average, by small values, and small values by large values.

"Large" and "small" are relative terms. If the values can be positive or negative, positive dependency means that, on average, positive values are followed by positive values, and negative values by negative values.

A run test is a means of testing whether dichotomous data are dependent. A run is a group of consecutive or successful events; for example, in the series below, where each event follows the events to its left, there are 26 events:

+ + – – 0 + + 0 + + – + – + – – 0 + + 0 – + – + – –

However, when the ties, which are indicated by zeros, are dropped, there are 22 events and 14 runs:

+ + – – + + + + – + – + – – + + – + – + – –

The procedure for testing for dependency will now be described.

1. Decide whether to test for positive dependency, negative dependency, or both.

2. Select a level of significance $(1 - \alpha)$.

3. Calculate Z. If only positive or negative dependency is to be tested for, Z = (1 – α). If both positive and negative dependency are to be tested for, Z = (1 – α)/2.

4. Locate $\tilde{Z}$. $\tilde{Z}$ is the number of standard deviations from the mean that has a probability of Z. These values can be found in Table 2 in Appendix 1.

5. Calculate K.

$$K = \frac{N(r - 0.5) - 2n_1n_2}{\sqrt{\frac{2n_1n_2(2n_1n_2 - N)}{N - 1}}}$$

where N = the sample size
r = the number of runs
n_1 = one of the two types of events
n_2 = the other type of event.

(Naturally, $n_1 + n_2 = N$)

6. a. Positive dependency is significant at the (1 – α) level of confidence if

$$K > \tilde{Z}$$

Otherwise, it is not.

b. Negative dependency is significant at the (1 – α) level if

$$K < \tilde{Z}$$

Otherwise, it is not.

c. Positive or negative dependency is significant at the (1 – α) level if

$$K > |\tilde{Z}|$$

where the horizontal bars indicate that the absolute value of $\tilde{Z}$ is to be considered. In other words, a negative sign for $\tilde{Z}$ should be ignored. If K is not larger than the absolute value of $\tilde{Z}$, there is no significant dependency at the $(1 - \alpha)$ level.

For example, if all of a trader's decisions are optimal, his or her profits and losses will be independent. Contrariwise, if his profits and losses are not independent, the trader can change his behavior to incorporate this information and improve his reward/risk ratio. Assume that a trader has had a series of profitable and unprofitable trades that could be represented by the data given above. Assume, also, that the trader will not change his trading behavior unless the results are significant at the $(1 - \alpha)$ or 0.10 level. If both negative and positive dependency are to be tested for:

$$Z = (1 - 0.90)/2$$
$$= 0.1/2$$
$$= 0.05$$

$$\tilde{Z} = 1.65$$

Using the data above and assigning 12 to n_1, then:

$$N = 22,\ n_1 = 12,\ n_2 = 10, \text{ and } r = 14. \text{ Thus:}$$

$$2n_1n_2 = 2 \cdot 12 \cdot 10$$
$$2n_1n_2 = 240$$

$$K = \frac{22(14 - 0.5) - 240}{\sqrt{\dfrac{240(240 - 22)}{22 - 1}}}$$

$$= \frac{22(13.5) - 240}{\sqrt{\frac{240(218)}{21}}}$$

$$= \frac{297 - 240}{\sqrt{\frac{52320}{21}}}$$

$$= \frac{57}{\sqrt{2491.428571}}$$

$$= \frac{57}{49.91421212}$$

$$= 1.141959325$$

Because 1.141959325 is not larger than the absolute value of 1.65, the trader should not change his trading behavior.

The relationship between one dichotomous variable and another is frequently important. For example, it might be interesting to know how often an indicator that allegedly forecasts the direction of next week's T-bond futures closing-prices actually does forecast next week's price changes.

Clearly, four pieces of information are needed to estimate the relationship. The information needed is a, the number of times the index correctly forecasted a price rise; b, the number of times the index incorrectly forecasted a price rise; c, the number of times the index incorrectly forecasted a price decline; and d, the number of times the index correctly forecasted a price decline. This information can be tabled as in Figure 8–11.

The relationship between the two dichotomous variables can be estimated by the adjusted correlation coefficient C if it can be assumed that:

1. Each event can be classified into one of two groups; Y and ~Y, by each of two independent criteria.

Figure 8–11

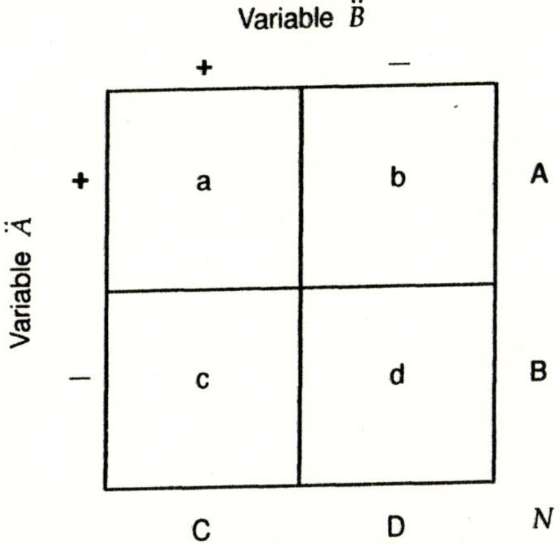

a, b, c, and d represent sample information and A, B, C, and D represent the margin totals. *N* is the sample size.

2. The probability **P** of an event being classified Y remains constant from event to event for each of the two criteria.

3. The *N* events are independent.

4. The *N* events have been randomly selected.

5. a, b, c, and d or their expected values are all greater than or equal to 1. The expected value of, say, b, that is, EX(b) is equal to the product of the appropriate marginal totals divided by the sample size. Thus:

$$EX(a) = A \cdot C/N$$

$$EX(b) = A \cdot D/N$$

$$EX(c) = B \cdot C/N$$

$$EX(d) = B \cdot D/N$$

where A, B, C, and D are all marginal totals. For example, using the data in Figure 8–12:

$$\text{EX(b)} = 5 \cdot 2/7$$
$$= 1.4$$

Figure 8–12

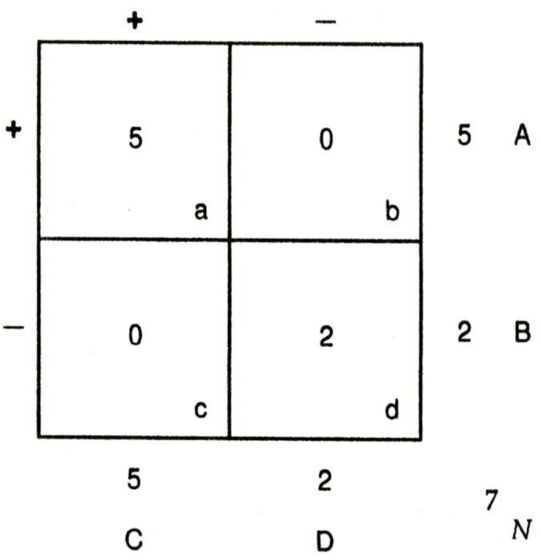

Naturally, when C = 0, there is no relationship between the sample variables; when C = 1, the relationship is perfect. The relationship will be positive if ad > bc, negative if ad < bc, and nonexistent if ad = bc. The adjusted correlation-coefficient is calculated as follows (Figure 8–12):

$$C = \sqrt{\frac{\chi^2}{\chi^2 + N}} \Big/ .707$$

when

$$\chi^2 = \frac{N\left(|ad - bc| - \frac{N}{2}\right)^2}{(a + b)(c + d)(a + c)(b + d)}$$

N = the sample size

These formulas are actually quite easy to use. Let us assume, for example, that over the last 90 weeks, a trader has counted the number of times a given index has and has not forecasted the weekly change in December T-bond futures and arranged the information in Figure 8–13.

Figure 8–13

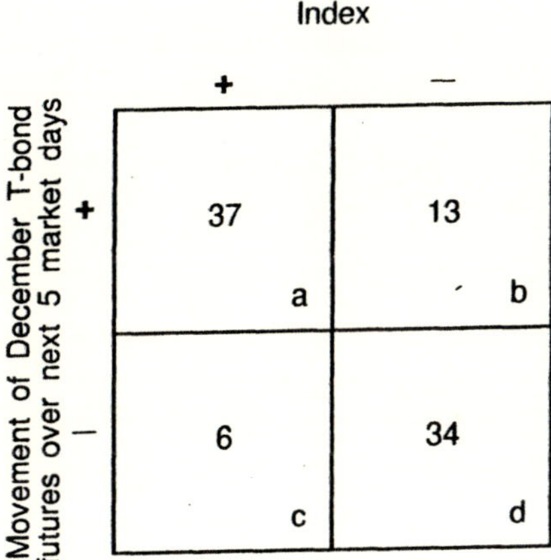

Therefore:

$$\chi^2 = \frac{90\left(|37 \cdot 34 - 13 \cdot 6| - \frac{90}{2}\right)^2}{(37 + 13)(6 + 34)(37 + 6)(13 + 34)}$$

$$= \frac{90\,(|\,1{,}258 - 78\,| - 45)^2}{4{,}042{,}000}$$

$$= \frac{90(|1{,}180| - 45)^2}{4{,}042{,}000}$$

$$= \frac{90(1{,}135)^2}{4{,}042{,}000}$$

$$= \frac{90 \cdot 1{,}288{,}225}{4{,}042{,}000}$$

$$= \frac{115{,}940{,}250}{4{,}042{,}000}$$

$$= 28.68388174$$

Therefore:

$$C = \sqrt{\frac{28.68388174}{28.68388174 + 90}} \Big/ .707$$

$$= \frac{\sqrt{0.2416830434}}{0.707}$$

$$= \frac{0.4916126965}{0.707}$$

$$= 0.6953503487$$

Clearly, C may or may not be significant. If the assumptions above were satisfied and if the actual or expected values of a, b, c, and d are all greater than or equal to 5, the significance can easily be determined. This technique will be described shortly. However, if all of the actual or expected values are not greater than 5, the following, and more tedious, technique must be used:

1. Decide whether to test for only positive or negative relationships, or both.
2. If you decided to test for a positive or a negative relationship but not both, check to see that the sign of the

relationship is the same as the sign of C. If it is not, there is no relationship.

3. Select a level of significance ($1 - \alpha$).

4. Calculate Z. If you have decided to test for both positive and negative relationships, $Z = (1 - \alpha)/2$. If you have decided to test for either positive or negative relationships, but not both, $Z = 1 - \alpha$.

5. Determine the sample values a + b and c + d.

6. Find the sample values a + b in Table 3 in Appendix 1 under the heading "Totals in the Right Margin."

7. In the same section of the table, but to the right, locate the sample values c + d under that heading.

8. To the right, in the next section of the table, locate the sample value b. If the sample value b is not available, go to step 8 (Alternative).

9. If the sample value d is equal to or less than the value in the column under the chosen value of Z in the row identified with the sample values for a + b, c + d, and b, the data are significant at level of significance ($1 - \alpha$).

8. *(Alternative)* In the same section of the table where the sample value b was found, locate sample value a.

9. *(Alternative)* If the sample value c is equal to or less than the value in the column under the chosen values of Z and in the row identified with the sample values for a + b, c + d, and a, the data are significant at that level.

For example, suppose a trader has observed the behavior of an index and the subsequent behavior of platinum and tabled the data as in Figure 8–12. Let us also assume that the trader has decided to use the index if it demonstrates positive dependency and 0.95 significance during the test period. In this case, therefore, $Z = 0.95$.

Using the data in Figure 8–12, $a + b = 5$ and $c + d = 2$. In this case, b does not equal 5, but a does. After locating the proper rows and columns on Table 3 in Appendix 1, we find that the sample value for c must be equal to or less than 0 for the data to be significant at the $(1 - \alpha)$ level.

If, in fact, the actual or expected values are all greater than or equal to 5, the procedure is as follows.

1. Decide whether to test for a positive relationship or negative relationship, or both.

2. If you have decided to test for a positive or a negative relationship but not both, check to see that the sign of the relationship is the same as the sign of C. If it is not, there is no relationship.

3. Select a level of significance $(1 - \alpha)$.

4. Calculate Z. If you have decided to test for either a positive or negative relationship, $Z = \alpha$. If you have decided to test for both positive and negative relationships, $Z = 1 - [(1 - \alpha)/2]$.

5. Locate ZZ on Table 4 in Appendix 1. ZZ is the value opposite Z.

6. If the value of χ^2 calculated above is equal to or larger than ZZ, then C is significant at the $(1 - \alpha)$ level.

For example, assume that a trader wanted 0.90 certainty before he used the method that generated the data in Figure 8–13. Let us assume that he wanted to test for positive or negative relationships. The expected values are all obviously over 5, so the technique above can be used. $Z = 0.95$ and Table 4 in Appendix 1 reveals that the χ^2 value must be larger than or equal to 3.84 for the trader to be 0.95 certain that the method is valid. As the χ^2 generated was, in fact, 28.6, the method seems to be valid.

One of the most frequent and important research tasks is estimating an average value. Unless, for example, trading can be expected to be profitable on average, it clearly makes no sense to trade.

There are several ways to estimate X, if it can be assumed that:

1. The data can be measured on a ratio scale. That is, a scale with a zero point and with constant differences between any two numbers. Price and weight are examples.
2. The true mean X is the same for each event.
3. The *N* events are independent.
4. The *N* events have been randomly selected.

A useful and obvious estimator for the population's arithmetic mean X is the sample's arithmetic mean X′. This is simply the sum of the sample value divided by the sample size. For example: 500, 300, –950, 45, –50, –150, 200, 400 has a total of 295 and a sample size of 8. The arithmetic mean is, therefore, 295/8 = 36.88.

Another estimator is the sample median X″. The sample median is the sample's middle value when the sample has been ordered by magnitude and the sample size is odd. When the sample size is even, the median is the arithmetic average of the middle two values. Ranking the data above produces the following: –950, –150, –50, 45, 200, 300, 400, 500. The median in the sample is (45 + 200)/2 = 122.5.

Note that the mean and the median differ in the example above. This will happen whenever the sample is not symmetric, that is, it is skewed. Because the mean gives more weight to extreme values than the median does, it will shift more than the median will in the direction of the extreme values, that is, in the direction of the skew (see Chapter 9, Figure 9–1).

In many ways, the sample mean is the most desirable average. After all, we are generally interested in the population mean, not the population median. However, because the mean is more affected by extreme values than the median is, it is a less stable and, therefore, in many ways a less desirable measure of location. The sample median can be used in any situation where the mean can be used, but the converse is not true.

A third estimator is the 50 percent truncated mean. This is not half of the mean, but the mean of inner half of the sample. The sample values are ordered by magnitude and the largest quarter of the values and the smallest quarter of the values are discarded. The 50 percent mean is the arithmetic mean of the remaining values. For example, using the same values as above, and discarding the largest and smallest fourths of the sample leaves: –50, 45, 200, 300. The arithmetic mean of these values is 123.75.

When the underlying distribution is normal, the 50 percent truncated mean is almost as good an estimator as the arithmetic mean, and considerably better than the median. When the underlying distribution is Cauchey, the 50 percent truncated mean performs exceedingly well, much better than the median, while the arithmetic mean fails utterly.[5] Notice that the 50 percent truncated mean excludes the most extreme values, which are most likely to be random fluctuations, or just plain wrong.

Measures of dispersion indicate how wide a distribution is. By far, the most popular measure is the sample range. The range is easy to understand and calculate, but it does not have many other virtues. Put less positively, the range is dependent on the sample values most likely to be wrong.[6]

A popular alternative is the standard deviation(s), or the variance, which is the standard deviation squared. The standard deviation is calculated as follows:

1. Calculate the mean of the sample.

2. Subtract each value in the sample from the mean.

3. Square each deviation from the mean.
4. Sum the squares.
5. Divide the sum just calculated by the sample size minus one.
6. Take the square root of the resulting calculation.

For example, the standard deviation of 500, 300, –950, 45, –50, –150, 200, 400 is calculated as follows:

Sample Size = 8
Mean = (500 + 300 – 950 + 45 – 50 – 150 + 200 + 400)/8 = 36.88

Obs		Mean		Difference	Difference Squared
500	–	36.88	=	463.12	214,480.13
300	–	36.88	=	263.12	69,232.13
–950	–	36.88	=	–986.88	973,932.13
45	–	36.88	=	8.12	65.93
–50	–	36.88	=	–86.88	7,548.13
–150	–	36.88	=	–186.88	34,924.13
200	–	36.88	=	163.12	26,608.13
400	–	36.88	=	363.12	131,856.13
		Sum of Squares			1,458,646.88
		Divided by (8 –1 = 7)			208,378.13
		Square Root			456.48

The standard deviation has a number of lovely mathematical attributes. It is relatively easy to calculate, and if the underlying distribution is normally distributed, it is the best possible measure of dispersion. Unfortunately, it is almost as dependent on the extreme sample values as the range. An alternative is the mean absolute deviation (MAD). The mean absolute deviation is calculated by subtracting each value in the sample, in turn, from the mean. All signs are then dropped. Finally, the average of the resulting values is calculated.

An alternative is to use the mean and confidence intervals based on the mean absolute deviation (MAD).

This technique assumes that the population is distributed normally, or approximately normally. A technique for constructing confidence intervals will now be described:

1. Decide whether an upper confidence limit, a lower confidence limit, or both are to be calculated.

2. Decide on a confidence coefficient α.

3. Calculate Z. If only one confidence limit is to be calculated, $Z = \alpha$. If both confidence limits are to be calculated, $Z = 1 - [(1 - \alpha)/2]$.

4. Calculate the sample size *N*.

5. Compute the sample mean X′.

6. Compute the sample mean absolute deviation (MAD). This is calculated by subtracting each value in the sample, in turn, for the mean. Second, all negative signs are dropped. Finally, the average of all the resulting values is calculated.

7. Find HNZ in Table 5 in Appendix 1. Move down the far left column until you find the sample size *N*. Then move across the row until you find the column under the value Z.

8. Calculate X′U(α) and/or X′L(α).

$$X'U(\alpha) = X' + [(MAD \cdot HNZ)/\sqrt{N}\,]$$

$$X'L(\alpha) = X' - [(MAD \cdot HNZ)/\sqrt{N}\,]$$

For example, assume that a trader was willing to trade gold only if he could be 0.95 percent confident that his trading method was profitable on a net basis. Let us also assume that during the trial run, the method produced the following profits and losses: 50, 150, 350, –200, –75, 300, –25, 250. Using the above data, the trader need calculate only a lower confidence limit, $Z = 0.95$ and $N = 8$. Therefore:

$$\text{HNZ} = 3.092$$

$$\sqrt{8} = 2.8284271$$

50	–	100	=	| 50|	=	50
150	–	100	=	| 150|	=	50
350	–	100	=	| 250|	=	250
–250	–	100	=	|–300|	=	300
–75	–	100	=	|–175|	=	175
300	–	100	=	| 200|	=	200
–25	–	100	=	|–125|	=	125
250	–	100	=	| 150|	=	150
800						1,300
÷ 8						÷ 8
X′ = 100						MAD = 162.5

Therefore:

$$\text{XL}(\alpha) = 100 - \frac{162.5 \cdot 3.092}{2.828471}$$
$$= 100 - 177.64014$$
$$= -77.64014$$

Confidence intervals for the median cannot generally be set without extensive tables. This is unfortunate, as these techniques, unlike the above techniques, do not demand that the population be distributed even approximately normally. However, if the trader is willing to construct both limits and to limit himself to one of three confidence coefficients, then limits can be easily calculated. We shall describe the method now.

1. Decide on a confidence coefficient α.

2. Select the appropriate value for $\exists$.

α	$\exists$
0.90	0.80
0.95	1.00
0.99	1.30

3. Arrange the sample in order of rank and give each value a rank from R(1) for the smallest to R(*N*) for the largest. *N* is, of course, also the sample size.

4. Calculate Π.

$$\Pi = \frac{N+1}{2} - \exists\sqrt{N}$$

rounded off to the nearest integer.

5. Calculate $\Pi\,\Pi$

$$\Pi\,\Pi = (N+1) - \Pi$$

6. $X''U(\alpha) = R(\Pi\,\Pi)$

$X''L(\alpha) = R(\Pi)$

For example, assume that a trader wishes to construct 0.90 confidence intervals for the trial run of a new stock-options trading method, and that his sample is: 50, 150, 350, –200, –75, 300, –25, 250.

In this case, $\exists$ = 0.8. The sample is ranked below:

R(8) = 350

R(7) = 300

R(6) = 250

R(5) = 150

$$R(4) = 50$$

$$R(3) = -25$$

$$R(2) = -75$$

$$R(1) = -200$$

$$\Pi = \frac{8+1}{2} - 0.8\sqrt{8}$$
$$= \frac{9}{2} - 0.8 \cdot 2.8284271$$
$$= 4.5 - 2.2627416$$
$$= 2$$

$$\Pi\,\Pi = (8+1) - 2$$
$$= 9 - 2$$
$$= 7$$

$$X''U(\alpha) = R(7)$$
$$= 300$$

$$X''L(\alpha) = R(2)$$
$$= -75$$

It is often useful to know the relationship between two variables. One method of doing this is to plot the data on a dot chart called a scatter diagram. In Figure 8–14 each dot represents the relationship between the level of a proprietary indicator and the net change in the price of gold over the next week. In this case, the relationship is positive, that is, large values of one variable are accompanied or followed, on average, by large values of the other variable, and small values of one variable by small values

Figure 8–14. A scattergram of a positive relationship

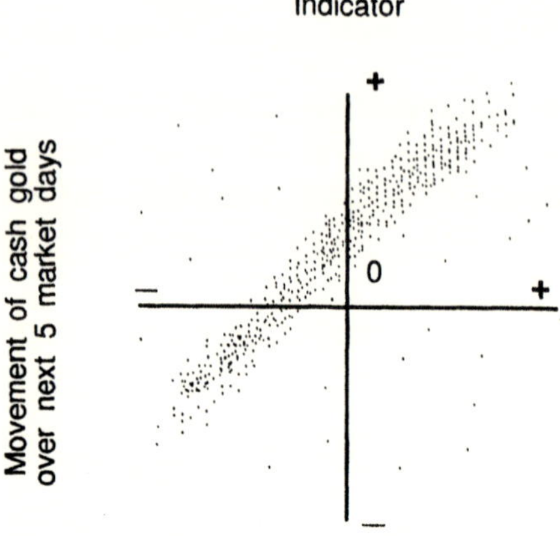

of the other. Figure 8-15 illustrates a negative relationship, that is, large values of one variable are accompanied or followed, on average, by small values of the other variable, and small values of one variable by large values of the other. Figure 8-16 illustrates a third alternative, that is, that there is no relationship at all between the variables.

Figure 8–15. A scattergram of a negative relationship

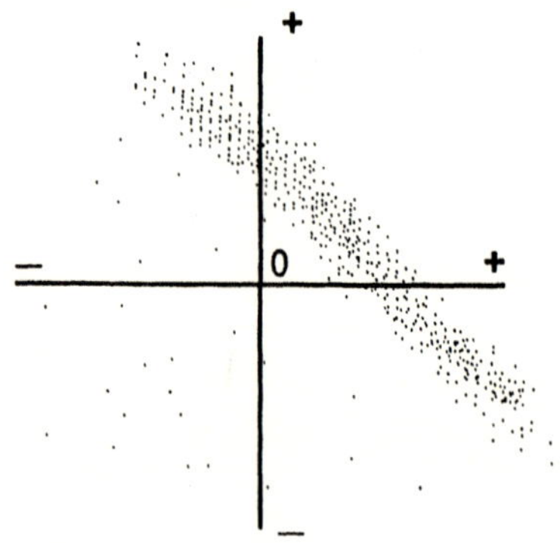

Figure 8–16. A scattergram of a nonexistent relationship

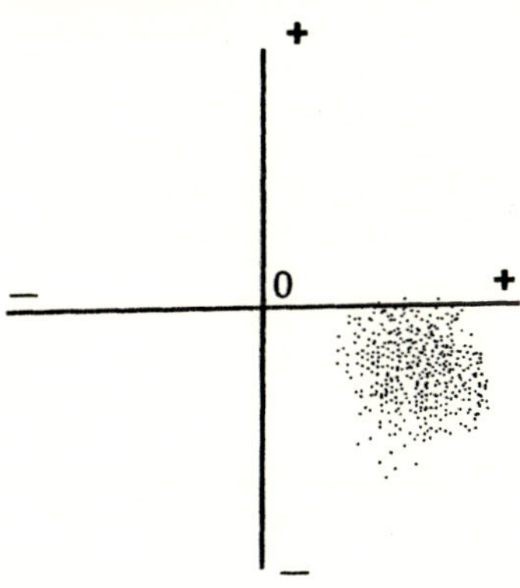

Despite the usefulness of the scatter diagram, it does not provide a measure of the relationship of the two variables.

One way to express this relationship is with the Pearson correlation coefficient. This coefficient expresses the relationship between two numbers by means of a number from negative one to one inclusive. If the coefficient is one, this indicates a perfect positive correlation between the variables. For example:

X	*Y*
6	70
5	60
4	50
3	40

Notice that the location and scale of X and Y differ. If the coefficient is minus one, this indicates a perfect negative correlation between the variables. For example:

X	*Y*
6	40
5	50
4	60
3	70

If the coefficient is zero, this indicates no correlation between the variable. An approximate example is:

X	Y
6	60
5	30
4	30
3	60

The formula for the Pearson correlation coefficient is:

$$T_p = \frac{\Sigma(x_i - \bar{x})(y_i - \bar{y})}{\sqrt{\Sigma(x_i - \bar{x})^2 \cdot \Sigma(y_i - \bar{y})^2}}$$

In words, the procedure is as follows:

1. Calculate the mean of the X and Y variables.
2. Subtract each value, in turn, from that variable mean.
3. Multiply the differences.
4. Sum the values multiplied. The result is the numerator.
5. Square each difference calculated in instruction 2.
6. Sum the squares for each variable.
7. Multiply the resulting sum.
8. Take the square root of the result. The result is the denominator.
9. Divide the numerator by the denominator.

For example, suppose a trader has an index that he or she believes can forecast the changes in the rates for collateralized mortgage obligations, in basis points, over some specified period. The index values are listed in the X column in the table below, and the corresponding change in the CMO in the Y column. Thus:

	X	Y	$X-\bar{X}$	$Y-\bar{Y}$	$(X-\bar{X})(Y-\bar{Y})$
	150	25	35	–15	–525
	95	–100	–20	–140	2,800
	125	300	10	260	2,600
	80	250	–35	210	–7,350
	140	–200	25	–240	–6,000
	100	–35	–15	–75	1,125
Mean	115	40			
Sum	690	240			–7,350

	X	Y	$X-\bar{X}$	$Y-\bar{Y}$	$(X-\bar{X})^2$	$(Y-\bar{Y})^2$
	150	25	35	–15	1,225	225
	95	–100	–20	–140	400	19,600
	125	300	10	260	100	67,600
	80	250	–35	210	1,225	44,100
	140	–200	25	–240	625	57,600
	100	–35	–15	–75	225	5,625
Mean	115	40				
Sum	690	240			3,800	194,750

$$-7{,}350/\sqrt{3{,}800 \cdot 194{,}750}$$
$$-7{,}350/\sqrt{740{,}050{,}000}$$
$$-7{,}350/27{,}203$$
$$-0.27$$

The Pearson correlation coefficient is, by far, the most popular of the correlation coefficients. Indeed, if a correlation coefficient is used but not named, it is almost certainly the Pearson's coefficient. Fortunately, there are other measures, for the trust so many put in this measure is almost certainly misplaced. Notice that the mean and standard deviation are part of Pearson's measure. This means the measure is easily affected by extreme values.

Spearman's rank correlation coefficient (r_s) is one of the most useful alternatives. This coefficient expresses the relationship between pairs of ranked variables, X(i) and Y(i), by means of a number from negative one to positive one inclusive. If the coefficient is one, this indicates perfect positive correlation between the variables. For example:

X(I)	Y(I)
6	6
5	5
4	4
3	3
2	2
1	1

Negative and zero correlations have the same meaning that they have for Pearson's correlation coefficient. I will now describe the calculation of this coefficient.

1. If the data is not already in ranked form, it must be reduced to ranked form.

2. For each pair of ranked data, calculate di. The difference between the ranks is di.

3. Calculate di^2 for each value. This is simply the di value squared.

4. Calculate Σdi^2. This is the sum of all the di^2 values.

5. Multiply di^2 by 6.

6. Take the sample size N and cube it, that is, multiply it by itself twice.

7. The result is N^3. Subtract N from N^3.

8. Divide the results of step 5 by the results of step 7.

9. If the results of step 8 are subtracted from 1, the result is the Spearman correlation coefficient (r_s). Algebraically, this is:

$$r_s = 1 - \frac{6 \cdot \Sigma di^2}{N^3 - N}$$

For example, let us suppose that a trader has invented an index that he or she believes can forecast the gold market over the next three days. The index values are listed in the X(i) column in the matrix below, and the corresponding changes in the gold price over the next three days are listed in column Y(i). In other words, when the index registered 150, the net change in the gold price over the next three days was $25. In the next two columns, R(X) and R(Y), the variables X and Y are ranked. The next column, di, calculates the difference between columns R(X) and R(Y), and the column next to that, di^2, squares the difference. The sum of these squares is then calculated and multiplied by 6. The result is the numerator. The sample size, which is also the largest rank, is subtracted from the sample size cubed. The result is the denominator. The resulting ratio is then subtracted from 1.

X(i)	Y(i)	R(X)	R(Y)	di	di^2
150	25	6	4	2	4
90	–100	2	2	0	0
125	300	4	6	–2	4
70	250	1	5	–4	16
140	–200	5	1	4	16
100	–50	3	3	0	0
160	500	7	7	0	0

$\Sigma di^2 = 40$

$$7^3 = 7 \cdot 7 \cdot 7$$
$$= 343$$
$$r_s = 1 - \frac{6 \cdot 40}{343 - 7}$$
$$= 0.2857$$

Of course, r_s is a statistic, and may or may not equal the parameter r_s. Fortunately, it is relatively easy to test the significance of r_s. The procedure will now be described.

1. Select a level of significance $(1 - \alpha)$.
2. Decide whether the test will be for positive relationships, negative relationships, or both.
3. If both relationships are to be tested for, the available values of $(1 - \alpha)$ are in the top row of Table 6 of Appendix 1. If only positive or negative relationships but not both are to be tested for, the second row gives the available values.
4. Note the sample size *N*. The far left column contains all available sample sizes between 6 and 100. Locate the row with the appropriate sample size.
5. Move across the row until you locate the right-most value that is smaller than the absolute value of r_s.
6. Move up this column to whichever of the top two rows is appropriate. If the $(1 - \alpha)$ level is larger than or equal to the $(1 - \alpha)$ level selected earlier, the data are not significant at the selected level.

For example, if a trader decides to conduct a two-sided test of the problem above with a significance of $(1 - 0.95)$ or 0.05, the appropriate value in Table 6 in Appendix 1 is 0.786. As the value for the sample only equals 0.2857, r_s is not significant at the 0.05 level.

Endnotes

1. Allen W. Wallis, and Harry V. Roberts, *Statistics: A New Approach* (New York: The Free Press, 1956): 3. (This, inciden-

tally, is the best introductory book on statistics I know of. Statistics books age slowly.)

2. Actually, there are situations where accepting a 1 to 100 bet is rational. Such a bet is rational, for example, for an individual who owned only $100 and who had no prospect of obtaining more but who needed a minimum of $101 for a project of life-and-death importance. Such situations are rare, of course. The example given is not a counterexample to the idea that making wise decisions is important. It only shows that utility values rather than dollar values must be used. Unfortunately, giving an example in terms of utility values rather than in dollars would obscure rather than clarify the point.
3. The logic of confidence intervals can be more obscure than the logic of standard errors, as, for example, when confidence intervals for the standard deviation are being constructed. In my opinion, however, it is unlikely that the trader will need such tools.
4. Investment statistics almost never have to be adjusted for sample size. The only obvious exceptions are auditing and data correction applications.
5. See Chapter 9 for a discussion of the Cauchey distribution and its investment implications. See Thomas C. Rothenberg, Franklin M. Fisher, and C. B. Tilanus, "A Note on Estimation from a Cauchey Sample," *Journal of the American Statistical Society* (June 1964): 460–463.
6. This is a virtue in some situations, such as quality control analysis. In most other situations, it is not.

9

Avoiding Catastrophic Risk

How Serious Is the Risk?

One of the most serious problems facing the trader is the possibility of catastrophic loss. A catastrophic loss is a loss much larger than the trader budgeted for, much larger than the investment or the margin demanded by the exchange. Traders have been financially ruined by a single bad trade. Without a doubt, it will happen again.

There seem to be two popular attitudes toward catastrophic risk. The first is that the probability of a trader actually being afflicted is so small it is hardly worth considering. The second attitude is that the mere possibility of decimating a large portion of one's wealth should be sufficient to discourage all but the most foolhardy.

Both attitudes contain an element of truth. Clearly, every trader and potential trader should seriously consider the possibility of sustaining a catastrophic loss. It is also clear that those who find the possibility unbearable should not accept such risks.

Catastrophic risk is the risk the trader accepts in addition to the risk of losing trading capital. Obviously, if the trader commits all of her assets to trading, she is accepting no catastrophic risk. Many young traders are in this situation. A trader who has $130,000 in assets and commits $100,000 to trading need worry little about catastrophic loss. If the trader sustains, say, a $500,000 loss, she goes bankrupt, but bankruptcy will be little different than a long series of losing trades. This approach would not be prudent for most traders, especially for most older or corporate traders, of course.

For most traders, a more useful approach would be to shelter some assets from seizure. I am informed that individual investors can shelter assets in several ways. For example, money kept in a qualified retirement plan is safe from seizure until retirement; money kept in a short-term trust is safe from seizure until the money reverts to its settler-creator; and money transferred to other family members before a loss takes place is safe from seizure, but the money is no longer the giver's.

Alternatively, a wholly owned corporation, rather than the trader, can do the trading. Barring fraud of some kind by a stockholder/officer of the firm, a corporation's stockholders are liable only for paid-in capital and any guarantees they may make. Of course, the trader may already be a corporation of some kind, say a pension plan or an endowment fund, that does not want to put its entire capital at risk, in which case, the corporation can spin off a wholly owned subsidiary. As the law is far more capricious than the market, the trader should consult a lawyer before depending on any legal method of sheltering money.

The trader who cannot shelter the majority of his assets should take half an hour or so and imagine what would happen if he lost ten times the amount he was willing to risk. How would he feel? How would his wife feel? How would his children and neighbors feel? If he is a corporate employee, how would his boss or board of directors feel? What actions would these people take? How would he feel about how they felt? What actions would he have to take?

Without a doubt, catastrophic loss is horrible. For many, no potential profit is worth the risk. For others, trading can be worth the risk—if the probability of sustaining a catastrophic loss is small enough. This is an important advantage. Many traders will emphatically not accept such risks. Indeed, many traders are reading this chapter because they do not want such risks. But this does not make the risks go away. Someone else must accept them. Most of the time, this is not an act of charity. If the trader is lucky, it is an act of stupidity. More often, the person or firm accepting the risk is getting paid for it. Considering how emphatic most investors are about avoiding such risk, the investors accepting such risk are probably getting well paid.

But selling something like catastrophic risk insurance to other traders is only worth the money if the premiums are large relative to the risks. How large are the risks?

At one time, economists thought they knew exactly how likely price changes of any given size would be. At that time, economists believed stock and commodity price changes were normally distributed. If price changes were, in fact, normally distributed and if the mean and standard deviation of the distribution were known, *everything* that could be known about that distribution would be known.

Figure 8–3 in Chapter 8 is a drawing of a normal distribution. Like all such drawings, it is incorrect. It is incorrect because the tails of the distribution do not go to infinity, which they should, theoretically. Unfortunately, the publisher, showing a remarkable lack of sympathy for your personal needs, refuses to include any pages of infinite size in this book. In practice, of course, this is scarcely important; beyond, say, three standard deviations from the mean, the tails can hardly be seen.

Indeed, if price changes were, in fact, distributed normally, price changes larger than three standard deviations from the mean should occur fewer than 0.01 of the time; whereas, changes larger than ten standard deviations should almost never happen. If price changes were normally distributed, catastrophic risk would not be a serious problem.

Unfortunately, catastrophic risk is a serious problem.

It came as quite a shock to economists when Mandelbrot announced that certain speculative prices were not normally distributed.[1] The distributions looked normal. Moreover, there were strong mathematical reasons why these distributions should be normal. Nevertheless, Mandelbrot insisted they were not. What Mandelbrot had noticed was that the tails of these distributions were much thicker than they would have been if the distributions were, in fact, normal; therefore, the distributions were not, in fact, normal.

Mandelbrot believed that the appropriate distribution was the stable Paretian family. This announcement was not greeted with any particular pleasure. The mathematics of the normal distribution had been thoroughly studied; the mathematics of the stable Paretian family were hardly understood at all.

Indeed, the distribution is really understood in only three special cases: the coin toss, the normal, and the Cauchy, which we will discuss later. These cases are actually relatively simple. Indeed, all three distributions can be completely described by two variables, such as the mean and standard deviations.

On the other hand, the stable Paretian family requires four variables to describe it: location, scale, skewness, and kurtosis. Location is the central tendency of a distribution; it might be measured by the mean or median. Scale is the width or dispersion of the distribution; it might be measured by the standard deviation or the mean absolute deviation. Skewness is the symmetry of a distribution (see Figure 9–1), and kurtosis is the thickness of the distribution tails (see Figure 9–2).

The most important of the distribution's variables is kurtosis. *The kurtosis of the distribution determines which statistical tools can be used to measure the other three variables.* The kurtosis ($\mathcal{X}$) of a stable Paretian distribution is measured on a scale of zero to two, exclusive of zero, inclusive of two. When the distribution is symmetrical and when $\mathcal{X}$ equals two, the distribution is normal. When the distribution is normal, the mean is a valid measure of location, and the standard deviation is a valid measure of dispersion.

However, as $\mathcal{X}$ drops below two, the standard deviation rapidly becomes meaningless. Fortunately, the mean absolute deviation is a valid measure of dispersion as long as $\mathcal{X}$ is larger than one; unfortunately, the mean absolute deviation and even the mean itself are only valid measures as long as $\mathcal{X}$ is larger than

Figure 9–1

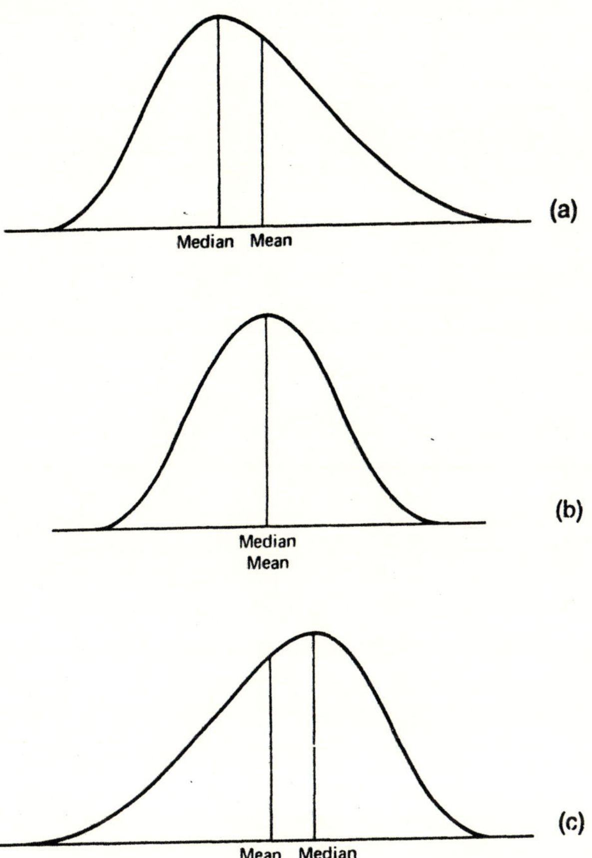

Skewness can be positive (a), nonexistent (b), or negative (c).

one. When χ equals one and when the distribution is symmetrical, the distribution is Cauchy. When the distribution is Cauchy or, more generally, when χ is equal to or smaller than one, it becomes extremely difficult to trade rationally (see Figure 9–3).

Figure 9–2

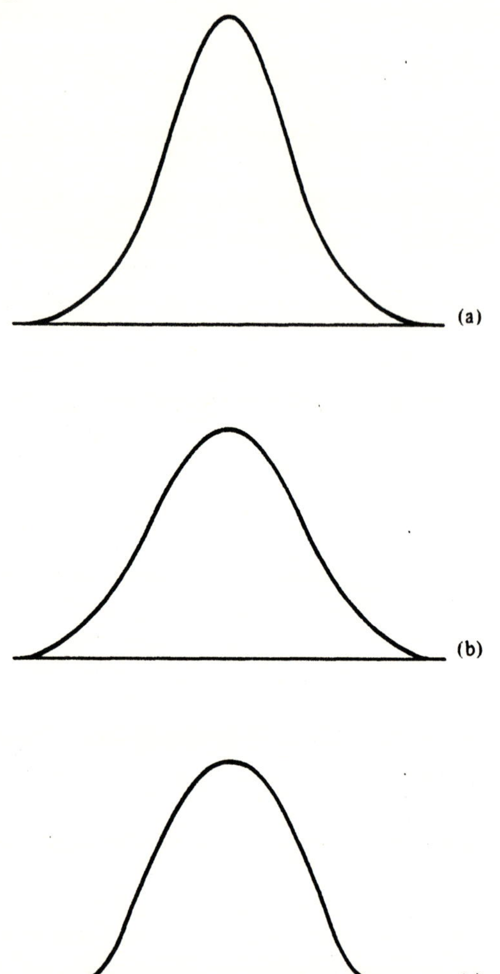

Kurtosis can be peaked (a), nonexistent (b), or flat-topped (c).

The problem is that there is no really desirable, generally usable, valid measure of location for Cauchy-like distributions.

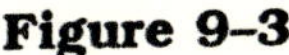

Figure 9–3

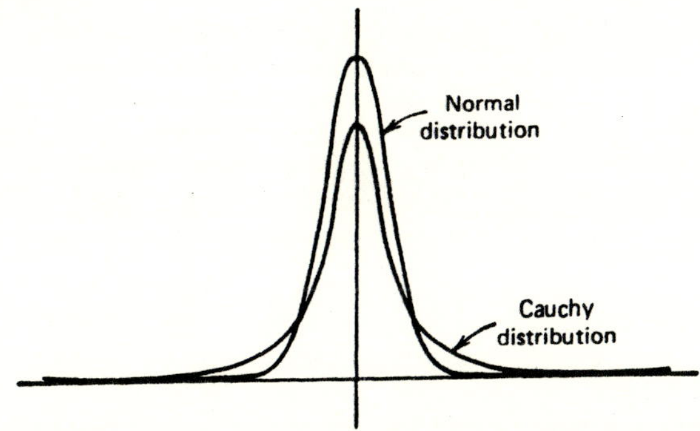

The proper commodity price distribution seems to be somewhere between the normal and the Cauchy, at least if skewness can be ignored. Unfortunately, the student's *t* distribution, the stable Paretian family of distributions, and perhaps other distributions and families of distributions subsume this range.

The most desirable measure of location would be the arithmetic average, the mean. But when $\mathcal{X}$ is equal to or smaller than 1, the mean is not a valid measure. This means that a trading method that had been profitable on average would give *no* assurance whatsoever that the method could be expected to remain profitable. A sample size of a billion would be as useful or useless as a sample size of one.

Location can still be measured. The median is still a valid measure of location for Cauchy-like distributions, for example. However, the median is not really a desirable measure because it does not really tell the trader what he or she wants to know; it is simply available while the mean is not.

Fortunately, prices do not appear to have a Cauchy distribution; at least, no published study of price behavior that I am aware of has found one. Unfortunately, estimates of $\mathcal{X}$ vary radically from sample to sample, so it is difficult to say exactly what $\mathcal{X}$ is, though it seems to be somewhere between one and two (see Table 9–1).

Table 9–1

	Estimates of Degrees of Freedom for Student Model		Estimates of the Characteristic Exponent for the Stable Model		Log-Likelihood Ratios for
	Daily Data	Weekly Data	Daily Data	Weekly Data	Daily Data
Union Carbide	7.6562	23.315	1.71	1.80	14.46
Dupont	6.1215	8.267	1.67	1.76	12.81
Procter and Gamble	3.3021	5.937	1.52	1.80	14.64
Sears	2.8021	4.089	1.55	1.62	9.61
Standard Oil of California	4.8368	5.206	1.62	1.84	17.72
Standard Oil of New Jersey	3.5694	27.040	1.61	1.76	7.85
Swift	4.3281	14.417	1.60	1.78	17.03
Texaco	5.3455	9.657	1.65	1.83	15.48
Bethlehem Steel	4.7830	6.175	1.64	1.77	10.75
Chrysler	6.3715	9.666	1.73	1.77	10.04
Eastman Kodak	5.3542	3.598	1.72	1.47	7.88
United Aircraft	4.8455	10.394	1.66	1.89	8.71
U.S. Steel	13.2600	13.452	1.87	1.80	2.99
Westinghouse	6.1128	8.929	1.73	1.75	10.50
General Electric	4.8368	7.287	1.66	1.70	14.38
General Foods	5.0955	5.281	1.67	1.77	10.19
General Motors	5.0955	6.493	1.68	1.78	9.29
Goodyear	4.8368	11.162	1.65	1.77	8.24
International Harvester	5.1042	8.570	1.72	1.73	4.72
International Nickel	3.8194	6.044	1.58	1.65	11.30
International Paper	5.1042	8.096	1.68	1.60	10.78
Johns Manville	5.8542	8.783	1.77	1.72	6.54
Allied Chemical	5.0417	89.984	1.73	1.94	7.43
Alcoa	4.8368	5.725	1.67	1.86	8.16
American Can	3.3198	4.735	1.65	1.61	7.89
American Telephone and Telegraph	2.5347	2.349	1.45	1.45	10.29
American Tobacco	2.8021	3.351	1.49	1.59	14.29
Anaconda	8.9323	6.731	1.76	1.61	11.27
Woolworth	3.3194	2.561	1.60	1.45	12.61
Owens Illinois	4.5781	9.182	1.60	1.66	14.10

Table 9–1 (continued)

Estimated results for daily rate of return. Notice that in all cases the log-likelihood ratio favors the student's distribution. (A ratio below one would favor the stable model.) Notice also that in 26 of 30 cases, the distribution becomes more normal, that is, the degrees of freedom increase as the sum size or the differencing interval increases. Reprinted from R. Blattberg and N. J. Gonedes. A comparison of the Stable and Student Distributions as Statistical Models for Stock Prices, *The Journal of Business*, Volume 47, No. 2, April 1974, pp. 244–280, by permission of University of Chicago Press © 1974, University of Chicago Press.

Interestingly enough, the stable Paretian family is not the only distribution that provides descriptions ranging from the normal to the Cauchy, inclusive. The student's distribution, which is far better known and understood, does so, also.[2]

The student's distribution, which is invariably symmetrical, requires only three variables to describe it: location, scale, and kurtosis. Location and scale can be measured the same way they can be for the stable Paretian distribution. Kurtosis, however, is measured by a variable known as the degrees of freedom (v) which can take any value from one to infinity, inclusive. When $v = 1$, the distribution is Cauchy; when v is infinite, the distribution is normal.

The stable Paretian distribution and the student's distribution differ in several ways. The most obvious is that the stable distribution can describe skewed data, which the student's distribution cannot. A more important difference is that the standard deviation of the stable Paretian distributions rapidly becomes a meaningless measure of scale as $\mathcal{X}$ drops below two. On the other hand, the standard deviation of the student's distribution only becomes meaningless when v is relatively close to one. This allows the trader to use many more powerful statistical tools.

Another important difference is that the stable Paretian distribution is stable; whereas, the student's distribution is not. If the distribution is stable, kurtosis will remain constant, regardless of the differencing interval, that is, the time period between the events being measured. On the other hand, location, scale, and skewness will increase in proportion to any increase in the differencing interval. For example, if the distribution is stable and if the mean daily price change is $\ddot{X}$, the standard deviation of the mean daily price change is $\ddot{S}$, and the kurtosis is $\ddot{\mathcal{X}}$, the mean weekly (five-day) price change will be $5\ddot{X}$, the standard deviation of the weekly price change will be $5\ddot{S}$, and the kurtosis of the weekly price change will be $\ddot{\mathcal{X}}$.

On the other hand, if the distribution is not stable, that is, if it converges, the distribution's kurtosis will decrease as the differencing interval increases. This will have no effect on the mean, which will remain stable, but the skewness and standard deviation will decrease as the differencing interval increases. For example, if the distribution is not stable and if the mean daily price change is $\ddot{X}$, the standard deviation is $\ddot{S}$, and the kurtosis is $\ddot{\mathcal{X}}$, the mean weekly price change will be $5\ddot{X}$, the standard deviation will be less than $5\ddot{S}$, and the kurtosis will be less than $\ddot{\mathcal{X}}$.

Interestingly enough, academic studies of stock-price behavior have found that the distributions converge. Although there is considerable kurtosis in daily price-data, there is considerably less in weekly data (Table 9–1). Indeed, when monthly data are considered, kurtosis may disappear almost completely.

The available evidence indicates that stock and probably commodity-price distributions resemble a student's distribution more closely than they do a stable Paretian distribution. Unfortunately, stock-price distributions and possibly commodity-price distributions are frequently skewed.[3] As the student's distribution cannot describe skewed data, the student's distribution cannot adequately describe some price behavior.

The fact is that no one knows how prices are *really* distributed, and without this information it is impossible to accurately calculate risk, either catastrophic or otherwise. In other words, *part of the risk a trader must accept is not knowing the full extent of the risk.*

On the other hand, if the trader plans carefully, the probability of sustaining a catastrophic loss might be smaller than the above analysis suggests. In other words, to some extent catastrophic loss is probably avoidable.

There are both strategic and tactical approaches to eliminating or minimizing catastrophic risk. Strategic approaches do not involve forecasting; tactical approaches do. Strategic approaches will be discussed first.

Eliminating Catastrophic Risk

A trader with exposed assets can eliminate catastrophic risk only by legally shifting the risk to someone else or by trading only certain limited-risk speculations. Some money managers and brokerage firms are willing to limit the trader's risk to his or her investment, in effect insuring the trader against catastrophic loss. In return, they demand large advisory fees or commissions and partial or total control over trading.

Limited-risk speculations allow the trader considerably more control. These speculations include options and certain spreads. The trader obviously should restrict him- or herself to those options and spreads that can be expected to be profitable on average. Whether this can be expected of any given option will depend on the price the investor paid for it and the probability of the underlying investment moving as forecasted. In recent years a great deal of work, academic and otherwise, has been done on option pricing;[4] the trader should become familiar with it before buying his or her first option.

Spreads, per se, are neither more nor less dangerous than outright positions; however, certain spreads, which are known as carrying-charge spreads, will indeed limit the trader's risk. Unfortunately, the logic and location of these spreads are so well known that there is little point in describing them here. If there is little risk in trading them, there is also little reason. Indeed, there are so many traders trying to exploit these spreads, it would be remarkable if there were any profit potential left.

The problem with these techniques is that they are quite expensive in terms of profit potential. It is clearly pointless, for example, to buy an option that is so expensive there is no chance or almost no chance of selling it profitably. This, unfortunately, is all too often the case. In such cases, the trader would be better off either accepting the risk of catastrophic loss or foregoing trading altogether.

There are at least two strategies that will reduce catastrophic risk, although they will not eliminate it. One strategy is to minimize the time the trader is in the market. This will be discussed shortly. The other strategy is to limit trading to times and places where limits are enforced. Currently, this limits trading to American exchanges.

American exchanges enforce several types of price limits. For example, currently the S&P 500 cannot change more than 500 points in the first five minutes of trading. If it does, the market is shut down for five minutes. Another type of limit prevents a price from moving more than a certain amount above or below the previous day's close. There are still other types.

Trading need not stop when the price hits a limit. Occasionally, for example, the price will hit an upper and lower limit during a day's trading, sometimes more than once. A rational price change larger than the limits allow will still happen, but it will happen over several days' time. For example, it took the Mexican peso five days to drop from .078 to .048. Presumably, without limits, it would have dropped that distance in a single day (see Figure 9–4).

On the other hand, limits *will* impede large irrational price changes. Suppose, for example, the Mexican peso's proper price was .070, but the peso was already at .060. A limit would allow investors time to take advantage of the bargain. The more time investors have, the less likely it is that the price will drop as far as it would without limits.

Figure 9–4

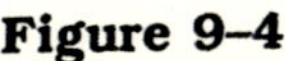

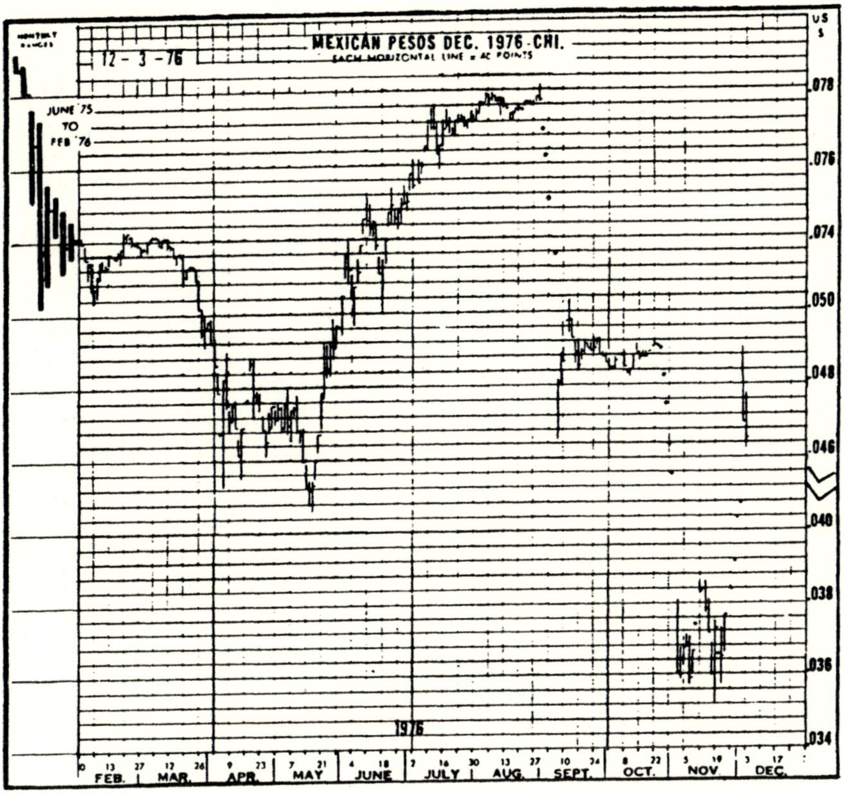

December 1976 Mexican Peso (International Money Market). From Commodity Chart Service.

This is not necessarily a virtue, however. Profits can only be made when the market acts irrationally; a more rational market will be a less potentially profitable one. Nevertheless, if the trader is willing to give up some profit potential, he or she will find the risks of catastrophic loss less on exchanges that enforce price limits.

Unfortunately, not all exchanges have price limits. British exchanges, for example, do not. Furthermore, many American exchanges do not enforce price limits during the last month a contract is traded. Therefore, prices are unusually volatile during this time, and it is not a prudent time to trade (see Figure 9–5).

The second strategy for reducing catastrophic risk is to minimize the time the trader is in the market. For example, a futures trader should try to minimize and aggregate the number of contract-days held. For foreign-exchange, risk-arbitrage traders, and others, the terms change, but the concepts are the same. The number of contract-days held, over some period of time, is the sum of the number of contracts the trader holds on each day that he or she holds one or more. For example, if a trader buys three contracts on Monday's opening and sells them on Tuesday's opening, and then buys one contract on Wednesday's opening and sells it on the following Monday's opening, he or she has held eight contract-days over the calendar week.

All other things being equal, the greater the number of contract days a trader holds, the greater the catastrophic risk. All other things being equal, the trader who buys eight contracts on Wednesday's open and sells them all on the next open is accepting the same catastrophic risk as the trader above.

But all other things are never equal. If a catastrophic loss is likely to bankrupt the trader, it may make more sense to aggregate the number of contract-days held as much as possible. This minimizes the probability of a catastrophic loss but increases the size of the loss if, in fact, a loss takes place. But then, the magnitude of the loss need not concern the trader if he or she goes bankrupt; legally, going bankrupt with $50,000 in debts is exactly the same as going bankrupt with $5,000,000 in debts.[5] On the other hand, if catastrophic losses are not likely to bankrupt the trader, but only cause considerable pain, it makes more sense to equally distribute the number of contract-days held as much as possible. This will maximize the probability of being affected but will minimize the effect if, in fact, a disaster takes place.

Figure 9-5

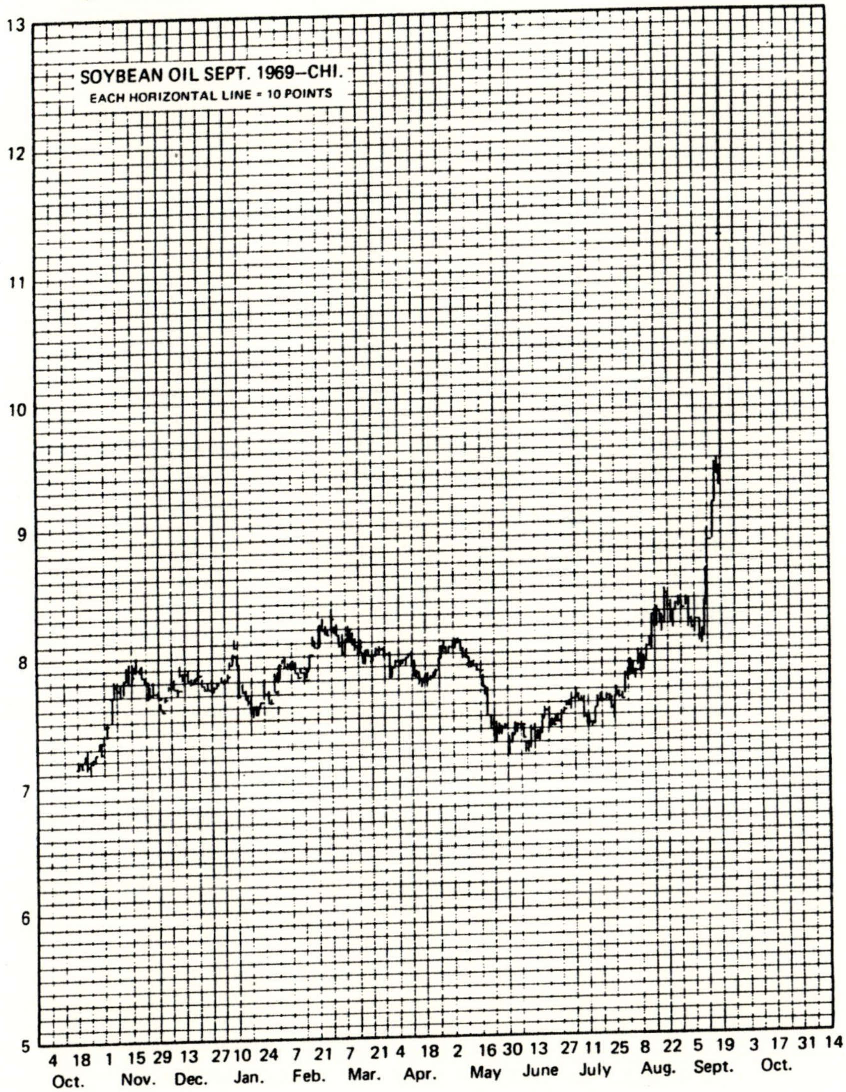

September 1969 Soybean Oil (Chicago Board of Trade). From Commodity Chart Service.

Notice that aggregating the number of contract-days held is likely to increase the noncatastrophic risk, which is really much more important than the catastrophic risk. Thus, the two strategies described above are likely to be of marginal benefit.

Tactical approaches involve forecasting the market. These will be discussed next.

Forecasting Catastrophic Risk

The extent to which the market can successfully be forecasted is the extent to which its causes can be understood. Because massive changes in price are caused by massive changes in the fundamentals, it is necessary to study these. Case studies of catastrophic price changes reveal at least four different types of fundamental change.

The first, most obvious, and most unpleasant type of massive fundamental change is a sudden emergence or disappearance of a powerful source of supply or demand. The 1973 wheat market (see Figure 9–6) is an example.

The sharp increase in the price of wheat was caused by a sharp increase in the foreign demand for wheat. Russian demand for wheat had not been an important market factor for years, and there was no reason to believe it would be then. Russian buying, in effect, was a powerful, random, exogenous shock to the market.

A second, less obvious, but more predictable type of massive fundamental change is the sudden but conditional emergence or disappearance of a source of supply or demand. The 1977 orange freeze provides an example of this type of catastrophe (see Figure 9–7). At certain times of the year the orange crop is susceptible to frost damage; at other times it is not. If a trader can forecast the seasons, he can forecast the danger of being in the orange juice market; he need not be able to forecast the weather. An orange freeze is, in effect, a powerful, conditional, exogenous shock to the market.[6]

Figure 9-6

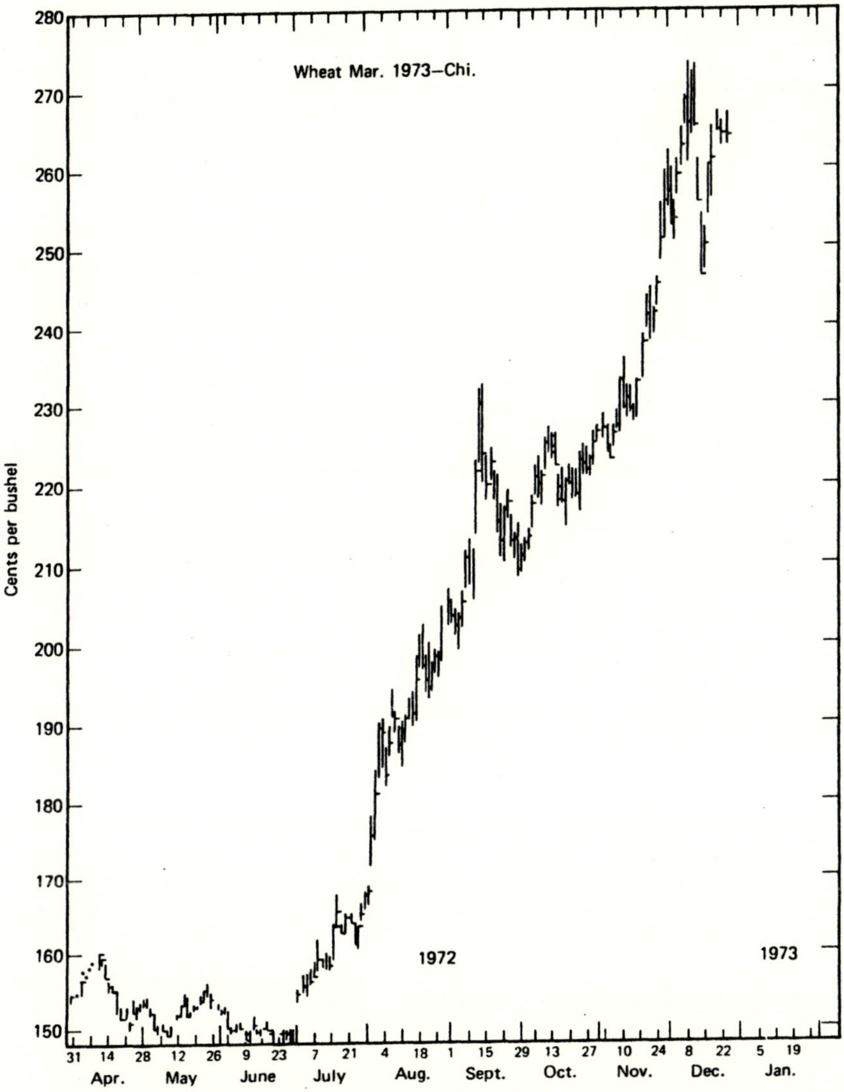

March 1973 Wheat (Chicago Board of Trade). From Commodity Chart Service.

Figure 9–7

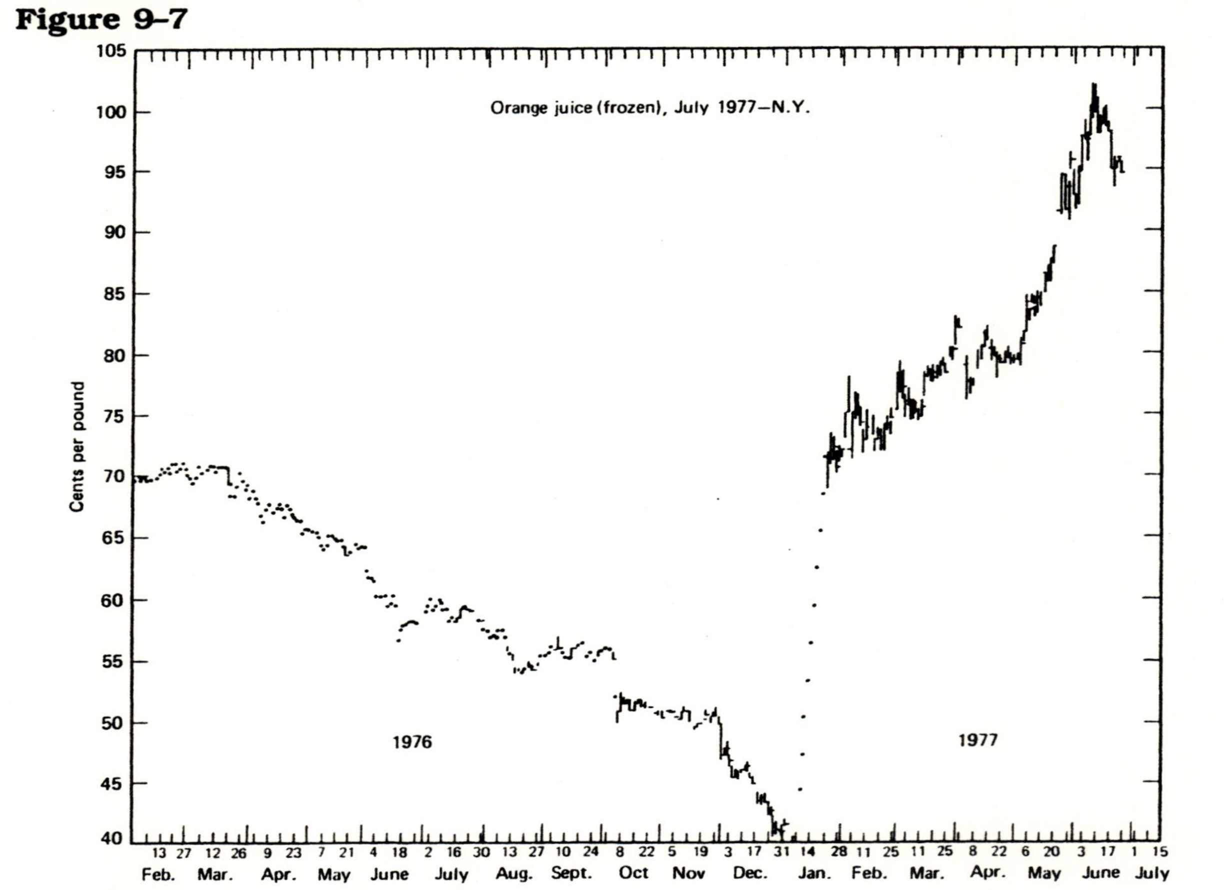

July 1977 Orange Juice. From Commodity Chart Service.

A third, still less obvious, but still more predictable type of massive fundamental change is a *gradual* change in the fundamentals that causes a sudden emergence or disappearance of a form of supply or demand. The trader will find it easier to understand this concept if she takes the time to make and play with the toy in Figure 9–8.

Figure 9–8

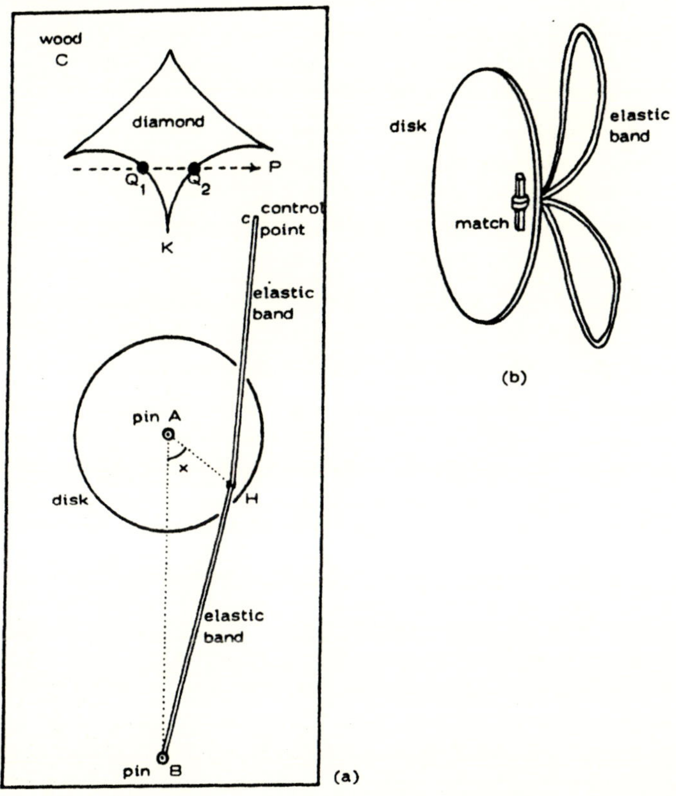

(a) a catastrophe machine; (b) how to attach the elastic bands. From E.C. Zeeman, *Catastrophe Theory Selected Papers, 1972-1977*, Addison-Wesley, Reading, MA, 1977, p. 9.

The materials needed are two elastic bands, two drawing pins, half a matchstick, a piece of cardboard, and a piece of wood. Taking the unstretched length of an elastic band as our unit of length, cut out a cardboard disk of diameter about one unit. Attach the two elastic bands to a point near the edge of the disk. The easiest way to do this is to pierce a small hole at H, push little loops of the elastic bands through the hole, and secure them by slipping the matchstick through the loops and pulling tight (as in Figure 9–8). Now pin the center of the disk to the piece of wood with drawing pin A (with the elastic bands on the top and the matchstick underneath), and make sure that it spins freely. Fix the other drawing pin B into the wood, so that AB is about two units, and then hook one of the elastic bands over B. The machine is now ready to go.

Hold the other end of the other elastic band; where you hold it is the *control point* C. Therefore, the control space C is the surface of the wood. Meanwhile, the *state* of the machine is in the position of the disk, and this is measured by the angle X = BAH. When the control C is moved smoothly, the state X will follow suit, except that sometimes instead of moving smoothly, it will suddenly jump.[7]

The control point corresponds to the market's fundamentals and the state to the market price. The sudden jump corresponds to a catastrophic price change.

A real-world example is the 1976 Mexican peso devaluation (see Figure 9–4). For decades, the Mexican government had pegged the price of the peso to the U.S. dollar by buying pesos whenever they fell below the price of $.078 per peso. At the same time, the Mexican government had inflated the money supply relative to that of the United States. Although in terms of the U.S. dollar the price of the peso was stable, its value was steadily eroding. It was obvious, therefore, that if the peso was devalued, anyone holding pesos at that time would lose a great deal. It was also obvious that unless radical and unlikely changes in the fundamentals took place, sooner or later the Mexican government would have to devalue the peso. When the Mexican government finally devalued the peso, prices collapsed.

A fourth, more obvious, and still more predictable type of massive fundamental change is one that takes place in a market so unstable that one massive fundamental change can be expected to follow another. A real-world example is the 1979–80 gold market (see Figure 9–9). In one sense, the cause of each catastrophic price-change differed: Each change was caused by a different radical change in the international political economy. However, in another sense, the causes were the same: international political instability. The trader need not have understood

Figure 9–9

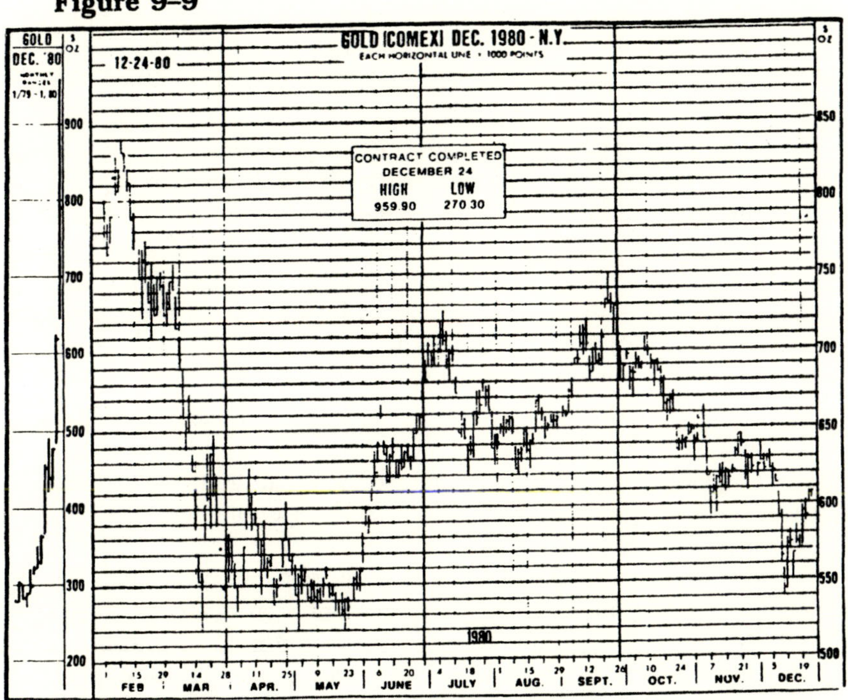

December 1980 Gold (International Money Market). From Commodity Chart Service.

international political economics to have understood the danger of trading gold.

The above analysis permits or demands several conclusions. The first is that the degree to which a trader can avoid catastrophic risk depends on his knowledge of market fundamentals.

Prudent trading demands fundamental analysis. In most of the cases above, the technical trader could not have avoided catastrophe.

This seriously limits the trader's ability to diversify. As few traders understand the fundamentals of more than a few investments in any depth, few traders can trade more than one or two investments with relative safety. If the trader accepts a smaller portfolio to reduce the probability of sustaining a catastrophic loss, she will have to make larger commitments per investment. All other things being equal, this will increase the size of the loss, if a loss takes place.

On the other hand, the trader does not need to know what the fundamentals imply on average, he need only know what the extreme implications are. The trader does not even have to do the research himself. He can buy the research from a brokerage firm or investment advisory service. If there are no extreme implications, or if he can live with them, then all is well. But if there is an extreme implication he cannot live with, he needs to know about it and take appropriate action. For example, a bond arbitrager does not have to be able to interpret the Federal Reserve Bureau's esoteric pronouncements. But he does need to know enough about Federal Reserve Bureau policy to understand a Fed watcher when he says there is a chance of a large increase or decrease in rates.

A lower level of knowledge provides less protection, of course. On the other hand, the trader can then diversify more, which is more important. For example, a technical futures-market trader need not understand Fed policy or weather in depth, but he does need to know enough to understand those who do understand these issues. And he needs to use them to understand when his positions are in danger, and how much danger they are in.

A second conclusion is that efforts to avoid catastrophic risk are clearly subject to diminishing returns (see Chapter 12, Figure 12–1). Some catastrophic risks may be easily avoided; for example, even the most cursory examination of the 1979–80 gold market would have revealed the danger of trading in it. Indeed, the most cursory glance at the price charts should have revealed the market's instability.

Unfortunately, the charts would not reveal the danger of trading the Mexican peso. Fortunately, the fundamentals would. Clearly, as long as the peso was pegged to the dollar, the *only* purpose a futures contract for the peso could have had was to provide a place to hedge against, or to gamble on, the peso's potential devaluation. It should have been clear at the time that those who best understood the economics believed there was a reasonable chance of a devaluation. Otherwise, why a contract?

Interestingly enough, if the trader read the financial press, she would have seen that the devaluation was imminent. Several weeks before the devaluation, the Mexican government took out full-page ads in *The Wall Street Journal* and other publications to announce that the peso would not be devalued. Such announcements frequently precede devaluations.

In the case of orange juice, the situation is somewhat different. A freeze is a mere possibility, not an inevitability. However, the fact that oranges are subject to periodic freezes is well known; thus a trader who had made a reasonably thorough study of the fundamentals should have been able to avoid this disaster.

Unfortunately, in the case of the 1973 wheat market or the October 1987 stock market, there is simply no reason to believe the average trader could have anticipated the risk. Indeed, with the exceptions of the governments of the United States and what was then the Soviet Union and, perhaps some of the larger grain companies, no one was aware of the potential turmoil in the wheat market until it was too late.

Clearly, if an individual is going to trade, he is going to have to accept some risk of catastrophic loss. As more and more risk is avoided, it clearly will become progressively harder to avoid what remains, until finally there will be risk that can be avoided only at an excessive price, if it can be avoided at all.

The problem, of course, is not avoiding risk, but selecting the "right" risks, that is, risks that promise an adequate reward. This is not an easy task.

Endnotes

1. B. Mandelbrot, "The Variation of Certain Speculative Prices," *Journal of Business*, Vol. 36, No. 4 (1963): 394–419.
2. P.D. Praetz, "The Distribution of Share Price Changes," *Journal of Business*, Vol. 45 (January 1972). Pages 49–55 appear to describe the first research on this topic; unfortunately, however, Praetz's work is seriously flawed. More reliable is R.C. Blattberg and H.J. Gomedes, "A Comparison of the Stable and Student Distributions as Statistical Models for Stock Prices," *Journal of Business*, Vol. 47, No. 2 (April 1974): 244–280.
3. "Asymmetric Stable Distributed Security Returns," *Journal of the American Statistical Association* (June 1980): 306–312.
4. For example, R.A. Jarrow and A.R. Rudd, *Option Pricing* (Homewood, IL: Dow Jones-Irwin, 1983). There are many excellent options books available.
5. Planning for a possible bankruptcy is *not* fraud as long as the trader honestly presents his or her financial position to the brokerage firm. Brokerage firms are very well aware of the risk of catastrophic loss and are free to reject the account. Incidentally, the behavior of most brokerage firms is less than honorable here. Many firms will not open accounts for individuals whose total assets do not substantially exceed the amount they will devote to trading. This protects the com-

pany against a default if the trader suffers a catastrophic loss, and, of course, there is nothing unethical about this. What is unethical is the implication that this practice is enforced only for the protection of the trader, not for the mutual protection of the trader and the firm. Worse, most brokerage firms give little or no warning of the risks involved.

6. The October 19, 1987, stock-market meltdown seems to me to have been caused, to a large extent, by a conditional emergence of supply-portfolio insurance. On the other hand, many of the smartest people in the industry say quite frankly that they have no idea what caused the meltdown.
7. E.C. Zeeman, *Catastrophe Theory: Selected Papers, 1972–1977*, (Reading, MA: Addison-Wesley, 1977): 8, 10.

10

Avoiding Avoidable Risk through Portfolio Theory

Theory

The virtue of applying portfolio theory to trading has been lauded at length—and well it should be. Modern portfolio theory is almost the only area of trading where there is certainty. Unfortunately, it is possible to abuse even the most powerful techniques. In recent years, the promotional literature of several brokerage firms and advisory services have implied that portfolio trading will produce certain or near certain profits. Of course, it will do no such thing.

Portfolio investing need be nothing more than making several simultaneous *investments*.[1] Portfolio theory, on the other hand, is the use of probability theory to account and budget for certain types of risk. As there are few facts more well established about investing or trading than its risk, this task is critical. However, trading a portfolio will no more ensure market success than will having an accountant.

Although portfolio theory is an important tool, it is not the only tool needed. Claims to the contrary notwithstanding, portfolio theory will not forecast the market. But given forecasts and their probable error, it will suggest the amount and type of diversification advisable.

Assuming that none of the streams of profits and losses from the investments are perfectly correlated with each other (see Figure 10–1), that each of the investments can be traded profitably, and that costs are nonexistent, it can be proven that trading yet another investment will always lower risk. Alternatively, the same risk can be taken for a higher expected return (see Figure

Figure 10–1

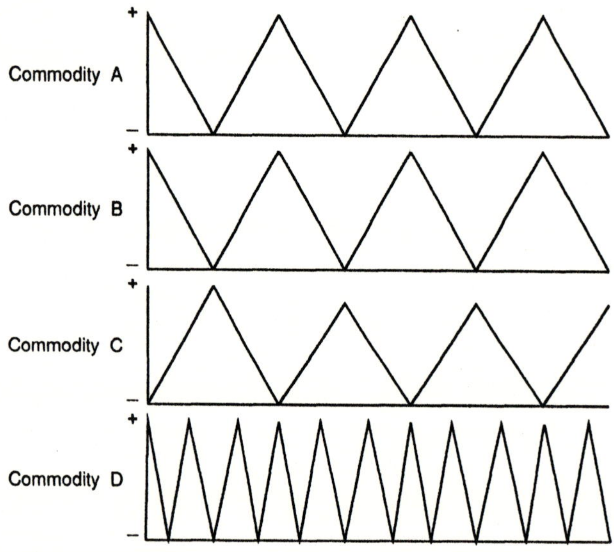

The correlation coefficient C expresses the relationship between two variables by a number from +1 to –1 inclusive. Profits and losses from trading commodities *A* and *B* are perfectly correlated (C = + 1); a $500 profit in Commodity *A* would be accompanied by a $500 profit in Commodity *B*, for example. Trading profits and losses from *B* and *C* are negatively correlated (C = –1); a $500 profit in Commodity *B* would be accompanied by a $500 loss in Commodity *C*. Profits and losses in *C* and *D* have no correlation (C = 0). For a more general explanation, see Chapter 8.

Figure 10–2

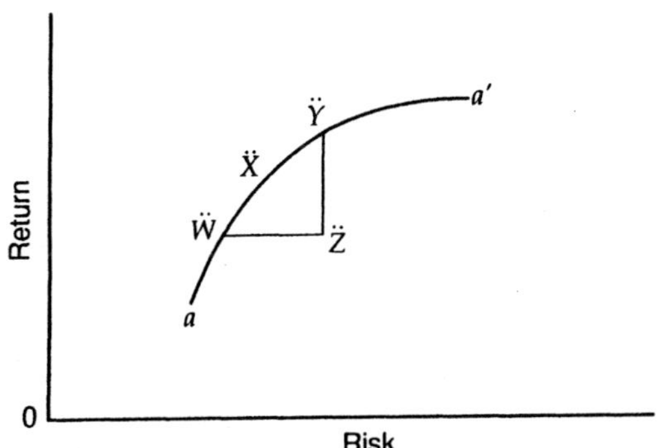

Of all conceivable combinations of risk and return, only those on or to the right of line *a–a′* are obtainable by investor Ä. If investor Ä holds portfolio Z̈, he can acquire a portfolio with a higher return, a lower risk, or both.

10–2). How serious are these caveats? Profits are never or almost never perfectly correlated. As we shall see below, costs are a serious, but not fatal, problem. But if an investor cannot invest profitably, he is in serious trouble. If an investor cannot invest profitably, on average, diversification will only ensure ruin. If such an investor must invest, the most reasonable plan would be to trade infrequently. An even better plan, of course, would be to give up trading.

Strictly speaking, proper diversification demands quadratic programming, a hideously complicated mathematical technique. Quadratic programming takes as input the expected returns and risks and the correlations between the investments or trades that will be in the portfolio. Then the program suggests weightings for the investments or trades based on the trader's objectives and constraints, which the trader must state in mathematical form. In one sense, quadratic programming is fairly easy to use: A number of software vendors sell quadratic programming products.

By pointing the program at the data and hitting a few keys, anyone can produce a report.

In another sense, this technique is extremely difficult to use. Quadratic programs will sometimes produce unbalanced portfolios; such a program might well put 75 percent of the trader's money into one investment. More, quadratic programs sometimes radically shift the weighting of the investments in the portfolio from month to month. The weighting in a particular investment media might go from 5 percent to 30 percent to 2 percent, when nothing much has changed in the economy.

Typically, a trader will try to fix such problems by setting an upper limit to the amount he or she will commit to a particular investment in the portfolio or by using a moving average of the recommended portfolio commitments.[2] Other problems have similar fixes. But all such fixes avoid the real problem, which is that some of the data are probably unrealistic. If the data *are* realistic, the suggested actions are correct, of course. But if the data are *not* realistic, the data should be changed.

But which of the data? Part of the problem is the amount of data a quadratic program demands: Estimates of the returns and risks for each investment and a correlation coefficient for about half of each pair of investments.[3] For example, a quadratic program demands 65 estimates for a ten-investment portfolio. The other part of the problem is that it is impossible to know which of the numbers are likely to be important without understanding the mathematics of the method, which most traders find occult. I therefore recommend other, more transparent, techniques.

Edwin Elton and Martin Gruber, both of New York University, have shown that the Sharpe ratio for a group of investments can be used to allocate funds. Sharpe's Ratio (*SR*) is one method of adjusting for risk and reward.[4] Here reward is the expected mean return per investment (*EX*), and risk is the standard deviation of returns (*SD*). In addition, a measure is needed of the riskless rate of return, that is, the rate that could be earned without trading (*I*). By definition, the Sharpe ratio of any investment is

$$SR = (EX - I)/SD$$

What follows is a simplification and adaptation of the work of Elton and Gruber.[5] Assuming the correlation coefficients of a group of investments are all equal and the Sharpe ratios for a group of investments are all positive, Elton, Gruber, and Padbury suggest summing the Sharpe ratios for the various investments and then dividing the Sharpe ratio for each investment by the resulting sum. The resulting proportion for a given investment is the proportion of the available funds that should be allocated to it (see Figure 10–3).

Assuming the Sharpe ratio is positive is not a particularly dangerous assumption. If the Sharpe ratio for a particular investment is zero, the trader does not trade that investment. Theoretically, if the Sharpe ratio for a particular investment is negative, the trader might reverse the signs of the investment, buying when he or she would have sold, and vice versa. This is not always possible.

Assuming the correlation coefficients of a group of investments are all equal is more serious. This is never true, but neither is it a fatal problem. As long as the correlation coefficients are fairly close, a group average can be used. For a small or medium-sized portfolio, one approach would be to select the investment with the highest Sharpe ratio from each group of related investment (meats, currencies, etc.) and construct the portfolio from these investments.

Another approach is to use the techniques above to construct portfolios for each group of related investments and then to combine these portfolios into a single portfolio by using the same technique again. In this case, each subportfolio would consist of one or more investments but perhaps not all of the investments that might be included. But if not all of the available investments, how many?

Portfolio theory suggests that under all but the most extreme situations, every investment that can be traded profitably

Figure 10–3

Investment	Mean Return	Standard Deviation of Return(s)	Sharpe Ratio	Portfolio Weighting
A	50	100 =	0.5000 ÷ 3.9166 =	0.1277
B	75	90 =	0.8333 ÷ 3.9166 =	0.2128
C	60	80 =	0.7500 ÷ 3.9166 =	0.1915
D	100	75 =	1.3333 ÷ 3.9166 =	0.3404
C	40	80 =	0.5000 ÷ 3.9166 =	0.1276
Total			3.9166	1.0000

The Sharpe ratio is the mean return of an investment divided by its standard deviation of returns. The portfolio weighting for an investment is its Sharpe ratio divided by the sum of the Sharpe ratios.

However, assume that the trader will commit no more than 0.25 of available funds to any investment. Investment D is therefore assigned a weighting of 0.25 and the other investments recalculated. Divide the Sharpe ratio for an investment by the sum of the Sharpe ratios for those investments not assigned a weighting. Multiply this by the proportion of the portfolio that remains to be allocated. Because one investment already has been set at 0.25, the remaining investments must be multiplied by (1 – 0.25) = 0.75.

Investment	Set at Upper Boundary	Sharpe Ratio	Portfolio Weight of Remaining Investments	Portfolio Weighting
A		0.5000 ÷ 2.5833 = 0.1936 × 0.75 =	0.1452	0.1452
B		0.8333 ÷ 2.5833 = 0.3226 × 0.75 =	0.2419	0.2419
C		0.7500 ÷ 2.5833 = 0.2903 × 0.75 =	0.2177	0.2177
D	0.25			0.25
E	____	0.5000 ÷ 2.5833 = 0.1936 × 0.75 =	0.1452	0.1452
Total	0.25	2.5833	0.7500	1.0000

should be traded to some extent. In the real world, this is simply not possible. Trades are not infinitely divisible, as classic theory demands—they can be acquired only in fairly large "lumps." Moreover, because diversification costs, additional diversification beyond a certain point may lower the return and only minimally reduce risk. There is no easy way to determine the optimal amount of diversification. Currently, the best that can be done is to set up a spreadsheet where each column represents the costs and benefits of trading one more investment.

The benefits of diversification come in the form of increased return, or reduced risk, or both. Theoretically, it is possible to collapse return and risk into one number. One way to do this is to estimate the average *geometric* return over the next period. The geometric return times the amount of money under management tells how much the trader can expect to earn next period. This number should go up with diversification, irrespective of whether the trader tries to increase return or reduce risk.

In the geometric return, N sample values are multiplied together and the Nth root taken. If $N = 2$, the square root is taken. If $N = 10$, the tenth root is taken. Thus, if the sample is: 1.25, 0.95, 1.15, 1.5 then $N = 4$ then, the product of the four numbers is 2.0484 and the fourth root is: 1.19. Notice that the N sample values must be proportional returns, not percentage returns. A return of 0.95 indicates a 5 percent loss, not a gain of just under 1 percent. The geometric average shows how fast earnings under risk will compound. The geometric average can be found on some pocket calculators and spreadsheets.

The two primary costs of diversification are research costs and transaction costs. Marginal research costs may be minimal if the trader or fund manager has a computerized trading method that does not vary from investment to investment. On the other hand, marginal costs may be extensive if the trader must personally analyze each investment's fundamentals. Transaction costs consist of commission and execution costs. Commissions may go up as the dollars committed per investment go down, which will happen with diversification. Execution costs depend on the liquidity of the market. If the trader is trading in large amounts, execution costs will go down with diversification.

If we assume that the risks, returns, and profit correlations for all investments are equal (see Figure 10–4) and that N is the number of investments traded, Bierman[6] shows that the propor-

Figure 10-4

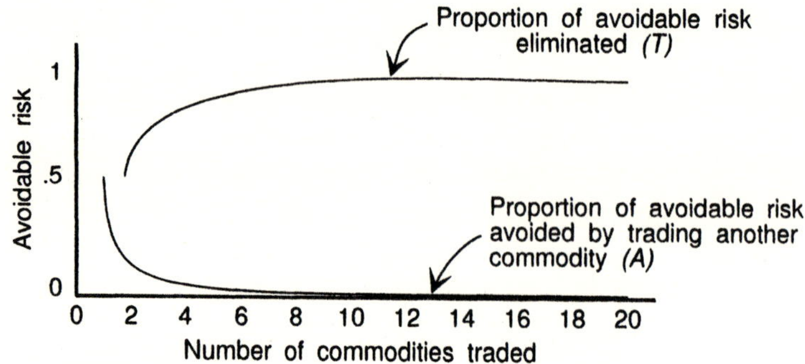

The amount that each additional commodity reduces the "avoidable" risk diminishes quickly.

tion of the risk eliminated of the total avoidable risk (T) is (see Figure 10–5)

$$T = (N - 1)/N$$

The proportion of the total avoidable risk avoided by trading another investment (A) is

$$A = 1/[N(N + 1)]$$

Thus, if $N = 5$ then $T = 0.8$ and $A = 0.03$

The amount of avoidable risk is a function of the portfolio correlation coefficient. A correlation coefficient is a number between one and minus one, inclusive, where one indicates a perfect and positive correlation, minus one indicates a negative correlation, and zero indicates no correlation at all. Bierman assumes that negative correlations do not exist, which is almost certainly true.

The total avoidable risk can never be lowered below the portfolio's correlation coefficient—no matter how large a portfo-

Figure 10–5

Number of Investments Traded								
	1	1	1.00	1.00	1.0000	1.0000	1.0000	1.000
	2	1	0.90	0.75	0.6250	0.6000	0.5500	0.500
	3	1	0.87	0.67	0.5000	0.4664	0.3997	0.333
	4	1	0.85	0.63	0.4375	0.4000	0.3250	0.250
	5	1	0.84	0.60	0.4000	0.3600	0.2800	0.200
	10	1	0.82	0.55	0.3250	0.2800	0.2400	0.100
	20	1	0.82	0.53	0.2875	0.2400	0.1900	0.050
	∞	1	0.80	0.50	0.2500	0.2000	0.1000	0.000
		1	0.80	0.50	0.2500	0.2000	0.1000	0.000

Correlation Coefficient of Investments Traded

Amount of remaining "avoidable" risk. From H. Bierman, "Diversification: Is There Safety in Numbers?" Reprinted with permission of *The Journal of Portfolio Management,* Fall 1978, Vol. 5, No. 1, p. 30.

lio is traded. If the risk and return for all investments in the portfolio are equal and the correlation coefficient is 0.8, the risk can never be lowered below 0.8 of the risk on a single investment. An examination of Figure 10–5 shows, in this case, that there is little reason to diversify beyond two or three investments. As the average correlation coefficient drops, additional diversification makes more sense. For some traders the only way to determine the number of investments to trade is to glare at Figure 10–5 and guess.

Practice

One problem in using techniques such as those presented above is that they all make assumptions known to be false. Unfortunately, there is no alternative to using such formulas except guessing. There are at least four problems in using portfolio-management techniques: catastrophic risk, changing market conditions, new money, and problems coordinating portfolio-management and market-commitment techniques. I will discuss each of these problems in turn.

Catastrophic Risk

A substantially capitalized and diversified account could withstand even catastrophic loss as long as such losses are rare and independent. As perusal of any historical chart book will demonstrate, catastrophic losses are rare—or at least catastrophic price changes are. More important, catastrophic risk is often foreseeable. Techniques for managing catastrophic risk are discussed in Chapter 9.

For the most part, price movements do seem to be independent. However, monetary and political pressures can cause diverse investments to move together. At such times, diversification is of little use. If the trader cannot forecast such changes, he or she can at least hedge against them by keeping a considerable proportion of his or her assets in cash. In such a case, it is probably prudent to commit even less capital to the market than the formulas in Chapter 11 recommend.

A more interesting, difficult, costly, but safer technique is to risk approximately the same amount on the long and short sides at any given time. One reason it is difficult to use this technique is that there are other, often conflicting, criteria for choosing which investment to trade.

Changing Market Conditions

Strictly speaking, most portfolio-management techniques assume that the portfolio will be optimized once. But trades only last a little while, while everything else changes constantly. Thus, some kind of reoptimization must be done on a regular or irregular basis.

In order to minimize costs, as much reoptimization as possible should be done when trades are normally done, when buy and sell signals are generated, or when action is taken because an asset has matured. In many cases, this will not be enough. Frequently, prices or fundamentals will move enough to unbalance the portfolio, without moving enough to generate buy and sell signals.

When the portfolio must be reoptimized between buy and sell signals, as little as possible should be done. This implies that the trader must tolerate a certain slack in the system, a certain distance between the optimal and actual weights. This in turn implies that the trader will optimize the portfolio when the slack becomes intolerable, not on a calendar basis.

The amount of slack a trader must tolerate depends partly on how much it costs to rebalance the portfolio, partly on how often the trader trades naturally, and partly on the relationship between what I call the trader's external and internal portfolio. All traders have an external portfolio, a portfolio of assets or investments they might trade. Typically, this is two to ten times the size of their internal portfolio, that is, the portfolio they are trading at any given time. There are exceptions, of course. At one extreme, some hedge funds claim they will trade anything. At the other extreme, some trend followers must have a position in every investment in their external portfolio; their external and internal portfolios are the same.

The bigger the difference between a trader's external and internal portfolios, the more slack must be allowed in the system. For many trading styles, money committed to the market must wait until a trade is available. For example, for a portfolio that allows trades in gold, silver, and platinum only and long, short, or neutral positions, a neutral position in platinum means money committed to the market will actually stay idle. Alternatively, for a portfolio that allows trades in grains, energy contracts, and meats only, the lack of a meat trade may mean the first meat-trade that comes along gets all of the money committed to that part of the portfolio. Multiple meat-trades may not come along often enough to let money sit idle.

There is no obvious formula for determining how much slack the portfolio should have. This means that the trader must depend on complicated Monte Carlo simulations or make a judgment call. In many cases, the amount of slack needed is surprisingly large, which is why I stress transparent techniques rather than quadratic programming. Indeed, at some point portfolio theory becomes more a metaphor than a technique. Nevertheless, it should be a disciplined metaphor, one the trader has thought through before making his or her first trade.

New Money

Typically, a trader does not decide on a new set of trades on the day an investor opens an account. Typically, if the trader has other similar accounts, some trades have been open for some time. This means that either the trader must buy and sell in order to match his other portfolios, or he has to wait until his system generates new signals and place the investor at that time.

Unfortunately, no matter what the trader does, the investor will notice, and probably won't like it. If the trader waits and commits money only when he has a fresh set of signals, he will trade an underdiversified portfolio, which means he will be taking more risk than he has to for the money he has committed to the market.

If the trader commits the investor's money immediately, he will more or less match the performance of his other account. Unfortunately, if the trader is skillful, he will not be putting money in the market at the best possible time, which means he will underperform his other accounts. If it was the best possible time to put money in the market, he would have had a fresh set of signals.

Given the choices, I am firmly on the side of waiting and placing the money only as a trader's system generates signals. Of the two types of trading risks, this is the smaller. In some cases, the marketing risk, that is, the risk the investor might object to, may actually be higher. But that is not the trader's problem. At least, it shouldn't be.[7]

Coordination

To use the techniques above, a trader needs to know how much money he will commit to the market. This depends on his goals and the properties of his portfolio. I discuss this problem in Chapter 11. But regardless of the trader's goals, how much money he should commit to trading depends on the construction of his portfolio!

Iterative or trial-and-error techniques provide one method of avoiding this paradox. The trader can assume a dollar commitment to the market and then construct a portfolio to fit it. That portfolio can then be used to calculate the trader's market commitment, and the process can be repeated until the answer stabilizes.

Suppose, by way of analogy, that the trader wished to calculate the square root of $\ddot{X}$ but lacked any method of doing it exactly. One solution would be to divide $\ddot{X}$ by an arbitrary number $\ddot{Y}$. If the result $\ddot{Z}$ does not equal $\ddot{Y}$, then $\ddot{X}$ should be divided by the average of $\ddot{Y}$ and $\ddot{Z}$ and the process repeated until $\ddot{Y}$ is arbitrarily close to $\ddot{Z}$.

For example, assume the trader wishes to find the square root of 81, which is 9, of course. Dividing 81 by, say, 5 produces 16.2. As the numbers are not even approximately equal, the process should be repeated by dividing 81 by (5 + 16.2)/2 = 10.6. The result this time is 7.641509434. As the numbers are still not approximately equal, the process should be continued by dividing 81 by (10.6 + 7.641509434)/2 = 9.120754717. The result this time is 8.880844022.

Notice that the result draws progressively closer to the correct answer, but that with each iteration the improvement becomes more trivial. With enough repetitions, the result can be brought arbitrarily close. How close is close enough depends on how much work each iteration is and how much each iteration changes the answer.

Estimating Portfolio Parameters

To use some of the formulas in Chapter 11, the proportion of time the portfolio is profitable must be known, as well as the profit expected when the portfolio is profitable and the loss expected when it is not.

If the portfolio is equally weighted among the investments traded, if the risk and reward of trading the investments are identical, and if the profits and losses are independent, this can be calculated easily.

For a properly constructed, small or medium-sized portfolio, independence is probably a reasonable assumption. Identity of reward and risk is probably not a reasonable assumption for any portfolio. However, the technique is usable and conservative if the trader uses the investment with the *lowest* reward/risk ratio. Similarly, equal weighting is not a reasonable assumption, but the technique is usable and conservative if the trader uses n rather than N in the formulas that follow; n is calculated by dividing 1 by the portfolio's largest weighting and rounding the answer down to the largest whole number. For example, in Figure 10–3, the largest portfolio weighting is 0.3404. In this case, $n = 1/0.3404 = 2$, rounded down. If the upper boundary is set at 0.25, $n = 1/0.25 = 4$.

These techniques make two pessimistic or, if you will, conservative assumptions. The techniques assume, first, that the portfolio is, in effect, only as large as it would be if all the investments were weighted as heavily as the most heavily weighted one. Second, they assume that none of the investments has a higher reward/risk ratio than the investment with the least favorable one.

There are, of course, techniques that make more reasonable assumptions, but they are much more difficult and tedious to use.

The objects of the calculations to follow are:

- P = the proportion of the time the portfolio is profitable
- W = the average winnings if, in fact, the portfolio is profitable
- L = the average losses if, in fact, the portfolio is not profitable

The data used are:

- p = the probability of a given trade for a given investment being profitable
- w = the average winnings if, in fact, the trade is profitable
- l = the average losses if, in fact, the trade is not profitable

Clearly, the amount won or lost any time the portfolio is traded (G) will depend on how many of the investments have been traded profitably (K). There are obviously $n + 1$ possible values for K and G, and these values can easily be calculated and tabled. In fact

$$G = (wK) - [l(\mathrm{n} - K)]$$

where k is, in turn, each number from 0 to n, inclusive. Figure 10–6 displays the tabled values for $p = 0.4$, $w = \$200$, $l = \$100$ and $n = 5$.

The probability of any given K occurring (Q) can be extracted from a table of binomial probabilities if p, K, and n are known. The appropriate values for Figure 10–6 have been extracted from Table 7 in Appendix 1.

The probability of the portfolio being profitable is the sum of the probabilities of all the different ways the portfolio might be profitable. Reading down the table in Figure 10–6, we see that the lowest positive value for G is 1, at which value $K = 2$. Therefore, if the portfolio is to be traded profitably, $K \geq 2$. The probability

Figure 10–6

K	G		Q		M	
0	–500.00	×	0.078	=	–39.00	
1	–200.00	×	0.259	=	–51.80	–90.80
2	100.00	×	0.346	=	34.60	
3	400.00	×	0.230	=	92.00	
4	700.00	×	0.077	=	53.90	
5	1,000.00	×	0.010	=	10.00	190.50

K is in turn each of the numbers from 0 to n, inclusive. G is calculated from K by inserting ar, l, n, and K into the formula:

$$G = (wK) - [l\ (n - K)]$$

Q is extracted from the table of binomial probabilities (Table 7 in Appendix 1). M is calculated by multiplying $G \times Q$.

that the portfolio will be profitable (P) is the sum of all the Q values from $K = n$ to $K = 2$, inclusive. In this particular case, $P = (0.010 + 0.077 + 0.230 + 0.346) = 0.663$. P can also be extracted from a table of cumulative binomial probabilities (see Table 8 in Appendix 1).

Given the above assumptions, if the portfolio is profitable, the profit will be one of the positive G values. However, for budgeting purposes a probability-weighted average of the positive G values should be used. For each value of K, and μ value, which is the product of the G and Q values, must be calculated. For $K = 5$, for example, $\mu = G \times Q = 1000 \times 0.010 = 10.00$. These values are also tabled in Figure 10–6. The sum of all the μ values for $K \geq 2$ (that is, for all cases where the portfolio would be traded profitably) divided by P is the probability-weighted average for winning, or W. In the example above

$$W = \frac{(10.00 + 53.90 + 92.00 + 34.60)}{0.663}$$

$$= 287.33$$

Similarly, the sum of all μ values for $K \leq 1$ (that is, for all cases where the portfolio would be traded unprofitably) divided by $1 - P$ is the probability-weighted average for losing, or L. In the example above

$$L = \frac{(51.80 + 39.00)}{0.337}$$

$$= 269.43$$

Endnotes

1. Strictly speaking, I should refer to assets or investment media, rather than investments, since it is possible to trade anything speculatively. On the other hand, speculative trades tend to be more complex than investments or than buying stocks or bonds for the long haul. This complexity affects how portfolio theory is implemented, which I will address later in this chapter.
2. Some software packages allow you to edit the estimates. This makes a lot less sense than it sounds. It is almost impossible to edit a set of return, risk, and correlation coefficients and still have a set of estimates that might possibly be produced by real-world investments. A better approach is to edit the rate of return numbers directly. This is difficult to do badly and almost impossible to do well, but at least the results would be possible in the real world.
3. Actually, the trader needs $2N + (N(N\text{-}1))/2$ estimates, where N is the number of investments.
4. William F. Sharpe, "Capital Asset Prices: A Theory of Market Equilibrium under Conditions of Risk," *Journal of Finance* (September 1964): 425–444.
5. Edwin Elton and Martin Gruber, *Modern Portfolio Theory and Investment Analysis* (New York: Wiley, 1991). Elton and

Gruber present a variety of techniques with varying assumptions. Something here ought to work for you.

6. H. Bierman, "Diversification: Is There Safety in Numbers?" *Journal of Portfolio Management* (Fall 1978): 29–32.
7. When money is professionally managed, the marketing and trading functions should be separate, if at all possible. Naturally, the investor should be prepared, and possibly fees should be deferred until a fully diversified portfolio is acquired. The investor owns the portfolio and must be listened to. But part of the investment management's job is preventing the investor from doing anything stupid.

11

Portfolio Commitment Strategies

Introduction

Every trader must decide what proportion of the money allocated to trading to commit to the market at any one time. But many traders are not aware of this. Many beginning traders commit everything to every trade. One loss can wipe out the account. In the case of Orange County, the loss was over two billion dollars.[1] At the other extreme, the trader commits no money to the market. In this case, it is difficult to make any money trading. Of course, for many traders, such as that bozo in the office across the hall, this is the right thing to do.

All of this is moderately obvious. What is not obvious is how to make the choice. Or even what the exact choice is. Over the last 15 years or so, traders and investment scholars have developed a technology for allocating money between cash and one or more risky assets.[2] In this chapter, we will first discuss several properties of the most viable market commitment strategies. We will then discuss a number of strategies in detail. Finally, we will discuss a number of technicalities involved in using any of these strategies.

Basic Properties of All Portfolio Commitment Strategies

Portfolio commitment strategies were created by a heterogeneous group of traders and scholars whom, I suspect, were not on speaking terms. Certainly, many of the strategies have little in common. Risk of ruin strategies are designed to calculate a trader's risk of losing all his trading capital or enough that he quits trading. This allows the trader to maximize account growth subject to the risk of ruin not exceeding some specified probability. Optimal *f* strategies are designed to maximize the trader's (*e* log) account growth. Given a set of portfolio parameters, the formula calculates how much should be committed to the market at any one time so that the account grows at the fastest possible rate. Drawdown management-strategies are designed to ensure that the largest drawdown over some period does not exceed some specified level. A drawdown is a retracement of account equity from a high point. Hopefully, a temporary high point.

Hopefully, one of the strategies presented has the same goals the trader does. If not, the trader must use whatever strategy best fits his goals and adapt as best he can.[3] Playing what-if games with the selected strategy can give insight as to what is, and what is not, a prudent use of a particular strategy. Several Monte Carlo studies are explained in this chapter. Any well-defined strategy can be studied in this way.

Most of the assumptions the various portfolio commitment strategies make are peculiar to the strategy. I will describe these assumptions as I describe the strategies. But by necessity, all useful strategies, and others that are not useful, make the following assumptions:

1. The portfolio's distribution of wins and losses, or at least, certain properties of the distribution, are known with certainty.

2. The portfolio is a good bet.

3. The trader will actually take the actions the strategy demands.

We will consider these assumptions in turn.

1. The portfolio's distribution of wins and losses, or at least certain properties of the distribution, are known with certainty. Most of the techniques presented are not particularly robust. Typically, if a trader underestimates the power of his trading method, his account will not grow as fast as possible. If a trader overestimates the power of his trading method, and this error is *far* more common than not, he will be ruined. Assuming the trader is interested in avoiding ruin, he must use statistical techniques carefully and conservatively to estimate the distribution of profits and losses.

Some portfolio commitment techniques demand knowledge of the entire distribution of wins and losses. Other techniques demand less knowledge. Black and Jones's constant-proportion portfolio insurance, which will be discussed later, does not seem to make any assumptions about the portfolio's distribution of profits and losses, but of course it does. Black assumes the portfolio will make money on average. If not, portfolio insurance is a bad idea.

Black and Jones's technique is an extreme example. Still, most of the techniques do not demand full knowledge of the distribution of wins and losses. To the contrary, most of the techniques work on the basis of summary statistics of one kind or another. For example, allocations may be based on P, W, and L.

where P = the proportion of winning portfolios
W = the average amount won per portfolio
L = the average amount lost per portfolio

Strictly speaking, strategies based on such statistics are only valid when P, W, and L are constants, that is, fixed numbers, rather than variables. Thus, strictly speaking, if the average win might equal $1,200,000 or $1,200,000.01, the formulas are not acceptable.

In more practical terms, as long as the alternative estimates for *P*, *W*, and *L* are reasonably close together, this technique is acceptable. Conversely, if the range of values is large enough, such a technique is dangerous. Such a technique would work with many options trading strategies, for example. One way to check whether the technique would work with a particular investment method is to recalculate the numbers with varying values for *P*, *W*, and *L*. If the varying values generate roughly the same answer, that is the answer. If not, it is better to use a more sophisticated technique. Of course, if a trader checks too carefully, she will end up doing as much work as she would have if she'd used a more sophisticated technique. And her answer will still be less valuable.

2. The portfolio is a good bet. Mathematically sophisticated traders will wonder why it is necessary to say this. To them, it will seem obvious. But it is not obvious to all traders. Indeed, there is a large and bogus literature that claims to produce profits without such stringent requirements. But all trading involves the risk of ruin, the risk that the trader will lose his trading capital or a large enough portion of it that he will quit trading. If the trader accepts "bad" or even "fair" bets, ruin is inevitable. A bad bet is one where

$$PW < (1 - P)L$$

And where *P*, *W*, and *L* are defined as above.

The symbol $<$ indicates that the amount on the left is smaller than the amount on the right. A fair bet is one where the amount on the left is equal to the amount on the right. In either case, it is not a question of whether or not the trader will be ruined, it is a question of how long it will take. A trader could still get lucky, and die or quit before ruin, but this does not seem a prudent strategy. If for some reason, a trader must bet, perhaps because she is paid to do so, the best strategy is to bet infrequently.

If a trader accepts only "good" bets, ruin is no longer certain, but merely possible. The symbol > indicates that the amount on the left is larger than the amount on the right. A good bet is one where

$$PW > (1 - P)L$$

Clearly, the greater a trader's commitment to the market, that is, the more of his funds he commits to the market at any one time, the more quickly his account will grow, but the more likely it is that the trader will be ruined. How large a trader's risk of ruin is depends on how well capitalized he is relative to the risks of his portfolio. If a trader accepts only good bets and wishes to reduce his risk of ruin, he can do so merely by reducing his scale of trading. Of course, if the trader reduces the scale of trading far enough, trading will not be worth the effort.

3. The trader will actually take the actions the strategy demands. The trader may not be able to use the strategy he has decided on for psychological or political reasons. For example, the optimal *f* strategy is designed to achieve maximum capital growth with no risk of ruin. And if the assumptions underlying the method are satisfied, it will do just that. But even if the method works as advertised, there is no reason a trader could not lose, say, 95 percent of his trading capital on a temporary basis. A trader who does not understand this property of the method, a trader who does not have the discipline to ride out these losses, will all but ensure that his account is closed at a loss.[4]

Psychological and political problems can be redefined as technical problems, of course. For example, if a trader cannot stand a 95 percent drawdown, but can stand a 30 percent drawdown, another technique can be used. As long as the trader knows who he is, and knows who his clients are, if any, there is always something the trader can do. But if the trader does not know who he is and accepts clients who do not know who they are—he and his clients are doomed.

Risk of Ruin Strategies

Basic Properties

Probability theorists have studied risk of ruin strategies, which they often call gambler's ruin for obvious reasons, for a long time.[5] If the assumptions underlying the method are true, the technique will calculate the probability of ruin (*R*), that is, the probability that the investor will lose his trading capital, or a large enough portion of his trading capital that he will stop trading. This is a number worth knowing.

In the simplest case, wins equal losses, and the trader bets a fixed dollar-amount. For example, a trader opens a $1,000,000 account and bets $500,000 at a time, winning 55 percent of the bets. Notice that the investor initially has enough money for only two bets. These numbers are plugged into the following formula.

$$R = \left(\frac{1 - A}{1 + A}\right)^{\delta}$$

where $A = P - (1 - P)$
P = the proportion of winning trades
δ = the units of trading capital

Then $\delta = 2$, $P = .55$, and $A = .1$. This produces a risk of ruin of 67 percent, which seems a trifle large. If the investor finds this unacceptable, he or she can lower the risk of ruin by betting $50,000 at a time. In this case, the risk of ruin is 1.8 percent.

Presumedly, if the trader is not ruined, he is making money, which probably means his account is growing. As his account grows, the original risk of ruin strategy becomes overly conservative, if not completely irrelevant. Thus, unless a trader's goals are relatively modest or short term, risk of ruin probably makes more sense as a constraint than an objective. For example, a trader might decide to maximize account growth, as long as the risk of losing 50 percent or more of his initial capital is less than 1 percent. I will discuss such strategies later.

When Wins and Losses Are Constant

Blackjack expert and California State University professor Peter Griffin has developed a formula that approximates the risk of ruin when wins do not equal losses.[6] When wins do equal losses, the formula in the section above is

$$R = \Psi^{\Theta}$$

where $\Psi = \dfrac{1-\rho}{\rho}$

$\rho = 0.5 + \dfrac{EX}{2\sqrt{\Gamma}}$

EX = the expected mean return per trade

Γ = the expected squared mean return per trade

$\Theta = \dfrac{\zeta}{\sqrt{\Gamma}}$

ζ = the beginning capital minus the level of ruin

The expected mean return per trade (EX) is the probability weighted sum of all of the values that the trade might take. The expected squared mean return per trade (Γ) is the probability weighted sum of all of the squared values that the trade might take.

A trader's capital is the amount he has available for trading. Unfortunately, because some of this money must be allocated to margins and other costs, not all of it is available for trading. If funds that are not available for trading are lost, the trader is ruined. At the very least, a trader's level of ruin must be set high enough to cover the needed margins, commissions, executions costs, and other expenses. Therefore, a trader's "real" beginning capital ζ is his beginning capital minus those funds that are not available for trading, or his net power.

Some traders prefer to set higher levels of ruin. This, of course, increases the risk of ruin (*R*) but provides some insurance against catastrophic loss. The trader must decide for himself the value of this trade-off.

When Wins and Losses Are Variables

There is almost certainly no closed formula for calculating the risk of ruin, when wins and losses are variables. This means that *R* will have to be found by brute force, by a Monte Carlo simulation. The trader must decide on an initial level of capitalization, a ruin level, and an acceptable risk of ruin. Roughly speaking, this means trying one unit of capital and finding the risk of ruin, then two units of capital and finding the risk of ruin, and so on, until the risk of ruin drops below 5 percent or 1 percent or whatever risk of ruin is acceptable.

To risk one dollar means to buy a risky investment with a certain distribution of dollar profits and losses. If two dollars are at risk, the profits and losses are twice as large. And so on. Thus, three units of capital mean dividing the original capital by three. If the initial capital has not been decided, start with an arbitrary initial value, say, $1,000,000. Notice that the amount actually lost may be larger than or smaller than the amount at risk. The amount at risk is the amount committed to the market at any one time. Ideally, this should be the sum of the absolute differences between the current price of the various investments bought or sold short and their respective stops, plus various execution costs. If the trader does not use stops, the amount committed could be defined as the expected loss, that is, the mean loss if there is a loss.

In the first iteration of the simulation, one unit of capital is at risk. Draw a return at random from the distribution of wins and losses for the method of interest. Multiply this profit or loss by the number of units of capital, in this case one, divided by initial capital. Add the result to the initial capital. Repeat this until either 1) capital drops to whatever level means ruin, or 2) some designated horizon is reached. If a 20-year period is of interest, and the analyst is working with daily profit and loss data, repeat another 7,304 times.

Repeat this process 10,000 times and calculate the proportion of times the trader would have been ruined. If the risk of ruin is not acceptable, increase the units of capital by one and do the whole thing again. Continue until the risk of ruin drops to an acceptable level or someone else demands to use the computer.

Optimal *f* Strategies

Basic Properties

The optimal *f* strategy was developed by blackjack expert and University of California professor Edward O. Thorp.[7] If the assumptions underlying the method are true, the technique will minimize the average time necessary for the account to grow by any given amount. Alternatively, the account will grow as fast as it can. Indeed, there is a severe profit penalty for not using it.

If the trader wants to maximize his account growth, and if the assumptions underlying the method are true, assumptions which will be discussed shortly, the trader should bet a fixed fraction *f* of his trading capital every time. In the simplest case, a portfolio's wins must equal its losses, and the proportion of winning portfolios, which is designated P, must be larger than .5. I've never actually seen this happen, but I suppose it must happen every now and then. In this case, the formula is

$$f = P - (1 - P)$$

for example, if $P = .6$ then

$$\begin{aligned} f &= 0.6 - (1 - 0.6) \\ &= 0.6 - 0.4 \\ &= 0.2 \end{aligned}$$

Thus, if the trader has a $10,000,000 account, he should commit $2,000,000 to the market. If he loses the $2,000,000, he should commit $1,600,000. On the other hand, if the account grows to, say, $12,000,000, he should commit $2,400,000.

Optimal *f* is a powerful and useful strategy, but as is the case with all powerful and useful strategies, and many strategies that are not powerful and useful, there are problems with using them. Optimal *f* strategies come in several flavors, all of which make the following assumptions.

1. The trader wants to maximize his or her (*e* log) account growth.

2. The trader is willing to lose almost all of his or her capital, on a temporary basis.

3. Capital is infinitely divisible.

The first assumption should not provoke any worry. If the trader has another goal he flips the page, if he has not already flipped it.

The second assumption is worth some thought. If the trader is worried about large temporary losses, he has a decision to make. Large temporary losses are a cost of using this technique; they are a price paid for maximizing growth. This means temporary capital losses of, say 30–95 percent. If the other assumptions underlying this technique are true, the losses must be temporary, and the capital will be regained. Of course, this may be cold comfort to a trader who has lost 98 percent of his capital, not to mention his wife and job, and has to wait 17 years to regain the capital. If a trader or investor is uncomfortable with this possibility, he must use another technique.

The third assumption is worth some thought, too. If all of the other assumptions are true, there is no risk of ruin, no risk of losing all trading capital, or enough trading capital that the trader gives up trading. But even if all of the other assumptions are true, as long as capital is not infinitely divisible, there is some risk of ruin. In this case, as long as the trader knows how many units of capital he has, he can calculate his risk of ruin, using techniques discussed later in this chapter. Assuming wins are a reciprocal of the losses, the number of units of capital (*N*) is

$$N = \frac{Ln(Y/X)}{Ln(1-\Delta)}$$

where X = upper limit
Y = lower limit
Δ = proportion lost when portfolio suffers loss
Ln = log function

For example, assume an investor commits $1,000,000 to the market, but instructs his trader to close the account if equity drops to $500,000. Further, assume the investor loses 20 percent or wins 25 percent on the entire portfolio each time he wins or loses. In this case, the trader has

$$\begin{aligned} N &= \frac{Ln(1{,}000{,}000/500{,}000)}{Ln(1-.2)} \\ &= \frac{Ln(2)}{Ln(.8)} \\ &= \frac{-0.693147181}{-0.223143551} \\ &= 3.1062837195 \end{aligned}$$

The log function can be found on many pocket calculators and most spreadsheets. Often several logs are available (base 2, 10, *e*). It does not matter which log type is used as long as the same type is used in both the numerator and denominator.

More reasonable assumptions probably demand simulations.

When Wins and Losses Are Constant

In the unlikely event that wins equal losses, the trader can use the formula in the previous section. When wins do not equal losses, and even when they do, the proper formula is

$$f = e/B$$

where
$$e = (B+1)P - 1$$
$$B = W/L$$

where
P = proportion of time portfolio wins
W = amount won if trade wins
L = amount lost if trade loses

For example, if $P = .6$, $W = \$1{,}200{,}000$, and $L = \$800{,}000$, then

$$\begin{aligned} B &= 1{,}200{,}000/800{,}000 \\ &= 1.5 \end{aligned}$$

$$\begin{aligned} e &= (1.5+1)\,0.6 - 1 \\ &= 2.25 \cdot 0.6 - 1 \\ &= 1.5 - 1 \\ &= 0.5 \end{aligned}$$

$$\begin{aligned} f &= 0.5/0.6 \\ &= 0.8 \end{aligned}$$

If $f < 0$, then it is prudent not to trade, and if $f > 0.5$, it is probably prudent to use 0.5 instead.

When Wins and Losses Are Variables

In most real-world cases, the distribution of wins and losses resembles a normal or stable Paretian distribution (see Chapter 9). In this case, the techniques described above are of little value.

Worse, there is almost certainly no closed formula for calculating *f*. This means that *f* will have to be found by brute force. This means trying values from zero to one and seeing which works best.

Since there are an infinite number of numbers between zero and one, or at least, there used to be, only a few of them can be tested in any reasonable period. In most cases, testing each hundredth from .01 to .99 is sufficient. For each of these *f* values, a return and risk statistic is calculated over some reasonable time horizon. Assuming the distribution is based on daily portfolio returns, assuming the trader is going to use the method for 20 years, and assuming the calendar does not change noticeably during that period, this means a horizon of 7,305 periods.[8]

For a trader interested in maximizing return, the proper return statistic is the median terminal value. Start a portfolio with an arbitrary initial value of $1,000,000. Draw a return at random from the distribution of wins and losses for the method of interest. Multiply the initial value by the return. Draw a return at random from the distribution of wins and losses for the method of interest. This return may or may not be the return just drawn. Multiply the current value of the portfolio by the return just drawn. Repeat another 7,303 times.

Drawing a return at random can be done in several ways. If actual historical or simulated returns are used, this means selecting a historical or simulated return at random. This means numbering the returns between one and whatever the sample size is, generating a random number between one and whatever the sample size is, and then using that number's return.[9] This is done again and again. If an estimated distribution is used, a random number between zero and 100 is generated, and the estimated return at that percentile is used. For technical reasons, I strongly recommend using an estimated distribution rather than an actual one. In either case, the distribution will be based on a sample, and the value of that sample will depend on the skill used in taking it.

You now have the first of, say, 10,000 terminal values. Generate another 9,999 and take the median of those terminal values.

The procedure described above for generating terminal values mimics the way real-world account values are generated. Just like real-world account values, the terminal value is sometimes abnormally affected by a small number of extreme return values. The median should be used, rather than another statistic, because it is the most robust measure of location.

If drawdowns or other risk measures are of no interest, the *f* value with the highest median terminal value is the optimal *f* value. Assuming some random variation in median terminal values unrelated to their real merit, which is as safe an assumption as it is possible to make, it is better to chart the average terminal value against the various *f* values and visually choose *f* rather than just choose the highest value (see Figure 11–1).

Figure 11–1

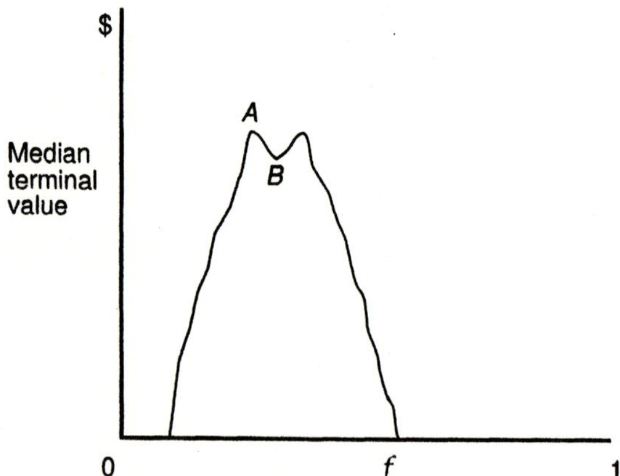

Optimal *f* is at point B, not at point A.

Judging by the complaints of traders interested in maximizing account growth, the proper measure of risk is maximum account drawdown. As a real-time measure of performance, which is how it is often used, maximum account drawdown is a silly measure because it is all too likely to be affected by a small number of chance events. Nevertheless, this measurement is quite common, and likely to be more common for those maximizing return than for others. Worse, investors who say they are not interested in drawdown are likely to be affected by it.

The only obvious alternative to maximum drawdown is a high-percentile drawdown. Thus, if the trader chooses the 90th percentile, the maximum drawdown over the time horizon of interest will be larger 10 percent of the time. Calculating the 90th percentile means ranking the drawdowns and counting down from the smallest drawdown to the largest. The 90th percentile is the rank with 90 percent of the values above it and 10 percent of the values below it. If the 90th percentile is between two ranks, an average of the two surrounding values is used.[10] For example, if the 90th percentile maximum drawdown over a 7,285-day period is 34 percent, then, if the study is done correctly, there is only a 10 percent chance of a drawdown larger than 34 percent over the next 7,285 days.

Assuming drawdowns are of interest, the trader can decide what maximum drawdown he will accept and the maximum probability he will accept of a drawdown that size. The trader then chooses the *f* value with the highest median terminal value and an acceptable probability of the drawdown occurring.

Drawdown Management-Strategies

Bizarrely enough, drawdown management-techniques are a practical application of one of Zeno's paradoxes. In one paradox, Zeno (500–440 B.C.) argued that an arrow will never reach its target because, very roughly speaking, it would first have to cover half the distance to the target, then half the remaining half, and so on. Since this series never ends, the arrow must always be some distance from the target. Drawdown management-techniques use the same principle to prevent account equity from dropping below any specified amount.

Assuming costs are zero, that prices do not jump, and that the trader can react with the necessary speed, the protection is absolute. Of course, making similar assumptions no trader can use this technique. To use it, a trader would have to read this section of the book, or some similar explanatory material, but that cannot be done. Before a trader completed reading this section, he would have to read the first half of this section, and then half of what remained, and so on forever without ever finishing. Under less than ideal conditions, it is possible to read this section of the book and use this method. The protection might not be absolute, but it might still be worth having.

Constant-proportion portfolio insurance was apparently invented by Fisher Black and Robert Jones.[11] Compared to other forms of portfolio insurance, constant proportion is remarkably easy to understand and use. In this model, the amount at risk is called the market exposure (*e*). This is the amount the trader expects to lose if all the trades in the portfolio go bad. That is

$$e = m\,(V - \mathrm{F})$$

where m = trader-chosen multiple
V = current portfolio value
F = trader-chosen portfolio floor value

Assume that a trader opens a $100,000,000 account, does not want the account's value to drop below $70,000,000, and for various occult reasons chooses the multiple 0.5. In this case

$$e = 0.5\,(100{,}000{,}000 - 70{,}000{,}000)$$
$$e = 0.5\,(30{,}000{,}000)$$
$$e = 15{,}000{,}000$$

If the value of the account drops to $80,000,000, the exposure should equal $5,000,000. Conversely, if the account rises to $200,000,000, the amount at risk rises to $65,000,000. At this point, the trader is still protecting the investor against a drop in equity below $70,000,000, which is becoming progressively less of a worry. But notice that nothing in the model prevents the trader from changing his mind about m or F. Thus, protecting against a drop below $140,000,000, say, is a simple matter of raising F, recalculating e and moving money to the riskless asset. In general, drawdown management means selecting a percentage retracement from the high and recalculating e every time that trading funds hit a new high. Thus

$$e = m(V - (\mathrm{H}(1 - \mathrm{P})))$$

where H = highest portfolio value to date
P = trader-chosen percentage floor

For example, if H = 200,000,000, V = 190,000,000, and P = .25, then

$$e = 0.5\,(190{,}000{,}000 - (200{,}000{,}000\,(1 - 0.25)))$$
$$e = 0.5\,(190{,}000{,}000 - (200{,}000{,}000\,(0.75)))$$
$$e = 0.5\,(190{,}000{,}000 - (150{,}000{,}000))$$
$$e = 0.5\,(40{,}000{,}000)$$
$$e = 20{,}000{,}000$$

In this case, the trader should risk $20,000,000.

Which value of m should the trader use? Notice the similarity between the optimal f strategy and constant-proportion portfolio insurance. Note that f and m are almost the same thing. There is only one obvious difference: for the optimal f strategy the floor is zero, which is somewhat lower than the floor most users of constant-proportion portfolio insurance demand. Nevertheless, under certain circumstances it is possible to set m equal to f. This can be done when

$$m > \frac{l}{(1/f)^1} + \frac{l}{(1/f)^2} + \frac{l}{(1/f)^3} + \ldots$$

The dots at the end of the equation above indicate the equation goes on forever, which means most of the equation is off the right side of the page and therefore difficult to read. Note that $1/f$ is raised to the power of one, two, three, and so on, so the rest of the formula is remarkably dull reading. The right side of the formula represents an infinite series of losses, where each loss is f of the remaining capital. Oddly enough, the sum of an infinite series is sometimes quite small. For example, if $m = .3$ and $f = .1$ then

$$0.3 > \frac{1}{(1/0.1)^1} + \frac{1}{(1/0.1)^2} + \frac{1}{(1/0.1)^3} + \dots$$

$$0.3 > \frac{1}{10^1} + \frac{1}{10^2} + \frac{1}{10^3} + \dots$$

$$0.3 > \frac{1}{10} + \frac{1}{100} + \frac{1}{1000} + \dots$$

$$0.3 > 0.1 + 0.01 + 0.001 + \dots$$

$$0.3 > 0.111 \dots$$

The sum of this infinite series is 1/9, so f can be safely substituted for m. If the sum is less than the drawdown the trader is trying to avoid, the trader gets the best of all possible worlds. The trader need not add all of the numbers in the series, which would take more time than the project is worth. The sum of the first four or five numbers gives an excellent approximation of the final answer.

Unfortunately, in more cases than not, the trader will find that the sum of the series is larger than m. This is painfully obvious when f is larger than m, as it often is. In this case, the trader must make a decision. If the trader wants his account to grow as quickly as possible, or if he wants his account to grow as quickly as possible subject to a certain risk of ruin, he is in the wrong section of this chapter. Alternatively, if the trader can estimate certain parameter values and understands something about his tolerance for risk, he can use Grossman and Zhou's optimal drawdown formula.[12] Failing that, if the trader wants to preserve his capital at all costs, subject to the assumptions of this model, he must still select *m*.

Black and Jones provide some help in selecting *m*. Obviously, the larger *m* is, the more volatile the account will be, the faster the account will grow when you are making money, and the faster the account will shrink when you are losing. The larger *m* is, the more aggressive the program. If the account value goes up or down a lot, the trader will benefit from a large *m*. If the account whipsaws, if it goes up and then down or down and then up, the trader will benefit from a small *m*. More, the larger *m* is, the larger the costs of using this method. Prudence therefore argues for a small *m*. Simulations similar to the ones used in selecting *f* should be of value here.

Implementation

Much of the literature on market commitment strategies has an oddly abstract quality. Some of the literature ignores the fact that taking action costs. Other literature seems to assume the investor does not do anything other than invest. Unfortunately, from the trader's point of view, investors do more than write checks. Investors do things that affect how much money they can invest, when they can invest it, and when they will want it back. Traders are likely to find the last possibility especially distressing, but that cannot be helped. Thus, the trader must deal with at least four problems: controlling costs, determining the proper size of the account, adding money to the account, and taking money away from the account. I will discuss each of these subjects in turn.

First, many market commitment strategies assume that transaction costs do not exist. Transaction costs are the direct costs of taking action: commissions, bid-ask spreads, administrative costs, and so on. Oddly enough, this lack of realism is not quite as fatal as it might at first seem. Cost can be built into the model by lowering profit estimates and increasing loss estimates.

Transaction costs depend on the investment strategy used, the investments used, and the frequency of action. Thus, a trader specializing in bankrupt or illiquid securities will almost certainly not be able to find a useful market commitment strategy. On the other hand, a trader specializing in the futures markets will find liquid markets and relatively low costs.

Nevertheless, even in liquid markets, the costs may be excessive. A lot of small costs can add up to a very large total. Constant-proportion portfolio insurance, for example, assumes action is taken at every infinitesimal change in price, which means that if transaction costs are not infinitesimal, which they are not, total costs will be substantial. In practice, therefore, the trader cannot afford to act until the price moves some moderately large amount. How large is moderately large? In an interesting study of option-based portfolio insurance, Ethan Etziono considered three alternative rebalancing strategies:

1. Fully rebalance to the required stock/cash mix at regular time intervals of various lengths (the "time discipline")

2. Fully rebalance to the required mix every time the market has a prespecified percentage move since the last adjustment (the "market move discipline")

3. Rebalance only when the actual mix lags the required mix by more than a prespecified lag factor in either direction, and then rebalance only to the extent of bringing the actual mix up to a lag factor away from the required mix (the "lag discipline")[13]

On the basis of certain simulations, which were performed using a portfolio-insurance strategy, Ethan Etziono recommended the third alternative. Conceivably, for other market commitment strategies, other rebalancing strategies might be of value. If the trader is going to commit real money, it is certainly worth finding out.

Second, the investor may not have enough money to use the strategy, or alternatively he may have too much. A popular tool for analyzing problems of scale is the break-even chart. The horizontal scale measures dollars under management. Traditionally, the vertical scale measures dollar profits or losses. Thus, profits and losses must be risk adjusted, if the technique is to be meaningful. This means the investor must find the certainty equivalent of his or her return on capital.[14]

A certainty equivalent is the fee an investor would charge to give up a trade. Thus, the right to win $1,000,000 or lose $500,000 with equal likelihood might be worth $100,000 to a particular investor. The investor must be indifferent to whether he owns the certainty equivalent or the trade. Indifference means he would let his worst enemy decide. In a break-even analysis the investor must find the certainty equivalent of his return on his dedicated capital. Thus, a risky return of .30 on capital might be worth a certain return of .20 to a particular investor.

Break-even analysis generally divides costs into two types: fixed and variable. Fixed costs are those that do not vary with the amount of trading, the cost of a chart service would be an example. In turn, variable costs are those that do depend on the amount of trading, commissions would be an example.

Clearly, if trading is profitable, it is because trading revenues are larger than trading costs. If revenues and costs are linear functions of the amount of funds dedicated to trading, then the amount that must be dedicated to trading can easily be calculated as follows

$$BK = FC/(TR - VC)$$

where

$$BK = \text{break-even point}$$

$$FC = \text{fixed costs}$$

$$TR = \text{total revenue}$$

$$VC = \text{variable costs}$$

(When several letters constitute one symbol, the letters are placed closely together and printed in roman type.)

For example, if over the next year, the investor's fixed costs are \$120,000, and he expects to gross 0.2 on his dedicated capital, but to pay out about 0.1 in commissions and execution costs, then

$$\begin{aligned} BK &= \$120{,}000 / (0.2 - 0.1) \\ &= \$120{,}000 / 0.1 \\ &= \$1{,}200{,}000 \end{aligned}$$

In other words, if the investor cannot afford to dedicate at least \$1,200,000 to trading, he should not trade. If the investor and trader are the same person, he should get a real job and let someone else manage his money. If the investor and trader are not the same person, the trader needs to help the investor find someone he can afford. If this kind of thing happens frequently, the trader has probably priced himself out of the market.

The break-even chart (see Figure 11–2) illustrates this relationship. Notice that the traditional break-even chart implies that the more money that is dedicated to trading, the more profitable trading will be. Unfortunately, this is simply not true.

Consider costs, for example. Costs rarely increase in the simple fashion that the above analysis assumes. In fact, some trading costs will increase and others will decrease with the amount of trading.

Technically, trading involves economies of scale when costs decrease as trading is done on a larger basis; for example, when large funds are dedicated to trading, it may be cost effective to employ extremely sophisticated cash-management techniques and to employ an accountant to handle the paperwork. The proportional costs of cash management and accounting will be smaller for the large trader than the small trader because the large trader can afford specialists that the small trader cannot.

Figure 11-2

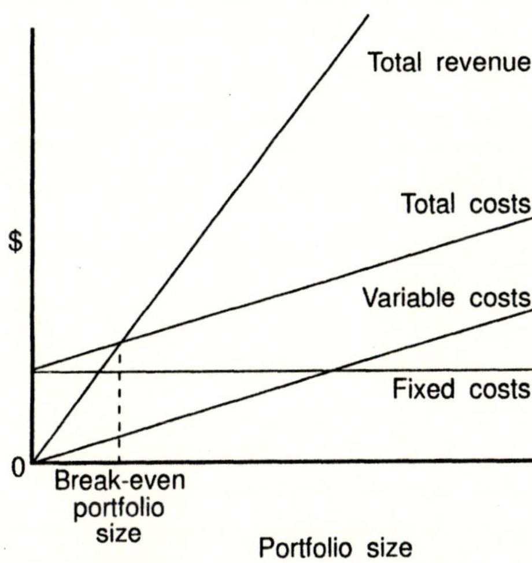

Traditional break-even analysis implies that trading is pointless if the amount dedicated to trading is too small and that profits will grow without limit as trading funds grow. The latter conclusion is wrong.

On the other hand, as more funds are dedicated to trading, it will become increasingly difficult to coordinate activities and to react to changing conditions. These are diseconomies of scale.

The net effect of this analysis is that if not enough money is dedicated to trading, trading will not be successful. On the other hand, trading will not succeed if too much money is dedicated to it, either.

One implication of the above analysis is that there is, theoretically, an optimum amount that should be dedicated to trading. However, that amount may be larger than the trader can afford, either financially or psychologically. In practice, therefore, the amount that is dedicated to trading should be a function of the trader's capital and his taste for risk.

Still, the trader should realize, other things being equal, that economic theory suggests that the return from an investment will be a function of the investment's size. Economic theory assumes, however, that among the things "being equal" are brains, discipline, and the capacity for hard work. This may not be true, but there is no evidence that these are a function of portfolio size either.

Third, bizarrely enough, adding money to an investment program is not as straightforward as investment professionals make it seem. If a trader adds the money thoughtlessly, he or she adds extra risk. Small investors generally commit all the money that they are going to commit to a speculative venture in one lump. Given the amount of money they can commit, this is often their only option. This presents no new problems. In contrast, large investors often stagger their commitments. They do this for a variety of reasons, some of which they may have no control over. For example, the investor's cash flows may demand it. But large traders will also stagger cash commitments because the investor is not completely convinced the investment program will work, and he or she wants to see it work with small change before trusting it with serious money.[15]

Oddly enough, prudence presents a serious problem here. At least, staggered investments do. Consider an investor who commits money to a convertibles-and-warrants fund. Each year the fund does well on average, although it has bad months. The investor not only lets his money ride, he puts new money in the fund. Then one month the fund does not do well, and the investor withdraws his money. Unfortunately, while the percentage drawdown was only a little worse than it had been, the investor had more money at risk than ever before. As a result, in one month he lost more than he made in the investment over a period of years.

One solution to this problem is to never have a bad period. Another solution is to never remove money from a fund that will eventually recover its losses.[16] Failing the insights necessary to implement these solutions, the investor must live with the risk.

There is no way to avoid it. The best an investor can do is to become more conservative as he or she grows richer, and to alter or adjust his or her cash-commitment strategy as necessary.

Adding money will not affect optimal *f* strategies or drawdown management-strategies; that is, it will not require the strategies to be rethought or recalculated. For example, the amount of money multiplied by *f* will change, but *f* will not. In contrast, adding money will affect risk of ruin strategies and most portfolio-insurance strategies.

If funds are added after an account is opened, and no other action is taken, the risk of ruin formula above will overestimate the risk from the date the funds are added. If the risk of ruin formula above gives an acceptable answer, the only necessary change is to recalculate every time new funds are added and to take larger risks. If the formula does not give an acceptable answer, one of the formulas in the section on removing money from an account should be used. The investor is just removing a negative amount of money. When money is added, portfolio insurance must be recalculated. With constant-proportion portfolio insurance, the adjustments are obvious and trivial.

Fourth, assuming the investor actually wants to do something with the money he or she earns (if the investor earns any, that is), he or she must remove it from the account. But doing so thoughtlessly can destroy the trader's portfolio commitment strategy.

Mathematically, the most straightforward approach is to set a date on which to close the account and spend the money. Setting a date to close the account only makes sense if the trader is planning to retire, or has some large project that must be funded on a particular date, which is sometimes the case. Setting a date and closing the account on that date will not affect optimal *f* strategies, risk of ruin strategies, or drawdown management-strategies. On the other hand, using these strategies under those circumstances does not make much sense.

Another straightforward approach is to wait until the portfolio grows to some acceptable level and then close the account. This will not affect optimal *f* strategies, or drawdown management-strategies. It will affect risk of ruin strategies. In fact, it will lower the risk. The new formula demands £, which is the trader's desired capital minus his or her level of ruin. If Professor Griffin's formula above gave an acceptable answer, the more complicated formula below will, too. In which case, formula is

$$R = 1 - \frac{\Psi^{\Theta} - 1}{\Psi^{\xi} - 1}$$

where $\xi = \frac{£}{\sqrt{\Gamma}}$

and where Ψ, Θ, EX, Γ, and φ are defined as above.

An example may make the use of Professor Griffin's technique clearer. Assume that a trader was interested in opening a $50,000,000 account. Previous research had convinced him that he would need to devote $1,500,000 to margins and other fixed expenses; that he could expect his portfolio to be profitable 60 percent of the time on a weekly basis; and that his portfolio would produce profits of $750,000, on average, when it was profitable, and losses of $250,000, on average, when it was not. Assume also that the trader had decided to abandon trading if his balance declined to $20,000,000 and to retire from trading if his balance reached $100,000,000.

Given the information above, but presenting the amounts in thousands, for clarity

$$\begin{aligned} \zeta &= 5{,}000 - 2{,}000 \\ &= 3000 \end{aligned}$$

$$\begin{aligned} £ &= 10{,}000 - 2{,}000 \\ &= 8000 \end{aligned}$$

Possible Value $\ddot{X}$	Probability $P(\ddot{X})$	$\ddot{X} \cdot P(\ddot{X})$	$\ddot{X}^2 \cdot P(\ddot{X})$
750	0.6	450	337,500
–250	0.4	–100	25,000
	1.0	EX = 350	Γ = 362,500

Therefore:

$$= 0.5 + \frac{350}{2\sqrt{362{,}500}}$$

$$= 0.5 + \frac{350}{2 \cdot 602.0797289}$$

$$= 0.5 + \frac{350}{1204.159458}$$

$$= 0.5 + 0.2906591795$$

$$= 0.7906591795$$

$$\Psi = \frac{1 - 0.7906591795}{0.7906591795}$$

$$= \frac{0.2093408205}{0.7906591795}$$

$$= 0.2647674573$$

$$\Theta = \frac{3{,}000}{\sqrt{362{,}500}}$$

$$= \frac{3{,}000}{602.0797289}$$

$$= 4.982728791$$

$$\xi = \frac{8{,}000}{\sqrt{362{,}500}}$$

$$= \frac{8{,}000}{602.0797289}$$

$$= 13.28727678$$

$$R = 1 - \frac{0.2647674573^{4.982728791} - 1}{0.2647674573^{13.28727678} - 1}$$

$$= 1 - \frac{0.001331345728 - 1}{0.00000002145073926 - 1}$$

$$= 1 - \frac{-0.9986686543}{-0.9999999786}$$

$$= 1 - 0.9986686757$$

$$= 0.0013313243$$

Although the calculations are tedious, the answer is important. Knowing that the risk of ruin is relatively small can provide valuable peace of mind during the inevitable runs of losing trades. Notice that the simplified formula still gives an acceptable answer:

$$R = 0.2647674573^{4.982728791}$$

$$= 0.001331345728$$

An alternative is to remove an amount equal to the average loss (L) every t trades. This effectively reduces the proportion of winning trades and increases the risk of ruin, all other things being equal. Of course, the effective proportion of winning trades (EP) must now be used instead of the proportion of winning trades (P) in the formulas above. The relationship is

$$\text{EP} = \frac{P}{1 + \frac{1}{t}}$$

If, for example, $P = 0.6$ and $t = 5$, then

$$\text{EP} = \frac{0.6}{1 + \frac{1}{5}}$$

$$= \frac{0.6}{1 + 0.2}$$

$$= \frac{0.6}{1.2}$$

$$= 0.5$$

A fifth, and easier, alternative is to allow the trading capital to build up to some predetermined level ξ and then to withdraw enough money to drop the capital to C. This would have no effect on optimal f strategies, portfolio-insurance strategies, or drawdown management-strategies. If the trader's risk of ruin between withdrawals is R, then if N withdrawals are made the risk of being ruined at least once (NRR) is

$$\text{NRR} = 1 - (1 - R)^N$$

For example, if $R = 0.05$ and $N = 10$, then

$$\text{NRR} = 1 - (1 - 0.05)^{10}$$

$$= 1 - (0.95)^{10}$$

$$= 1 - 0.60$$

$$= 0.40$$

Again, removing trading funds sharply increases the chance of ruin, but then a trader who has repeatedly removed capital from the market may not care.

Endnotes

1. If reports in the financial press about the Orange County investment-fund debacle can be trusted, the fund's single fatal mistake was to risk more money at one time than it should have. The fund made wrong individual trades, including some that seem stupid in retrospect, but everyone does that.
2. I do not describe these techniques, or the options-based portfolio-insurance techniques that these techniques are based on, because I have doubts about how useful traders will find these techniques. For a different viewpoint, see Oldrich Vasicek "The Best-Return Strategy" in Donald L. Luskin, Ed., *Portfolio Insurance: A Guide to Dynamic Hedging* (New York: Wiley): 101–112.
3. Investment consultants can develop portfolio commitment strategies for any need, so there is no need to use dubious commitment strategies. This was not the case 15 or 20 years ago, when the literature of bogus portfolio commitment strategies was larger than the literature of legitimate strategies. Unfortunately, these strategies are still in use. This is understandable, as it is not easy for the nonspecialist to tell the difference between high- and low-quality work. Almost all high-quality work is first published in peer reviewed professional journals. In almost all cases, the strategy is mathematically derived from assumptions about investors' utility for profits and losses. In contrast, low-quality work is privately published and the justification, when there is one, is empirical.
4. Individuals and organizations with the skills necessary to trade successfully often lose for psychological or sociological reasons. There is an interesting and useful literature devoted to individual investment psychology. See for example, Van K. Tharpe, *The Investment Psychology Guides* (Glendale, CA: Investment Psychology Consultants 1984, 1985). Unfortu-

nately, there is no literature devoted to psychological problems of investment organizations.

5. Gamblers ruin or risk of ruin has been studied by James Bernoulli, De Moivre, Lagrange, Laplace, and others. The first investment use I know of is in *The Commodity Futures Game.* See Richard J. Teweles, Charles V. Harlow, and Herbert L. Stone, *The Commodity Futures Game* (New York: McGraw-Hill): 260.
6. Peter Griffin, *The Theory of Blackjack* (Las Vegas: Gamblers Press, 1981). Dr. Griffin's formulas, alas, are only approximations. When wins do not equal losses, the true risk of ruin can only be calculated using difference equations, which are too complicated to explain here.
7. Edward O. Thorp, "The Kelly Money Management System," *Gambling Times* (December 1980): 91–92. Ralph Vince has probably done more work on this method than anyone else. See Ralph Vince, *Portfolio Management Formulas* (New York: Wiley, 1990), *The Mathematics of Money Management: Risk Analysis for Traders* (New York: Wiley, 1992), and probably half a dozen other books by the time this gets to press.
8. For preliminary studies, monthly data are probably sufficient. For definitive studies, interday data are necessary. In the real world, intraday drawdowns count.
9. This is usually done by generating a series of random numbers between zero and one and then mapping those numbers from one to the sample size (N). If the random number generated is below $1/N$, the first value in the sample is chosen. If the random number generated is below $2/N$ but equal to or above $1/N$, the second value in the sample is chosen, and so on.
10. For a more detailed explanation, see almost any introductory statistics text. An explanation of the median is given in Chapter 8. The median is 50th percentile.
11. Fisher Black and Robert Jones, "Simplifying Portfolio Insurance," *Journal of Portfolio Management* (Fall 1987): 48–51. Inci-

dentally, Zeno's paradox implies that Black and Jones did not create this method, and the *Journal of Portfolio Management* did not publish their article, all evidence to the contrary notwithstanding. The proof of these statements is left to the reader as an exercise.

12. Stanford J. Grossman and Zhongquan Zhou, "Optimal Investment Strategies for Controlling Drawdowns," *Mathematical Finance* (July 1993): 241–276. Grossman and Zhou's techniques are marginally more complicated than the ones suggested here. These techniques demand estimates of the expected return minus risk-free return, the standard deviation of expected return, and trader selected maximum drawdown and utility function.
13. Ethan Etolli, "Rebalance Disciplines for Portfolio Insurance," the *Journal of Portfolio Management* (Fall 1986): 59–62.
14. Certainty equivalents and risk-adjusted returns are popular investment-management tools. I do not believe they are anywhere near as useful as many investment professionals believe. I will discuss my reasons in a forthcoming book tentatively titled, *Fact-Based Approaches to Hiring and Firing Money Managers*.
15. The quality-control techniques discussed in Chapter 7 are useful here.
16. Bizarrely enough, I have repeatedly heard experienced investment professionals suggest such solutions. See, for example, Bruce Babcock, Jr. and Joe Bristor, *Equity Curve Conqueror, Advanced Trading Seminars*, Inc. (California: Sacramento, 1987). I suspect the problem is that experienced traders learn to trust their judgment but do not learn when experience and judgment do not count. See footnote three this chapter. Incidentally, Mr. Babcock produces an interesting newsletter that reviews trading methods.

12

Managing the Work of Risk Management

If you have gotten this far, you have either a bizarre sense of what constitutes fun reading or you actually want to do something about managing your trading risks. But what? Where are you to start?

Sometimes, it's obvious where to start; commissions may be too high, the portfolio may be underdiversified, or the computer room may be on fire. Even when where to start is not obvious, what needs to be done may be. In this case, whatever obvious actions need to be taken should be taken.

But often it is not obvious where to start. In which case, the place to start is with a probabilistic risk assessment (see Chapter 3). This will tell you where your risks are. Follow this with a review of technology available for managing those risks, after which, you will know what your problems are and what is available to solve them. Such a review, and this can be said dogmatically, will show too many things that need doing, all of which have to be done now, and all too many of which are difficult, or expensive, or both. What do you do first? How much time and money do you spend on the first project before moving on? How much time and money do you spend on the project after that? When do you stop?

Somehow, the trader must set priorities. Naturally, there are no right priorities. As one wit put it, "There are no decision rules with which to choose decision rules."[1] Setting priorities is a matter of judgment. Occasionally, the judgment calls will be obvious. More often, they will not. In which case, the trader will have to guess. Economic theory will, at least, help the trader guess what the right projects to work on are. If a trader guesses, he or she should guess in the right way.

A critical distinction must be made between marginal and total analysis. Let's consider the law of diminishing returns in this context. The law of diminishing returns refers to the relationship between the marginal input of any one production factor, such as capital or labor, and the marginal output of the resulting good or service, such as profitable trades. The marginal input is the smallest extra input that can be added. The marginal output is the extra output that the marginal input generates. Often, the input or output will be reasonably large, but, for theoretical reasons, we will pretend or assume that it is infinitesimal.

Figure 12–1 shows what happens to the output when an input is marginally increased. Notice that while the total output continues to increase, the marginal output first increases, then remains constant, then decreases. The law of diminishing returns holds that although the marginal output may at first increase, eventually it must decrease.

Much economic analysis is the use of marginal analysis in an attempt to maximize, minimize, or otherwise optimize some value. Indeed, in most beginning microeconomic classes, a student can answer, "marginal costs equal marginal results" to almost any question and get at least partial credit. More to the point, the economic theory of the firm demonstrates that profits will be their greatest when the firm produces until its marginal cost equals its marginal revenue. The marginal revenue, of course, is the extra revenue produced by the last unit sold of good or service $\ddot{A}$. Marginal cost is the cost of producing that unit. All other things being equal, the marginal revenue of one unit will always be less than or equal to the marginal revenue of

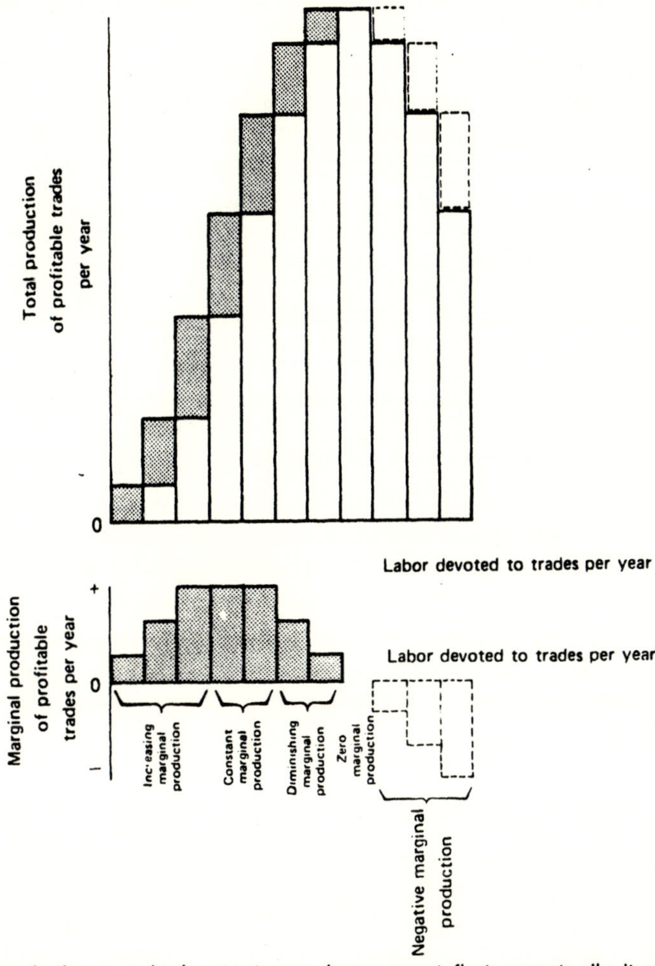

Although the marginal output may increase at first, eventually it must diminish.

the preceding unit. In the real world, in fact, the trader will almost certainly find marginal revenue continually dropping. On the other hand, marginal costs will continually rise, although they may drop somewhat in the beginning as economies of scale come into play.

As long as the marginal cost is less than the marginal revenue, the firm can still produce units profitably. On the other hand, when the marginal costs become larger than the marginal revenues, as they eventually will, the firm is producing some units at a loss. As Figure 12–2 demonstrates, the single place where earnings are greatest is where the marginal costs just equal the marginal revenue.

The implications of the analysis above should be fairly obvious. The trader should, ideally, devote effort to money management until the marginal reward of the effort in the form of lowered risk and increased return (*revenue* is perhaps not the proper term) just equals the marginal cost of the effort.

Marginal costs and marginal returns are products of various business factors. A factor is an economic term that refers to something that produces business results or costs, such as slippage or diversification. Economic theory suggests that the trader should break the rewards and costs of money management into a number of factors and estimate, separately, the marginal rewards and marginal costs of each factor. The trader can then upgrade each factor in turn until the marginal costs equal the marginal reward.

Factors should not be upgraded at random, of course. Factors with high marginal reward/cost ratios should be upgraded before those with lower ratios. Specifically, the factor with the highest marginal reward/cost ratio is located first and upgraded; then the factor with the next highest marginal reward/cost ratio, which may or may not be the same factor, is located and upgraded, until the trader reaches a factor with a marginal reward/cost ratio equal to or less than one. The trader then stops. Figure 12–3 may make this clearer.

The rule of working until marginal costs equal marginal benefits is a law of logic itself, not just a law of economics. Theoretically, therefore, marginal analysis will allow the trader to

Figure 12–2

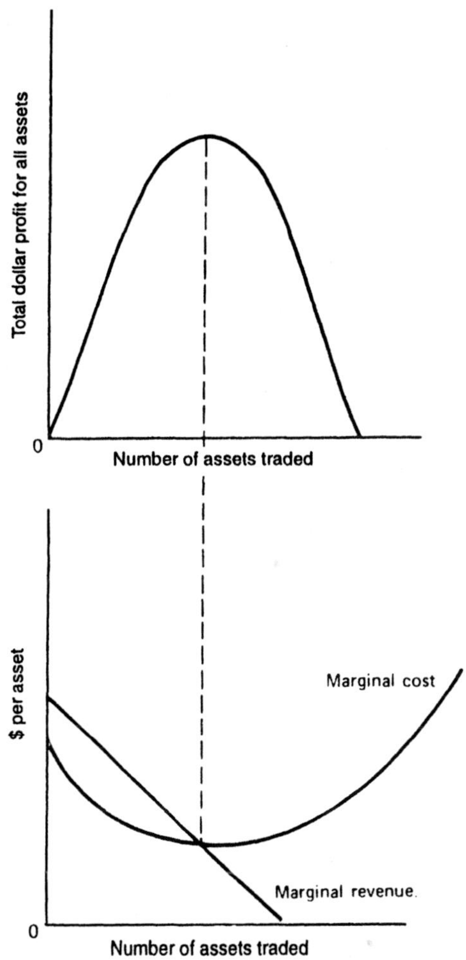

Profits will be their greatest when marginal costs just equal marginal benefits.

make the best possible use of his or her resources. Unfortunately, actually performing a marginal analysis is a lot harder, and less

Figure 12–3

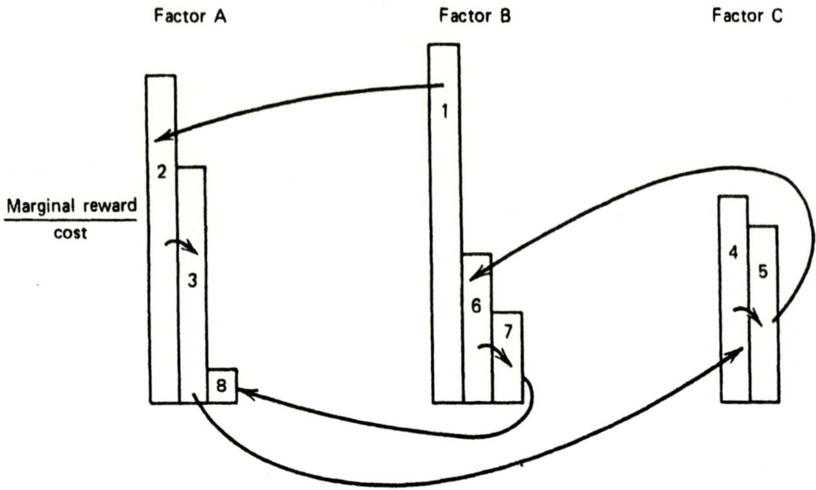

Factors should be upgraded in order of their marginal reward/cost ratios.

productive, than theory suggests. Still, marginal analysis has its virtues, if only as a metaphor. If a trader guesses, he or she should guess in the right way.

The problem is that differences between theory and the real world bring subtle and destructive biases into the analysis. Worse, these biases are the ones almost all of us have anyhow. They do not even have novelty value.

First, costs are always easier to estimate than benefits. More likely than not, a given factor unit will produce any of several rewards. One method of dealing with this problem is simply to assume that the reward will be the one most likely. A second method, and the one that is theoretically the best, is to use a probability-weighted average of all the possible values. A third method is to use a relatively simple probability-weighted average.

This average (λ) assumes that the unit factor can only produce one of two possible results, a minimum reward (M) and the most likely reward ($\mathcal{M}$). Also needed is the probability of the unit factor producing the most likely reward (P). A probability is a number from zero to one, inclusive, where zero indicates that there is no probability of success, and one indicates that success is certain. The formula, then, is

$$\lambda = P(\mathcal{M} - M) + M$$

For example, if $\lambda = 15$, $M = 10$, and $P = 0.6$, then

$$\lambda = 0.6\,(15 - 10) + 10 = 13$$

If the minimum reward is zero, which it will often be, the formula reduces to

$$\lambda = P\,\mathcal{M}$$

The λ values can be used as the numerator in the reward/cost ratio. This average works relatively well. But it does not change the nature of the estimates. Estimates of costs are crisp and relatively reliable, while estimates of benefits are not. Because of this, marginal analysis, benefit/cost analysis, and other similar techniques all have a bias toward inaction or "cost cutting," rather than, say, innovation and improving quality. The agents of entropy, that overpaid bozo down the hall, for example, can almost always argue that the prospective returns for whatever project interests you are not high enough or certain enough to justify the costs. The only way to counter these biases, which cannot be avoided, is with a strong bias toward action. Ready. Fire. Aim.

Second, marginal analysis assumes results, and costs come in small units, infinitely small units, actually. I personally have hardly ever been able to find infinitely small units, much less use them. In contrast, real-world work comes in fairly large chunks. As a matter of fact, work comes in chunks larger than the trader imagines, even when he or she considers that it comes in chunks larger than he or she imagines. Thus, marginal analysis has to be based on large estimates, not infinitesimal ones.

Moreover, far too often there is no benefit to doing part of a task. Thus, if a trader is not willing to devote substantial time and effort to a money-management task, he or she should probably not start. This means that unless a trader has a bias toward action, he or she will not act. Phrased more positively, experienced traders budget large amounts of time to projects of importance; they decide what they will do and what they will not do. And then they ruthlessly enforce that budget.

Figure 12–4

Marginal Factors	Benefits	Costs	Benefits/Costs
A	125	100	1.25
B	320	200	1.60
C	525	300	1.75
D	800	400	2.00
E	750	500	1.50
F	780	600	1.30

The marginal factors above are rearranged in order of benefits/costs below.

Marginal Factors	Benefits/ Costs	Benefits	Cumulative Benefits	Costs	Cumulative Costs
D	2.00	800	800	400	400
C	1.75	525	1325	300	700
B	1.60	320	1645	200	900
E	1.50	750	2395	500	1400
F	1.30	780	3175	600	2000
A	1.25	125	3300	100	2100

Ranking marginal factors by benefit/cost ratios and acquiring the marginal factors with the highest ratios first will produce the best or almost the best results possible. When there is a better ranking, it can often be found by inspecting the ranked data.

Because work comes in large chunks, effective traders work in a particular way. They do one thing at a time. They do it well. And then they move on.[2]

Understand? Now, *move*!

Endnotes

1. Anonymous, Bloggin's Working Rules, in *The Scientist Speculates*. I. J. Good, ed. (New York: Capricorn Books, 1962): 213.
2. There is a large and accessible literature on time management. See for example, Edwin Bliss, *Getting Things Done: The ABC's of Time Management*, (New York: Bantam, 1978). The literature on effectiveness, which is getting important things done, is smaller. The first book on this subject, and one of the most important management books ever written is Peter Drucker's, *The Effective Executive*, (London: Pan, 1966).

Appendix 1

Tables

Only working tables are included in this section. Expository tables are distributed throughout the text.

1. Selected Confidence Limits for the Binomial Distribution
2. Critical Values of the Unit Normal Distribution
3. Critical Values for d (or c) in the Fisher-Yates Test
4. Critical Values of the χ^2 Distribution for One Degree of Freedom
5. Critical Values of the Distribution of the Mean Absolute Deviation
6. Critical Values of Spearman's Rank Correlation Coefficient
7. Binomial Distribution—Individual Terms
8. Binomial Distribution—Cumulative Terms
9. Selected Values for the Exponential Distribution
10. Tables of Common Logarithms—Five Places
11. Tables of Natural or Naperian Logarithms, .01–11.09

Table 1. Selected Confidence Limits for the Binomial Distribution[a,b]

N	Y	Confidence Coefficient (z) .90	.95	.99
1	0	0.000	0.000	0.000
	1	.100	.050	.010
2	0	0.000	0.000	0.000
	1	.051	.025+	.005+
	2	.316	.224	.100
3	0	0.000	0.000	0.000
	1	.035–	.017	.003
	2	.196	.135+	.059
	3	.464	.368	.215+
4	0	0.000	0.000	0.000
	1	.026	.013	.003
	2	.143	.098	.042
	3	.320	.249	.141
	4	.500	.473	.316
5	0	0.000	0.000	0.000
	1	.021	.010	.002
	2	.112	.076	.033
	3	.247	.189	.106
	4	.379	.343	.222
	5	.621	.500	.398
6	0	0.000	0.000	0.000
	1	.017	.009	.002
	2	.093	.063	.027
	3	.201	.153	.085–
	4	.333	.271	.173
	5	.458	.402	.294
	6	.655+	.598	.464
7	0	0.000	0.000	0.000
	1	.015–	.007	.001
	2	.079	.053	.023
	3	.170	.129	.071
	4	.279	.225+	.142
	5	.316	.341	.236
	6	.500	.446	.357
	7	.684	.623	.500
8	0	0.000	0.000	0.000
	1	.013	.006	.001
	2	.069	.046	.020
	3	.147	.111	.061
	4	.240	.193	.121
	5	.255–	.289	.198
	6	.418	.315+	.293
	7	.582	.500	.410
	8	.745+	.685–	.549

[a]Calculated by Edwin L. Crow, Eleanor G. Crow, and Robert S. Gardner according to a modification of a proposal of Theodore E. Sterne. Reprinted by permission of Biometrika Trustees.

[b]The observed proportion in a random sample of size n is Y/N. The table gives the lower confidence limit for the population proportion PL(Z), as a function of N and Y. The upper confidence limit PU(Z) = 1 – (lower confidence limit, entered with $N - Y$ instead of Y).

Table 1. *(continued)*

N	Y	Confidence Coefficient (Z)		
		.90	.95	.99
9	0	0.000	0.000	0.000
	1	.012	.006	.001
	2	.061	.041	.017
	3	.129	.098	.053
	4	.210	.169	.105+
	5	.232	.251	.171
	6	.390	.289	.250
	7	.485-	.442	.344
	8	.609	.557	.402
	9	.768	.711	.598
10	0	0.000	0.000	0.000
	1	.010	.005+	.001
	2	.055-	.037	.016
	3	.116	.087	.048
	4	.188	.150	.093
	5	.222	.222	.150
	6	.341	.267	.218
	7	.352	.381	.297
	8	.500	.397	.376
	9	.648	.603	.488
	10	.778	.733	.624
11	0	0.000	0.000	0.000
	1	.010	.005-	.001
	2	.049	.033	.014
	3	.105-	.079	.043
	4	.169	.135+	.084
	5	.197	.200	.134
	6	.302	.250	.194
	7	.315+	.333	.262
	8	0.423	0.369	0.340
	9	.577	.500	.407
	10	.685-	.631	.500
	11	.803	.750	.641
12	0	0.000	0.000	0.000
	1	.009	.004	.001
	2	.045+	.030	.013
	3	.096	.072	.039
	4	.154	.123	.076
	5	.184	.181	.121
	6	.271	.236	.175-
	7	.294	.294	.235-
	8	.398	.346	.302
	9	.500	.450	.321
	10	.602	.550	.445+
	11	.706	.654	.555-
	12	.816	.764	.679
13	0	0.000	0.000	0.000
	1	.008	.004	.001
	2	.042	.028	.012
	3	.088	.066	.036
	4	.142	.113	.069
	5	.173	.166	.111
	6	.246	.224	.159
	7	.276	.260	.213
	8	.379	.327	.273
	9	.455+	.413	.302
	10	.530	.480	.406
	11	.621	.566	.477
	12	.724	.673	.571
	13	.827	.755-	.698
14	0	0.000	0.000	0.000
	1	.007	.004	.001
	2	.039	.026	.011
	3	.081	.061	.033

Table 1. *(continued)*

N	Y	Confidence Coefficient (Z)		
		.90	.95	.99
	4	.131	.104	.064
	5	.163	.153	.102
	6	.224	.206	.146
	7	.261	.206	.195-
	8	0.355-	0.312	0.249
	9	.406	.371	.286
	10	.422	.389	.364
	11	.578	.500	.392
	12	.635-	.611	.500
	13	.739	.688	.608
	14	.837	.794	.714
15	0	0.000	0.000	0.000
	1	.007	.003	.001
	2	.036	.024	.010
	3	.076	.057	.031
	4	.122	.097	.059
	5	.154	.142	.094
	6	.205+	.191	.135-
	7	.247	.191	.179
	8	.325+	.294	.229
	9	.325+	.332	.273

N	Y	Confidence Coefficient (Z)		
		.90	.95	.99
	10	.400	.369	.328
	11	.500	.448	.373
	12	.600	.552	.461
	13	.675-	.631	.539
	14	.753	.698	.627
	15	.846	.809	.727
16	0	0.000	0.000	0.000
	1	.007	.003	.001
	2	.034	.023	.010
	3	.071	.053	.029
	4	.114	.090	.055+
	5	.147	.132	.088
	6	.189	.178	.125+
	7	.235+	.178	.166
	8	.299	.272	.212
	9	.305+	.272	.261
	10	.381	.352	.295+
	11	.450	.429	.357
	12	.550	.500	.421
	13	.619	.571	.475+
	14	.695-	.648	.549

N	Y	Confidence Coefficient (Z)		
		.90	.95	.99
	15	.765-	.728	.643
	16	.853	.822	.736
17	0	0.000	0.000	0.000
	1	.006	.003	.001
	2	.032	.021	.009
	3	.067	.050	.027
	4	.107	.085-	.052
	5	.140	.124	.082
	6	.175+	.166	.117
	7	.225+	.166	.155+
	8	.277	.253	.197
	9	.290	.254	.242
	10	.364	.337	.242
	11	.432	.406	.338
	12	.500	.456	.380
	13	.568	.511	.413
	14	.636	.583	.500
	15	.710	.663	.587
	16	.775-	.746	.654
	17	.860	.834	.758

Table 1. *(continued)*

N	Y	Confidence Coefficient (Z) .90	.95	.99
18	0	0.000	0.000	0.000
	1	.006	.003	.001
	2	.030	.020	.008
	3	.063	.047	.025+
	4	.101	.080	.049
	5	.135-	.116	.077
	6	.163	.156	.110
	7	.216	.157	.145+
	8	.257	.236	.184
	9	.277	.242	.226
	10	.349	.325-	.228
	11	.416	.375-	.314
	12	.464	.381	.318
	13	.518	.444	.397
	14	.581	.556	.466
	15	.651	.619	.534
	16	.723	.675+	.603
	17	.784	.758	.682
	18	.865+	.843	.772
19	0	0.000	0.000	0.000
	1	.006	.003	.001
	2	.028	.019	.008
	3	.059	.044	.024
	4	.095+	.075+	.046
	5	0.130	0.110	0.073
	6	.151	.147	.103
	7	.209	.150	.137
	8	.238	.222	.173
	9	.265+	.232	.212
	10	.337	.312	.218
	11	.386	.345-	.293
	12	.386	.365-	.305+
	13	.440	.426	.383
	14	.560	.500	.436
	15	.614	.574	.485-
	16	.663	.635+	.545-
	17	.735-	.684	.617
	18	.791	.768	.695-
	19	.870	.850	.782
20	0	0.000	0.000	0.000
	1	.005+	.003	.001
	2	.027	.018	.008
	3	.056	.042	.023
	4	.090	.071	.044
	5	.126	.104	.069
	6	.141	.140	.098
	7	.201	.143	.129
	8	.221	.209	.163
	9	.255-	.222	.200
	10	.325-	.293	.209
	11	.358	.293	.274
	12	.367	.351	.293
	13	.422	.411	.363
	14	.500	.467	.399
	15	.578	.533	.424
	16	.633	.589	.500
	17	.672	.649	.576
	18	.745+	.707	.625+
	19	.797	.778	.707
	20	.874	.857	.791
21	0	0.000	0.000	0.000
	1	.005+	.002	.000
	2	.026	.017	.007
	3	.054	.040	.022
	4	.086	.068	.041

Table 1. *(continued)*

N	Y	Confidence Coefficient (Z)		
		.90	.95	.99
	5	.121	.099	.065+
	6	0.130	0.132	0.092
	7	.191	.137	.122
	8	.191	.197	.155
	9	.245	.213	.189
	10	.306	.276	.201
	11	.306	.276	.257
	12	.353	.338	.283
	13	.407	.398	.339
	14	.458	.449	.347
	15	.542	.494	.409
	16	.593	.545	.466
	17	.647	.602	.534
	18	.694	.662	.591
	19	.755+	.724	.653
	20	.809	.787	.717
	21	.877	.863	.799
22	0	0.000	0.000	0.000
	1	.005–	.002	.000
	2	.024	.016	.007
	3	.051	.038	.021
	4	.082	.065–	.039

N	Y	Confidence Coefficient (Z)		
		.90	.95	.99
	5	.115–	.094	.062
	6	.115–	.126	.088
	7	.181	.132	.116
	8	.181	.187	.147
	9	.236	.205+	.179
	10	.289	.260	.194
	11	.289	.264	.242
	12	.340	.326	.273
	13	.393	.383	.318
	14	.444	.418	.334
	15	.500	.424	.396
	16	.556	.500	.450
	17	.607	.576	.495+
	18	.660	.611	.546
	19	.711	.674	.604
	20	.764	.736	.666
	21	.819	.795–	.727
	22	.885+	.868	.806
23	0	0.000	0.000	0.000
	1	.005–	.002	.000
	2	.023	.016	.007

N	Y	Confidence Coefficient (Z)		
		.90	.95	.99
	3	.049	.037	.020
	4	.078	.062	.038
	5	0.110	0.090	0.059
	6	.110	.120	.084
	7	.173	.127	.111
	8	.173	.178	.140
	9	.228	.198	.171
	10	.273	.247	.187
	11	.274	.255–	.229
	12	.328	.317	.265+
	13	.381	.360	.298
	14	.431	.360	.323
	15	.478	.409	.384
	16	.521	.457	.420
	17	.569	.543	.429
	18	.619	.591	.500
	19	.672	.640	.571
	20	.726	.683	.614
	21	.772	.745+	.677
	22	.827	.802	.735–
	23	.890	.873	.813

Table 1. (*continued*)

N	*Y*	Confidence Coefficient (Z) .90	.95	.99	*N*	*Y*	Confidence Coefficient (Z) .90	.95	.99	*N*	*Y*	Confidence Coefficient (Z) .90	.95	.99
24	**0**	0.000	0.000	0.000		**22**	.779	.754	.687		**18**	.568	.525+	.451
	1	.004	.002	.000		**23**	.835+	.809	.741		**19**	.611	.569	.500
	2	.022	.015+	.006		**24**	.895+	.878	.819		**20**	.638	.616	.549
	3	.047	.035–	.019	25	**0**	0.000	0.000	0.000		**21**	.693	.664	.597
	4	.075–	.059	.036		**1**	.004	.002	.000		**22**	.745+	.697	.648
	5	.105–	.086	.057		**2**	.021	.014	.006		**23**	.786	.762	.695+
	6	.105–	.115–	.080		**3**	.045–	.034	.018		**24**	.842	.815–	.755–
	7	.165–	.122	.106		**4**	.072	.057	.034		**25**	.899	.882	.825–
	8	.165–	.169	.133		**5**	.101	.082	.054	26	**0**	0.000	0.000	0.000
	9	.221	.191	.163		**6**	.101	.110	.077		**1**	.004	.002	.000
	10	.259	.234	.181		**7**	.158	.118	.101		**2**	.021	.014	.006
	11	.264	.246	.216		**8**	.158	.161	.127		**3**	.043	.032	.017
	12	.317	.308	.257		**9**	.214	.185+	.155+		**4**	.069	.054	.033
	13	.370	.339	.280		**10**	.246	.222	.175+		**5**	.097	.079	.052
	14	.413	.347	.313		**11**	.255–	.238	.205+		**6**	.097	.106	.073
	15	.447	.396	.362		**12**	.307	.296	.245+		**7**	.151	.114	.097
	16	.447	.443	.364		**13**	.360	.317	.245+		**8**	.151	.154	.122
	17	.553	.500	.416		**14**	.389	.336	.305–		**9**	.209	.180	.149
	18	.577	.557	.464		**15**	.389	.384	.342		**10**	.233	.212	.170
	19	.630	.604	.536		**16**	.432	.431	.352		**11**	.247	.230	.195–
	20	.683	.653	.584		**17**	.500	.475–	.403		**12**	.299	.282	.234
	21	.736	.692	.636										

Table 1. (*continued*)

N	*Y*	Confidence Coefficient (Z) .90	.95	.99
	13	.342	.282	.234
	14	.342	.325+	.298
	15	.377	.374	.322
	16	.419	.421	.342
	17	.460	.458	.393
	18	.540	.494	.438
	19	.581	.535–	.474
	20	0.623	0.579	0.513
	21	.658	.626	.558
	22	.701	.675–	.607
	23	.753	.718	.658
	24	.791	.770	.702
	25	.849	.820	.766
	26	.903	.886	.830
27	0	0.000	0.000	0.000
	1	.004	.002	.000
	2	.020	.013	.006
	3	.042	.031	.017
	4	.066	.052	.032
	5	.093	.076	.050
	6	.093	.101	.070
	7	.145+	.110	.093
	8	.145+	.148	.117
	9	.204	.175–	.143
	10	.221	.202	.166
	11	.239	.223	.185–
	12	.291	.269	.224
	13	.326	.269	.225–
	14	.326	.316	.284
	15	.365+	.364	.298
	16	.407	.402	.332
	17	.447	.430	.383
	18	.500	.437	.413
	19	.553	.500	.419
	20	.593	.563	.461
	21	.635–	.585+	.539
	22	.674	.636	.581
	23	.709	.684	.616
	24	.761	.731	.668
	25	.796	.777	.703
	26	.855–	.825+	.775+
	27	.907	.890	.834
28	0	0.000	0.000	0.000
	1	.004	.002	.000
	2	.019	.013	.005+
	3	.040	.030	.016
	4	.064	.050	.031
	5	0.089	0.073	0.048
	6	.089	.098	.068
	7	.139	.106	.089
	8	.139	.142	.112
	9	.197	.170	.137
	10	.208	.192	.162
	11	.232	.217	.175+
	12	.284	.258	.214
	13	.310	.259	.218
	14	.312	.307	.272
	15	.355–	.355–	.272
	16	.396	.381	.323
	17	.435+	.384	.364
	18	.473	.424	.364
	19	.527	.463	.408
	20	.565–	.537	.449
	21	.604	.576	.500

Table 1. (*continued*)

N	Y	Confidence Coefficient (Z) .90	.95	.99
	22	.645+	.616	.551
	23	.688	.643	.592
	24	.716	.693	.636
	25	.768	.741	.677
	26	.799	.783	.728
	27	.861	.830	.782
	28	.911	.894	.838
29	0	0.000	0.000	0.000
	1	.004	.002	.000
	2	.018	.012	.005+
	3	.039	.029	.015+
	4	.062	.049	.030
	5	.086	.070	.046
	6	.086	.094	.065+
	7	.134	.103	.086
	8	.134	.136	.108
	9	.189	.166	.132
	10	.189	.184	.157
	11	.225-	.211	.165+
	12	.276	.247	.206
	13	.294	.251	.211
	14	.303	.299	.260
	15	.345-	.339	.263
	16	.385+	.339	.316
	17	.425-	.374	.346
	18	.463	.413	.354
	19	.500	.451	.397
	20	0.537	0.500	0.438
	21	.575+	.549	.477
	22	.615-	.587	.523
	23	.655+	.626	.562
	24	.697	.661	.603
	25	.721	.701	.646
	26	.775+	.749	.684
	27	.811	.789	.737
	28	.866	.834	.789
	29	.914	.897	.840
30	0	0.000	0.000	0.000
	1	.004	.002	.000
	2	.018	.012	.005+
	3	.037	.028	.015-
	4	.059	.047	.028
	5	.083	.068	.045-
	6	.083	.091	.063
	7	.129	.100	.083
	8	.129	.131	.104
	9	.182	.163	.127
	10	.182	.175+	.151
	11	.219	.205+	.151
	12	.265-	.236	.198
	13	.265-	.244	.206
	14	.295-	.292	.249
	15	.336	.324	.256
	16	.376	.324	.308
	17	.416	.364	.329
	18	.446	.403	.345-
	19	.476	.440	.388
	20	.508	.476	.430
	21	.545-	.524	.462
	22	.584	.560	.495-
	23	.624	.597	.531
	24	.664	.636	.570
	25	.705+	.676	.612
	26	.735+	.708	.655+
	27	.781	.756	.690
	28	.818	.795-	.744
	29	.871	.837	.794
	30	.917	.900	.849

Table 2. Critical Values of the Unit Normal Distribution.[a,b,c]

Z	.00	.01	.02	.03	.04	.05	.06	.07	.08	.09
0.0	.0000	.0040	.0080	.0120	.0160	.0199	.0239	.0279	.0319	.0359
0.1	.0398	.0438	.0478	.0517	.0557	.0596	.0636	.0675	.0714	.0753
0.2	.0793	.0832	.0871	.0910	.0948	.0987	.1026	.1064	.1103	.1141
0.3	.1179	.1217	.1255	.1293	.1331	.1368	.1406	.1443	.1480	.1517
0.4	.1554	.1591	.1628	.1664	.1700	.1736	.1772	.1808	.1844	.1879
0.5	.1915	.1950	.1985	.2019	.2054	.2088	.2123	.2157	.2190	.2224
0.6	.2257	.2291	.2324	.2357	.2389	.2422	.2454	.2486	.2518	.2549
0.7	.2580	.2612	.2642	.2673	.2704	.2734	.2764	.2794	.2823	.2852
0.8	.2881	.2910	.2939	.2967	.2995	.3023	.3051	.3078	.3106	.3133
0.9	.3159	.3186	.3212	.3238	.3264	.3289	.3315	.3340	.3365	.3389
1.0	.3413	.3438	.3461	.3485	.3508	.3531	.3554	.3577	.3599	.3621
1.1	.3643	.3665	.3686	.3708	.3729	.3749	.3770	.3790	.3810	.3830
1.2	.3849	.3869	.3888	.3907	.3925	.3944	.3962	.3980	.3997	.4015
1.3	.4032	.4049	.4066	.4082	.4099	.4115	.4131	.4147	.4162	.4177
1.4	.4192	.4207	.4222	.4236	.4251	.4265	.4279	.4292	.4306	.4319
1.5	.4332	.4345	.4357	.4370	.4382	.4394	.4406	.4418	.4429	.4441
1.6	.4452	.4463	.4474	.4484	.4495	.4505	.4515	.4525	.4535	.4545
1.7	.4554	.4564	.4573	.4582	.4591	.4599	.4608	.4616	.4625	.4633
1.8	.4641	.4649	.4656	.4664	.4671	.4678	.4686	.4693	.4699	.4706
1.9	.4713	.4719	.4726	.4732	.4738	.4744	.4750	.4756	.4761	.4767
2.0	.4772	.4778	.4783	.4788	.4793	.4708	.4803	.4808	.4812	.4817
2.1	.4821	.4826	.4830	.4834	.4838	.4842	.4846	.4850	.4854	.4857
2.2	.4861	.4864	.4868	.4871	.4875	.4878	.4881	.4884	.4887	.4890
2.3	.4893	.4896	.4898	.4901	.4904	.4906	.4909	.4911	.4913	.4916
2.4	.4918	.4920	.4922	.4925	.49[illegible]	[illegible]	4931	.4932	.4934	.4936

2.5	.4938	.4940	.4941	.4943	.4945	.4946	.4948	.4949	.4951	.4952
2.6	.4953	.4955	.4956	.4957	.4959	.4960	.4961	.4962	.4963	.4964
2.7	.4965	.4966	.4967	.4968	.4969	.4970	.4971	.4972	.4973	.4974
2.8	.4974	.4975	.4976	.4977	.4977	.4978	.4979	.4979	.4980	.4981
2.9	.4981	.4982	.4982	.4983	.4984	.4984	.4985	.4985	.4986	.4986
3.0	.49865	.4987	.4987	.4988	.4988	.4989	.4989	.4989	.4990	.4990
3.1	.49903	.4991	.4991	.4991	.4992	.4992	.4992	.4992	.4993	.4993
3.2	.4993129	.4993	.4994	.4994	.4994	.4994	.4994	.4995	.4995	.4995
3.3	.4995166	.4995	.4995	.4996	.4996	.4996	.4996	.4996	.4996	.4997
3.4	.4996631	.4997	.4997	.4997	.4997	.4997	.4997	.4997	.4998	.4998
3.5	.4997674	.4998	.4998	.4998	.4998	.4998	.4998	.4998	.4998	.4998
3.6	.4998409	.4998	.4999	.4999	.4999	.4999	.4999	.4999	.4999	.4999
3.7	.4998922	.4999	.4999	.4999	.4999	.4999	.4999	.4999	.4999	.4999
3.8	.4999277	.4999	.4999	.4999	.4999	.4999	.4999	.5000	.5000	.5000
3.9	.4999519	.5000	.5000	.5000	.5000	.5000	.5000	.5000	.5000	.5000
4.0	.4999683									
4.5	.4999966									
5.0	.4999997133									

[a] From Croxton, Frederick E., and Cowden. Dudley J., *Practical Business Statistics*, Prentice-Hall, New York 1948, p. 511. Reprinted by permission of the publisher.

[b] Through Z = 2.99, from Rugg's *Statistical Methods Applied to Education*, by arrangement with the publishers, Houghton Mifflin Company. A much more detailed table of normal curve areas is given in Federal Works Agency. Work Projects Administration for the City of New York, *Tables of Probability Functions*, Natural Bureau of Standards, New York, 1942, Vol. II, pp. 2–238. In this appendix values for Z = 3.00 through 5.00 were computed from the latter source.

[c] Each entry in this table is the proportion of the total area under a normal curve which lies under the segment between the mean and Z standard deviations from the mean.

Table 3. Critical Values for d (or c) in the Fisher–Yates Test[a]

Totals in Right Margin		b (or a)[b]	Level of Significance			
			.05	.025	.01	.005
a + b = 3	c + d = 3	3	0	–	–	–
a + b = 4	c + d = 4	4	0	0	–	–
	c + d = 3	4	0	–	–	–
a + b = 5	c + d = 5	5	1	1	0	0
		4	0	0	–	–
	c + d = 4	5	1	0	0	–
		4	0	–	–	–
	c + d = 3	5	0	0	–	–
	c + d = 2	5	0	–	–	–
a + b = 6	c + d = 6	6	2	1	1	0
		5	1	0	0	–
		4	0	–	–	–
	c + d = 5	6	1	0	0	0
		5	0	0	–	–
		4	0	–	–	–
	c + d = 4	6	1	0	0	0
		5	0	0	–	–
	c + d = 3	6	0	0		
		5	0			
	c + d = 2	6	0		–	–
a + b = 7	c + d = 7	7	3	2	1	1
		6	1	1	0	0
		5	0	0	–	–
		4	0	–	–	–
	c + d = 6	77	2	2	1	1
		6	1	0	0	0
		5	0	0	–	–
		4	0	–	–	–
	c + d = 5	7	2	1	0	0
		6	1	0	0	–
		5	0	–	–	–
	c + d = 4	7	1	1	0	0
		6	0	0	–	–
		5	0	–	–	–

[a]Adapted from Finney, D. J., 1948. The Fisher–Yates test of significance in 2 × 2 contingency tables. *Biometrika*, 35, 149–154, with the kind permission of the author and the Biometrika Trustees.

[b]When b is entered in the middle column, the significance levels are for d. When a is used in place of b, the significance levels are for c.

Table 3. *(continued)*

Totals in Right Margin		b (or a)[b]	Level of Significance .05	.025	.01	.005
	c + d = 3	7	0	0	0	–
		6	0	–	–	–
	c + d = 2	7	0	–	–	–
a + b = 8	c + d = 8	8	4	3	2	2
		7	2	2	1	0
		6	1	1	0	0
		5	0	0	–	–
		4	0	–	–	–
	c + d = 7	8	3	2	2	1
		7	2	1	1	0
		6	1	0	0	–
		5	0	0	–	–
	c + d = 6	8	2	2	1	1
		7	1	1	0	0
		6	0	0	0	–
		5	0	–	–	–
	c + d = 5	8	2	1	1	0
		7	1	0	0	0
		6	0	0	–	–
		5	0	–	–	–
	c + d = 4	8	1	1	0	0
		7	0	0	–	–
		6	0	–	–	–
	c + d = 3	8	0	0	0	–
		7	0	0	–	–
	c + d = 2	8	0	0	–	–
a + b = 9	c + d = 9	9	5	4	3	3
		8	3	3	2	1
		7	2	1	1	0
		6	1	1	0	0
		5	0	0	–	–
		4	0	–	–	–
	c + d = 8	9	4	3	3	2
		8	3	2	1	1
		7	2	1	0	0
		6	1	0	0	–
		5	0	0	–	–
	c + d = 7	9	3	3	2	2
		8	2	2	1	0

Table 3. *(continued)*

Totals in Right Margin		b (or a)[b]	.05	.025	.01	.005
			Level of Significance			
		7	1	1	0	0
		6	0	0	–	–
		5	0	–	–	–
a + b = 9	c + d = 6	9	3	2	1	1
		8	2	1	0	0
		7	1	0	0	–
		6	0	0	–	–
		5	0	–	–	–
	c + d = 5	9	2	1	1	1
		8	1	1	0	0
		7	0	0	–	–
		6	0	–	–	–
	c + d = 4	9	1	1	0	0
		8	0	0	0	–
		7	0	0	–	–
		6	0	–	–	–
	c + d = 3	9	1	0	0	0
		8	0	0	–	–
		7	0	–	–	–
	c + d = 2	9	0	0	–	–
a + b = 10	c + d = 10	10	6	5	4	3
		9	4	3	3	2
		8	3	2	1	1
		7	2	1	1	0
		6	1	0	0	–
		5	0	0	–	–
		4	0	–	–	–
	c + d = 9	10	5	4	3	3
		9	4	3	2	2
		8	2	2	1	1
		7	1	1	0	0
		6	1	0	0	–
		5	0	0	–	–
	c + d = 8	10	4	4	3	2
		9	3	2	2	1
		8	2	1	1	0
		7	1	1	0	0
		6	0	0	–	–
		5	0	–	–	–

Table 3. *(continued)*

Totals in Right Margin		b (or a)[b]	Level of Significance .05	.025	.01	.005
	c + d = 7	10	3	3	2	2
		9	2	2	1	1
		8	1	1	0	0
		7	1	0	0	–
		6	0	0	–	–
		5	0	–	–	–
a + b = 10	c + d = 6	10	3	2	2	1
		9	2	1	1	0
		8	1	1	0	0
		7	0	0	–	–
		6	0	–	–	–
	c + d = 5	10	2	2	1	1
		9	1	1	0	0
		8	1	0	0	–
		7	0	0	–	–
		6	0	–	–	–
	c + d = 4	10	1	1	0	0
		9	1	0	0	0
		8	0	0	–	–
		7	0	–	–	–
	c + d = 3	10	1	0	0	0
		9	0	0	–	–
		8	0	–	–	–
	c + d = 2	10	0	0	–	–
		9	0	–	–	–
a + b = 11	c + d = 11	11	7	6	5	4
		10	5	4	3	3
		9	4	3	2	2
		8	3	2	1	1
		7	2	1	0	0
		6	1	0	0	–
		5	0	0	–	–
		4	0	–	–	–
	c + d = 10	11	6	5	4	4
		10	4	4	3	2
		9	3	3	2	1
		8	2	2	1	0
		7	1	1	0	0
		6	1	0	0	–
		5	0	–	–	–

Table 3. (*continued*)

Totals in Right Margin		b (or a)[b]	Level of Significance .05	.025	.01	.005
	c + d = 9	11	5	4	4	3
		10	4	3	2	2
		9	3	2	1	1
		8	2	1	1	0
		7	1	1	0	0
		6	0	0	–	–
		5	0	–	–	–
a + b = 11	c + d = 8	11	4	4	3	3
		10	3	3	2	1
		9	2	2	1	1
		8	1	1	0	0
		7	1	0	0	–
		6	0	0	–	–
		5	0	–	–	–
	c + d = 7	11	4	3	2	2
		10	3	2	1	1
		9	2	1	1	0
		8	1	1	0	0
		7	0	0	–	–
		6	0	0	–	–
	c + d = 6	11	3	2	2	1
		10	2	1	1	0
		9	1	1	0	0
		8	1	0	0	–
		7	0	0	–	–
		6	0	–	–	–
	c + d = 5	11	2	2	1	1
		10	1	1	0	0
		9	1	0	0	0
		8	0	0	–	–
		7	0	–	–	–
	c + d = 4	11	1	1	1	0
		10	1	0	0	0
		9	0	0	–	–
		8	0	–	–	–
	c + d = 3	11	1	0	0	0
		10	0	0	–	–
		9	0	–	–	–
	c + d = 2	11	0	0	–	–
		10	0	–	–	–

Table 3. *(continued)*

Totals in Right Margin		b (or a)[b]	Level of Significance .05	.025	.01	.005
a + b = 12	c + d = 12	12	8	7	6	5
		11	6	5	4	4
		10	5	4	3	2
		9	4	3	2	1
		8	3	2	1	1
		7	2	1	0	0
		6	1	0	0	–
		5	0	0	–	–
		4	0	–	–	–
a + b = 12	c + d = 11	12	7	6	5	5
		11	5	5	4	3
		10	4	3	2	2
		9	3	2	2	1
		8	2	1	1	0
		7	1	1	0	0
		6	1	0	0	–
		5	0	0	–	–
	c + d = 10	12	6	5	5	4
		11	5	4	3	3
		10	4	3	2	2
		9	3	2	1	1
		8	2	1	0	0
		7	1	0	0	0
		6	0	0	–	–
		5	0	–	–	–
	c + d = 9	12	5	5	4	3
		11	4	3	3	2
		10	3	2	2	1
		9	2	2	1	0
		8	1	1	0	0
		7	1	0	0	–
		6	0	0	–	–
		5	0	–	–	–
	c + d = 8	12	5	4	3	3
		11	3	3	2	2
		10	2	2	1	1
		9	2	1	1	0
		8	1	1	0	0
		7	0	0	–	–
		6	0	0	–	–

Table 3. (*continued*)

Totals in Right Margin		b (or a)[b]	Level of Significance .05	.025	.01	.005
	c + d = 7	12	4	3	2	2
		11	3	2	2	1
		10	2	1	1	0
		9	1	1	0	0
		8	1	0	0	–
		7	0	0	–	–
		6	0	–	–	–
a + b = 12	c + d = 6	12	3	3	2	2
		11	2	2	1	1
		10	1	1	0	0
		9	1	0	0	0
		8	0	0	–	–
		7	0	0	–	–
		6	0	–	–	–
	c + d = 5	12	2	2	1	1
		11	1	1	1	0
		10	1	0	0	0
		9	0	0	0	–
		8	0	0	–	–
		7	0	–	–	–
	c + d = 4	12	2	1	1	0
		11	1	0	0	0
		10	0	0	0	–
		9	0	0	–	–
		8	0	–	–	–
	c + d = 3	12	1	0	0	0
		11	0	0	0	–
		10	0	0	–	–
		9	0	–	–	–
	c + d = 2	12	0	0	–	–
		11	0	–	–	–
a + b = 13	c + d = 13	13	9	8	7	6
		12	7	6	5	4
		11	6	5	4	3
		10	4	4	3	2
		9	3	3	2	1
		8	2	2	1	0
		7	2	1	0	0
		6	1	0	0	–

Table 3. *(continued)*

Totals in Right Margin		b (or a)[b]	.05	.025	.01	.005
			Level of Significance			
		5	0	0	–	–
		4	0	–	–	–
	c + d = 12	13	8	7	6	5
		12	6	5	5	4
		11	5	4	3	3
		10	4	3	2	2
		9	3	2	1	1
		8	2	1	1	0
		7	1	1	0	0
		6	1	0	0	–
		5	0	0	–	–
a + b = 13	c + d = 11	13	7	6	5	5
		12	6	5	4	3
		11	4	4	3	2
		10	3	3	2	1
		9	3	2	1	1
		8	2	1	0	0
		7	1	0	0	0
		6	0	0	–	–
		5	0	–	–	–
	c + d = 10	13	6	6	5	4
		12	5	4	3	3
		11	4	3	2	2
		10	3	2	1	1
		9	2	1	1	0
		8	1	1	0	0
		7	1	0	0	–
		6	0	0	–	–
		5	0	–	–	–
	c + d = 9	13	5	5	4	4
		12	4	4	3	2
		11	3	3	2	1
		10	2	2	1	1
		9	2	1	0	0
		8	1	1	0	0
		7	0	0	–	–
		6	0	0	–	–
		5	0	–	–	–

Table 3. *(continued)*

Totals in Right Margin	b (or a)[b]	Level of Significance .05	.025	.01	.005
c + d = 8	13	5	4	3	3
	12	4	3	2	2
	11	3	2	1	1
	10	2	1	1	0
	9	1	1	0	0
	8	1	0	0	–
	7	0	0	–	–
	6	0	–	–	–
c + d = 7	13	4	3	3	2
	12	3	2	2	1
	11	2	2	1	1
	10	1	1	0	0
	9	1	0	0	0
	8	0	0	–	–
	7	0	0	–	–
	6	0	–	–	–

Table 4. Critical Values of the χ^2 Square Distribution for One Degree of Freedom

P	χ^2
.01	0.00016
.05	0.0039
.10	0.0158
.50	0.455
.90	2.71
.95	3.84
.99	6.63

Table 5. **Critical Values of the Distribution of the Mean Absolute Deviation**[a]

Sample	HNZ as a function of N and Z											
Size N	.10	.20	.30	.40	.50	.60	.70	.80	.90	.95	.98	.99
2	0.224	0.460	0.721	1.027	1.414	1.946	2.776	4.353	8.929	17.969	45.001	90.024
3	0.193	0.393	0.605	0.840	1.111	1.444	1.888	2.570	3.981	5.868	9.499	13.538
4	0.182	0.369	0.566	0.780	1.022	1.308	1.673	2.195	3.161	4.280	6.113	7.868
5	0.176	0.357	0.546	0.750	0.978	1.243	1.574	2.032	2.833	3.698	5.002	6.153
6	0.173	0.349	0.534	0.732	0.951	1.205	1.516	1.940	2.657	3.399	4.461	5.355
7	0.170	0.344	0.525	0.719	0.934	1.179	1.479	1.881	2.546	3.216	4.143	4.897
8	0.168	0.340	0.519	0.711	0.921	1.161	1.452	1.840	2.471	3.092	3.933	4.601
9	0.167	0.338	0.515	0.704	0.912	1.148	1.433	1.809	2.415	3.003	3.785	4.394
10	0.166	0.335	0.511	0.699	0.904	1.138	1.418	1.786	2.373	2.936	3.674	4.241
11	0.165	0.334	0.509	0.695	0.898	1.129	1.406	1.767	2.340	2.884	3.589	4.124
12	0.165	0.332	0.506	0.691	0.894	1.122	1.396	1.752	2.313	2.842	3.520	4.031
13	0.164	0.331	0.504	0.689	0.890	1.117	1.388	1.739	2.291	2.807	3.465	3.956
14	0.163	0.330	0.503	0.686	0.886	1.112	1.381	1.729	2.273	2.779	3.418	3.893
15	0.163	0.329	0.501	0.684	0.883	1.108	1.375	1.720	2.257	2.754	3.379	3.840
16	0.163	0.328	0.500	0.682	0.881	1.104	1.370	1.712	2.243	2.733	3.346	3.795
17	0.162	0.328	0.499	0.681	0.879	1.101	1.365	1.705	2.232	2.715	3.317	3.757
18	0.162	0.327	0.498	0.679	0.877	1.098	1.361	1.699	2.221	2.699	3.292	3.723
19	0.162	0.327	0.497	0.678	0.875	1.096	1.358	1.694	2.212	2.685	3.269	3.693
20	0.162	0.326	0.497	0.677	0.873	1.094	1.355	1.689	2.204	2.672	3.249	3.667

21	0.161	0.326	0.496	0.676	0.872	1.092	1.352	1.685	2.197	2.661	3.232	3.643
22	0.161	0.325	0.495	0.675	0.871	1.090	1.349	1.681	2.190	2.651	3.216	3.622
23	0.161	0.325	0.495	0.674	0.869	1.089	1.347	1.678	2.184	2.642	3.201	3.603
24	0.161	0.325	0.494	0.674	0.868	1.087	1.345	1.675	2.178	2.633	3.188	3.586
25	0.161	0.324	0.494	0.673	0.867	1.086	1.343	1.672	2.173	2.626	3.176	3.570
26	0.161	0.324	0.493	0.672	0.867	1.084	1.341	1.669	2.169	2.619	3.165	3.555
27	0.161	0.324	0.493	0.672	0.866	1.083	1.340	1.667	2.165	2.612	3.155	3.542
28	0.160	0.324	0.493	0.671	0.865	1.082	1.338	1.665	2.161	2.606	3.146	3.530
29	0.160	0.323	0.492	0.671	0.864	1.081	1.337	1.662	2.157	2.601	3.138	3.519
30	0.160	0.323	0.492	0.670	0.864	1.080	1.335	1.660	2.154	2.596	3.130	3.508
40	0.160	0.322	0.490	0.667	0.859	1.074	1.326	1.646	2.130	2.559	3.073	3.434
60	0.159	0.320	0.487	0.664	0.854	1.067	1.317	1.633	2.106	2.524	3.019	3.362
120	0.158	0.319	0.485	0.660	0.850	1.061	1.308	1.619	2.084	2.490	2.966	3.294
∞	0.157	0.318	0.483	0.657	0.845	1.055	1.299	1.606	2.062	2.456	2.916	3.228

[a]Adapted from Herrey. A. M. J., Percentage Points of the H-Distribution for Computing Confidence Limits or Performing t-Tests by Way of the Mean Absolute Deviation, *Journal of the American Statistical Association*, March 1971, p. 188.

Table 6. Critical Values of Spearman's Rank Correlation Coefficient[a]

N	$(1-\alpha)(2)$: 0.50 $(1-\alpha)(1)$: 0.25	0.20 0.10	0.10 0.05	0.05 0.025	0.02 0.01	0.01 0.005	0.005 0.00025	0.002 0.001	0.001 0.0005
4	0.600	1.000	1.000						
5	0.500	0.800	0.900	1.000	1.000				
6	0.371	0.657	0.829	0.886	0.943	1.000	1.000		
7	0.321	0.571	0.714	0.786	0.893	0.929	0.964	1.000	1.000
8	0.310	0.524	0.643	0.738	0.833	0.881	0.905	0.952	0.976
9	0.267	0.483	0.600	0.700	0.783	0.833	0.867	0.917	0.933
10	0.248	0.455	0.464	0.648	0.745	0.794	0.830	0.879	0.903
11	0.236	0.427	0.536	0.618	0.709	0.755	0.800	0.845	0.873
12	0.217	0.406	0.503	0.587	0.678	0.727	0.769	0.818	0.846
13	0.209	0.385	0.484	0.560	0.648	0.703	0.747	0.791	0.824
14	0.200	0.367	0.464	0.538	0.626	0.679	0.723	0.771	0.802
15	0.189	0.354	0.446	0.521	0.604	0.654	0.700	0.750	0.779
16	0.182	0.341	0.429	0.503	0.582	0.635	0.679	0.729	0.762
17	0.176	0.328	0.414	0.485	0.566	0.615	0.662	0.713	0.748
18	0.170	0.317	0.401	0.472	0.550	0.600	0.643	0.695	0.728
19	0.165	0.309	0.391	0.460	0.535	0.584	0.628	0.677	0.712
20	0.161	0.299	0.380	0.447	0.520	0.570	0.612	0.662	0.696
21	0.156	0.292	0.370	0.435	0.508	0.556	0.599	0.648	0.681
22	0.152	0.284	0.361	0.425	0.496	0.544	0.586	0.634	0.667
23	0.148	0.278	0.353	0.415	0.486	0.532	0.573	0.622	0.654

[a]Reproduced from Zar, Jerrold H., *Biostatistical Analysis*, Prentice-Hall, Englewood Cliffs, N.J., © 1974 pp. 498–499. Reprinted by permission of Prentice-Hall Inc.

Table 6. (*continued*)

$(1-\alpha)(2)$: N $(1-\alpha)(1)$:	0.50 0.25	0.20 0.10	0.10 0.05	0.05 0.025	0.02 0.01	0.01 0.005	0.005 0.00025	0.002 0.001	0.001 0.0005
24	0.144	0.271	0.344	0.406	0.476	0.521	0.562	0.610	0.642
25	0.142	0.265	0.337	0.398	0.466	0.511	0.551	0.598	0.630
26	0.138	0.259	0.331	0.390	0.457	0.501	0.541	0.587	0.619
27	0.136	0.255	0.324	0.382	0.448	0.491	0.531	0.577	0.608
28	0.133	0.250	0.317	0.375	0.440	0.483	0.522	0.567	0.598
29	0.130	0.245	0.312	0.368	0.433	0.475	0.513	0.558	0.589
30	0.128	0.240	0.306	0.362	0.425	0.467	0.504	0.549	0.580
31	0.126	0.236	0.301	0.356	0.418	0.459	0.496	0.541	0.571
32	0.124	0.232	0.296	0.350	0.412	0.452	0.489	0.533	0.563
33	0.121	0.229	0.291	0.345	0.405	0.446	0.482	0.525	0.554
34	0.120	0.225	0.287	0.340	0.399	0.439	0.475	0.517	0.547
35	0.118	0.222	0.283	0.335	0.394	0.433	0.468	0.510	0.539
36	0.116	0.219	0.279	0.330	0.388	0.427	0.462	0.504	0.533
37	0.114	0.216	0.275	0.325	0.383	0.421	0.456	0.497	0.526
38	0.113	0.212	0.271	0.321	0.378	0.415	0.450	0.491	0.519
39	0.111	0.210	0.267	0.317	0.373	0.410	0.444	0.485	0.513
40	0.110	0.207	0.264	0.313	0.368	0.405	0.439	0.479	0.507
41	0.108	0.204	0.261	0.309	0.364	0.400	0.433	0.473	0.501
42	0.107	0.202	0.257	0.305	0.359	0.395	0.428	0.468	0.495
43	0.105	0.199	0.254	0.301	0.355	0.391	0.423	0.463	0.490
44	0.104	0.197	0.251	0.298	0.351	0.386	0.419	0.458	0.484
45	0.103	0.194	0.248	0.294	0.347	0.382	0.414	0.453	0.479

Table 6. (*continued*)

$(1-\alpha)(2)$:	0.50	0.20	0.10	0.05	0.02	0.01	0.005	0.002	0.001
N $(1-\alpha)(1)$:	0.25	0.10	0.05	0.025	0.01	0.005	0.00025	0.001	0.0005
46	0.102	0.192	0.246	0.291	0.343	0.378	0.410	0.448	0.474
47	0.101	0.190	0.243	0.288	0.340	0.374	0.405	0.443	0.469
48	0.100	0.188	0.240	0.285	0.336	0.370	0.401	0.439	0.465
49	0.098	0.186	0.238	0.282	0.333	0.366	0.397	0.434	0.460
50	0.097	0.184	0.235	0.279	0.329	0.363	0.393	0.430	0.456
51	0.096	0.182	0.233	0.276	0.326	0.359	0.390	0.426	0.451
52	0.095	0.180	0.231	0.274	0.323	0.356	0.386	0.422	0.447
53	0.095	0.179	0.228	0.271	0.320	0.352	0.382	0.418	0.443
54	0.094	0.177	0.226	0.268	0.317	0.349	0.379	0.414	0.439
55	0.093	0.175	0.224	0.266	0.314	0.346	0.375	0.411	0.435
56	0.092	0.174	0.222	0.264	0.311	0.343	0.372	0.407	0.432
57	0.091	0.172	0.220	0.261	0.308	0.340	0.369	0.404	0.428
58	0.090	0.171	0.218	0.259	0.306	0.337	0.366	0.400	0.424
59	0.089	0.169	0.216	0.257	0.303	0.334	0.363	0.397	0.421
60	0.089	0.168	0.214	0.255	0.300	0.331	0.360	0.394	0.418
61	0.088	0.166	0.213	0.252	0.298	0.329	0.357	0.391	0.414
62	0.087	0.165	0.211	0.250	0.296	0.326	0.354	0.388	0.411
63	0.086	0.163	0.209	0.248	0.293	0.323	0.351	0.385	0.408
64	0.086	0.162	0.207	0.246	0.291	0.321	0.348	0.382	0.405
65	0.085	0.161	0.206	0.244	0.289	0.318	0.346	0.379	0.402
66	0.084	0.160	0.204	0.243	0.287	0.316	0.343	0.376	0.399
67	0.084	0.158	0.203	0.241	0.284	0.314	0.341	0.373	0.396

Table 6. *(continued)*

N	$(1-\alpha)(2)$: 0.50 $(1-\alpha)(1)$: 0.25	0.20 0.10	0.10 0.05	0.05 0.025	0.02 0.01	0.01 0.005	0.005 0.00025	0.002 0.001	0.001 0.0005
68	0.083	0.157	0.201	0.239	0.282	0.311	0.338	0.370	0.393
69	0.082	0.156	0.200	0.237	0.280	0.309	0.336	0.368	0.390
70	0.082	0.155	0.198	0.235	0.278	0.307	0.333	0.365	0.388
71	0.081	0.154	0.197	0.234	0.276	0.305	0.331	0.363	0.385
72	0.081	0.153	0.195	0.232	0.274	0.303	0.329	0.360	0.382
73	0.080	0.152	0.194	0.230	0.272	0.301	0.327	0.358	0.380
74	0.080	0.151	0.193	0.229	0.271	0.299	0.324	0.355	0.377
75	0.079	0.150	0.191	0.227	0.269	0.297	0.322	0.353	0.375
76	0.078	0.149	0.190	0.226	0.267	0.295	0.320	0.351	0.372
77	0.078	0.148	0.189	0.224	0.265	0.293	0.318	0.349	0.370
78	0.077	0.147	0.188	0.223	0.264	0.291	0.316	0.346	0.368
79	0.077	0.146	0.186	0.221	0.262	0.289	0.314	0.344	0.365
80	0.076	0.145	0.185	0.220	0.260	0.287	0.312	0.342	0.363
81	0.076	0.144	0.184	0.219	0.259	0.285	0.310	0.340	0.361
82	0.075	0.143	0.183	0.217	0.257	0.284	0.308	0.338	0.359
83	0.075	0.142	0.182	0.216	0.255	0.282	0.306	0.336	0.357
84	0.074	0.141	0.181	0.215	0.254	0.280	0.305	0.334	0.355
85	0.074	0.140	0.180	0.213	0.252	0.279	0.303	0.332	0.353
86	0.074	0.139	0.179	0.212	0.251	0.277	0.301	0.330	0.351
87	0.073	0.139	0.177	0.211	0.250	0.276	0.299	0.328	0.349
88	0.073	0.158	0.176	0.210	0.248	0.274	0.298	0.327	0.347
89	0.072	0.137	0.175	0.209	0.247	0.272	0.296	0.324	0.345
90	0.072	0.136	0.174	0.207	0.245	0.271	0.294	0.323	0.345

Table 6. *(continued)*

$(1-\alpha)(2)$: N $(1-\alpha)(1)$:	0.50 0.25	0.20 0.10	0.10 0.05	0.05 0.025	0.02 0.01	0.01 0.005	0.005 0.00025	0.002 0.001	0.001 0.0005
91	0.072	0.135	0.173	0.206	0.244	0.269	0.293	0.321	0.341
92	0.071	0.135	0.173	0.205	0.243	0.268	0.291	0.319	0.339
93	0.071	0.134	0.172	0.204	0.241	0.267	0.290	0.318	0.338
94	0.070	0.133	0.171	0.203	0.240	0.265	0.288	0.316	0.336
95	0.070	0.133	0.170	0.202	0.239	0.264	0.287	0.314	0.334
96	0.070	0.132	0.169	0.201	0.238	0.262	0.285	0.313	0.332
97	0.069	0.131	0.168	0.200	0.236	0.261	0.284	0.311	0.331
98	0.069	0.130	0.167	0.199	0.235	0.260	0.282	0.310	0.329
99	0.068	0.130	0.166	0.198	0.234	0.258	0.281	0.308	0.327
100	0.068	0.129	0.165	0.197	0.233	0.257	0.279	0.307	0.326

Table 7. Binomial Distribution—Individual Terms[a]

		p																				
N	K	.01	.02	.04	.05	.06	.08	.10	.12	.14	.15	.16	.18	.20	.22	.24	.25	.30	.35	.40	.45	.50	K
2	0	980	960	922	902	884	846	810	774	740	722	706	672	640	608	578	562	490	422	360	302	250	0
	1	020	039	077	095	113	147	180	211	241	255	269	295	320	343	365	375	420	455	480	495	500	1
	2	0+	0+	002	002	004	006	010	014	020	022	026	032	040	048	058	062	090	122	160	202	250	2
3	0	970	941	885	857	831	779	729	681	636	614	593	551	512	475	439	422	343	275	216	166	125	0
	1	029	058	111	135	159	203	243	279	311	325	339	363	384	402	416	422	441	444	432	408	375	1
	2	0+	001	005	007	010	018	027	038	051	057	065	080	096	113	131	141	189	239	288	334	375	2
	3	0+	0+	0+	0+	0+	001	001	002	003	003	004	006	008	011	014	016	027	043	064	091	125	3
4	0	961	922	849	815	781	716	656	600	547	522	498	452	410	370	334	316	240	179	130	092	063	0
	1	039	075	142	171	199	249	292	327	356	368	379	397	410	418	421	422	412	384	346	299	250	1
	2	001	002	009	014	019	033	049	067	087	098	108	131	154	177	200	211	265	311	346	368	375	2
	3	0+	0+	0+	0+	001	002	004	006	009	011	014	019	026	033	042	047	076	111	154	200	250	3
	4	0+	0+	0+	0+	0+	0+	0+	0+	0+	001	001	001	002	002	003	004	008	015	026	041	062	4
5	0	951	904	815	774	734	659	590	528	470	444	418	371	328	289	254	237	168	116	078	050	031	0
	1	048	092	170	204	234	287	328	360	383	392	398	407	410	407	400	396	360	312	259	206	156	1
	2	001	004	014	021	030	050	073	098	125	138	152	179	205	230	253	264	309	336	346	337	312	2
	3	0+	0+	001	001	002	004	008	013	020	024	029	039	051	065	080	088	132	181	230	276	312	3
	4	0+	0+	0+	0+	0+	0+	0+	001	002	002	003	004	006	009	013	015	028	049	077	113	156	4
	5	0+	0+	0+	0+	0+	0+	0+	0+	0+	0+	0+	0+	0+	001	001	001	002	005	010	018	031	5

[a]From Croxton, Frederick E., and Cowden, Dudley J., *Practical Business Statistics*, Prentice-Hall, New York, 1948, p. 511. Reprinted by permission of the publisher.

Table 7. (*continued*)

N	K	.01	.02	.04	.05	.06	.08	.10	.12	.14	.15	.16	.18	.20	.22	.24	.25	.30	.35	.40	.45	.50	K
												p											
6	0	941	886	783	735	690	606	531	464	405	377	351	304	262	225	193	178	118	075	047	028	016	0
	1	057	108	196	232	264	316	354	380	395	399	401	400	393	381	365	356	303	244	187	136	094	1
	2	001	006	020	031	042	069	098	130	161	176	191	220	246	269	288	297	324	328	311	278	234	2
	3	0+	0+	001	002	004	008	015	024	035	041	049	064	082	101	121	132	185	235	276	303	312	3
	4	0+	0+	0+	0+	0+	001	001	002	004	005	007	011	015	021	029	033	060	095	138	186	234	4
	5	0+	0+	0+	0+	0+	0+	0+	0+	0+	0+	001	001	002	002	004	004	010	020	037	061	094	5
	6	0+	0+	0+	0+	0+	0+	0+	0+	0+	0+	0+	0+	0+	0+	0+	0+	001	002	004	008	016	6
7	0	932	868	751	698	648	558	478	409	348	321	295	249	210	176	146	133	082	049	028	015	008	0
	1	066	124	219	257	290	340	372	390	396	396	393	383	367	347	324	311	247	185	131	087	055	1
	2	002	008	027	041	055	089	124	160	194	210	225	252	275	293	307	311	318	298	261	214	164	2
	3	0+	0+	002	004	006	013	023	036	053	062	071	092	115	138	161	173	227	268	290	292	273	3
	4	0+	0+	0+	0+	0+	001	003	005	009	011	014	020	029	039	051	058	097	144	194	239	273	4
	5	0+	0+	0+	0+	0+	0+	0+	0+	001	001	002	003	004	007	010	012	025	047	077	117	164	5
	6	0+	0+	0+	0+	0+	0+	0+	0+	0+	0+	0+	0+	0+	001	001	001	004	008	017	032	055	6
	7	0+	0+	0+	0+	0+	0+	0+	0+	0+	0+	0+	0+	0+	0+	0+	0+	0+	001	002	004	008	7
8	0	923	851	721	663	610	513	430	360	299	272	248	204	168	137	111	100	058	032	017	008	004	
	1	075	139	240	279	311	357	383	392	390	385	378	359	336	309	281	267	198	137	090	055	031	1
	2	003	010	035	051	070	109	149	187	222	238	252	276	294	305	311	311	296	259	209	157	109	2
	3	0+	0+	003	005	009	019	033	051	072	084	096	121	147	172	196	208	254	279	279	257	219	3
	4	0+	0+	0+	0+	001	002	005	009	015	018	023	033	046	061	077	087	136	188	232	263	273	4
	5	0+	0+	0+	0+	0+	0+	0+	001	002	003	003	006	009	014	020	023	047	081	124	172	219	5
	6	0+	0+	0+	0+	0+	0+	0+	0+	0+	0+	0+	001	001	002	003	004	010	022	041	070	109	6

Table 7. (*continued*)

		p																				
N	*K*	.01	.02	.04	.05	.06	.08	.10	.12	.14	.15	.16	.18	.20	.22	.24	.25	.30	.35	.40	.45	.50	*K*
	7	0+	0+	0+	0+	0+	0+	0+	0+	0+	0+	0+	0+	0+	0+	0+	0+	001	003	008	016	031	7
	8	0+	0+	0+	0+	0+	0+	0+	0+	0+	0+	0+	0+	0+	0+	0+	0+	0+	0+	001	002	004	8
9	0	914	834	693	630	573	472	387	316	257	232	208	168	134	107	085	075	040	021	010	005	002	0
	1	083	153	260	299	329	370	387	388	377	368	357	331	302	271	240	225	156	100	060	034	018	1
	2	003	013	043	063	084	129	172	212	245	260	272	291	302	306	304	300	267	216	161	111	070	2
	3	0+	001	004	008	013	026	045	067	093	107	121	149	176	201	224	234	267	272	251	212	164	3
	4	0+	0+	0+	001	001	003	007	014	023	028	035	049	066	085	106	117	172	219	251	260	246	4
	5	0+	0+	0+	0+	0+	0+	001	002	004	005	007	011	017	024	033	039	074	118	167	213	246	5
	6	0+	0+	0+	0+	0+	0+	0+	0+	0+	001	001	002	003	005	007	009	021	042	074	116	164	6
	7	0+	0+	0+	0+	0+	0+	0+	0+	0+	0+	0+	0+	0+	001	001	001	004	010	021	041	070	7
	8	0+	0+	0+	0+	0+	0+	0+	0+	0+	0+	0+	0+	0+	0+	0+	0+	0+	001	004	009	018	8
	9	0+	0+	0+	0+	0+	0+	0+	0+	0+	0+	0+	0+	0+	0+	0+	0+	0+	0+	0+	001	002	9
10	0	904	817	665	599	539	434	349	279	221	197	175	137	107	083	064	056	028	013	006	003	001	0
	1	091	167	277	315	344	378	387	380	360	347	333	302	268	235	203	188	121	072	040	021	010	1
	2	004	015	052	075	099	148	194	233	264	276	286	298	302	298	288	282	233	176	121	076	044	2
	3	0+	001	006	010	017	034	057	085	115	130	145	174	201	224	243	250	267	252	215	166	117	3
	4	0+	0+	0+	001	002	005	011	020	033	040	048	067	088	111	134	146	200	238	251	238	205	4
	5	0+	0+	0+	0+	0+	001	001	003	006	008	011	018	026	037	051	058	103	154	201	234	246	5
	6	0+	0+	0+	0+	0+	0+	0+	0+	001	001	002	003	006	009	013	016	037	069	111	160	205	6
	7	0+	0+	0+	0+	0+	0+	0+	0+	0+	0+	0+	0+	001	001	002	003	009	021	042	075	117	7
	8	0+	0+	0+	0+	0+	0+	0+	0+	0+	0+	0+	0+	0+	0+	0+	0+	001	004	011	023	044	8
	9	0+	0+	0+	0+	0+	0+	0+	0+	0+	0+	0+	0+	0+	0+	0+	0+	0+	001	002	004	010	9
	10	0+	0+	0+	0+	0+	0+	0+	0+	0+	0+	0+	0+	0+	0+	0+	0+	0+	0+	0+	0+	001	0

Table 7. (*continued*)

N	K	.01	.02	.04	.05	.06	.08	.10	.12	.14	.15	.16	.18	.20	.22	.24	.25	.30	.35	.40	.45	.50	K
												p											
11	0	895	801	638	569	506	400	314	245	190	167	147	113	086	065	049	042	020	009	004	001	0+	0
	1	099	180	293	329	355	382	384	368	341	325	308	272	236	202	170	155	093	052	027	013	005	1
	2	005	018	061	087	113	166	213	251	277	287	293	299	295	284	268	258	200	140	089	051	027	2
	3	0+	001	008	014	022	043	071	103	135	152	168	197	221	241	254	258	257	225	177	126	081	3
	4	0+	0+	001	001	003	008	016	028	044	054	064	086	111	136	160	172	220	243	236	206	161	4
	5	0+	0+	0+	0+	0+	001	002	005	010	013	017	027	039	054	071	080	132	183	221	236	226	5
	6	0+	0+	0+	0+	0+	0+	0+	001	002	002	003	006	010	015	022	027	057	099	147	193	226	6
	7	0+	0+	0+	0+	0+	0+	0+	0+	0+	0+	0+	001	002	003	005	006	017	038	070	113	161	7
	8	0+	0+	0+	0+	0+	0+	0+	0+	0+	0+	0+	0+	0+	0+	001	001	004	010	023	046	081	8
	9	0+	0+	0+	0+	0+	0+	0+	0+	0+	0+	0+	0+	0+	0+	0+	0+	001	002	005	013	027	9
	10	0+	0+	0+	0+	0+	0+	0+	0+	0+	0+	0+	0+	0+	0+	0+	0+	0+	0+	001	002	005	10
	11	0+	0+	0+	0+	0+	0+	0+	0+	0+	0+	0+	0+	0+	0+	0+	0+	0+	0+	0+	0+	0+	11
12	0	886	785	613	540	476	368	282	216	164	142	123	092	069	051	037	032	014	006	002	001	0+	0
	1	107	192	306	341	365	384	377	353	320	301	282	243	206	172	141	127	071	037	017	008	003	1
	2	006	022	070	099	128	183	230	265	286	292	296	294	283	266	244	232	168	109	064	034	016	2
	3	0+	001	010	017	027	053	085	120	155	172	188	215	236	250	257	258	240	195	142	092	054	3
	4	0+	0+	001	002	004	010	021	037	057	068	080	106	133	159	183	194	231	237	213	170	121	4
	5	0+	0+	0+	0+	0+	001	004	008	015	019	025	037	053	072	092	103	158	204	227	222	193	5
	6	0+	0+	0+	0+	0+	0+	0+	001	003	004	005	010	016	024	034	040	079	128	177	212	226	6
	7	0+	0+	0+	0+	0+	0+	0+	0+	0+	001	001	002	003	006	009	011	029	059	101	149	193	7
	8	0+	0+	0+	0+	0+	0+	0+	0+	0+	0+	0+	0+	001	001	002	002	008	020	042	076	121	8
	9	0+	0+	0+	0+	0+	0+	0+	0+	0+	0+	0+	0+	0+	0+	0+	0+	001	005	012	028	054	9

Table 7. (*continued*)

		p																					
N	*K*	.01	.02	.04	.05	.06	.08	.10	.12	.14	.15	.16	.18	.20	.22	.24	.25	.30	.35	.40	.45	.50	*K*
	10	0+	0+	0+	0+	0+	0+	0+	0+	0+	0+	0+	0+	0+	0+	0+	0+	0+	001	002	007	016	10
	11	0+	0+	0+	0+	0+	0+	0+	0+	0+	0+	0+	0+	0+	0+	0+	0+	0+	0+	0+	001	003	11
	12	0+	0+	0+	0+	0+	0+	0+	0+	0+	0+	0+	0+	0+	0+	0+	0+	0+	0+	0+	0+	0+	12
13	0	878	769	588	513	447	338	254	190	141	121	104	076	055	040	028	024	010	004	001	0+	0+	0
	1	115	204	319	351	371	382	367	336	298	277	257	216	179	145	116	103	054	026	011	004	002	1
	2	007	025	080	111	142	199	245	275	291	294	293	285	268	245	220	206	139	084	045	022	010	2
	3	0+	002	012	021	033	064	100	138	174	190	205	229	246	254	254	252	218	165	111	066	035	3
	4	0+	0+	001	003	005	014	028	047	071	084	098	126	154	179	201	210	234	222	184	135	087	4
	5	0+	0+	0+	0+	001	002	006	012	021	027	033	050	069	091	114	126	180	215	221	199	157	5
	6	0+	0+	0+	0+	0+	0+	001	002	004	006	008	015	023	034	048	056	103	155	197	217	209	6
	7	0+	0+	0+	0+	0+	0+	0+	0+	001	001	002	003	006	010	015	019	044	083	131	177	209	7
	8	0+	0+	0+	0+	0+	0+	0+	0+	0+	0+	0+	001	001	002	004	005	014	034	066	109	157	8
	9	0+	0+	0+	0+	0+	0+	0+	0+	0+	0+	0+	0+	0+	0+	001	001	003	010	024	050	087	9
	10	0+	0+	0+	0+	0+	0+	0+	0+	0+	0+	0+	0+	0+	0+	0+	0+	001	002	006	016	035	10
	11	0+	0+	0+	0+	0+	0+	0+	0+	0+	0+	0+	0+	0+	0+	0+	0+	0+	0+	001	004	010	11
	12	0+	0+	0+	0+	0+	0+	0+	0+	0+	0+	0+	0+	0+	0+	0+	0+	0+	0+	0+	0+	002	12
	13	0+	0+	0+	0+	0+	0+	0+	0+	0+	0+	0+	0+	0+	0+	0+	0+	0+	0+	0+	0+	0+	13
14		869	754	565	488	421	311	229	167	121	103	087	062	044	031	021	018	007	002	001	0+	0+	0
	1	123	215	329	359	376	379	356	319	276	254	232	191	154	122	095	083	041	018	007	003	001	1
	2	008	029	089	123	156	214	257	283	292	291	287	272	250	223	195	180	113	063	032	014	006	2
	3	0+	002	015	026	040	074	114	154	190	206	219	239	250	252	246	240	194	137	085	046	022	3
	4	0+	0+	002	004	007	018	035	058	085	100	115	144	172	195	214	220	229	202	155	104	061	4

Table 7. *(continued)*

N	K	.01	.02	.04	.05	.06	.08	.10	.12	.14	.15	.16	.18	.20	.22	.24	.25	.30	.35	.40	.45	.50	K
	5	0+	0+	0+	0+	001	003	008	016	028	035	044	063	086	110	135	147	196	218	207	170	122	5
	6	0+	0+	0+	0+	0+	0+	001	003	007	009	012	021	032	047	064	073	126	176	207	209	183	6
	7	0+	0+	0+	0+	0+	0+	0+	001	001	002	003	005	009	015	023	028	062	108	157	195	209	7
	8	0+	0+	0+	0+	0+	0+	0+	0+	0+	0+	0+	001	002	004	006	008	023	051	092	140	183	8
	9	0+	0+	0+	0+	0+	0+	0+	0+	0+	0+	0+	0+	0+	001	001	002	007	018	041	076	122	9
	10	0+	0+	0+	0+	0+	0+	0+	0+	0+	0+	0+	0+	0+	0+	0+	0+	001	005	014	031	061	10
	11	0+	0+	0+	0+	0+	0+	0+	0+	0+	0+	0+	0+	0+	0+	0+	0+	0+	001	003	009	022	11
	12	0+	0+	0+	0+	0+	0+	0+	0+	0+	0+	0+	0+	0+	0+	0+	0+	0+	0+	001	002	006	12
	13	0+	0+	0+	0+	0+	0+	0+	0+	0+	0+	0+	0+	0+	0+	0+	0+	0+	0+	0+	0+	001	13
	14	0+	0+	0+	0+	0+	0+	0+	0+	0+	0+	0+	0+	0+	0+	0+	0+	0+	0+	0+	0+	0+	14
15	0	860	739	542	463	395	286	206	147	104	087	073	051	035	024	016	013	005	002	0+	0+	0+	0
	1	130	226	339	366	378	373	343	301	254	231	209	168	132	102	077	067	031	013	005	002	0+	1
	2	009	032	099	135	169	227	267	287	290	286	279	258	231	201	171	156	092	048	022	009	003	2
	3	0+	003	018	031	047	086	129	170	204	218	230	245	250	246	234	225	170	111	063	032	014	3
	4	0+	0+	002	005	009	022	043	069	100	116	131	162	188	208	221	225	219	179	127	078	042	4
	5	0+	0+	0+	001	001	004	010	021	036	045	055	078	103	129	154	165	206	212	186	140	092	5
	6	0+	0+	0+	0+	0+	001	002	005	010	013	017	029	043	061	081	092	147	191	207	191	153	6
	7	0+	0+	0+	0+	0+	0+	0+	001	002	003	004	008	014	022	033	039	081	132	177	201	196	7
	8	0+	0+	0+	0+	0+	0+	0+	0+	0+	001	001	002	003	006	010	013	035	071	118	165	196	8
	9	0+	0+	0+	0+	0+	0+	0+	0+	0+	0+	0+	0+	001	001	003	003	012	030	061	105	153	9
	10	0+	0+	0+	0+	0+	0+	0+	0+	0+	0+	0+	0+	0+	0+	0+	001	003	010	024	051	092	10
	11	0+	0+	0+	0+	0+	0+	0+	0+	0+	0+	0+	0+	0+	0+	0+	0+	001	002	007	019	042	11

Table 7. *(continued)*

N	K	.01	.02	.04	.05	.06	.08	.10	.12	.14	.15	.16	.18	.20	.22	.24	.25	.30	.35	.40	.45	.50	K
	12	0+	0+	0+	0+	0+	0+	0+	0+	0+	0+	0+	0+	0+	0+	0+	0+	0+	0+	002	005	014	12
	13	0+	0+	0+	0+	0+	0+	0+	0+	0+	0+	0+	0+	0+	0+	0+	0+	0+	0+	0+	001	003	13
	14	0+	0+	0+	0+	0+	0+	0+	0+	0+	0+	0+	0+	0+	0+	0+	0+	0+	0+	0+	0+	0+	14
	15	0+	0+	0+	0+	0+	0+	0+	0+	0+	0+	0+	0+	0+	0+	0+	0+	0+	0+	0+	0+	0+	15
16	0	851	724	520	440	372	263	385	129	090	074	061	042	028	019	012	010	003	001	0+	0+	0+	16
	1	138	236	347	371	379	366	329	282	233	210	187	147	113	085	063	053	023	009	003	001	0+	1
	2	010	036	108	146	182	239	275	289	285	277	268	242	211	179	1480	134	073	035	015	006	002	2
	3	0+	003	021	036	054	097	142	184	216	229	238	248	246	236	218	208	146	089	047	022	009	3
	4	0+	0+	003	006	011	027	051	081	114	131	147	177	200	216	224	225	204	155	101	057	028	4
	5	0+	0+	0+	001	002	006	014	027	045	056	067	093	120	146	170	180	210	201	162	112	067	5
	6	0+	0+	0+	0+	0+	001	003	007	013	018	023	037	055	076	098	110	165	198	198	168	122	6
	7	0+	0+	0+	0+	0+	0+	0+	001	003	005	006	012	020	030	044	052	101	152	189	197	175	7
	8	0+	0+	0+	0+	0+	0+	0+	0+	001	001	001	003	006	010	016	020	049	092	142	181	196	8
	9	0+	0+	0+	0+	0+	0+	0+	0+	0+	0+	0+	001	001	002	004	006	019	044	084	132	175	9
	10	0+	0+	0+	0+	0+	0+	0+	0+	0+	0+	0+	0+	0+	0+	001	001	006	017	039	075	122	10
	11	0+	0+	0+	0+	0+	0+	0+	0+	0+	0+	0+	0+	0+	0+	0+	0+	001	005	014	034	067	11
	12	0+	0+	0+	0+	0+	0+	0+	0+	0+	0+	0+	0+	0+	0+	0+	0+	0+	001	004	011	028	12
	13	0+	0+	0+	0+	0+	0+	0+	0+	0+	0+	0+	0+	0+	0+	0+	0+	0+	0+	001	003	009	13
	14	0+	0+	0+	0+	0+	0+	0+	0+	0+	0+	0+	0+	0+	0+	0+	0+	0+	0+	0+	001	002	14
	15	0+	0+	0+	0+	0+	0+	0+	0+	0+	0+	0+	0+	0+	0+	0+	0+	0+	0+	0+	0+	0+	15
	16	0+	0+	0+	0+	0+	0+	0+	0+	0+	0+	0+	0+	0+	0+	0+	0+	0+	0+	0+	0+	0+	16

Table 7. *(continued)*

N	K	.01	.02	.04	.05	.06	.08	.10	.12	.14	.15	.16	.18	.20	.22	.24	.25	.30	.35	.40	.45	.50	K
17	0	843	709	500	418	349	242	167	114	077	063	052	034	023	015	009	008	002	001	0+	0+	0+	0
	1	145	246	354	374	379	358	315	264	213	189	167	128	096	070	051	043	017	006	002	001	0+	1
	2	012	040	118	158	194	249	280	288	279	267	255	225	191	158	128	114	058	026	010	004	001	2
	3	001	004	025	041	062	108	156	196	226	236	243	246	239	223	202	189	125	070	034	014	005	3
	4	0+	0+	004	008	014	033	060	094	129	146	162	189	209	221	223	221	187	132	080	041	018	4
	5	0+	0+	0+	001	002	007	017	033	054	067	080	108	136	162	183	191	208	185	138	087	047	5
	6	0+	0+	0+	0+	0+	001	004	009	018	024	031	047	068	091	116	128	178	199	184	143	094	6
	7	0+	0+	0+	0+	0+	0+	001	002	005	007	009	016	027	040	057	067	120	168	193	184	148	7
	8	0+	0+	0+	0+	0+	0+	0+	0+	001	001	002	004	008	014	023	028	064	113	161	188	185	8
	9	0+	0+	0+	0+	0+	0+	0+	0+	0+	0+	0+	001	002	004	007	009	028	061	107	154	185	9
	10	0+	0+	0+	0+	0+	0+	0+	0+	0+	0+	0+	0+	0+	001	002	002	009	026	057	101	148	10
	11	0+	0+	0+	0+	0+	0+	0+	0+	0+	0+	0+	0+	0+	0+	0+	001	003	009	024	052	094	11
	12	0+	0+	0+	0+	0+	0+	0+	0+	0+	0+	0+	0+	0+	0+	0+	0+	001	002	008	021	047	12
	13	0+	0+	0+	0+	0+	0+	0+	0+	0+	0+	0+	0+	0+	0+	0+	0+	0+	001	002	007	018	13
	14	0+	0+	0+	0+	0+	0+	0+	0+	0+	0+	0+	0+	0+	0+	0+	0+	0+	0+	0+	002	005	14
	15	0+	0+	0+	0+	0+	0+	0+	0+	0+	0+	0+	0+	0+	0+	0+	0+	0+	0+	0+	001	001	15
	16	0+	0+	0+	0+	0+	0+	0+	0+	0+	0+	0+	0+	0+	0+	0+	0+	0+	0+	0+	0+	0+	16
	17	0+	0+	0+	0+	0+	0+	0+	0+	0+	0+	0+	0+	0+	0+	0+	0+	0+	0+	0+	0+	0+	17
18	0	835	695	480	397	328	223	150	100	066	054	043	028	018	011	007	006	002	0+	0+	0+	0+	0
	1	152	255	360	376	377	349	300	246	194	170	149	111	081	058	041	034	013	004	001	0+	0+	1
	2	013	044	127	168	205	258	284	285	268	256	241	207	172	139	109	096	046	019	007	002	001	2
	3	001	005	028	047	070	120	168	207	233	241	244	243	230	209	184	170	105	055	025	009	003	3
	4	0+	0+	004	009	017	039	070	106	142	159	175	200	215	221	218	213	168	110	061	029	012	4

Table 7. *(continued)*

N	K	.01	.02	.04	.05	.06	.08	.10	.12	.14	.15	.16	.18	.20	.22	.24	.25	.30	.35	.40	.45	.50	K
	5	0+	0+	001	001	003	009	022	040	065	079	093	123	151	175	193	199	202	166	115	067	033	5
	6	0+	0+	0+	0+	0+	002	005	012	023	030	038	058	082	107	132	144	187	194	166	118	071	6
	7	0+	0+	0+	0+	0+	0+	001	003	006	009	013	022	035	052	071	082	138	179	189	166	121	7
	8	0+	0+	0+	0+	0+	0+	0+	001	001	002	003	007	012	020	031	038	081	133	173	186	167	8
	9	0+	0+	0+	0+	0+	0+	0+	0+	0+	0+	001	002	003	006	011	014	039	079	128	169	185	9
	10	0+	0+	0+	0+	0+	0+	0+	0+	0+	0+	0+	0+	001	002	003	004	015	038	077	125	167	10
	11	0+	0+	0+	0+	0+	0+	0+	0+	0+	0+	0+	0+	0+	0+	001	001	005	015	037	074	121	11
	12	0+	0+	0+	0+	0+	0+	0+	0+	0+	0+	0+	0+	0+	0+	0+	0+	001	005	015	035	071	12
	13	0+	0+	0+	0+	0+	0+	0+	0+	0+	0+	0+	0+	0+	0+	0+	0+	0+	001	004	013	033	13
	14	0+	0+	0+	0+	0+	0+	0+	0+	0+	0+	0+	0+	0+	0+	0+	0+	0+	0+	001	004	012	14
	15	0+	0+	0+	0+	0+	0+	0+	0+	0+	0+	0+	0+	0+	0+	0+	0+	0+	0+	0+	001	003	15
	16	0+	0+	0+	0+	0+	0+	0+	0+	0+	0+	0+	0+	0+	0+	0+	0+	0+	0+	0+	0+	001	16
	17	0+	0+	0+	0+	0+	0+	0+	0+	0+	0+	0+	0+	0+	0+	0+	0+	0+	0+	0+	0+	0+	17
	18	0+	0+	0+	0+	0+	0+	0+	0+	0+	0+	0+	0+	0+	0+	0+	0+	0+	0+	0+	0+	0+	18
19	0	826	681	460	377	309	205	135	088	057	046	036	023	014	009	005	004	001	0+	0+	0+	0+	0
	1	159	264	364	377	374	339	285	228	176	153	132	096	068	048	033	027	009	003	001	0+	0+	1
	2	014	049	137	179	215	265	285	280	258	243	226	190	154	121	093	080	036	014	005	001	0+	2
	3	001	006	032	053	078	131	180	217	238	243	244	236	218	194	166	152	087	042	017	006	002	3
	4	0+	0+	005	011	020	045	080	118	155	171	186	207	218	219	210	202	149	091	047	020	007	4
	5	0+	0+	001	002	004	012	027	048	076	091	106	137	164	185	199	202	192	147	093	050	022	5
	6	0+	0+	0+	0+	001	002	007	015	029	037	047	070	095	122	146	157	192	184	145	095	052	6
	7	0+	0+	0+	0+	0+	0+	001	004	009	012	017	029	044	064	086	097	153	184	180	144	096	7

Table 7. (*continued*)

		P																				
N	*K*	.01	.02	.04	.05	.06	.08	.10	.12	.14	.15	.16	.18	.20	.22	.24	.25	.30	.35	.40	.45	.50	*K*
	8	0+	0+	0+	0+	0+	0+	0+	001	002	003	005	009	017	027	041	049	098	149	180	177	144	8
	9	0+	0+	0+	0+	0+	0+	0+	0+	0+	001	001	003	005	009	016	020	051	098	146	177	176	9
	10	0+	0+	0+	0+	0+	0+	0+	0+	0+	0+	0+	001	001	003	005	007	022	053	098	145	176	10
	11	0+	0+	0+	0+	0+	0+	0+	0+	0+	0+	0+	0+	0+	001	001	002	008	023	053	097	144	11
	12	0+	0+	0+	0+	0+	0+	0+	0+	0+	0+	0+	0+	0+	0+	0+	0+	002	008	024	053	096	12
	13	0+	0+	0+	0+	0+	0+	0+	0+	0+	0+	0+	0+	0+	0+	0+	0+	001	002	008	023	052	13
	14	0+	0+	0+	0+	0+	0+	0+	0+	0+	0+	0+	0+	0+	0+	0+	0+	0+	001	002	008	022	14
	15	0+	0+	0+	0+	0+	0+	0+	0+	0+	0+	0+	0+	0+	0+	0+	0+	0+	0+	001	002	007	15
	16	0+	0+	0+	0+	0+	0+	0+	0+	0+	0+	0+	0+	0+	0+	0+	0+	0+	0+	0+	0+	002	16
	17	0+	0+	0+	0+	0+	0+	0+	0+	0+	0+	0+	0+	0+	0+	0+	0+	0+	0+	0+	0+	0+	17
	18	0+	0+	0+	0+	0+	0+	0+	0+	0+	0+	0+	0+	0+	0+	0+	0+	0+	0+	0+	0+	0+	18
	19	0+	0+	0+	0+	0+	0+	0+	0+	0+	0+	0+	0+	0+	0+	0+	0+	0+	0+	0+	0+	0+	19
20	0	818	668	442	358	290	189	122	078	049	039	031	019	012	007	004	003	001	0+	0+	0+	0+	0
	1	165	272	368	377	370	328	270	212	159	137	117	083	058	039	026	021	007	002	0+	0+	0+	1
	2	016	053	146	189	225	271	285	274	247	229	211	173	137	105	078	067	028	010	003	001	0+	2
	3	001	006	036	060	086	141	190	224	241	243	241	228	205	178	148	134	072	032	012	004	001	3
	4	0+	001	006	013	023	052	090	130	167	182	195	213	218	213	199	190	130	074	035	014	005	4
	5	0+	0+	001	002	005	015	032	057	087	103	119	149	175	192	201	202	179	127	075	036	015	5
	6	0+	0+	0+	0+	001	003	009	019	035	045	057	082	109	136	159	169	192	171	124	075	037	6
	7	0+	0+	0+	0+	0+	001	002	005	012	016	022	036	055	076	100	112	164	184	166	122	074	7
	8	0+	0+	0+	0+	0+	0+	0+	001	003	005	007	013	022	035	051	061	114	161	180	162	120	8
	9	0+	0+	0+	0+	0+	0+	0+	0+	001	001	002	004	007	013	022	027	065	116	160	177	160	9

Table 7. (*continued*)

		P																				
N	*K*	.01	.02	.04	.05	.06	.08	.10	.12	.14	.15	.16	.18	.20	.22	.24	.25	.30	.35	.40	.45	.50	*K*
	10	0+	0+	0+	0+	0+	0+	0+	0+	0+	0+	0+	001	002	004	008	010	031	069	117	159	176	10
	11	0+	0+	0+	0+	0+	0+	0+	0+	0+	0+	0+	0+	0+	001	002	003	012	034	071	119	160	11
	12	0+	0+	0+	0+	0+	0+	0+	0+	0+	0+	0+	0+	0+	0+	001	001	004	014	035	073	120	12
	13	0+	0+	0+	0+	0+	0+	0+	0+	0+	0+	0+	0+	0+	0+	0+	0+	001	004	015	037	074	13
	14	0+	0+	0+	0+	0+	0+	0+	0+	0+	0+	0+	0+	0+	0+	0+	0+	0+	001	005	015	037	14
	15	0+	0+	0+	0+	0+	0+	0+	0+	0+	0+	0+	0+	0+	0+	0+	0+	0+	0+	001	005	015	15
	16	0+	0+	0+	0+	0+	0+	0+	0+	0+	0+	0+	0+	0+	0+	0+	0+	0+	0+	0+	001	005	15
	17	0+	0+	0+	0+	0+	0+	0+	0+	0+	0+	0+	0+	0+	0+	0+	0+	0+	0+	0+	0+	001	16
	18	0+	0+	0+	0+	0+	0+	0+	0+	0+	0+	0+	0+	0+	0+	0+	0+	0+	0+	0+	0+	0+	17
	19	0+	0+	0+	0+	0+	0+	0+	0+	0+	0+	0+	0+	0+	0+	0+	0+	0+	0+	0+	0+	0+	19
	20	0+	0+	0+	0+	0+	0+	0+	0+	0+	0+	0+	0+	0+	0+	0+	0+	0+	0+	0+	0+	0+	20
21	0	810	654	424	341	273	174	109	068	042	033	026	015	010	005	003	002	001	0+	0+	0+	0+	0
	1	172	280	371	376	366	317	255	195	144	122	103	071	048	032	021	017	005	001	0+	0+	0+	1
	2	017	057	155	198	233	276	284	267	234	215	196	157	121	091	066	055	022	007	002	0+	0+	2
	3	001	007	041	066	094	152	200	230	242	241	236	218	192	162	132	117	058	024	009	003	001	3
	4	0+	001	008	016	027	059	100	141	177	191	202	215	216	205	187	176	113	059	026	009	003	4
	5	0+	0+	001	003	006	018	038	065	098	115	131	161	183	197	201	199	164	109	059	026	010	5
	6	0+	0+	0+	0+	001	004	011	024	043	054	067	094	122	148	169	177	188	156	105	057	026	6
	7	0+	0+	0+	0+	0+	001	003	007	015	020	027	044	065	089	114	126	172	180	149	101	055	7
	8	0+	0+	0+	0+	0+	0+	001	002	004	006	009	017	029	044	063	074	129	169	174	144	097	8
	9	0+	0+	0+	0+	0+	0+	0+	0+	001	002	002	005	010	018	029	036	080	132	168	170	140	9

Table 7. (*continued*)

N	K	.01	.02	.04	.05	.06	.08	.10	.12	.14	.15	.16	.18	.20	.22	.24	.25	.30	.35	.40	.45	.50	K
												P											
	10	0+	0+	0+	0+	0+	0+	0+	0+	0+	0+	001	001	003	006	011	014	041	085	134	167	168	10
	11	0+	0+	0+	0+	0+	0+	0+	0+	0+	0+	0+	0+	001	002	003	005	018	046	089	137	168	11
	12	0+	0+	0+	0+	0+	0+	0+	0+	0+	0+	0+	0+	0+	0+	001	001	006	021	050	093	140	12
	13	0+	0+	0+	0+	0+	0+	0+	0+	0+	0+	0+	0+	0+	0+	0+	0+	002	008	023	053	097	13
	14	0+	0+	0+	0+	0+	0+	0+	0+	0+	0+	0+	0+	0+	0+	0+	0+	0+	002	009	025	055	14
	15	0+	0+	0+	0+	0+	0+	0+	0+	0+	0+	0+	0+	0+	0+	0+	0+	0+	001	003	009	026	15
	16	0+	0+	0+	0+	0+	0+	0+	0+	0+	0+	0+	0+	0+	0+	0+	0+	0+	0+	001	003	010	16
	17	0+	0+	0+	0+	0+	0+	0+	0+	0+	0+	0+	0+	0+	0+	0+	0+	0+	0+	0+	001	003	17
	18	0+	0+	0+	0+	0+	0+	0+	0+	0+	0+	0+	0+	0+	0+	0+	0+	0+	0+	0+	0+	001	18
	19	0+	0+	0+	0+	0+	0+	0+	0+	0+	0+	0+	0+	0+	0+	0+	0+	0+	0+	0+	0+	0+	19
	20	0+	0+	0+	0+	0+	0+	0+	0+	0+	0+	0+	0+	0+	0+	0+	0+	0+	0+	0+	0+	0+	20
	21	0+	0+	0+	0+	0+	0+	0+	0+	0+	0+	0+	0+	0+	0+	0+	0+	0+	0+	0+	0+	0+	21
22	0	802	641	407	324	256	160	098	060	036	028	022	013	007	004	002	002	0+	0+	0+	0+	0+	0
	1	178	288	373	375	360	306	241	180	130	109	090	061	041	026	017	013	004	001	0+	0+	0+	1
	2	019	062	163	207	241	279	281	258	222	201	181	141	107	078	055	046	017	005	001	0+	0+	2
	3	001	008	045	073	103	162	208	235	241	237	230	207	178	146	116	102	047	018	006	002	0+	3
	4	0+	001	009	018	031	067	110	152	186	199	208	216	211	196	174	161	096	047	019	006	002	4
	5	0+	0+	001	003	007	021	044	075	109	126	143	170	190	199	197	193	149	091	046	019	006	5
	6	0+	0+	0+	001	001	005	014	029	050	063	077	106	134	159	177	183	181	139	086	043	018	6
	7	0+	0+	0+	0+	0+	001	004	009	019	025	033	053	077	102	128	139	177	171	131	081	041	7
	8	0+	0+	0+	0+	0+	0+	001	002	006	008	012	022	036	054	075	087	142	173	164	125	076	8
	9	0+	0+	0+	0+	0+	0+	0+	0+	001	002	004	007	014	024	037	045	095	145	170	164	119	9

Table 7. *(continued)*

N	K	.01	.02	.04	.05	.06	.08	.10	.12	.14	.15	.16	.18	.20	.22	.24	.25	.30	.35	.40	.45	.50	K
	10	0+	0+	0+	0+	0+	0+	0+	0+	0+	001	001	002	005	009	015	020	053	101	148	169	154	10
	11	0+	0+	0+	0+	0+	0+	0+	0+	0+	0+	0+	001	001	003	005	007	025	060	107	151	168	11
	12	0+	0+	0+	0+	0+	0+	0+	0+	0+	0+	0+	0+	0+	001	002	002	010	029	066	113	154	12
	13	0+	0+	0+	0+	0+	0+	0+	0+	0+	0+	0+	0+	0+	0+	0+	001	003	012	034	071	119	13
	14	0+	0+	0+	0+	0+	0+	0+	0+	0+	0+	0+	0+	0+	0+	0+	0+	001	004	014	037	076	14
	15	0+	0+	0+	0+	0+	0+	0+	0+	0+	0+	0+	0+	0+	0+	0+	0+	0+	001	001	016	041	15
	16	0+	0+	0+	0+	0+	0+	0+	0+	0+	0+	0+	0+	0+	0+	0+	0+	0+	0+	001	006	018	16
	17	0+	0+	0+	0+	0+	0+	0+	0+	0+	0+	0+	0+	0+	0+	0+	0+	0+	0+	0+	002	007	17
	18	0+	0+	0+	0+	0+	0+	0+	0+	0+	0+	0+	0+	0+	0+	0+	0+	0+	0+	0+	0+	002	18
	19	0+	0+	0+	0+	0+	0+	0+	0+	0+	0+	0+	0+	0+	0+	0+	0+	0+	0+	0+	0+	0+	19
	20	0+	0+	0+	0+	0+	0+	0+	0+	0+	0+	0+	0+	0+	0+	0+	0+	0+	0+	0+	0+	0+	20
	21	0+	0+	0+	0+	0+	0+	0+	0+	0+	0+	0+	0+	0+	0+	0+	0+	0+	0+	0+	0+	0+	21
	22	0+	0+	0+	0+	0+	0+	0+	0+	0+	0+	0+	0+	0+	0+	0+	0+	0+	0+	0+	0+	0+	22
23	0	794	628	391	307	241	147	089	053	031	024	018	010	006	003	002	001	0+	0+	0+	0+	0+	0
	1	184	295	375	372	354	294	226	166	117	097	079	053	034	021	013	010	003	001	0+	0+	0+	1
	2	020	066	172	215	248	281	277	249	209	188	166	127	093	066	046	038	013	004	001	0+	0+	2
	3	001	009	050	079	111	171	215	237	238	232	222	195	163	131	101	088	038	014	004	001	0+	3
	4	0+	001	010	021	035	074	120	162	194	204	211	214	204	185	160	146	082	037	014	004	001	4
	5	0+	0+	002	004	009	025	051	084	120	137	153	179	194	198	192	185	133	076	035	013	004	5
	6	0+	0+	0+	001	002	006	017	034	059	073	087	118	145	168	182	185	171	122	070	032	012	6
	7	0+	0+	0+	0+	0+	001	005	011	023	031	040	063	088	115	139	150	178	160	113	064	029	7
	8	0+	0+	0+	0+	0+	0+	001	003	008	011	015	028	044	065	088	100	153	172	151	105	058	8
	9	0+	0+	0+	0+	0+	0+	0+	001	002	003	005	010	018	030	046	056	109	155	168	143	097	9

Table 7. *(continued)*

N	K	.01	.02	.04	.05	.06	.08	.10	.12	.14	.15	.16	.18	.20	.22	.24	.25	.30	.35	.40	.45	.50	K
	10	0+	0+	0+	0+	0+	0+	0+	0+	0+	001	001	003	006	012	020	026	065	117	157	164	136	10
	11	0+	0+	0+	0+	0+	0+	0+	0+	0+	0+	0+	001	002	004	008	010	033	074	123	159	161	11
	12	0+	0+	0+	0+	0+	0+	0+	0+	0+	0+	0+	0+	0+	001	002	003	014	040	082	130	161	12
	13	0+	0+	0+	0+	0+	0+	0+	0+	0+	0+	0+	0+	0+	0+	001	001	005	018	046	090	136	13
	14	0+	0+	0+	0+	0+	0+	0+	0+	0+	0+	0+	0+	0+	0+	0+	0+	002	007	022	053	097	14
	15	0+	0+	0+	0+	0+	0+	0+	0+	0+	0+	0+	0+	0+	0+	0+	0+	0+	002	009	026	058	15
	16	0+	0+	0+	0+	0+	0+	0+	0+	0+	0+	0+	0+	0+	0+	0+	0+	0+	001	003	011	029	16
	17	0+	0+	0+	0+	0+	0+	0+	0+	0+	0+	0+	0+	0+	0+	0+	0+	0+	0+	001	004	012	17
	18	0+	0+	0+	0+	0+	0+	0+	0+	0+	0+	0+	0+	0+	0+	0+	0+	0+	0+	0+	001	004	18
	19	0+	0+	0+	0+	0+	0+	0+	0+	0+	0+	0+	0+	0+	0+	0+	0+	0+	0+	0+	0+	001	19
	20	0+	0+	0+	0+	0+	0+	0+	0+	0+	0+	0+	0+	0+	0+	0+	0+	0+	0+	0+	0+	0+	20
	21	0+	0+	0+	0+	0+	0+	0+	0+	0+	0+	0+	0+	0+	0+	0+	0+	0+	0+	0+	0+	0+	21
	22	0+	0+	0+	0+	0+	0+	0+	0+	0+	0+	0+	0+	0+	0+	0+	0+	0+	0+	0+	0+	0+	22
	23	0+	0+	0+	0+	0+	0+	0+	0+	0+	0+	0+	0+	0+	0+	0+	0+	0+	0+	0+	0+	0+	23
24	0	786	616	375	292	227	135	080	047	027	020	015	009	005	003	001	001	0+	0+	0+	0+	0+	0
	1	190	302	375	369	347	282	213	152	105	086	070	045	028	017	010	008	002	0+	0+	0+	0+	1
	2	022	071	180	223	255	282	272	239	196	174	153	114	081	056	038	031	010	003	001	0+	0+	2
	3	002	011	055	086	119	180	221	239	234	225	213	183	149	117	088	075	031	010	003	001	0+	3
	4	0+	001	012	024	040	082	129	171	200	209	213	211	196	173	146	132	069	029	010	003	001	4
	5	0+	0+	002	005	010	029	057	093	130	147	162	185	196	195	184	176	118	062	027	009	003	5
	6	0+	0+	0+	001	002	008	020	040	067	082	098	129	155	174	184	185	160	106	056	024	008	6
	7	0+	0+	0+	0+	0+	002	006	014	028	037	048	073	100	126	149	159	176	147	096	050	021	7

Table 7. *(continued)*

		p																				
N	*K*	.01	.02	.04	.05	.06	.08	.10	.12	.14	.15	.16	.18	.20	.22	.24	.25	.30	.35	.40	.45	.50	*K*
	8	0+	0+	0+	0+	0+	0+	001	004	010	014	019	034	053	076	100	112	160	168	136	087	044	8
	9	0+	0+	0+	0+	0+	0+	0+	001	003	004	007	013	024	038	056	067	122	161	161	126	078	9
	10	0+	0+	0+	0+	0+	0+	0+	0+	001	001	002	004	009	016	027	033	079	130	161	155	117	10
	11	0+	0+	0+	0+	0+	0+	0+	0+	0+	0+	0+	001	003	006	011	014	043	089	1137	161	149	11
	12	0+	0+	0+	0+	0+	0+	0+	0+	0+	0+	0+	0+	001	002	004	005	020	052	099	143	161	12
	13	0+	0+	0+	0+	0+	0+	0+	0+	0+	0+	0+	0+	0+	0+	001	002	008	026	061	108	149	13
	14	0+	0+	0+	0+	0+	0+	0+	0+	0+	0+	0+	0+	0+	0+	0+	0+	003	011	032	069	117	14
	15	0+	0+	0+	0+	0+	0+	0+	0+	0+	0+	0+	0+	0+	0+	0+	0+	001	004	014	038	078	15
	16	0+	0+	0+	0+	0+	0+	0+	0+	0+	0+	0+	0+	0+	0+	0+	0+	0+	001	005	017	044	16
	17	0+	0+	0+	0+	0+	0+	0+	0+	0+	0+	0+	0+	0+	0+	0+	0+	0+	0+	002	007	021	17
	18	0+	0+	0+	0+	0+	0+	0+	0+	0+	0+	0+	0+	0+	0+	0+	0+	0+	0+	0+	002	008	18
	19	0+	0+	0+	0+	0+	0+	0+	0+	0+	0+	0+	0+	0+	0+	0+	0+	0+	0+	0+	001	003	19
	20	0+	0+	0+	0+	0+	0+	0+	0+	0+	0+	0+	0+	0+	0+	0+	0+	0+	0+	0+	0+	001	20
	21	0+	0+	0+	0+	0+	0+	0+	0+	0+	0+	0+	0+	0+	0+	0+	0+	0+	0+	0+	0+	0+	21
	22	0+	0+	0+	0+	0+	0+	0+	0+	0+	0+	0+	0+	0+	0+	0+	0+	0+	0+	0+	0+	0+	22
	23	0+	0+	0+	0+	0+	0+	0+	0+	0+	0+	0+	0+	0+	0+	0+	0+	0+	0+	0+	0+	0+	23
	24	0+	0+	0+	0+	0+	0+	0+	0+	0+	0+	0+	0+	0+	0+	0+	0+	0+	0+	0+	0+	0+	24
25	0	778	603	360	277	213	124	072	041	023	017	013	007	004	002	001	001	0+	0+	0+	0+	0+	0
	1	196	308	375	365	340	270	199	140	094	076	061	038	024	014	008	006	001	0+	0+	0+	0+	1
	2	024	075	188	231	260	282	266	228	183	161	139	101	071	048	031	025	007	002	0+	0+	0+	2
	3	002	012	060	093	127	188	226	239	229	217	203	170	136	104	076	064	024	008	002	0+	0+	3
	4	0+	001	014	027	045	090	138	179	205	211	213	206	187	161	132	118	057	022	007	002	0+	4

Table 7. *(continued)*

	p																				
N K	.01	.02	.04	.05	.06	.08	.10	.12	.14	.15	.16	.18	.20	.22	.24	.25	.30	.35	.40	.45	.50 *K*
5	0+	0+	002	006	012	033	065	103	140	156	170	190	196	190	175	165	103	051	020	006	002 5
6	0+	0+	0+	001	003	010	024	047	076	092	108	139	163	179	184	183	147	091	044	017	005 6
7	0+	0+	0+	0+	0+	002	007	017	034	044	056	083	111	137	158	165	171	133	080	038	014 7
8	0+	0+	0+	0+	0+	0+	002	005	012	017	024	041	062	087	112	124	165	161	120	070	032 8
9	0+	0+	0+	0+	0+	0+	0+	001	004	006	009	017	029	046	067	078	134	163	151	108	061 9
10	0+	0+	0+	0+	0+	0+	0+	0+	001	002	003	006	012	021	034	042	092	141	161	142	097 10
11	0+	0+	0+	0+	0+	0+	0+	0+	0+	0+	001	002	004	008	015	019	054	103	147	158	133 11
12	0+	0+	0+	0+	0+	0+	0+	0+	0+	0+	0+	0+	001	003	005	007	027	065	114	151	155 12
13	0+	0+	0+	0+	0+	0+	0+	0+	0+	0+	0+	0+	0+	001	002	002	011	035	076	124	155 13
14	0+	0+	0+	0+	0+	0+	0+	0+	0+	0+	0+	0+	0+	0+	0+	001	004	016	043	087	133 14
15	0+	0+	0+	0+	0+	0+	0+	0+	0+	0+	0+	0+	0+	0+	0+	0+	001	006	021	052	097 15
16	0+	0+	0+	0+	0+	0+	0+	0+	0+	0+	0+	0+	0+	0+	0+	0+	0+	002	009	027	061 16
17	0+	0+	0+	0+	0+	0+	0+	0+	0+	0+	0+	0+	0+	0+	0+	0+	0+	001	003	012	032 17
18	0+	0+	0+	0+	0+	0+	0+	0+	0+	0+	0+	0+	0+	0+	0+	0+	0+	0+	001	004	014 18
19	0+	0+	0+	0+	0+	0+	0+	0+	0+	0+	0+	0+	0+	0+	0+	0+	0+	0+	0+	001	005 19
20	0+	0+	0+	0+	0+	0+	0+	0+	0+	0+	0+	0+	0+	0+	0+	0+	0+	0+	0+	0+	002 20
21	0+	0+	0+	0+	0+	0+	0+	0+	0+	0+	0+	0+	0+	0+	0+	0+	0+	0+	0+	0+	0+ 21
22	0+	0+	0+	0+	0+	0+	0+	0+	0+	0+	0+	0+	0+	0+	0+	0+	0+	0+	0+	0+	0+ 22
23	0+	0+	0+	0+	0+	0+	0+	0+	0+	0+	0+	0+	0+	0+	0+	0+	0+	0+	0+	0+	0+ 23
24	0+	0+	0+	0+	0+	0+	0+	0+	0+	0+	0+	0+	0+	0+	0+	0+	0+	0+	0+	0+	0+ 24
25	0+	0+	0+	0+	0+	0+	0+	0+	0+	0+	0+	0+	0+	0+	0+	0+	0+	0+	0+	0+	0+ 25

Table 8. **Binomial Distribution—Cumulative Terms**[a]

N	K	.01	.02	.04	.05	.06	.08	.10	.12	.14	.15	.16	.18	.20	.22	.24	.25	.30	.35	.40	.45	.50	K
2	0	1	1	1	1	1	1	1	1	1	1	1	1	1	1	1	1	1	1	1	1	1	0
	1	020	040	078	098	116	154	190	226	260	278	294	328	360	391	422	438	510	578	640	698	750	1
	2	0+	0+	002	002	004	006	010	014	020	022	026	032	040	048	058	062	090	122	160	202	250	2
3	0	1	1	1	1	1	1	1	1	1	1	1	1	1	1	1	1	1	1	1	1	1	0
	1	030	059	115	143	169	221	271	319	364	386	407	449	488	525	561	578	657	725	784	834	875	1
	2	0+	001	005	007	010	018	028	040	053	061	069	086	104	124	145	156	216	282	352	425	500	2
	3	0+	0+	0+	0+	0+	001	001	002	003	003	004	006	008	011	014	016	027	043	064	091	125	3
4	0	1	1	1	1	1	1	1	1	1	1	1	1	1	1	1	1	1	1	1	1	1	0
	1	039	078	151	185	219	284	344	400	453	478	502	548	590	630	666	684	760	821	870	908	938	1
	2	001	002	009	014	020	034	052	073	097	110	123	151	181	212	245	262	348	437	525	609	688	2
	3	0+	0+	0+	0+	001	002	004	006	010	012	014	020	027	036	045	051	084	126	179	241	312	3
	4	0+	0+	0+	0+	0+	0+	0+	0+	0+	001	001	001	002	002	003	004	008	015	026	041	062	4
5	0	1	1	1	1	1	1	1	1	1	1	1	1	1	1	1	1	1	1	1	1	1	0
	1	049	096	185	226	266	341	410	472	530	556	582	629	672	711	746	763	832	884	922	950	969	1
	2	001	004	015	023	032	054	081	112	147	165	183	222	263	304	346	367	472	572	663	744	812	2
	3	0+	0+	001	001	002	005	009	014	022	027	032	044	058	074	093	104	1163	235	317	407	500	3
	4	0+	0+	0+	0+	0+	0+	0+	001	002	002	003	004	007	010	013	016	031	054	087	131	188	4
	5	0+	0+	0+	0+	0+	0+	0+	0+	0+	0+	0+	0+	0+	001	001	001	002	005	010	018	031	5

[a]From Croxton, Frederick E., and Cowden, Dudley J., *Practical Business Statistics*, Prentice-Hall, New York, 1948, p. 511. Reprinted by permission of the publisher.

Table 8. *(continued)*

		P																				
N	*K*	.01	.02	.04	.05	.06	.08	.10	.12	.14	.15	.16	.18	.20	.22	.24	.25	.30	.35	.40	.45	.50	*K*
6	0	1	1	1	1	1	1	1	1	1	1	1	1	1	1	1	1	1	1	1	1	1	0
	1	059	114	217	265	310	394	469	536	595	623	649	696	738	775	807	822	882	925	953	972	984	1
	2	001	006	022	033	046	077	114	156	200	224	247	296	345	394	442	466	580	681	767	836	891	2
	3	0+	0+	001	002	004	009	016	026	039	047	056	076	099	125	154	169	256	353	456	558	656	3
	4	0+	0+	0+	0+	0+	001	001	003	005	006	007	012	017	024	033	038	070	117	179	255	344	4
	5	0+	0+	0+	0+	0+	0+	0+	0+	0+	0+	001	001	002	003	004	005	011	022	041	069	109	5
	6	0+	0+	0+	0+	0+	0+	0+	0+	0+	0+	0+	0+	0+	0+	0+	0+	001	002	004	008	016	6
7	0	1	1	1	1	1	1	1	1	1	1	1	1	1	1	1	1	1	1	1	1	1	0
	1	068	132	249	302	352	442	522	591	652	679	705	751	790	824	854	867	918	951	972	985	992	1
	2	002	008	029	044	062	103	150	201	256	283	311	368	423	478	530	555	671	766	841	898	938	2
	3	0+	0+	002	004	006	014	026	042	062	074	087	115	148	184	223	244	353	468	580	684	773	3
	4	0+	0+	0+	0+	0+	001	003	005	009	012	015	023	033	046	062	071	126	200	290	392	500	4
	5	0+	0+	0+	0+	0+	0+	0+	0+	001	001	002	003	005	007	011	013	029	056	096	153	227	5
	6	0+	0+	0+	0+	0+	0+	0+	0+	0+	0+	0+	0+	0+	001	001	001	004	009	019	036	062	6
	7	0+	0+	0+	0+	0+	0+	0+	0+	0+	0+	0+	0+	0+	0+	0+	0+	0+	001	002	004	008	7
8	0	1	1	1	1	1	1	1	1	1	1	1	1	1	1	1	1	1	1	1	1	1	0
	1	077	149	279	337	390	487	570	640	701	728	752	796	832	863	889	900	942	968	983	992	996	1
	2	003	010	038	057	079	130	187	248	311	343	374	437	497	554	608	633	745	831	894	937	965	2
	3	0+	0+	003	006	010	021	038	061	089	105	123	161	203	249	297	321	448	572	685	780	855	3
	4	0+	0+	0+	0+	001	002	005	010	017	021	027	040	056	076	100	114	194	294	406	523	637	4

Table 8. (*continued*)

N	K	.01	.02	.04	.05	.06	.08	.10	.12	.14	.15	.16	.18	.20	.22	.24	.25	.30	.35	.40	.45	.50	K
	5	0+	0+	0+	0+	0+	0+	0+	001	002	003	004	007	010	016	023	027	058	106	174	260	363	5
	6	0+	0+	0+	0+	0+	0+	0+	0+	0+	0+	0+	001	001	002	003	004	011	025	050	088	145	6
	7	0+	0+	0+	0+	0+	0+	0+	0+	0+	0+	0+	0+	0+	0+	0+	0+	001	004	009	018	035	7
	8	0+	0+	0+	0+	0+	0+	0+	0+	0+	0+	0+	0+	0+	0+	0+	0+	0+	0+	001	002	004	8
9	0	1	1	1	1	1	1	1	1	1	1	1	1	1	1	1	1	1	1	1	1	1	0
	1	086	166	307	370	427	528	613	684	743	768	792	832	866	893	915	925	960	979	990	995	998	1
	2	003	013	048	071	098	158	225	295	366	401	435	501	564	622	675	700	804	879	929	961	980	2
	3	0+	001	004	008	014	030	053	083	120	141	163	210	262	316	371	399	537	663	768	850	910	3
	4	0+	0+	0+	001	001	004	008	016	027	034	042	062	086	114	148	166	270	391	517	639	746	4
	5	0+	0+	0+	0+	0+	0+	001	002	004	006	007	012	020	029	042	049	099	172	267	379	500	5
	6	0+	0+	0+	0+	0+	0+	0+	0+	0+	001	001	002	003	005	008	010	025	054	099	166	254	6
	7	0+	0+	0+	0+	0+	0+	0+	0+	0+	0+	0+	0+	0+	001	001	001	004	011	025	050	090	7
	8	0+	0+	0+	0+	0+	0+	0+	0+	0+	0+	0+	0+	0+	0+	0+	0+	0+	001	004	009	020	8
	9	0+	0+	0+	0+	0+	0+	0+	0+	0+	0+	0+	0+	0+	0+	0+	0+	0+	0+	0+	001	002	9
10	0	1	1	1	1	1	1	1	1	1	1	1	1	1	1	1	1	1	1	1	1	1	0
	1	096	183	335	401	461	566	651	721	779	803	825	863	893	917	936	944	972	987	994	997	999	1
	2	004	016	058	086	118	188	264	342	418	456	492	561	624	682	733	756	851	914	954	977	989	2
	3	0+	001	006	012	019	040	070	109	155	180	206	263	322	383	444	474	617	738	833	900	945	3
	4	0+	0+	0+	001	002	006	013	024	040	050	061	088	121	159	201	224	350	486	618	734	828	4
	5	0+	0+	0+	0+	0+	001	002	004	007	010	013	021	033	048	067	078	150	249	367	496	623	5
	6	0+	0+	0+	0+	0+	0+	0+	0+	001	001	002	004	006	010	016	020	047	095	166	262	377	6
	7	0+	0+	0+	0+	0+	0+	0+	0+	0+	0+	0+	0+	001	002	003	004	011	026	055	102	172	7

Table 8. (*continued*)

N	K	.01	.02	.04	.05	.06	.08	.10	.12	.14	.15	.16	.18	.20	.22	.24	.25	.30	.35	.40	.45	.50	K
	8	0+	0+	0+	0+	0+	0+	0+	0+	0+	0+	0+	0+	0+	0+	0+	0+	002	005	012	027	055	8
	9	0+	0+	0+	0+	0+	0+	0+	0+	0+	0+	0+	0+	0+	0+	0+	0+	0+	001	002	005	011	9
	10	0+	0+	0+	0+	0+	0+	0+	0+	0+	0+	0+	0+	0+	0+	0+	0+	0+	0+	0+	0+	001	10
11	0	1	1	1	1	1	1	1	1	1	1	1	1	1	1	1	1	1	1	1	1	1	
	1	105	199	362	431	494	600	686	755	810	833	853	887	914	935	951	958	980	991	996	999	1−	1
	2	005	020	069	102	138	218	303	387	469	508	545	615	678	733	781	803	887	939	970	986	994	2
	3	0+	001	008	015	025	052	090	137	191	221	252	316	383	449	513	545	687	800	881	935	967	3
	4	0+	0+	001	002	003	009	019	034	056	069	085	120	161	208	260	287	430	574	704	809	887	4
	5	0+	0+	0+	0+	0+	001	003	006	012	016	021	033	050	072	099	115	210	332	467	603	726	5
	6	0+	0+	0+	0+	0+	0+	0+	001	002	003	004	007	012	019	028	034	078	149	247	367	500	6
	7	0+	0+	0+	0+	0+	0+	0+	0+	0+	0+	0+	001	002	004	006	008	022	050	099	174	274	7
	8	0+	0+	0+	0+	0+	0+	0+	0+	0+	0+	0+	0+	0+	0+	001	002	004	012	029	061	113	8
	9	0+	0+	0+	0+	0+	0+	0+	0+	0+	0+	0+	0+	0+	0+	0+	0+	001	002	006	015	033	9
	10	0+	0+	0+	0+	0+	0+	0+	0+	0+	0+	0+	0+	0+	0+	0+	0+	0+	0+	001	002	006	10
	11	0+	0+	0+	0+	0+	0+	0+	0+	0+	0+	0+	0+	0+	0+	0+	0+	0+	0+	0+	0+	0+	11
12	0	1	1	1	1	1	1	1	1	1	1	1	1	1	1	1	1	1	1	1	1	1	0
	1	114	215	387	460	524	632	718	784	836	858	877	908	931	949	963	968	986	994	998	999	1−	1
	2	006	023	081	118	160	249	341	432	517	557	595	664	725	778	822	842	915	958	980	992	997	2
	3	0+	002	011	020	032	065	111	167	230	264	299	370	442	511	578	609	747	849	917	958	981	3
	4	0+	0+	001	002	004	012	026	046	075	092	111	155	205	261	320	351	507	653	775	866	927	4
	5	0+	0+	0+	0+	0+	002	004	009	018	024	031	049	073	102	138	158	276	417	562	696	806	5

Table 8. *(continued)*

		P																					
N	*K*	.01	.02	.04	.05	.06	.08	.10	.12	.14	.15	.16	.18	.20	.22	.24	.25	.30	.35	.40	.45	.50	*K*
	6	0+	0+	0+	0+	0+	0+	001	001	003	005	006	012	019	030	045	054	118	213	335	473	613	6
	7	0+	0+	0+	0+	0+	0+	0+	0+	0+	001	001	002	004	007	011	014	039	085	158	261	387	7
	8	0+	0+	0+	0+	0+	0+	0+	0+	0+	0+	0+	0+	001	001	002	003	009	026	057	112	194	8
	9	0+	0+	0+	0+	0+	0+	0+	0+	0+	0+	0+	0+	0+	0+	0+	0+	002	006	015	036	073	9
	10	0+	0+	0+	0+	0+	0+	0+	0+	0+	0+	0+	0+	0+	0+	0+	0+	0+	001	003	008	019	10
	11	0+	0+	0+	0+	0+	0+	0+	0+	0+	0+	0+	0+	0+	0+	0+	0+	0+	0+	0+	001	003	11
	12	0+	0+	0+	0+	0+	0+	0+	0+	0+	0+	0+	0+	0+	0+	0+	0+	0+	0+	0+	0+	0+	12
13	0	1	1	1	1	1	1	1	1	1	1	1	1	1	1	1	1	1	1	1	1	1	0
	1	122	231	412	487	553	662	746	810	859	879	896	924	945	960	972	976	990	996	999	1–	1–	1
	2	007	027	093	135	181	279	379	474	561	602	640	708	766	815	856	873	936	970	987	995	998	2
	3	0+	002	014	025	039	080	134	198	270	308	346	423	498	570	636	667	798	887	942	973	989	3
	4	0+	0+	001	003	006	016	034	061	097	118	141	194	253	316	382	416	579	722	831	907	954	4
	5	0+	0+	0+	0+	001	002	006	014	026	034	044	068	099	137	182	206	346	499	647	772	867	5
	6	0+	0+	0+	0+	0+	0+	001	002	005	008	010	018	030	046	068	080	165	284	426	573	709	6
	7	0+	0+	0+	0+	0+	0+	0+	0+	001	001	002	004	007	012	019	024	062	129	229	356	500	7
	8	0+	0+	0+	0+	0+	0+	0+	0+	0+	0+	0+	001	001	002	004	006	018	046	098	179	291	8
	9	0+	0+	0+	0+	0+	0+	0+	0+	0+	0+	0+	0+	0+	0+	001	001	004	013	032	070	133	9
	10	0+	0+	0+	0+	0+	0+	0+	0+	0+	0+	0+	0+	0+	0+	0+	0+	001	003	008	020	046	10
	11	0+	0+	0+	0+	0+	0+	0+	0+	0+	0+	0+	0+	0+	0+	0+	0+	0+	0+	001	004	011	11
	12	0+	0+	0+	0+	0+	0+	0+	0+	0+	0+	0+	0+	0+	0+	0+	0+	0+	0+	0+	001	002	12
	13	0+	0+	0+	0+	0+	0+	0+	0+	0+	0+	0+	0+	0+	0+	0+	0+	0+	0+	0+	0+	0+	13

Table 8. *(continued)*

N	K	.01	.02	.04	.05	.06	.08	.10	.12	.14	.15	.16	.18	.20	.22	.24	.25	.30	.35	.40	.45	.50	K
14	0	1	1	1	1	1	1	1	1	1	1	1	1	1	1	1	1	1	1	1	1	1	0
	1	131	246	435	512	579	689	771	833	879	897	913	938	956	969	979	982	993	998	999	1–	1–	1
	2	008	031	106	153	204	310	415	514	603	643	681	747	802	847	884	899	953	979	992	997	999	2
	3	0+	002	017	030	048	096	158	232	311	352	393	474	552	624	689	719	839	916	960	981	994	3
	4	0+	0+	002	004	008	021	044	077	121	147	174	235	302	372	443	479	645	779	876	937	971	4
	5	0+	0+	0+	0+	001	004	009	020	036	047	059	091	130	176	230	258	416	577	721	833	910	5
	6	0+	0+	0+	0+	0+	0+	001	004	008	012	016	027	044	066	095	112	219	359	514	663	788	6
	7	0+	0+	0+	0+	0+	0+	0+	001	001	002	003	006	012	020	031	038	093	184	308	454	605	7
	8	0+	0+	0+	0+	0+	0+	0+	0+	0+	0+	001	001	002	005	008	010	031	075	150	259	395	8
	9	0+	0+	0+	0+	0+	0+	0+	0+	0+	0+	0+	0+	0+	001	002	002	008	024	058	119	212	9
	10	0+	0+	0+	0+	0+	0+	0+	0+	0+	0+	0+	0+	0+	0+	0+	0+	008	006	018	043	090	10
	11	0+	0+	0+	0+	0+	0+	0+	0+	0+	0+	0+	0+	0+	0+	0+	0+	0+	001	004	011	029	11
	12	0+	0+	0+	0+	0+	0+	0+	0+	0+	0+	0+	0+	0+	0+	0+	0+	0+	0+	001	002	006	12
	13	0+	0+	0+	0+	0+	0+	0+	0+	0+	0+	0+	0+	0+	0+	0+	0+	0+	0+	0+	0+	001	13
	14	0+	0+	0+	0+	0+	0+	0+	0+	0+	0+	0+	0+	0+	0+	0+	0+	0+	0+	0+	0+	0+	14
15	0	1	1	1	1	1	1	1	1	1	1	1	1	1	1	1	1	1	1	1	1	1	0
	1	140	261	458	537	605	714	794	853	896	913	927	949	965	976	984	987	995	998	1–	1–	1–	1
	2	010	035	119	171	226	340	451	552	642	681	718	781	833	874	906	920	965	986	995	998	1–	2
	3	0+	003	020	036	057	113	184	265	352	396	439	523	602	673	736	764	873	938	973	989	996	3
	4	0+	0+	002	005	010	027	056	096	148	177	209	278	352	427	502	539	703	827	909	958	982	4
	5	0+	0+	0+	001	001	005	013	026	048	062	078	117	164	219	281	314	485	648	783	880	941	5
	6	0+	0+	0+	0+	0+	001	002	006	012	017	023	039	061	090	127	148	278	436	597	739	849	6

Table 8. *(continued)*

N	K	.01	.02	.04	.05	.06	.08	.10	.12	.14	.15	.16	.18	.20	.22	.24	.25	.30	.35	.40	.45	.50	K
	7	0+	0+	0+	0+	0+	0+	0+	001	002	004	005	010	018	030	046	057	131	245	390	548	696	7
	8	0+	0+	0+	0+	0+	0+	0+	0+	0+	001	001	002	004	008	013	017	050	113	213	346	500	8
	9	0+	0+	0+	0+	0+	0+	0+	0+	0+	0+	0+	0+	001	002	003	004	015	042	095	182	304	9
	10	0+	0+	0+	0+	0+	0+	0+	0+	0+	0+	0+	0+	0+	0+	001	001	004	012	034	077	151	10
	11	0+	0+	0+	0+	0+	0+	0+	0+	0+	0+	0+	0+	0+	0+	0+	0+	001	003	009	025	059	11
	12	0+	0+	0+	0+	0+	0+	0+	0+	0+	0+	0+	0+	0+	0+	0+	0+	0+	0+	002	006	018	12
	13	0+	0+	0+	0+	0+	0+	0+	0+	0+	0+	0+	0+	0+	0+	0+	0+	0+	0+	0+	001	004	13
	14	0+	0+	0+	0+	0+	0+	0+	0+	0+	0+	0+	0+	0+	0+	0+	0+	0+	0+	0+	0+	0+	14
	15	0+	0+	0+	0+	0+	0+	0+	0+	0+	0+	0+	0+	0+	0+	0+	0+	0+	0+	0+	0+	0+	15
16	0	1	1	1	1	1	1	1	1	1	1	1	1	1	1	1	1	1	1	1	1	1	0
	1	149	276	480	560	628	737	815	871	910	926	939	958	972	981	988	990	997	999	1–	1–	1–	1
	2	011	040	133	189	249	370	485	588	677	716	751	811	859	897	925	937	974	990	997	999	1–	2
	3	001	004	024	043	067	131	211	300	393	439	484	570	648	717	777	803	901	955	982	993	998	3
	4	0+	0+	003	007	013	034	068	116	176	210	246	322	402	481	558	595	754	866	935	972	989	4
	5	0+	0+	0+	001	002	007	017	035	062	079	099	146	202	265	334	370	550	711	833	915	962	5
	6	0+	0+	0+	0+	0+	001	003	008	017	024	032	053	082	119	164	190	340	510	671	802	895	6
	7	0+	0+	0+	0+	0+	0+	001	002	004	006	008	015	027	043	066	080	175	312	473	634	773	7
	8	0+	0+	0+	0+	0+	0+	0+	0+	001	001	002	004	007	013	021	027	074	159	284	437	598	8
	9	0+	0+	0+	0+	0+	0+	0+	0+	0+	0+	0+	001	001	003	006	007	026	067	142	256	402	9
	10	0+	0+	0+	0+	0+	0+	0+	0+	0+	0+	0+	0+	0+	001	001	002	007	023	058	124	227	10
	11	0+	0+	0+	0+	0+	0+	0+	0+	0+	0+	0+	0+	0+	0+	0+	0+	002	006	019	049	105	11

Table 8. *(continued)*

N	K	.01	.02	.04	.05	.06	.08	.10	.12	.14	.15	.16	.18	.20	.22	.24	.25	.30	.35	.40	.45	.50	K
	12	0+	0+	0+	0+	0+	0+	0+	0+	0+	0+	0+	0+	0+	0+	0+	0+	0+	001	005	015	038	12
	13	0+	0+	0+	0+	0+	0+	0+	0+	0+	0+	0+	0+	0+	0+	0+	0+	0+	0+	001	003	011	13
	14	0+	0+	0+	0+	0+	0+	0+	0+	0+	0+	0+	0+	0+	0+	0+	0+	0+	0+	0+	001	002	14
	15	0+	0+	0+	0+	0+	0+	0+	0+	0+	0+	0+	0+	0+	0+	0+	0+	0+	0+	0+	0+	0+	15
	16	0+	0+	0+	0+	0+	0+	0+	0+	0+	0+	0+	0+	0+	0+	0+	0+	0+	0+	0+	0+	0+	16
17	0	1	1	1	1	1	1	1	1	1	1	1	1	1	1	1	1	1	1	1	1	1	0
	1	157	291	500	582	651	758	833	886	923	937	948	966	977	985	991	992	998	999	1−	1−	1−	1
	2	012	045	147	208	272	399	518	622	710	748	781	838	882	915	940	950	981	993	998	999	1−	2
	3	001	004	029	050	078	150	238	335	432	480	527	613	690	758	812	836	923	967	988	996	999	3
	4	0+	0+	004	009	016	042	083	138	207	244	284	367	451	533	611	647	798	897	954	982	994	4
	5	0+	0+	0+	001	003	009	022	045	078	099	122	178	242	313	388	426	611	765	874	940	975	5
	6	0+	0+	0+	0+	0+	001	005	011	023	032	042	069	106	151	205	235	403	580	736	853	928	6
	7	0+	0+	0+	0+	0+	0+	001	002	006	008	012	022	038	060	089	107	225	381	552	710	834	7
	8	0+	0+	0+	0+	0+	0+	0+	0+	001	002	003	006	011	019	032	040	105	213	359	526	685	8
	9	0+	0+	0+	0+	0+	0+	0+	0+	0+	0+	0+	001	003	005	009	012	040	099	199	337	500	9
	10	0+	0+	0+	0+	0+	0+	0+	0+	0+	0+	0+	0+	0+	001	002	003	013	038	092	183	315	10
	11	0+	0+	0+	0+	0+	0+	0+	0+	0+	0+	0+	0+	0+	0+	0+	001	003	012	035	083	166	11
	12	0+	0+	0+	0+	0+	0+	0+	0+	0+	0+	0+	0+	0+	0+	0+	0+	001	003	011	030	072	12
	13	0+	0+	0+	0+	0+	0+	0+	0+	0+	0+	0+	0+	0+	0+	0+	0+	0+	001	003	009	025	13
	14	0+	0+	0+	0+	0+	0+	0+	0+	0+	0+	0+	0+	0+	0+	0+	0+	0+	0+	0+	002	006	14
	15	0+	0+	0+	0+	0+	0+	0+	0+	0+	0+	0+	0+	0+	0+	0+	0+	0+	0+	0+	0+	001	15

Table 8. *(continued)*

N	K	.01	.02	.04	.05	.06	.08	.10	.12	.14	.15	.16	.18	.20	.22	.24	.25	.30	.35	.40	.45	.50	K
	16	0+	0+	0+	0+	0+	0+	0+	0+	0+	0+	0+	0+	0+	0+	0+	0+	0+	0+	0+	0+	0+	16
	17	0+	0+	0+	0+	0+	0+	0+	0+	0+	0+	0+	0+	0+	0+	0+	0+	0+	0+	0+	0+	0+	17
18	0	1	1	1	1	1	1	1	1	1	1	1	1	1	1	1	1	1	1	1	1	1	0
	1	165	305	520	603	672	777	850	900	934	946	957	972	982	989	993	994	998	1–	1–	1–	1–	1
	2	014	050	161	226	294	428	550	654	740	776	808	861	901	931	952	961	986	995	999	1–	1–	2
	3	001	005	033	058	090	170	266	369	471	520	567	654	729	792	843	865	940	976	992	997	999	3
	4	0+	0+	005	011	020	051	098	162	238	280	323	411	499	582	659	694	835	922	967	988	996	4
	5	0+	0+	001	002	003	012	028	056	096	121	148	212	284	361	441	481	667	811	906	959	985	5
	6	0+	0+	0+	0+	0+	002	006	015	031	042	055	089	133	187	249	283	466	645	791	892	952	6
	7	0+	0+	0+	0+	0+	0+	001	003	008	012	017	031	051	080	117	139	278	451	626	774	881	7
	8	0+	0+	0+	0+	0+	0+	0+	001	002	003	004	009	016	028	046	057	141	272	437	609	760	8
	9	0+	0+	0+	0+	0+	0+	0+	0+	0+	001	001	002	004	008	015	019	060	139	263	422	593	9
	10	0+	0+	0+	0+	0+	0+	0+	0+	0+	0+	0+	0+	001	002	004	005	021	060	135	253	407	10
	11	0+	0+	0+	0+	0+	0+	0+	0+	0+	0+	0+	0+	0+	0+	001	001	006	021	058	128	240	11
	12	0+	0+	0+	0+	0+	0+	0+	0+	0+	0+	0+	0+	0+	0+	0+	0+	001	006	020	054	119	12
	13	0+	0+	0+	0+	0+	0+	0+	0+	0+	0+	0+	0+	0+	0+	0+	0+	0+	001	006	018	048	13
	14	0+	0+	0+	0+	0+	0+	0+	0+	0+	0+	0+	0+	0+	0+	0+	0+	0+	0+	001	005	015	14
	15	0+	0+	0+	0+	0+	0+	0+	0+	0+	0+	0+	0+	0+	0+	0+	0+	0+	0+	0+	001	004	15
	16	0+	0+	0+	0+	0+	0+	0+	0+	0+	0+	0+	0+	0+	0+	0+	0+	0+	0+	0+	0+	001	16
	17	0+	0+	0+	0+	0+	0+	0+	0+	0+	0+	0+	0+	0+	0+	0+	0+	0+	0+	0+	0+	0+	17
	18	0+	0+	0+	0+	0+	0+	0+	0+	0+	0+	0+	0+	0+	0+	0+	0+	0+	0+	0+	0+	0+	18

Table 8. (*continued*) Binom

N	K	P: .01	.02	.04	.05	.06	.08	.10	.12	.14	.15	.16	.18	.20	.22	.24	.25	.30	.35	.40	.45	.50	K
19	0	1	1	1	1	1	1	1	1	1	1	1	1	1	1	1	1	1	1	1	1	1	0
	1	174	319	540	623	691	795	865	912	943	954	964	977	986	991	995	996	999	1−	1−	1−	1−	1
	2	015	055	175	245	317	456	580	683	767	802	832	881	917	943	962	969	990	997	999	1−	1−	2
	3	001	006	038	067	102	191	295	403	509	559	606	691	763	822	869	889	954	983	995	998	1−	3
	4	0+	0+	006	013	024	060	115	187	271	316	362	455	545	628	703	737	867	941	977	992	998	4
	5	0+	0+	001	002	004	015	035	069	116	144	176	248	327	410	494	535	718	850	930	972	990	5
	6	0+	0+	0+	0+	001	003	009	020	040	054	070	111	163	225	295	332	526	703	837	922	968	6
	7	0+	0+	0+	0+	0+	0+	002	005	011	016	023	041	068	103	149	175	334	519	692	827	916	7
	8	0+	0+	0+	0+	0+	0+	0+	001	003	004	006	013	023	040	063	077	182	334	512	683	820	8
	9	0+	0+	0+	0+	0+	0+	0+	0+	001	001	001	003	007	013	022	029	084	185	333	506	676	9
	10	0+	0+	0+	0+	0+	0+	0+	0+	0+	0+	0+	001	002	003	007	009	033	087	186	329	500	10
	11	0+	0+	0+	0+	0+	0+	0+	0+	0+	0+	0+	0+	0+	001	002	002	011	035	088	184	324	11
	12	0+	0+	0+	0+	0+	0+	0+	0+	0+	0+	0+	0+	0+	0+	0+	0+	003	011	035	087	180	12
	13	0+	0+	0+	0+	0+	0+	0+	0+	0+	0+	0+	0+	0+	0+	0+	0+	001	003	012	034	084	13
	14	0+	0+	0+	0+	0+	0+	0+	0+	0+	0+	0+	0+	0+	0+	0+	0+	0+	001	003	011	032	14
	15	0+	0+	0+	0+	0+	0+	0+	0+	0+	0+	0+	0+	0+	0+	0+	0+	0+	0+	001	003	010	15
	16	0+	0+	0+	0+	0+	0+	0+	0+	0+	0+	0+	0+	0+	0+	0+	0+	0+	0+	0+	001	002	16
	17	0+	0+	0+	0+	0+	0+	0+	0+	0+	0+	0+	0+	0+	0+	0+	0+	0+	0+	0+	0+	0+	17
	18	0+	0+	0+	0+	0+	0+	0+	0+	0+	0+	0+	0+	0+	0+	0+	0+	0+	0+	0+	0+	0+	18
	19	0+	0+	0+	0+	0+	0+	0+	0+	0+	0+	0+	0+	0+	0+	0+	0+	0+	0+	0+	0+	0+	19
20	0	1	1	1	1	1	1	1	1	1	1	1	1	1	1	1	1	1	1	1	1	1	0
	1	182	332	558	642	710	811	878	922	951	961	969	981	988	993	996	997	999	1−	1−	1−	1−	1

Table 8. *(continued)*

N	K	.01	.02	.04	.05	.06	.08	.10	.12	.14	.15	.16	.18	.20	.22	.24	.25	.30	.35	.40	.45	.50	K
		P																					
	2	017	060	190	264	340	483	608	711	792	824	853	898	931	954	970	976	992	998	999	1–	1–	2
	3	001	007	044	075	115	212	323	437	545	595	642	725	794	849	891	909	965	988	996	999	1–	3
	4	0+	001	007	016	029	071	133	213	304	352	401	497	589	671	743	775	893	956	984	995	999	4
	5	0+	0+	001	003	006	018	043	083	137	170	206	285	370	458	544	585	762	882	949	981	994	5
	6	0+	0+	0+	0+	001	004	011	026	051	067	087	136	196	266	343	383	584	755	874	945	979	6
	7	0+	0+	0+	0+	0+	001	002	007	015	022	030	054	087	130	184	214	392	583	750	870	942	7
	8	0+	0+	0+	0+	0+	0+	0+	001	004	006	009	018	032	054	083	102	228	399	584	748	868	8
	9	0+	0+	0+	0+	0+	0+	0+	0+	001	001	002	005	010	019	032	041	113	238	404	586	748	9
	10	0+	0+	0+	0+	0+	0+	0+	0+	0+	0+	0+	001	003	005	010	014	048	122	245	409	588	10
	11	0+	0+	0+	0+	0+	0+	0+	0+	0+	0+	0+	0+	001	001	003	004	017	053	128	249	412	11
	12	0+	0+	0+	0+	0+	0+	0+	0+	0+	0+	0+	0+	0+	0+	001	001	005	020	057	131	252	12
	13	0+	0+	0+	0+	0+	0+	0+	0+	0+	0+	0+	0+	0+	0+	0+	0+	001	006	021	058	132	13
	14	0+	0+	0+	0+	0+	0+	0+	0+	0+	0+	0+	0+	0+	0+	0+	0+	0+	002	006	021	058	14
	15	0+	0+	0+	0+	0+	0+	0+	0+	0+	0+	0+	0+	0+	0+	0+	0+	0+	0+	002	006	021	15
	16	0+	0+	0+	0+	0+	0+	0+	0+	0+	0+	0+	0+	0+	0+	0+	0+	0+	0+	0+	002	006	16
	17	0+	0+	0+	0+	0+	0+	0+	0+	0+	0+	0+	0+	0+	0+	0+	0+	0+	0+	0+	0+	001	17
	18	0+	0+	0+	0+	0+	0+	0+	0+	0+	0+	0+	0+	0+	0+	0+	0+	0+	0+	0+	0+	0+	18
	19	0+	0+	0+	0+	0+	0+	0+	0+	0+	0+	0+	0+	0+	0+	0+	0+	0+	0+	0+	0+	0+	19
	20	0+	0+	0+	0+	0+	0+	0+	0+	0+	0+	0+	0+	0+	0+	0+	0+	0+	0+	0+	0+	0+	20
21	0	1	1	1	1	1	1	1	1	1	1	1	1	1	1	1	1	1	1	1	1	1	0
	1	190	346	576	659	727	826	891	932	958	967	974	985	991	995	997	998	999	1–	1–	1–	1–	1

Table 8. *(continued)*

											P											
N K	.01	.02	.04	.05	.06	.08	.10	.12	.14	.15	.16	.18	.20	.22	.24	.25	.30	.35	.40	.45	.50	*K*
2	019	065	204	283	362	509	635	736	814	845	872	913	943	962	976	981	994	999	1–	1–	1–	2
3	001	008	050	085	128	234	352	470	580	630	676	756	832	872	910	925	973	999	998	999	1–	3
4	0+	001	009	019	034	082	152	240	338	389	440	538	630	710	779	808	914	967	989	997	999	4
5	0+	0+	001	003	007	023	052	098	161	197	237	323	414	505	592	633	802	908	963	987	996	5
6	0+	0+	0+	0+	001	005	014	033	063	083	106	162	231	308	391	433	637	799	904	961	987	6
7	0+	0+	0+	0+	0+	001	003	009	020	029	039	068	109	160	222	256	449	643	800	904	961	7
8	0+	0+	0+	0+	0+	0+	001	002	005	008	012	024	043	070	108	130	277	464	650	803	905	8
9	0+	0+	0+	0+	0+	0+	0+	0+	001	002	003	007	014	026	044	056	148	294	476	659	808	9
10	0+	0+	0+	0+	0+	0+	0+	0+	0+	0+	001	002	004	008	016	021	068	162	309	488	669	10
11	0+	0+	0+	0+	0+	0+	0+	0+	0+	0+	0+	0+	001	002	005	006	026	077	174	321	500	11
12	0+	0+	0+	0+	0+	0+	0+	0+	0+	0+	0+	0+	0+	001	001	002	009	031	085	184	332	12
13	0+	0+	0+	0+	0+	0+	0+	0+	0+	0+	0+	0+	0+	0+	0+	0+	002	011	035	091	192	13
14	0+	0+	0+	0+	0+	0+	0+	0+	0+	0+	0+	0+	0+	0+	0+	0+	001	003	012	038	095	14
15	0+	0+	0+	0+	0+	0+	0+	0+	0+	0+	0+	0+	0+	0+	0+	0+	0+	001	004	013	039	15
16	0+	0+	0+	0+	0+	0+	0+	0+	0+	0+	0+	0+	0+	0+	0+	0+	0+	0+	001	004	013	16
17	0+	0+	0+	0+	0+	0+	0+	0+	0+	0+	0+	0+	0+	0+	0+	0+	0+	0+	0+	001	004	17
18	0+	0+	0+	0+	0+	0+	0+	0+	0+	0+	0+	0+	0+	0+	0+	0+	0+	0+	0+	0+	001	18
19	0+	0+	0+	0+	0+	0+	0+	0+	0+	0+	0+	0+	0+	0+	0+	0+	0+	0+	0+	0+	0+	19
20	0+	0+	0+	0+	0+	0+	0+	0+	0+	0+	0+	0+	0+	0+	0+	0+	0+	0+	0+	0+	0+	20
21	0+	0+	0+	0+	0+	0+	0+	0+	0+	0+	0+	0+	0+	0+	0+	0+	0+	0+	0+	0+	0+	21

Table 8. *(continued)*

		P																				
N	*K*	.01	.02	.04	.05	.06	.08	.10	.12	.14	.15	.16	.18	.20	.22	.24	.25	.30	.35	.40	.45	.50	*K*
22	0	1	1	1	1	1	1	1	1	1	1	1	1	1	1	1	1	1	1	1	1	1	0
	1	198	359	593	676	744	840	902	940	964	972	978	987	993	996	998	998	1–	1–	11–	1–	1–	1
	2	020	071	219	302	384	535	661	760	834	863	888	926	952	970	981	985	996	999	1–	1–	1–	2
	3	001	009	056	095	142	256	380	502	612	662	707	785	846	892	926	939	979	994	998	1–	1–	3
	4	0+	001	011	022	040	094	172	267	372	425	477	578	668	746	810	838	932	975	992	998	1–	4
	5	0+	0+	002	004	009	027	062	115	186	226	270	363	457	550	637	677	835	928	973	992	998	5
	6	0+	0+	0+	001	002	006	018	041	077	100	127	191	267	351	439	483	687	837	928	973	992	6
	7	0+	0+	0+	0+	0+	001	004	012	026	037	050	085	133	193	263	301	506	698	842	929	974	7
	8	0+	0+	0+	0+	0+	0+	001	003	008	011	017	032	056	090	135	162	329	526	710	848	933	8
	9	0+	0+	0+	0+	0+	0+	0+	001	002	003	005	010	020	036	060	075	186	353	546	724	857	9
	10	0+	0+	0+	0+	0+	0+	0+	0+	0+	001	001	003	006	012	022	030	092	208	376	565	738	10
	11	0+	0+	0+	0+	0+	0+	0+	0+	0+	0+	0+	001	002	004	007	010	039	107	228	396	584	11
	12	0+	0+	0+	0+	0+	0+	0+	0+	0+	0+	0+	0+	0+	001	002	003	014	047	121	246	416	12
	13	0+	0+	0+	0+	0+	0+	0+	0+	0+	0+	0+	0+	0+	0+	0+	001	004	018	055	133	262	13
	14	0+	0+	0+	0+	0+	0+	0+	0+	0+	0+	0+	0+	0+	0+	0+	0+	001	006	021	062	143	14
	15	0+	0+	0+	0+	0+	0+	0+	0+	0+	0+	0+	0+	0+	0+	0+	0+	0+	002	007	024	067	15
	16	0+	0+	0+	0+	0+	0+	0+	0+	0+	0+	0+	0+	0+	0+	0+	0+	0+	0+	002	008	026	16
	17	0+	0+	0+	0+	0+	0+	0+	0+	0+	0+	0+	0+	0+	0+	0+	0+	0+	0+	0+	002	008	17
	18	0+	0+	0+	0+	0+	0+	0+	0+	0+	0+	0+	0+	0+	0+	0+	0+	0+	0+	0+	0+	002	18
	19	0+	0+	0+	0+	0+	0+	0+	0+	0+	0+	0+	0+	0+	0+	0+	0+	0+	0+	0+	0+	0+	19
	20	0+	0+	0+	0+	0+	0+	0+	0+	0+	0+	0+	0+	0+	0+	0+	0+	0+	0+	0+	0+	0+	20

Table 8. (*continued*)

		P																					
N	*K*	.01	.02	.04	.05	.06	.08	.10	.12	.14	.15	.16	.18	.20	.22	.24	.25	.30	.35	.40	.45	.50	*K*
	21	0+	0+	0+	0+	0+	0+	0+	0+	0+	0+	0+	0+	0+	0+	0+	0+	0+	0+	0+	0+	0+	21
	22	0+	0+	0+	0+	0+	0+	0+	0+	0+	0+	0+	0+	0+	0+	0+	0+	0+	0+	0+	0+	0+	22
23	0	1	1	1	1	1	1	1	1	1	1	1	1	1	1	1	1	1	1	1	1	1	0
	1	206	372	609	693	759	853	911	947	969	976	982	990	994	997	998	999	1–	1–	1–	1–	1–	1
	2	022	077	234	321	405	559	685	781	852	880	902	937	960	975	985	988	997	999	1–	1–	1–	2
	3	002	011	062	105	157	278	408	533	643	692	736	810	867	909	939	951	984	996	999	1–	1–	3
	4	0+	001	012	026	046	107	193	295	405	460	514	615	703	778	838	863	946	982	995	999	1–	4
	5	0+	0+	002	005	011	033	073	133	212	256	303	401	499	593	678	717	864	945	981	995	999	5
	6	0+	0+	0+	001	002	008	023	050	092	119	150	222	305	395	487	532	731	869	946	981	995	6
	7	0+	0+	0+	0+	0+	002	006	015	033	046	062	104	160	227	305	346	560	747	876	949	983	7
	8	0+	0+	0+	0+	0+	0+	001	004	010	015	022	042	072	113	166	196	382	586	763	885	953	8
	9	0+	0+	0+	0+	0+	0+	0+	001	003	004	007	014	027	048	078	096	229	444	612	780	895	9
	10	0+	0+	0+	0+	0+	0+	0+	0+	001	001	002	004	009	017	031	041	120	259	444	636	798	10
	11	0+	0+	0+	0+	0+	0+	0+	0+	0+	0+	0+	001	003	005	011	015	055	142	287	472	661	11
	12	0+	0+	0+	0+	0+	0+	0+	0+	0+	0+	0+	0+	001	001	003	005	021	068	164	313	500	12
	13	0+	0+	0+	0+	0+	0+	0+	0+	0+	0+	0+	0+	0+	0+	001	001	007	028	081	184	339	13
	14	0+	0+	0+	0+	0+	0+	0+	0+	0+	0+	0+	0+	0+	0+	0+	0+	002	010	035	094	202	14
	15	0+	0+	0+	0+	0+	0+	0+	0+	0+	0+	0+	0+	0+	0+	0+	0+	001	003	013	041	105	15
	16	0+	0+	0+	0+	0+	0+	0+	0+	0+	0+	0+	0+	0+	0+	0+	0+	0+	001	004	015	047	16
	17	0+	0+	0+	0+	0+	0+	0+	0+	0+	0+	0+	0+	0+	0+	0+	0+	0+	0+	001	005	017	17
	18	0+	0+	0+	0+	0+	0+	0+	0+	0+	0+	0+	0+	0+	0+	0+	0+	0+	0+	0+	001	005	18
	19	0+	0+	0+	0+	0+	0+	0+	0+	0+	0+	0+	0+	0+	0+	0+	0+	0+	0+	0+	0+	001	19

Table 8. *(continued)*

N	K	.01	.02	.04	.05	.06	.08	.10	.12	.14	.15	.16	.18	.20	.22	.24	.25	.30	.35	.40	.45	.50	K
	20	0+	0+	0+	0+	0+	0+	0+	0+	0+	0+	0+	0+	0+	0+	0+	0+	0+	0+	0+	0+	0+	20
	21	0+	0+	0+	0+	0+	0+	0+	0+	0+	0+	0+	0+	0+	0+	0+	0+	0+	0+	0+	0+	0+	21
	22	0+	0+	0+	0+	0+	0+	0+	0+	0+	0+	0+	0+	0+	0+	0+	0+	0+	0+	0+	0+	0+	22
	23	0+	0+	0+	0+	0+	0+	0+	0+	0+	0+	0+	0+	0+	0+	0+	0+	0+	0+	0+	0+	0+	23
24	0	1	1	1	1	1	1	1	1	1	1	1	1	1	1	1	1	1	1	1	1	1	0
	1	214	384	625	708	773	865	920	953	973	980	985	991	995	997	999	999	1–	1–	1–	1–	1–	1
	2	024	083	249	339	427	583	708	801	869	894	915	946	967	980	988	991	998	1–	1–	1–	1–	2
	3	002	012	069	116	172	301	436	563	673	720	763	833	885	924	950	960	988	997	999	1–	1–	3
	4	0+	001	014	030	053	121	214	324	439	495	550	650	736	807	862	885	958	987	996	999	1–	4
	5	0+	0+	002	006	013	039	085	153	239	287	337	439	540	634	717	753	889	958	987	996	999	5
	6	0+	0+	0+	001	002	010	028	060	109	139	174	254	344	439	533	578	771	896	960	987	999	6
	7	0+	0+	0+	0+	0+	002	007	019	041	057	076	126	189	264	349	393	611	789	904	964	989	7
	8	0+	0+	0+	0+	0+	0+	002	005	013	020	028	053	089	138	199	234	435	642	808	914	968	8
	9	0+	0+	0+	0+	0+	0+	0+	001	004	006	009	019	036	062	099	121	275	474	672	827	924	9
	10	0+	0+	0+	0+	0+	0+	0+	0+	001	002	002	006	013	024	042	055	153	313	511	701	846	10
	11	0+	0+	0+	0+	0+	0+	0+	0+	0+	0+	001	002	004	008	016	021	074	183	350	546	729	11
	12	0+	0+	0+	0+	0+	0+	0+	0+	0+	0+	0+	0+	001	002	005	007	031	094	213	385	581	12
	13	0+	0+	0+	0+	0+	0+	0+	0+	0+	0+	0+	0+	0+	001	001	002	012	042	114	242	419	13
	14	0+	0+	0+	0+	0+	0+	0+	0+	0+	0+	0+	0+	0+	0+	0+	001	004	016	053	134	271	14
	15	0+	0+	0+	0+	0+	0+	0+	0+	0+	0+	0+	0+	0+	0+	0+	0+	001	005	022	065	154	15
	16	0+	0+	0+	0+	0+	0+	0+	0+	0+	0+	0+	0+	0+	0+	0+	0+	0+	002	008	027	076	16
	17	0+	0+	0+	0+	0+	0+	0+	0+	0+	0+	0+	0+	0+	0+	0+	0+	0+	0+	002	010	032	17

Table 8. *(continued)*

		P																				
N	K	.01	.02	.04	.05	.06	.08	.10	.12	.14	.15	.16	.18	.20	.22	.24	.25	.30	.35	.40	.45	.50	K
	18	0+	0+	0+	0+	0+	0+	0+	0+	0+	0+	0+	0+	0+	0+	0+	0+	0+	0+	001	003	011	18
	19	0+	0+	0+	0+	0+	0+	0+	0+	0+	0+	0+	0+	0+	0+	0+	0+	0+	0+	0+	001	003	19
	20	0+	0+	0+	0+	0+	0+	0+	0+	0+	0+	0+	0+	0+	0+	0+	0+	0+	0+	0+	0+	001	20
	21	0+	0+	0+	0+	0+	0+	0+	0+	0+	0+	0+	0+	0+	0+	0+	0+	0+	0+	0+	0+	0+	21
	22	0+	0+	0+	0+	0+	0+	0+	0+	0+	0+	0+	0+	0+	0+	0+	0+	0+	0+	0+	0+	0+	22
	23	0+	0+	0+	0+	0+	0+	0+	0+	0+	0+	0+	0+	0+	0+	0+	0+	0+	0+	0+	0+	0+	23
	24	0+	0+	0+	0+	0+	0+	0+	0+	0+	0+	0+	0+	0+	0+	0+	0+	0+	0+	0+	0+	0+	24
25	0	1	1	1	1	1	1	1	1	1	1	1	1	1	1	1	1	1	1	1	1	1	0
	1	222	397	640	723	787	876	928	959	977	983	987	993	996	998	999	999	1−	1−	1−	1−	1−	1
	2	026	089	264	358	447	605	729	820	883	907	926	955	973	984	991	993	998	1−	1−	1−	1−	2
	3	002	013	076	127	187	323	463	591	700	746	787	853	902	936	959	968	991	998	1−	1−	1−	3
	4	0+	001	017	034	060	135	236	352	471	529	584	683	766	832	883	904	967	990	998	1−	1−	4
	5	0+	0+	003	007	015	045	098	173	267	318	371	477	579	672	752	786	910	968	991	998	1−	5
	6	0+	0+	0+	001	003	012	033	071	127	162	200	288	383	482	577	622	807	917	971	991	998	6
	7	0+	0+	0+	0+	001	003	009	024	051	070	092	149	220	303	393	439	659	827	926	974	993	7
	8	0+	0+	0+	0+	0+	001	002	007	017	025	036	066	109	166	235	273	488	694	846	936	978	8
	9	0+	0+	0+	0+	0+	0+	0+	002	005	008	012	025	047	079	123	149	323	533	726	866	946	9
	10	0+	0+	0+	0+	0+	0+	0+	0+	001	002	003	008	017	033	056	071	189	370	575	758	885	10
	11	0+	0+	0+	0+	0+	0+	0+	0+	0+	0+	001	002	006	012	022	030	098	229	414	616	788	11
	12	0+	0+	0+	0+	0+	0+	0+	0+	0+	0+	0+	001	002	004	008	011	044	125	268	457	655	12
	13	0+	0+	0+	0+	0+	0+	0+	0+	0+	0+	0+	0+	0+	001	002	003	017	060	154	306	500	13
	14	0+	0+	0+	0+	0+	0+	0+	0+	0+	0+	0+	0+	0+	0+	001	001	006	025	078	183	345	14

15	0+	0+	0+	0+	0+	0+	0+	0+	0+	0+	0+	0+	0+	0+	0+	0+	002	009	034	096	212	15
16	0+	0+	0+	0+	0+	0+	0+	0+	0+	0+	0+	0+	0+	0+	0+	0+	0+	003	013	044	115	16
17	0+	0+	0+	0+	0+	0+	0+	0+	0+	0+	0+	0+	0+	0+	0+	0+	0+	001	004	017	054	17
18	0+	0+	0+	0+	0+	0+	0+	0+	0+	0+	0+	0+	0+	0+	0+	0+	0+	0+	001	006	022	18
19	0+	0+	0+	0+	0+	0+	0+	0+	0+	0+	0+	0+	0+	0+	0+	0+	0+	0+	0+	002	007	19
20	0+	0+	0+	0+	0+	0+	0+	0+	0+	0+	0+	0+	0+	0+	0+	0+	0+	0+	0+	0+	002	20
21	0+	0+	0+	0+	0+	0+	0+	0+	0+	0+	0+	0+	0+	0+	0+	0+	0+	0+	0+	0+	0+	21
22	0+	0+	0+	0+	0+	0+	0+	0+	0+	0+	0+	0+	0+	0+	0+	0+	0+	0+	0+	0+	0+	22
23	0+	0+	0+	0+	0+	0+	0+	0+	0+	0+	0+	0+	0+	0+	0+	0+	0+	0+	0+	0+	0+	23
24	0+	0+	0+	0+	0+	0+	0+	0+	0+	0+	0+	0+	0+	0+	0+	0+	0+	0+	0+	0+	0+	24
25	0+	0+	0+	0+	0+	0+	0+	0+	0+	0+	0+	0+	0+	0+	0+	0+	0+	0+	0+	0+	0+	25

Table 9. Selected Values for the Exponential Distribution

P	Δ	P	Δ	P	Δ
0.01	0.010050	0.34	0.415515	0.67	1.108662
0.02	0.020203	0.35	0.430783	0.68	1.139434
0.03	0.030459	0.36	0.446287	0.69	1.171183
0.04	0.040822	0.37	0.462035	0.70	1.203973
0.05	0.051293	0.38	0.478036	0.71	1.237874
0.06	0.061875	0.39	0.494296	0.72	1.272966
0.07	0.072571	0.40	0.510826	0.73	1.309333
0.08	0.083382	0.41	0.527633	0.74	1.347073
0.09	0.094311	0.42	0.544727	0.75	1.386294
0.10	0.105360	0.43	0.562119	0.76	1.427116
0.11	0.116534	0.44	0.579818	0.77	1.469676
0.12	0.127833	0.45	0.597837	0.78	1.514128
0.13	0.139262	0.46	0.616186	0.79	1.560648
0.14	0.150823	0.47	0.634878	0.80	1.609438
0.15	0.162519	0.48	0.653926	0.81	1.660731
0.16	0.174353	0.49	0.673344	0.82	1.714798
0.17	0.186330	0.50	0.693147	0.83	1.771957
0.18	0.198451	0.51	0.713350	0.84	1.832581
0.19	0.210721	0.52	0.733969	0.85	1.897120
0.20	0.223144	0.53	0.755023	0.86	1.966113
0.21	0.235722	0.54	0.776529	0.87	2.040220
0.22	0.248461	0.55	0.798508	0.88	2.120263
0.23	0.261365	0.56	0.820980	0.89	2.207275
0.24	0.274437	0.57	0.843970	0.90	2.302585
0.25	0.287682	0.58	0.867501	0.91	2.407945
0.26	0.301105	0.59	0.891598	0.92	2.525728
0.27	0.314711	0.60	0.916291	0.93	2.659259
0.28	0.328504	0.61	0.941608	0.94	2.813411
0.29	0.342490	0.62	0.967584	0.95	2.995732
0.30	0.356675	0.63	0.994252	0.96	3.218875
0.31	0.371064	0.64	1.021651	0.97	3.506557
0.32	0.385662	0.65	1.049822	0.98	3.912021
0.33	0.400478	0.66	1.078810	0.99	4.605165

Table 10. Table of Common Logarithms—Five Place[a]

N	L0	1	2	3	4	5	6	7	8	9
0	$-\infty$	00 000	30 103	47 712	60 206	69 897	77 815	84 510	90 309	95 424
1	00 000	04 139	07 918	11 394	14 613	17 609	20 412	23 04$\bar{5}$	25 527	27 875
2	30 103	32 222	34 242	36 173	38 021	39 794	41 497	43 136	44 716	46 240
3	47 712	49 136	50 515	51 851	53 148	54 407	55 630	56 820	57 978	59 106
4	60 206	61 278	62 32$\bar{5}$	63 347	64 345	65 321	66 276	67 210	68 124	69 020
5	69 897	70 757	71 600	72 428	73 239	74 036	74 819	75 587	76 343	77 085
6	77 815	78 533	79 239	79 934	80 618	81 291	81 954	82 607	83 251	83 885
7	84 510	85 126	85 733	86 332	86 923	87 506	88 081	88 649	89 209	89 763
8	90 309	90 849	91 381	91 908	92 428	92 942	93 4$\bar{5}$0	93 952	94 448	94 939
9	95 424	95 904	96 379	96 848	97 313	97 772	98 227	98 677	99 123	99 564
10	00 000	00 432	00 860	01 284	01 703	02 119	02 531	02 938	03 342	03 743
11	04 139	04 532	04 922	05 308	05 690	06 070	06 446	06 819	07 188	07 55$\bar{5}$
12	07 918	08 279	08 636	08 991	09 342	09 691	10 037	10 380	10 721	11 059
13	11 394	11 727	12 057	12 385	12 710	13 033	13 354	13 672	13 988	14 301
14	14 613	14 922	15 229	15 534	15 836	16 137	16 435	16 732	17 026	17 319
15	17 609	17 898	18 184	18 469	18 752	19 033	19 312	19 590	19 866	20 140
16	20 412	20 683	20 952	21 219	21 484	21 748	22 011	22 272	22 531	22 789
17	23 04$\bar{5}$	23 300	23 553	23 80$\bar{5}$	24 05$\bar{5}$	24 304	24 551	24 797	25 042	25 285
18	25 527	25 768	26 007	26 245	26 482	26 717	26 951	27 184	27 416	27 646
19	27 875	28 103	28 330	28 556	28 780	29 003	29 226	29 447	29 667	29 885

[a]Tables on pp. 2 and 3 in LOGARITHMIC AND TRIGONOMETRIC TABLES TO FIVE PLACES by Kai L. Nielsen (Barnes & Noble).

Table 10. (*continued*)

N	L0	1	2	3	4	5	6	7	8	9
20	30 103	30 320	30 535	30 7$\bar{5}$0	30 963	31 175	31 387	31 597	31 806	32 01$\bar{5}$
21	32 222	32 428	32 634	32 838	33 041	33 244	33 445	33 646	33 846	34 044
22	34 242	34 439	34 635	34 830	35 02$\bar{5}$	35 218	35 411	35 603	35 793	35 984
23	36 173	36 361	36 549	36 736	36 922	37 107	37 291	37 47$\bar{5}$	37 658	37 840
24	38 021	38 202	38 382	38 561	38 739	38 917	39 094	39 270	39 445	39 620
25	39 794	39 907	40 140	40 312	40 483	40 654	40 824	40 993	41 162	41 330
26	41 497	41 664	41 830	41 996	42 160	42 32$\bar{5}$	42 488	42 651	42 813	42 975
27	43 136	43 297	43 457	43 616	43 775	43 933	44 091	44 248	44 404	44 560
28	44 716	44 871	45 02$\bar{5}$	45 179	45 332	45 484	45 637	45 788	45 939	46 090
29	46 240	46 389	46 538	46 687	46 83$\bar{5}$	46 982	47 129	47 276	47 422	47 567
30	47 712	47 857	48 001	48 144	48 287	48 430	48 572	48 714	48 855	48 996
31	49 136	49 276	49 415	49 554	49 693	49 831	49 969	50 106	50 243	50 379
32	50 51$\bar{5}$	50 651	50 786	50 920	51 05$\bar{5}$	51 188	51 322	51 45$\bar{5}$	51 587	51 720
33	51 851	51 983	52 114	52 244	5237$\bar{5}$	52 504	52 634	52 763	52 892	53 020
34	53 148	53 275	53 493	53 529	53 656	53 782	53 908	54 033	54 158	54 283
35	54 407	54 531	54 654	54 777	54900	55 023	55 14$\bar{5}$	55 267	55 388	55 509
36	55 630	55 751	55 871	55 991	56 110	56 229	56 348	56 467	56 58$\bar{5}$	56 703
37	56 820	56 937	57 054	57 171	57 287	57 403	57 519	57 634	57 749	57 864
38	57 928	58 092	58 206	58 320	58 433	58 546	58 659	58 771	58 883	58 99$\bar{5}$
39	59 106	59 218	59 329	59 439	59 5$\bar{5}$0	59 660	59 770	59 879	59 988	60 097

Table 10. (*continued*)

N	L0	1	2	3	4	5	6	7	8	9
40	60 206	60 314	60 423	60 531	60 638	60 746	60 853	60 959	61 066	61 172
41	61 278	61 384	61 490	61 595	61 700	61 80$\bar{5}$	61 909	62 014	62 118	62 271
42	62 32$\bar{5}$	62 428	62 531	62 634	62 737	62 839	62 941	63 043	63 144	63 246
43	63 347	63 448	63 548	63 649	63 749	63 849	63 949	64 048	64 147	64 246
44	64 345	64 444	64 542	64 640	64 738	64 836	64 933	65 031	65 128	65 22$\bar{5}$
45	65 321	05 418	65 514	65 610	65 706	65 801	65 896	65 992	66 087	66 181
46	66 276	66 370	66 464	66 558	66 652	66 745	66 839	66 932	67 02$\bar{5}$	67 117
47	67 210	67 302	67 394	67 486	67 578	67 669	67 761	67 852	67 943	68 034
48	68 124	68 21$\bar{5}$	68 30$\bar{5}$	68 39$\bar{5}$	68 48$\bar{5}$	68 574	68 664	68 753	68 842	68 931
49	69 020	69 108	69 197	69 28$\bar{5}$	69 373	69 461	69 548	69 636	69 723	69 810
50	69 897	69 984	70 070	70 157	70 243	70 329	70 415	70 501	70 586	70 672
51	70 757	70 842	70 927	71 012	71 096	71 181	71 26$\bar{5}$	71 349	71 433	71 517
52	71 600	71 684	71 767	71 850	71 933	72 016	72 009	72 181	72 263	72 346
53	72 428	72 509	72 591	72 673	72 754	72 835	72 916	72 997	73 078	73 159
54	73 239	73 320	73 400	73 480	73 560	73 640	73 719	73 799	73 878	73 957
55	74 036	74 115	74 194	74 273	74 351	74 429	74 507	74 586	74 663	74 741
56	74 819	74 896	74 974	75 051	75 128	75 20$\bar{5}$	75 282	75 358	75 43$\bar{5}$	75 511
57	75 587	75 664	75 740	75 815	75 891	75 967	76 042	76 118	76 193	76 268
58	76 345	76 418	76 492	76 567	76 641	76 716	76 790	76 864	76 938	77 012
59	77 085	77 159	77 232	77 395	77 379	77 452	77 52$\bar{5}$	77 597	77 670	77 743

Table 10. *(continued)*

N	L0	1	2	3	4	5	6	7	8	9
60	77 815	77 887	77 960	78 032	78 104	78 176	78 247	78 319	78 390	78 462
61	78 533	78 604	78 675	78 746	78 817	78 888	78 958	79 029	79 009	79 169
62	79 239	79 309	79 379	79 449	79 518	79 588	79 657	79 727	79 796	79 865
63	79 934	80 003	80 072	80 140	80 209	80 277	80 346	80 414	80 482	80 550
64	80 618	80 686	80 754	80 821	80 889	80 956	81 023	81 090	81 158	81 224
65	81 291	81 358	81 42$\bar{5}$	81 491	81 558	81 624	81 690	81 757	81 823	81 889
66	81 954	82 020	82 086	82 151	82 217	82 282	82 347	82 413	82 478	82 543
67	82 607	82 672	82 737	82 808	82 866	82 930	82 99$\bar{5}$	83 059	83 123	83 187
68	83 251	83 31$\bar{5}$	83 378	83 442	83 506	83 569	83 632	83 696	83 759	83 822
69	83 88$\bar{5}$	83 948	84 011	84 073	84 136	84 198	84 261	84 323	84 386	84 448
70	84 510	84 572	84 634	84 696	84 757	84 819	84 880	84 942	85 003	85 06$\bar{5}$
71	85 126	85 187	85 248	85 309	85 370	85 431	85 491	85 552	85 612	85 673
72	85 733	85 794	85 854	85 914	85 974	86 034	86 094	86 153	86 213	86 273
73	86 332	86 392	86 451	86 510	86 570	86 629	86 688	86 747	86 806	86 864
74	86 923	86 982	87 040	87 099	87 157	87 216	87 274	87 332	87 390	87 448
75	87 506	87 564	87 622	87 679	87 737	87 79$\bar{5}$	88 423	88 480	88 536	88 593
76	88 081	88 138	88 195	88 252	88 309	88 366	88 423	88 480	88 536	88 593
77	88 649	88 705	88 762	88 818	88 874	88 930	88 986	89 042	89 098	89 154
78	89 209	89 265	89 321	89 376	89 432	89 487	89 542	89 597	89 653	89 708
79	89 763	89 818	89 873	89 927	89 982	90 037	90 091	90 146	90 200	90 25$\bar{5}$

Table 10. *(continued)*

N	L0	1	2	3	4	5	6	7	8	9
80	90 309	90 363	90 417	90 472	90 526	90 580	90 634	90 687	90 741	90 79$\bar{5}$
81	90 849	90 902	90 956	91 009	91 062	91 116	91 169	91 222	91 275	91 328
82	91 381	91 434	91 487	91 540	91 593	91 645	91 698	91 751	91 803	91 855
83	91 908	91 960	92 012	92 06$\bar{5}$	92 117	92 169	92 221	92 273	92 324	92 376
84	92 428	92 480	92 531	92 583	92 634	92 686	92 737	92 788	92 840	92 891
85	92 942	92 993	93 044	93 09$\bar{5}$	93 146	93 197	93 247	93 298	93 349	93 399
86	93 4$\bar{5}$0	93 500	93 551	93 601	93 651	93 702	93 752	93 802	93 852	93 902
87	93 952	94 002	94 052	94 101	94 151	94 201	94 250	94 300	94 349	94 399
88	94 448	94 498	94 547	94 506	94 645	94 694	94 743	94 792	94 841	94 890
89	94 939	94 988	95 036	95 086	95 134	95 182	95 231	95 279	95 328	95 376
90	95 424	95 472	95 521	95 569	95 617	95 66$\bar{5}$	95 713	95 761	95 809	95 856
91	95 904	95 952	95 999	96 047	96 09$\bar{5}$	96 142	96 100	96 237	96 284	96 332
92	96 379	96 426	96 473	96 520	96 567	96 614	96 661	96 708	96 75$\bar{5}$	96 802
93	96 848	96 89$\bar{5}$	96 942	96 988	97 03$\bar{5}$	97 081	97 128	97 174	97 220	97 267
94	97 313	97 359	97 405	97 451	97 497	97 543	97 589	97 63$\bar{5}$	97 681	97 727
95	97 772	97 818	97 864	97 909	97 95$\bar{5}$	98 000	98 046	98 091	98 137	98 182
96	98 227	98 272	98 318	98 363	98 408	98 453	98 498	98 543	98 588	98 632
97	93 677	98 722	98 767	98 811	98 856	98 900	98 94$\bar{5}$	98 989	99 034	99 078
98	99 123	99 167	99 211	99 255	99 300	99 344	99 388	99 432	99 476	99 520
99	99 564	99 607	99 651	99 69$\bar{5}$	99 739	99 782	99 826	99 870	99 913	99 957
100	00 000	00 043	00 087	00 130	00 173	00 217	00 260	00 303	00 346	00 389

Table 11. Table of Natural or Naperian Logarithms, .01–11.09[a,b]

A. 0.00–0.99[b]

N	.00	.01	.02	.03	.04	.05	.06	.07	.08	.09
0.0		5.395	6.088	6.493	6.781	7.004	7.187	7.341	7.474	7.592
0.1	7.697	7.793	7.880	7.960	8.034	8.103	8.167	8.228	8.285	8.339
0.2	8.391	8.439	8.486	8.530	8.573	8.614	8.653	8.691	8.727	8.762
0.3	8.796	8.829	8.861	8.891	8.921	8.950	8.978	9.006	9.032	9.058
0.4	9.084	9.108	9.132	9.156	9.179	9.201	9.223	9.245	9.266	9.287
0.5	9.307	9.327	9.346	9.365	9.384	9.402	9.420	9.438	9.455	9.472
0.6	9.489	9.506	9.522	9.538	9.554	9.569	9.584	9.600	9.614	9.629
0.7	9.643	9.658	9.671	9.685	9.699	9.712	9.726	9.739	9.752	9.764
0.8	9.777	9.789	9.802	9.814	9.826	9.837	9.849	9.861	9.872	9.883
0.9	9.805	9.906	9.917	9.927	9.938	9.949	9.959	9.970	9.980	9.990

B. 1.00–10.09

–N	.00	.00	.01	.02	.03	.04	.05	.06	.07	.08	.09
1.0	0.0	0000	0995	1980	2956	3922	4879	5827	6766	7696	8618
1.1		9531	*0436	*1333	*2222	*3103	*3976	*4842	*4700	*6551	*7395
1.2	0.1	8232	9062	9885	*0701	*1511	*2314	*3111	*2902	*4686	*5464

[a]Reprinted with permission from *Mathematical Tables*. copyright Chemical Rubber Publishing Co., CRC Press, Inc., 2000 Corporate Blvd. NW. Boca Raton, FL 33431, 1941, pp. 139–142.

[b]To find the natural logarithm of a number which is 1/10 or 10 times a number whose logarithm is given, subtract from or add to the given logarithm is given, subtract from or add to the given logarithm the logarithm of 10.

[t]–10 should be appended to each logarithm.

Table 11. (*continued*)

B. 1.00–10.09

N	.00	.01	.02	.03	.04	.05	.06	.07	.08	.09
1.3	0.2 6236	7003	7763	8518	9267	*0010	*0748	*1481	*2208	*2930
1.4	0.3 3647	4359	5066	5767	6464	7156	7844	8526	9204	9878
1.5	0.4 0547	1211	1871	2527	3176	3825	4469	5108	5742	6373
1.6	7000	7623	8243	8858	9470	*0078	*0682	*1282	*1879	*2473
1.7	0.5 3063	3649	4232	4812	5389	5962	6531	7098	7661	8222
1.8	8779	9333	9884	*0432	*0977	*1519	*2058	*2594	*3127	*3658
1.9	0.6 4185	4710	5233	5752	6269	6783	7294	7803	8310	8813
2.0	9315	9813	*0310	*0804	*1295	*1784	*2271	*2755	*3237	*3716
2.1	0.7 4194	4669	5142	5612	6081	6547	7011	7473	7932	8390
2.2	8846	9299	9751	*0200	*0648	*1093	*1536	*1978	*2418	*2855
2.3	0.8 3291	3725	4157	4587	5015	5442	5866	6289	6710	7129
2.4	7547	7963	8377	8789	9200	9609	*0016	*0422	*0826	*1228
2.5	0.9 1629	2028	2426	2822	3216	3609	4001	4391	4779	5166
2.6	5551	5935	6317	6698	7078	7456	7833	8208	8582	8954
2.7	9325	9695	*0063	*0430	*0796	*1160	*1523	*1885	*2245	*2604
2.8	1.0 2962	3318	3674	4028	4380	4732	5082	5431	5779	6126
2.9	6471	6815	7158	7500	7841	8181	8519	8856	9192	9527
3.0	9861	*0194	*0526	*0856	*1186	*1514	*1841	*2168	*2493	*2817
3.1	1.1 3140	3462	3783	4103	4422	4740	5057	5373	5688	6002
3.2	6315	6627	6938	7248	7557	7865	8173	8479	8784	9089
3.3	9392	9695	9996	*0297	*0597	*0896	*1194	*1491	*1788	*2083
3.4	1.2 2378	2671	2964	3256	3547	3837	4127	4415	4703	4990
3.5	5276	5562	5846	6130	6413	6695	6976	7257	7536	7815
3.6	8093	8371	8647	8923	9198	9473	9746	*0019	*0291	*0563

Table 11. *(continued)*

B. 1.00–10.09

N	.00	.01	.02	.03	.04	.05	.06	.07	.08	.09
3.7	1.3 0833	1103	1372	1641	1909	2176	2442	2708	2972	3237
3.8	3500	3763	4025	4286	4547	4807	5067	5325	5584	5841
3.9	6098	6354	6609	6864	7118	7372	7624	7877	8128	8379
4.0	8629	8879	9128	9377	9624	9872	*0118	*0364	*0610	*0854
4.1	1.4 1099	1342	1585	1828	2070	2311	2552	2792	3031	3270
4.2	3508	3746	3984	4220	4456	4692	4927	5161	5395	5629
4.3	5862	6094	6326	6557	6787	7018	7247	7476	7705	7933
4.4	8160	8387	8614	8840	9065	9290	9515	9739	9962	0185
4.5	1.5 0408	0630	0851	1072	1293	1513	1732	1951	2170	2388
4.6	2606	2823	3039	3256	3471	3687	3902	4116	4330	4543
4.7	4756	4969	5181	5393	5604	5814	6025	6235	6444	6653
4.8	6862	7070	7277	7485	7691	7898	8104	8309	8515	8719
4.9	8924	9127	9331	9534	9737	9939	*0141	*0342	*0543	*0744
5.0	1.6 0944	1144	1343	1542	1741	1939	2137	2334	2531	2728
5.1	2924	3120	3315	3511	3705	3900	4094	4287	4481	4673
5.2	4866	5058	5250	5441	5632	5823	6013	6203	6393	6582
5.3	6771	6959	7147	7335	7523	7710	7896	8083	8269	8455
5.4	8640	8825	9010	9194	9378	9562	9745	9928	*0111	*0293
5.5	1.7 0475	0656	0838	1019	1199	1380	1560	1740	1919	2098
5.6	2277	2455	2633	2811	2988	3166	3342	3519	3695	3871
5.7	4047	4222	4397	4572	4746	4920	5094	5267	5440	5613
5.8	5786	5958	6130	6302	6473	6644	6815	6985	7156	7326
5.9	7495	7665	7834	8002	8171	8339	8507	8675	8842	9009
6.0	9176	9342	9509	9675	9840	*0006	*0171	*0336	*0500	*0665

Table 11. (*continued*)

B. 1.00–10.09										
N	.00	.01	.02	.03	.04	.05	.06	.07	.08	.09
6.1	1.8 0829	0993	1156	1319	1482	1645	1808	1970	2132	2294
6.2	2455	2616	2777	2938	3098	3258	3418	3578	3737	3896
6.3	4055	4214	4372	4530	4688	4845	5003	5160	5317	5473
6.4	5630	5786	5942	6097	6253	6408	6563	6718	6872	7026
6.5	7180	7334	7487	7641	7794	7947	8099	8251	8403	8555
6.6	8707	8858	9010	9160	9311	9462	9612	9762	9912	*0061
6.7	1.9 0211	0360	0509	0658	0806	0954	1102	1250	1398	1545
6.8	1692	1839	1986	2132	2279	2425	2571	2716	2862	3007
6.9	3152	3297	3442	3586	3730	3874	4018	4162	4305	4448
7.0	4591	4734	4876	5019	5161	5303	5445	5586	5727	5869
7.1	6009	6150	6291	6431	6571	6711	6851	6991	7130	7269
7.2	7408	7547	7685	7824	7962	8100	8238	8376	8513	8650
7.3	8787	8924	9061	9198	9334	9470	9606	9742	9877	*0013
7.4	2.0 0148	0283	0418	0553	0687	0821	0956	1089	1223	1357
7.5	1490	1624	1757	1890	2022	2155	2287	2419	2551	2683
7.6	2815	2946	3078	3209	3340	3471	3601	3732	3862	3992
7.7	4122	4252	4381	4511	4640	4769	4898	5027	5156	5284
7.8	5 5412	5540	5668	5796	5924	6051	6179	6306	6433	6560
7.9	6686	6813	6939	7065	7191	7317	7443	7568	7694	7819
8.0	7944	8069	8194	8318	8443	8567	8691	8815	8939	9063
8.1	9186	9310	9433	9556	9679	9802	9924	*0047	*0169	*0291
8.2	2.1 0413	0535	0657	0779	0900	1021	1142	1263	1384	1505
8.3	1626	1746	1866	1986	2106	2226	2346	2465	2585	2704
8.4	2823	2942	3061	3180	3298	3417	3535	3653	3771	3889
8.5	4007	4124	4242	4359	4476	4593	4710	4827	4943	5060
8.6	5176	5292	5409	5524	5640	5756	5871	5987	6102	6217
8.7	6332	6447	6562	6677	6791	6905	7020	7134	7248	7361

Table 11. *(continued)*

B. 1.00–10.09 (Concluded)										
N	0	1	2	3	4	5	6	7	8	9
8.8	7475	7589	7702	7816	7929	8042	8155	8267	8380	8493
8.9	8605	8717	8830	8942	9054	9165	9277	9389	9500	9611
9.0	9722	9834	9944	*0055	*0166	*0276	*0387	*0497	*0607	*0717
9.1	2.2 0827	0937	1047	1157	1266	1375	1485	1594	1703	1812
9.2	1920	2029	2138	2246	2354	2462	2570	2678	2786	2894
9.3	3001	3109	3216	3324	3431	3538	3645	3751	3858	3965
9.4	4071	4177	4284	4390	4496	4601	4707	4813	4918	5024
9.5	5129	5234	5339	5444	5549	5654	5759	5863	5968	6072
9.6	6176	6280	6384	6488	6592	6696	6799	6903	7006	7109
9.7	7213	7316	7419	7521	7624	7727	7829	7932	8034	8136
9.8	8238	8340	8442	8544	8646	8747	8849	8950	9051	9152
9.9	9253	9354	9455	9556	9657	9757	9858	9958	*0058	*0158
10.0	2.3 0259	0358	0458	0558	0658	0757	0857	0956	1055	1154
1	2.30259	39790	48491	56495	63906	70805	77259	83321	89037	94444
2	99573	*04452	*09104	*13549	*17805	*21888	*25810	*29584	*33220	*36730
3	3.40120	43399	46574	49651	52636	55535	58352	61092	63759	66356
4	68888	71357	73767	76120	78419	80666	82864	85015	87120	89182
5	91202	93183	95124	97029	98898	*00733	*02535	*04305	*06044	*07754
6	4.09434	11087	12713	14313	15888	17439	18965	20469	21951	23411
7	24850	26268	27667	29046	30407	31749	33073	34381	35671	36945
8	38203	39445	40672	41884	43082	44265	45435	46591	47734	48864
9	49981	51086	52179	53260	54329	55388	56435	57471	58497	59512

Appendix 2

Fuzzy Decision Making

The popular press has had a lot of articles about fuzzy logic recently, some of which seem to imply that while it will be used in many ways in the future, its use right now is limited to controlling washing machines and the Sendai subway. Since few investment professionals control the Sendai subway, and not enough control washing machines, fuzzy logic might not seem to merit a place in this book.

Actually, fuzzy logic is a powerful and general discipline for managing uncertainty. Or at least certain types of uncertainty, such as vagueness. In classic logic, a meaningful statement is either true or it is not.[1] For example, it is true or false that John is tall. As long as we can locate and measure John, and as long as we know what we mean by "tall," there is no problem. But tall is a vague term. One way of dealing with this problem is to establish some kind of cut point. Anyone six feet or over, say, is tall. Anyone under six feet is not. With fuzzy logic we do not need a cut point. Instead, we say how likely it is that John is tall. The probability, excuse me, the possibility that John is tall might be 60 percent, as opposed to classic logic where the probability has to be 0 percent or 100 percent.

Alternatively, we might say, It is *likely* that John is tall. Or perhaps, John is *almost certainly* tall. Or, John is *not too tall*. Notice that the output is words. Words are inherently less precise than numbers. This is not a virtue if the data and analytic techniques are precise. Moreover, for psychological reasons, the use of fuzzy techniques can make it harder to develop precise data. Excuses are where you find them. On the other hand, it is no virtue to pretend that conclusions are more precise than they are. Pretending that conclusions are more precise than they are is standard investment-industry practice, unfortunately. When investment data are imprecise, which is all too often the case, investment technology should show the imprecision. This means the trader must use words and pictures more often than numbers, or at least more often than he or she uses numbers right now.

All of this is obvious. What is not obvious is how to generate the right words and pictures. While fuzzy logic deals with fuzzy statements or fuzzy data, the technology is not fuzzy at all. The technology is quite crisp, which, in fuzzy jargon, is the opposite of fuzzy. Perhaps it would be better to say that there are fuzzy technologies. In many cases, there are competing techniques. And in many areas of some passing interest to investment managers, such as calculating averages, there are currently no generally accepted techniques.

Still, the technology is developed well enough to do a few useful things. We will consider a problem similar to the problem of the money manager with the four bond-arbitrage systems we looked at in Chapter 3. We will assume that the trader is less certain of the actual numbers than he was in the example in Chapter 3. On the other hand, we will assume that the trader has some idea of how probable the various states of nature are.

Estimates or forecasts are still required, but the requirements are now more modest. Instead of requiring the manager to numerically estimate how profitable a method will be on average, we will allow him to use words. So, instead of requiring the manager to say that the method will produce, say, average profits of "$152,521.28" per trade, we might allow him to say that the average profits per trade will be "reasonably high."

More, instead of requiring the trader to estimate how profitable a method will be, we will only require him to estimate how profitable it might be. Strictly speaking, this requires the trader to estimate what is possible rather than what is probable. On the other hand, strictly speaking, anything is possible. In practice, what is required are upper and lower estimates of profitability. Upper and lower can be defined in a lot of different ways.[2] Fortunately, it probably does not matter much how upper and lower are defined, as long as the trader is consistent. Thus, the trader can get away with saying that he expects the average profit per trade "might range from break-even to some loss." The requirements for estimating the probability that a state of nature will occur are similarly relaxed. This information is presented in Figure A2–1. This is new information. Can we use it to make a better decision?

In Chapter 3 we described a standard probability-weighted decision analysis. The technique we will describe now is an extension to situations where we don't know what the probabilities really are, or much of anything else. The first step is to transform

Figure A2–1

	State J	**State K**	**State L**
	Likely–Possible	Possible–Highly Unlikely	Possible–Impossible
Investment A	Break-even–Average loss	Some profit–Extremely large loss	Large profit–Average loss
Investment B	Average loss–Average loss	Break-even–Break-even	Some profit–Average loss
Investment C	Some profit–Break-even	Large profit–Break-even	Large loss–Extremely large loss

Verbal descriptions of profits and losses and probabilities. Which is the best investment?

Figure A2–2

Certain	100%
Highly Likely	90%
Likely	70%
Possible	50%
Unlikely	30%
Highly Unlikely	10%
Impossible	0%

This is one possible mapping of likelihood descriptions to probabilities. Any mapping the user is comfortable with is right.

Figure A2–3

Extremely large profit	10,000,000
Large profit	7,000,000
Average profit	5,000,000
Some profit	3,000,000
Break-even	0
Some loss	–3,000,000
Average loss	–5,000,000
Large loss	–7,000,000
Extremely large loss	–10,000,000

This is one possible mapping of profit descriptions to dollar amounts. Any mapping the user is comfortable with is right.

the words to numbers. Given the current state of the art, it's not too easy to add words.[3] Figure A2–2 presents a mapping of words to probability or weighting values. As long as the decision maker uses words honestly and consistently, these transformations, "mapping" in the technical jargon, present no problems. Figure A2–3 can also be used to map payoff values to words. The principle is the same. In Figure A2–4 the verbal descriptions are mapped to numbers.

Figure A2–4

	State J	State K	State L
	70%–50%	50%–10%	50%–0%
Investment A	0– –5,000,000	3,000,000 –10,000,000	7,000,000– –5,000,000–
Investment B	–5,000,000– –5,000,000	0 0	3,000,000– –5,000,000
Investment C	3,000,000– 0	7,000,000– 0	7,000,000– –10,000,000

Because upper and lower bounds are used, rather than estimates, there is no simple mathematical solution to the problem. Instead, we will perform a Monte Carlo simulation.[4] In a simulation, we substitute raw computing power for technique. Instead of performing the calculations in Figure A2–4 once, we perform the calculations, say, a hundred thousand times. Each time, the numbers will be different because they will be chosen by chance. The first step is to figure out what the probabilities really are. By definition, probabilities must add up to one. But the upper and lower probability estimates are under no such constraints. A number is selected at random for each of the states of nature. In practice, this means running a computer program that generates pseudo-random numbers between zero and one inclusive. These numbers are then scaled so that they lie between the upper and lower probability estimates of whatever state of nature is of interest. This is done by dividing the random number by the higher estimate minus the lower estimate. The lower estimate is then added back. The result is then rounded to, say, .01. This procedure is then repeated for the next state of nature, and so on until random numbers have been generated for all of them. If the probabilities add up to one, which should happen on occasion, the probabilities are acceptable. If the probabilities do not add up to one, they are thrown out, and the procedure is started again.

How often the probabilities add up will depend on how they are rounded and how consistent the original probability descriptions were. If the original upper and lower probability-boundaries were ill-considered, there may be no way the probabilities can add to one. The program must check that there is more than one way that the probabilities can add to one.

The second step is to multiply an acceptable probability for a state of nature by a randomly generated payoff. The payoff for a particular investment and state of nature is generated by the same random number program, with a different scaling procedure. The randomly generated number between zero and one is multiplied by the range of the estimates, then the lower estimate is added. This is done for each investment for each of the states of nature. The results for each investment are added. The total for a particular investment is an estimate of expected value of that investment. And the investment with the highest total is the best investment for this iteration of the procedure (see Figure A2–3).

The procedure described above is then repeated a couple hundred thousand times. Each time, the results will be slightly different. At least, if the random-number generator works they will be.

The third step is to find the investment that was most frequently the best and find out how frequently it was the best. At the same time, we can find out what the average expected value was for the various investments.

Endnotes

1. Not all statements are meaningful. For example, "The number five is red" is neither true nor false, but meaningless, when "five" refers to a number, not a representation of a number. Meaningful ideas are always risky. If there is no way an idea can be wrong, there is no way an idea can be right. See discussion on operational definitions in Chapter 7.

For an introduction see Daniel McNeill and Paul Freiberger, *Fuzzy Logic,* (New York: Simon & Schuster, 1993).

2. A second alternative is to rank the probabilities. In this case, the upper and lower bounds refer to zero, 100 percent, or the probability of some other state of nature occurring.
3. As I read it, fuzzy decision-making technology is going in at least three different directions. One is to map words to numbers and then back again, which is the approach I discuss in this appendix. Another approach is to use verbal variables. The final approach is a new type of mathematics with slightly different assumptions than the ones that probability theory uses. Of course, more than 6,000 books and papers have been written on fuzzy set theory, not all of which I have read, so there could be other approaches. The second and third approaches are the most interesting, but I have not seen any practical results yet. Fuziware (Knoxville, TN) makes a spreadsheet program for fuzzy arithmetic. The version I have does not restrict probabilities so they sum to one. As is common practice, its fuzzy numbers require at least three parameters.
4. Bradley Efron and Gail Gong, "A Leisurely Look at the Bootstrap, the Jackknife, and Cross-Validation," *The American Statistician,* 1983, Vol. 36, pp. 36–48.

Index

P

T

U

V

W

X

Printed in the United States
21285LVS00001B/175-207